Security and Risk Analysis for Intelligent Cloud Computing

This edited book is a compilation of scholarly articles on the latest developments in the field of AI, Blockchain, and ML/DL in cloud security. This book is designed for security and risk assessment professionals and to help undergraduate, postgraduate students, research scholars, academicians, and technology professionals who are interested in learning practical approaches to cloud security. It covers practical strategies for assessing the security and privacy of cloud infrastructure and applications and shows how to make cloud infrastructure secure to combat threats, attacks, and prevent data breaches. The chapters are designed with a granular framework, starting with the security concepts, followed by hands-on assessment techniques based on real-world studies. Readers will gain detailed information on cloud computing security that—until now—has been difficult to access.

This book:

- Covers topics such as AI, Blockchain, and ML/DL in cloud security.
- Presents several case studies revealing how threat actors abuse and exploit cloud environments to spread threats.
- Explains the privacy aspects you need to consider in the cloud, including how they compare with aspects considered in traditional computing models.
- Examines security delivered as a service—a different facet of cloud security.

Security and Risk Analysis for Intelligent Cloud Computing

Methods, Applications, and Preventions

Edited by Ajay Kumar, Sangeeta Rani, Sarita Rathee, and Surbhi Bhatia

CRC Press
Taylor & Francis Group
Boca Raton London New York

CRC Press is an imprint of the
Taylor & Francis Group, an **Informa** business

Cover Image Credit: Shutterstock

First edition published 2024
by CRC Press
6000 Broken Sound Parkway NW, Suite 300, Boca Raton, FL 33487-2742

and by CRC Press
4 Park Square, Milton Park, Abingdon, Oxon, OX14 4RN

CRC Press is an imprint of Taylor & Francis Group, LLC

Library of Congress Cataloging-in-Publication Data
Names: Ajay Kumar, editor. | Rani, Sangeeta, editor. | Sarita, Ms., editor. | Bhatia, Surbhi, 1988– editor.
Title: Security and risk analysis for intelligent cloud computing : methods, applications, and prevention / edited by: Ajay Kumar, Sangeeta Rani, Sarita, Surbhi Bhatia.
Description: First edition. | Boca Raton : CRC Press, 2024. | Includes bibliographical references.
Identifiers: LCCN 2023027002 (print) | LCCN 2023027003 (ebook) | ISBN 9781032360300 (hardback) | ISBN 9781032360362 (paperback) | ISBN 9781003329947 (ebook)
Subjects: LCSH: Cloud computing—Security measures. | Artificial intelligence.
Classification: LCC QA76.585 .S435 2023 (print) | LCC QA76.585 (ebook) | DDC 004.67/82—dc23/eng/20231006
LC record available at https://lccn.loc.gov/2023027002
LC ebook record available at https://lccn.loc.gov/2023027003

ISBN: 9781032360300 (hbk)
ISBN: 9781032360362 (pbk)
ISBN: 9781003329947 (ebk)

DOI: 10.1201/9781003329947

Typeset in Sabon
by Apex CoVantage, LLC

Contents

Acknowledgements

The editors are grateful to CRC Press for showing their interest in publishing this book in the popular research field of security and risk analysis in intelligent cloud computing. The editors express their personal appreciation and gratitude to Ms. Gabriella Williams (Editor) for giving consent to publish this work. It is thanks to her and her team's systematic and methodical support that the editors have been able to compile and finalize this manuscript.

The editors wish to thank all the chapter authors who contributed their valuable research and experience to compile this volume. The chapter authors, corresponding authors in particular, deserve special acknowledgements for bearing with the editors, who persistently bothered them with deadlines and their remarks.

The editors, Ms. Sangeeta Rani, Ms. Sarita, and Dr. Surbhi Bhatia wish to thank Dr. Ajay Kumar for his unreserved support, valuable suggestions, and encouragement in nurturing this work. Dr. Ajay Kumar is a wonderful person and the epitome of simplicity, forthrightness, and strength, and he served as a valuable role model for his cohort of editors.

Finally, the editors obligate this work to the divine creator and express their indebtedness to the Almighty for gifting them power to bring their ideas and concepts into substantial manifestation. The editors believe that this book will enlighten readers about the features and characteristics of cloud computing.

Dr. Ajay Kumar
Ms. Sangeeta Rani
Ms. Sarita
Dr. Surbhi Bhatia

Preface

An internet service known as cloud computing provides information technology facilities, platforms, and software. It is being gradually adopted by organizations as a private, public, and hybrid cloud to fulfil a long-term dream called "Computing for Use." A large part of its purpose is to let users pay only for the services they need, regardless of what infrastructure or software they need. However, much security work is still needed to minimize cloud computing's shortcomings, even though it is considered to be a significant IT infrastructure shift. Cloud security issues and vulnerabilities need to be identified and mitigated since a significant amount of personal and corporate information is stored in cloud data centres. Internet protocols and the cloud infrastructure itself are based on a common internet architecture. This book is expected to provide the compiled comprehensive in the niche area of emerging technologies such as AI, blockchain, and ML/DL in cloud security.

In addition to the aforementioned various case studies of the latest research and development in niche technologies of AI, blockchain, and ML/DL are covered to help students of undergraduate, postgraduate and research scholars, academicians, professionals, and technology professionals.

This compilation will bring to its readers the latest developments/advancements in cloud computing, AI, blockchain, and ML/DL, which is currently not available at one place. This book will bridge the gap between R&D in smart manufacturing and professionals.

This book is an outcome of the extensive research accomplished by various researchers, academicians, scientists, and industrialists in different technologies. The area is under-explored and the outcomes are worth the research effort. Since the information related to security and risk analysis is scattered into patents and research publications and not at one place in a systematic form, editors recognize their ethical responsibility to compile, share, and spread the knowledge accumulated and technology developed, with the students, researchers, and industry people, to draw the benefits of this work in the form of a book and gain technical competence in the frontal area.

The book consists of 15 chapters that describe perspectives of security analysis for intelligent cloud computing. Chapter 1 outlines cloud data security and storage security domains from the perspective of cloud data owners and service providers. Chapter 2 presents several countermeasures to mitigate security attacks and privacy leakages. Different deployment techniques are suggested as ways to mitigate and enhance security and privacy shortcomings. Chapter 3 investigates various strategies and plans for cloud data security and privacy. Chapter 4 integrates the blockchain under the cloud storage system to reduce the issues related to business customers' data security and privacy. Chapter 5 provides a thorough analysis of the various ML and DL models applied to data security and privacy, along with several real-world case studies. The research issues faced during the development of ML and DL algorithms in the area of data privacy and security is also discussed. Chapter 6 explores the approach of big data analytics in machine to machine communications; blackout-loose strength generation and distribution; extreme-yield agriculture; safe and fast evacuation in reaction to herbal or man-made disasters; perpetual existence assistants for busy, older, or disabled people. Chapter 7 provides insights into how blockchain technology and cryptocurrencies are shaping the future of transactions in India and how businesses can leverage these technologies to gain a competitive edge. Chapter 8 validates the capability of the ML-based multiple linear regression (LR) model to analyze and predict the number of cases affected during the second wave of Covid-19 in India (2021). Chapter 9 presents a study to use reduction, iterative reduction, and hierarchical clustering techniques to detect renal disease from the input data. With early detection, CKD can be managed more effectively, which in turn reduces the risk of further complications and improves the quality of life for those affected. Chapter 10 proposes a data-mining-based methodological approach for forecasting the performance metrics of content posted on business brands' Facebook pages. Chapter 11 explains the way clustering can be used to analyze the role of various lexicons in social text stream. Chapter 12 stresses the importance of AI and ML in the modern business landscape and highlights their potential to drive growth and success. It also highlights the need for businesses to embrace these technologies with caution, and to ensure that their use aligns with ethical standards and regulations. Chapter 13 focuses on applied perspective of machine learning with an emphasis on algorithms that are actively used in the field of remote sensing such as support vector machines, single decision trees (DTs), random forests, boosted DTs, artificial neural networks, and k-nearest neighbors (k-NN). Chapter 14 has relevance for academics as AI technology develops, marketing and sales functionalities as well as job markets are expected to change significantly, and this report intends to give a complete study and documentation of such changes. Chapter 15 presents a novel framework proposed to solve the early classification problems for accurate prediction of the stock market using Two-Layered Bidirectional Long Short Term Memory (TL-BLSTM) with transfer learning.

This book is intended for both academia and industry. The postgraduate students, doctoral students, and researchers in universities and institutions, who are involved in the areas of cloud computing, AI, blockchain, and ML/DL, will find this compilation useful.

The editors acknowledge the professional support received from CRC Press and express their gratitude for this opportunity.

Reader's observations, suggestions, and queries are welcome,

Editors

Dr. Ajay Kumar
Ms. Sangeeta Rani
Ms. Sarita
Dr. Surbhi Bhatia

About the Editors

Dr. Ajay Kumar is currently serving as Associate Professor in the Mechanical Engineering Department, School of Engineering and Technology, JECRC University, Jaipur, Rajasthan, India. He received his doctorate in the field of advanced manufacturing from Guru Jambheshwar University of Science & Technology, Hisar, India, after his bachelor of technology (Hons.) in mechanical engineering and master of technology (Distinction) in manufacturing and automation. His areas of research include Incremental Sheet Forming, Artificial Intelligence, Sustainable Materials, Additive Manufacturing, Smart Manufacturing, Industry 4.0, Waste Management, and Optimization Techniques. He has over 65 publications in international journals of repute which are listed in SCOPUS, Web of Science, and SCI indexed databases and has refereed international conferences. He has more than 20 national and international patents to his credit. He has also co-authored and co-edited many books and proceedings including:

- Authored Book, Ajay Kumar and R K Mittal, *Incremental Sheet Forming Technologies: Principles, Merits, Limitations, and Applications*; CRC Press, Taylor and Francis; ISBN 9780367276744
- Managing Guest Editor of Journal Proceedings, Ajay Kumar, *Journal of Physics: Conference Series,* vol. 1950, International Conference on Mechatronics and Artificial Intelligence (ICMAI) 27 February 2021, Gurgaon, India
- Edited book, Ajay Kumar, R K Mittal, Abid Haleem (2023). *Advancements in Additive Manufacturing: Artificial Intelligence, Nature Inspired and Bio-manufacturing*; ISBN: 9780323918343, ELSEVIER
- Edited book, Ajay Kumar, Parveen, Sharif Ahmad, Jyotsna Sharma, Victor Gambhir. *Handbook of Sustainable Materials: Modelling, Characterization, and Optimization*; CRC Press, Taylor and Francis; ISBN: 978-1-032-28632-7
- Edited book, Ajay, Parveen, R K Mittal, Rajesh Goel (2022). *Waste Recovery and Management: An Approach Towards Sustainable Development Goals*; CRC Press, Taylor and Francis; ISBN: 9781032281933

- Edited book, Ajay Kumar, Parveen, Bandar AlMangour, Hari Singh (2023). *Smart Manufacturing: Forecasting the Future of Industry 4.0*; CRC Press, Taylor and Francis; ISBN: 9781032363431

He has organized various national and international events including an international conference on mechatronics and artificial intelligence (ICMAI-2021) as conference chair. He has supervised more than eight master technology and doctorate scholars and numerous undergraduate projects and thesis. He has a total of 15 years of experience in teaching and research. He is Guest Editor and Review Editor of the reputed journals including *Frontiers in Sustainability*. He has contributed to many international conferences and symposiums as a session chair, expert speaker, and member of the editorial board. He has won several proficiency awards during the course of his career, including merit awards, best teacher awards, and so on.

He is life member of Quality Circle Forum of India and has also authored many in-house course notes, lab manuals, monographs, and invited chapters in books. He has organized a series of faculty development programs, international conferences, workshops, and seminars for researchers, doctor of philosophy, undergraduate, and post-graduate level students. He is associated with many research, academic, and professional societies in various capacities.

ORCID ID: https://orcid.org/0000-0001-7306-1902
https://scholar.google.co.in/citations?user=TmZS4JIAAAAJ&hl=en
https://www.webofscience.com/wos/author/record/D-5813-2019
Publons Profile: https://publons.com/researcher/1596469/ajay-kumar/
Research Gate: https://www.researchgate.net/profile/Ajay_Kumar349
ResearcherID: D-5813-2019
http://www.researcherid.com/rid/D-5813-2019

Ms. Sangeeta Rani is currently serving as Assistant Professor in the department of Computer Science and Engineering, World College of Technology and Management, Gurgaon, Haryana, India. She is pursuing her doctorate from Amity University, Manesar, Gurugram. She completed her master of technology from Maharshi Dayanand University, Rohtak, India. Her areas of research include cloud computing and machine learning. She has over 15 research publications in international journals of repute and has refereed international conferences and co-authored more than five book chapters. She has guided several master of technology scholars. She has a total of nine years of experience in teaching. She has won the best paper awards in various international conferences.

She has also organized a series of faculty development programmes, workshops, and seminars for undergraduate and post-graduate level students. She teaches the following courses at the graduate and postgraduate level: Analysis and Design of Algorithms, Cloud Computing, Theory of Computation, Compiler Design, Programming in Python, Machine Learning, etc.

Ms. Sangeeta at:

- Scopus ID: Scopus preview—Scopus—Search for an author profile
- Google Scholar: https://scholar.google.com/citations?user=Hy5v3VQ AAAAJ&hl=en
- ORCID ID: https://orcid.org/0000-0002-7540-6342

Ms. Sarita Rathee received her M.Tech (Distinction) in the field of Electrical and Electronics Engineering from Maharshi Dayanand University, Rohtak, India after B.Tech. (Hons.) in electrical engineering. She is pursuing her doctorate from JECRC University, Jaipur, India, in smart security systems and control panels. She started her career as a project scheduler at Sage Metals Ltd., India. She continues her growth in the industrial industry having worked for eight years in different verticals of quality and environmental function and now as project manager, control systems and panels at Sage Metals Ltd., India. She is responsible for task management, reporting to stakeholders, overseeing budgets, and schedules. She also worked in business excellence for a year and worked on a project of business excellence sustainability task (BEST), with the integration of all control system and panels (QMS + EMS + OHSAS+ Social Accountability). The project has been awarded Siemens Excellence Award. Her areas of interest are cyber data security, virtual and augmented reality, industrial internet of things, PLC, and SCADA. She has more than five national and international patents. She has delivered many workshops on different aspects of smart learning, cyber security of control panels, smart instrumentation, and manufacturing techniques under the Government of India

Ms. Sarita is currently serving as an Assistant Professor in Department of Electrical and Electronics Engineering, School of Engineering and Technology, JECRC University, Jaipur, Rajasthan, India. Her areas of research include Artificial Intelligence, IOT, cloud computing, Industry 4.0, and optimization techniques. She has over 10 publications in international journals of repute including Scopus and Web of Science database and refereed international conferences.

She has more than 07 national and international patents to her credit. She has supervised more than 4 M.Tech scholars and numerous undergraduate projects/thesis. She has a total of 05 years of experience in teaching and research. She has won several proficiency awards during the course of his career, including merit awards, best teacher awards, and so on.

She has also authored many in-house course notes, lab manuals, monographs and invited chapters in books. She has attended a series of Faculty Development Programs, International Conferences, workshops, and seminars for researchers, PhD, UG and PG level students. She teaches the following courses at the graduate and postgraduate level: instrumentation engineering, IOT, FACTS devices, Power electronics, electric vehicles and so on. She is associated with many research, academic, and professional societies in various capacities.

https://scholar.google.com/citations?user=CqYbcTkAAAAJ&hl=en&authuser=2

Dr. Surbhi Bhatia holds a doctorate in computer science and engineering from Banasthali University, 2018, in the area of machine learning and social media analytics. She earned the Project Management Professional Certification from the reputed Project Management Institute, USA. She is currently an assistant professor in the Department of Information Systems, College of Computer Sciences and Information Technology, King Faisal University, Saudi Arabia. She has more than 10 years of teaching experience in different universities in India and Saudi Arabia. She is also working as a consultant in the Research Lab, India. She is an editorial board member with Inderscience Publishers in the *International Journal of Hybrid Intelligence* and in *SN Applied Sciences*, Springer. She has published 12 national and international patents from India, Australia, and the US. She has published many papers in reputed journals and conferences in high indexing databases (SCI, SCIE, Scopus, Web of Science, ESCI). She is currently serving as a guest editor of special issues in reputed journals of Springer (*SN Applied Sciences*, Indexing ESCI), *Computer, Materials and Continua* (Indexing SCI, Scopus), *Internet of Things* (Indexing: SCIE, Elsevier), Hindawi, Bentham Science, and in many international conferences (indexing: Springer, IEEE, IOP). She has delivered talks as keynote speaker in IEEE conferences and in faculty development programs. She has conducted workshops in AICTE programmers and chaired technical sessions in many conferences. She has successfully authored two books from Springer and Wiley. She has also edited eight books from IGI Global, Wiley, CRC Press, Elsevier, and Springer. She has been selected in the prestigious "Best Young National Award" by IRDP group of journals in India. She has many projects approved by the Ministry of Education, Saudi Arabia, and Deanship of Scientific Research in Saudi Arabia, and from SEED, DST, India. Her areas of interest are data mining, machine learning, sentiment analysis, natural language processing, and data analytics.

- Scopus Author ID: 56655934600
- Google Scholar: https://scholar.google.com/citations?user=C4EUDAw AAAAJ&hl=en&oi=ao
- LinkedIn: https://www.linkedin.com/in/dr-surbhi-bhatia-pmp%C2%AE-79a68b50/
- ORCID ID: https://orcid.org/0000-0003-3097-6568

Navigating the Landscape of Security Threat Analysis in Cloud Computing environments

[1]Vineeta Singh and [2]Vandana Dixit Kaushik

[1]Department of Computer Engineering and Applications,
GLA University 17km Stone, NH-
[2]Mathura-Delhi Road P.O. Chaumuhan, Mathura-281 406 (U.P.) Mathura,
India and Department of Computer Science and Engineering, Harcourt Butler
Technical University, HBTU East Campus, Nawabganj, Kanpur, Uttar Pradesh
208002, India

1.1 INTRODUCTION

Recently cloud computing research has faced a lot of technical advancements facilitating the ease in delivery of information technology (IT) solution services. Cloud computing is an internet-based computing service that is dynamic as well as involves both customers and cloud service providers. It is becoming increasingly well-liked in the IT sector globally, which promotes more opportunities in the commercial sector [1, 2]. Numerous advantages of this technology include cost savings, enhanced scalability, security, integrity, simplicity of use, and risk mitigation for businesses [3].

Systems for cloud computing are shown to be effective in addressing the diverging expectations with respect to distributed sharing services and resources of computing. In recent years, the scientific, education, and research sectors have benefited greatly from this breakthrough integral computing platform in information technology due to its unmatched computing capacity and adaptability in distributed community computing [3].

As a community cloud, the private cloud application enables its use in a variety of institutions for research and education. Numerous application types and usage situations, such as online applications, blogs, Web hosting, networking, and services for scattered data storage, have also been investigated. A cloud system of this kind can also perform provisioning tasks, such as software, platform development, and computer infrastructure to meet scientist as well as researchers' expectations [4]. In a network community, it is also a method by which users can utilize their own computational resources [5]. Despite its advantages, cloud computing has a number of technological, managerial, and financial issues that must be resolved, including privacy and

DOI: 10.1201/9781003329947-1

security [6, 7] and resource scheduling [7]. The community model has advantages to perceived risks, shared resources, and cost savings, is an essential component of cloud computing and is essential for its adaptability as well as expansion, especially in the community cloud model because of accessibility for its users. In cloud computing information systems, the issues and challenges facing the community have been examined from a number of angles [8, 9].

Along with these other aspects of cloud computing, it offers a great contribution in the area of security storage, resource distribution, as well as security communication [10]. As a result, improved approaches must be used to address these issues, with community cloud computing as one among them. Between private and public clouds is the community cloud. While likely to a private cloud, the infrastructure and computing services are shared by two or more businesses with similar privacy, security, data integrity, identification, as well as regulatory considerations [11, 12]. However, irrespective of the fact of the existence of community cloud computing, the restriction that has been imposed is thorough systematic study and information background with respect to the model and architecture connected for utilizing the community cloud in the HEI that poses certain constraints.

In order to identify the important frameworks, models, and architecture, this study's contribution is to ascertain how the general public views cloud computing while also reviewing the existing systematic literature review. The study also identifies the questions being looked at and their pertinent findings.

1.2 CLOUD COMPUTING: A BASIC INTRODUCTION

Cloud computing is defined as "access to computing resources which are owned as well as managed via a third-party provider on a consolidated basis" [13]. On-demand service provider and pay-as-you-utilize billing for resources make cloud computing distinguishable from other types of computing. Such characteristics lessen capital expenditures; transforms operating costs into real utilization while reducing cost of labour. It operates like a platform as well as a specific kind of application to yield computational services along with infrastructures. The platform can dynamically facilitate, configure/ reconfigure as well as de-provision servers, whether they are virtual or real computers. It creates a massive change from delivering computation technology like a purchased object to delivering computing as a service offered to clients over the internet through large databases or the cloud. The cloud infrastructure based facilities involves information technology services to be more beneficial, available virtually, customizable as well as ease of accessibility.

Platform for cloud computing as well as services eliminate the needed support for hardware as well as maintenance for middleware and applications.

The way applications are developed and business choices are made are changing as a result of cloud computing [13].

As per various kinds of services provided, three basic services offered via cloud may be considered:

(1) SaaS (software as a service) (SaaS). Customers who utilize SaaS may access the provider's cloud-based apps, whereas controlling power with respect to cloud operations, networks or infrastructure is not with the consumers. SaaS is like a delivery model and it will enable technologies supporting Web services along with SOA, that is, service-oriented architecture. Google's Gmail as well as Yahoo are two examples [11, 14].

(2) SaaS platform (PaaS). PaaS allows users to deploy apps to cloud infrastructure while using the provider's applications. Although the cloud infrastructure is not included in this arrangement, the customer does have some control over the distributed applications (networks, server, and storage). Examples include Azure from Microsoft and Force.com from Salesforce [11, 14]. Additionally, PaaS offers an uncompromised user experience while combining features like built-in security, scalability, as well as dependability. It also makes developer collaboration easier [15].

(3) Infrastructure as a service (IaaS). IaaS permits customers to access storage, networks, and provider-owned processes as the need arises. The end-user may install and utilise the software but the management of physical cloud infrastructure is not accompanied through the consumer in this architecture, such as Elastic Compute Cloud (EC2) of Amazon [11, 14].

1.3 DEPLOYMENT FRAMEWORKS IN CLOUD COMPUTING

There are four different cloud deployment technologies: private clouds, community clouds, hybrid clouds, and public clouds.

(1) Open cloud. Here via an open network, cloud services are facilitated to everyone and the technology is known as a public cloud which is a form of cloud hosting. One such example of this service is Google App Engine [11] that can be offered free of cost or as a pay-per-single use basis.

(2) Personal cloud. A private cloud is a specific cloud computing concept that consists of a safe cloud and a distinct cloud-based infrastructure. Here a specified client possesses complete control over this environment. In the form of service, here computational capability is yielded within a virtual environment via private clouds which utilise real

computing resources. The resources for cloud in the model are only accessible to an organization that possess control over privacy. One example would be VMware Private Cloud [13].

(3) Hybrid cloud. This form of cloud computing combines both private and public clouds and is integrated [16]. A hybrid cloud is constituted through combining two distinct clouds into a single one. It may involve either public as well as private cloud servers or both virtual as well as physical hardware. For offering a unified service, the several clouds are integrated [13]. Private data with public clouds are a specific kind of pairing. There are three main cloud service providers in this area, Microsoft System Center, Azure and Windows Server.

(4) Community cloud. When various organizations seek the same infrastructure and are willing to share it, a community cloud is formed. Cloud computing benefits may be enhanced via pooling resources. Expenditures involved with community cloud are dispersed to a few users in comparison to public cloud; dispursed to a renter or a person, however. Subsequently it is more costly despite of providing a great level security, privacy, and policy compliance [13]. Google has developed the Govcloud, which is an example of a community cloud [11].

1.3.1 Literature Survey

The IoT (Internet of Things) has created a new method for connecting people and machines in order to improve and make life much easier. IoT has shown to be a huge possibility in smart offices, smart homes, warehouses etc., which is the key draw for upgrading the industry related to healthcare by this novel innovation. IoT can therefore greatly enhance the healthcare field. Health-related information from the healthcare sensor includes blood pressure, ECG, blood glucose, blood temperature, as well as other measurements. These devices generate enormous volumes of data, which must be analyzed [17], filtered, and properly stored. Here they have covered the full architecture of the upcoming day's healthcare system using healthcare related IoT sensor as well as fog computing along with difficulties associated and security issues. This research also involved some strategies provided by different researchers for addressing the privacy as well as security concerns with respect to IoT, cloud computing environment as well as fog computing [18]

For designers, organizations, as well as integrators tasked with managing these new entities, the intricate and interrelated structure of smart cities poses substantial technical, political, as well as socioeconomic obstacles. Studies focused on security challenges pertaining to information security as well as the problems in smart city infrastructure with respect to the administration as well as processing of personal data are highly focusing to the safety, confidentiality, and vulnerabilities inside smart cities. In this paper, authors examined some of such issues, facilitate an invaluable synthesis of the appropriate major literature, and build up a paradigm for interacting smart city.

This study focuses on important topics in the field of smart cities research, including: the utilization as well as adoption of smart facilities via citizens; the safety and privacy of smart phones, gadgets, and services; power systems, smart city infrastructure, and healthcare; frameworks, techniques, and best practices to strengthen safety and privacy; operational risks for smart cities. This comprehensive study provides an insightful perspective on a number of urgent problems and gives crucial direction for future research. The finding outcomes of the study can be utilized as valuable direction for future exploration and as a source of information for both academics and practitioners [19].

Smart cities, 5G internet as well as the Internet of Things (IoT) all require cloud-based computing services for storing as well as processing much data. As a result, the diversity of the new businesses using the aforementioned technologies would increase the cloud paradigm's risks and security vulnerabilities. At the moment, cloud computing includes every element, including infrastructures, networks as well as access management. Without a clear understanding of the cloud infrastructure, security communities deal with issues including data duplication, slow detection of security issues, and losing control over access to data and protection in order to meet compliance with regulations.

We anticipate a quick change in the computational needs that cloud computing technologies can meet as it becomes a part of our everyday lives and digital computing world. Through this study researchers presented a cloud computing architecture overview, covering its key features, deployment strategies, services models, as well as cloud data centre automation. By conducting a thorough survey, they characterized and summarized the efforts put in the literature to discover answers to such security concerns. They also presented frameworks as well as security challenges for cloud computing. They also classified the numerous cloud cyber attacks and privacy issues and provided a summary of the initiatives taken in the research to provide preventive and safeguards strategies for vulnerability assessments. At the last they provided an overview for unresolved difficulties, open challenges for cloud security, and moreover future directions were also given [16].

Cloud computing is gaining popularity these days due to its ability to conduct business dispersed computing, offer facilities like data storage and resource sharing, as well as deliver services that are affordable, simple, and adaptable. Cyber security issues in cloud computing are brought on by data movement and apps from outside customers' administrative domains. Because security plays such a big part in cloud computing, it is crucial to look into the threats, vulnerabilities, and issues in various network layers.

This study will identify, assess, and categorise the current difficulties of various network levels in cloud computing. System designers can use the approaches provided by the categorization of security challenges associated with cloud computing as from network layers approach to offer a methodical process for a greater understanding and later, identifying, and mitigating security risks. This research also introduces new preventive techniques and emerging solutions that have the potential to lessen network layer vulnerabilities [20].

With the introduction of cloud computing, many consumers and companies are now able to utilise systems and corporate resources more effectively. The main advantages of cloud computing are lower service prices and the lack of a need for consumers to purchase pricey computing hardware. People and businesses shift their programmes, data, and resource to cloud-based storage services because of the accessibility of its services, resources, and adaptability for consumer computational activities. There are many privacy concerns and difficulties that come with a shift from localized to remote data processing for both service providers and users. Cloud computing does have one important disadvantage, though: a third-party is in charge of your storage of data. The privacy issue created by the sharing of resources with cloud computing is among the most difficult issues with offering powerful data storage and processing as on-demand services. Companies and governments all across the world are adopting cloud computing, whether from scratch or as a part of current infrastructure, due to rising productivity and improved performance. In this study authors discussed the risks and difficulties of cloud computing and moreover steps taken for assisting protection to the cloud against security threats [21].

The development of current cutting-edge innovation is being devoted towards cloud computing, helping to enhance how well governments operate as well as provide services for citizens as well as other businesses. Due to the growing number of advantages, such as scalability, safety, adaptability, dependability, pay-per-use, confidentiality, and dynamicity to distribute services of IT, it has acquired significant popularity. The goal of this work is to categorize the dispersed communities engaged in information technology research on cloud computing through an examination of a comprehensive review of the literature.

Fifty-one relevant publications published from 2010 to 2020 that dealt with the introduction of community cloud computing via different organizations are included to this study. Publications have been grouped according to the eleven main contributing factors relied over a detailed structured literature evaluation as well as a grounded theory strategy: cost, performance, security, QoS, accuracy, trust, ease of use, architecture, utility, framework, and model. Such variables further combined to a final one to envision aspects as well as concepts affecting adoption of community cloud computing. As a result it will enable the reader to investigate thoroughly the concept of community cloud computing. This is a novel effort for depicting variations in critical cloud computing parameters in various community settings including their causal links amongst some of the variables taken into consideration.

The results of the long-term comprehensive study will help with a number of factors that affect how widely community clouds services are used and with whom.

It might provide as a starting point for theoretical exploration of community cloud computing in the context of information systems. By offering comprehensive insights and prospective exploratory strategies, this study contributes and facilitates the identification of various research gaps already present. It is predicted that these strategies will produce a solid, model to implement community cloud services within higher education institutions abbreviated as HEIs [22].

Cloud computing is becoming more popular as a result of its ability to perform business dispersed computing, offer facilities like data storage and resource sharing, as well as deliver services that are affordable, simple, and adaptable. Various security issues in cloud computing are brought on by data movement and apps beyond the customers' administrative domains. Because protection plays such a big part in cloud computing, it is crucial to look into the risks, issues, and vulnerabilities in various network layers. This study has identified, assess, and categorize the current difficulties of various network levels in cloud computing. System designers can use the approaches provided by the categorization of security issues associated with cloud computing from the network layers aspect to offer a structured method for a deeper knowledge and later, identifying and minimizing threats and vulnerabilities. This research has introduced new preventive techniques and emerging solutions that have the potential to lessen network layer vulnerability [23].

Most issues faced by organizations are due to a lack of adoption of cloud computing in terms of resource sharing, while they are continually seeking to adopt new and effective innovations, like solutions for business intelligence for becoming much smarter and much more adaptable. The business intelligence solution is regarded as a cost-effective and simple-to-implement option. With businesses that process a lot of data, it has gained a lot of popularity. As a result, researches considered employing the cloud computing model for transferring the business intelligence system utilizing modified models and frameworks to process the data so that it is efficient and makes solution much accessible. The main objective involves satisfying users to provide accessibility and information security. Utilizing a cloud-based business intelligence solution has several advantages, particularly to yield savings. Through this study, the authors have illustrated cloud computing as well as business intelligence in a standard definition along with their significance, and the strategy through which both of them may be combined to create cloud BI. They also explain about management risks as well as solutions and compare established scenarios with their approaches for discussing the challenges and benefits of cloud computing [24].

Users now have a new method of accessing computing resources including software, data storage, and processing power anytime and wherever they need it courtesy of cloud computing. It's one of the quickly expanding industries under the technologies of information and communication that has significantly transformed our daily lives. Nowadays, the incorporation of cloud computing has helped smart grids, a much smarter and advanced version of the traditional power grid predecessor. They discuss how the development of the electrical grid resulting in the smart grid development and illustrate the enhancement of both sectors.

In Saudi Arabia's vision 2030, how smart grid techniques will perform is a significant part that is discussed in detail [25].

Cloud security is a major issue across the globe where computational processes are demanding and optimal solutions are needed. It is common knowledge that the cloud is a wide-ranging industry where data is essential, and subsequently, it attracts cyber criminals to join and infiltrate thereby creating a virtual threat to governments, organizations, and the technologies offered through cloud computing. Additionally, security risks and issues in different applications are discussed here. It also discusses cloud computing principles. After mentioning a few cloud based apps, this study also examines how security continues to pose a potential risk for cloud users all over the world. They also examine some workable methods and privacy precautions that could aid us in understanding cloud security concerns.

The solutions are evaluated and have significant analytical approach towards rendering the solutions to be more effective in every scenario. A number of cloud security options that can help businesses to cut costs while also increasing security. The study found that if the dangers are considered right away, the topic of solutions may be categorised into four pillars identified as network defence, visibility, computer-based security, and identity security that helps us to get a much broader understanding [26].

To get access to a large group of people with the least amount of effort and less expense, an increasing number of facilities and services are now being launched over the internet due to involvement of all these as a part of daily lives. Online resources are also used by healthcare organizations to educate themselves so they can treat patients' ailments effectively. Since health care systems utilise internet-based tools such as cloud computing as well as the Internet of Things (IoT) to assist people, words like e-health or smart health care are widely used. In addition to such advantages, these frameworks are vulnerable to risks or attacks to data security as well as invasions of user privacy, especially given the volume of false or unreliable information about health issues that is disseminated across the internet. The advantages as well as difficulties of deploying a cloud-integrated, IoT-based smart health care model are discussed throughout this study. A highly effective e-health solution may be produced by integrating these two advanced technologies [27].

Due to the continually expanding requirements, cloud computing has received great interest for decades. There are many benefits for businesses using cloud data storage options. These include cost-effective cloud computing schemes, effective IT administration, and enabling accessibility from anywhere in the world with reliable network connectivity. Further research is required to address related privacy and security concerns in the cloud. Scientists across academic communities, standard domains, as well as industry were given a potential solutions to such issues by the prior published studies. In this study the authors provide descriptive assessments of the issues, vulnerabilities, specifications, and threats associated with cloud security. The purpose of this study involves investigating the many elements of cloud computing as well as current privacy and security concerns. The authors, through this research, offer an in-depth analysis related to security threats associated with multiple cloud computing factors. The report also suggests a fresh categorization of developing security mechanisms relevant to this field. It mainly concentrates on and investigates the specific security challenges that cloud enterprises, involving cloud users, cloud service providers, as well as data owners, face [28].

Smart contracts as well as blockchain involves the potential to change the current structure of cloud industries through enabling the development of fully decentralised cloud/fog systems that lower costs through generating consistent results without the necessity for any mediator. The establishment of whole integrated as well as decentralized cloud solutions that will enable major companies to comply with such solutions and prevent exclusive hardware is also encouraged by many. We contend that certain evaluation advances cloud platforms through identifying operational issues, suggesting alternate approaches to problems encountered during exploration and development, as well as assessing established regulations and outlining excellent opportunities towards compatibility [29].

In the past few years, cloud computing has developed into a revolutionary innovation that provides businesses a number of advantages. Nevertheless, like any other innovation, it comes with inherent risks. Businesses may gain an edge over their competitors if companies engage with cloud computing while concurrently searching for fresh opportunities as well as utilizing their existing skills and knowledge. Concerns associated with cloud computing, meanwhile, may limit such skills. Here researchers show by using ambidexterity theoretical lens, that prospective cloud technology concerns have a big impact on how well businesses achieve in two key areas of exploitative as well as explorative technology. Fuzzy VIKOR technology uses language variables to let specialists express their viewpoints and rate the hazards of cloud computing while taking into account ambidexterity criteria, have been implemented to meet these aims. The findings demonstrate that every cloud computing vulnerability might prevent businesses from performing innovatively [30].

Recent years have seen a lot of interest regarding cloud computing because of its affordability as well as superior operations. Through its goods and services, cloud services had inexorably impacted both enterprises as well as people's daily lives during the past ten years. Pay-per-use and on-demand features enable firms to export a portion of their operations in order to increase value and speed up services. A recent financial movement favouring cloud settings, which began in 2019, points to a thriving inclination in the following few years. Regardless of the fact that using the cloud computing platform has many advantages for both enterprises and consumers, security concerns are still expected to be the most significant cloud concern in 2020. Despite the fact that many factors influence cloud computing tools, security like virtualization as well as scalability, along with their on-demand features, open up new safety entry points for malicious actions. To determine the present situation of the field, researchers carried out an analysis of service-based secure cloud computing challenges through this research. Here researchers mainly provided a review of cloud computing safety during past ten years as well as the provision of a standardised classification of security concerns across the three-layer paradigm, that is, IaaS, SaaS as well as PaaS [31].

Cloud computing had grown substantially in terms of business solutions. It consists of a collection of computing resources which can be made accessible online. Numerous research problems in the subject of cloud security, which is riddled with difficulties and has significant practical implications, remain unresolved. Cloud computing has been extremely beneficial in the IT industry. It resembles the next stage in the evolution of the internet and features a robust data storage network of administration with limitless potential. The data may be accessed by regulators without needing to be installed on the user's computer by utilizing internet services.

With the help of the cloud, shared or community access to customised computing resources is possible on request. You can maximise the use of a computer's resources by installing numerous operating systems on it. In this sense, it entails the creation of virtual versions of services like virtual operating systems, storage devices, hosting software, or applications over the cloud. The same is true regarding cloud computing where it has both benefits and drawbacks. A few of the repercussions include cloud security, manageability, trustworthiness, data loss, fraud, etc. In order to determine security concerns for implementing cloud computing, researchers' analyzed several obstacles as well as concerns relating to data security via the cloud through this research [32].

An increasingly popular internet-based innovation is cloud computing. It provides on-demand cloud-based services. Although it has many advantages, cloud computing poses a much more complicated situation in terms of key management, data security, data privacy, anomaly detection, cloud computing security and sharing, and vendor lock-in. Due to these issues, cloud computing adoptions are becoming difficult nowadays. Additionally, data integrity, privacy, and security are the biggest issue. Many scholars have conducted several surveys and published several papers related to the security of cloud computing. However, there was still a gap between cloud computing issues and their solutions because some researchers have discussed data security issues and the rest have discussed virtualization issues. But we tried to make an effort to outline all the security issues, and we have been delivered a proper and clear way. We have discussed many challenges and security threats regarding cloud computing and suggested possible solutions in our paper. We extracted the most common challenges and explain those and also compare them in a tabular form [33].

When using cloud resources to offer services, security is a criterion that modifies overall efficiency due to potential dangers. Protection as well as performance show how dependable cloud computing is when measuring the scale of a cloud's development. Artificial intelligence (AI) is the study of computing methods for improving natural reality. They explain the issues with and worries about cloud services for one or many AI technologies, including supervised, semi-controlled, uncontrolled, and improved cloud security issues. The future framework introduces a brand new paradigm for cloud data protection that makes use of cutting-edge techniques. The definition of this innovation describes it as a branch of computer science that focuses on developing intelligent machines which behave as well as react similar to people while enhancing security as well as privacy in cloud environments. Voice recognition, planning decision making, machine learning, as well as problem-solving solutions are the main areas of interest for AI. AI is a major sector for technologically advanced activities [34].

Big data is crucial in the modern world because more datasets are falling in its domain. The term refers to the enormously growing complex heterogeneous datasets requiring powerful technologies and algorithms. It is identified by its huge volume, high velocity of generation, and variety of data formats; identified as 3Vs. Data can be from smart grids, e-health systems, IoT, transportation, or government monitoring data, which must be sorted, analyzed, and stored. The challenge arises in storing and managing unlimited data while coping with high read and write rates flexibly and efficiently while dealing with various data models. Cloud computing, an open standard model, enabling ubiquitous computing with shared network access of a group of computing assets, serves to manage the big data resources. However, the use of distributed resources also poses a threat to the integrity as well as security of data. An active area of research that is of the utmost importance is the security and integrity of big data resources. This chapter will introduce big data, the need for cloud and distributed computing, data storage on the cloud resources, and the security concerns with its storage. Under these emblems, different datasets that form the big data will be discussed, along with the complexities in handling these datasets. Cloud computing architecture will be presented along with different types of clouds and services in current designs. The chapter will also outline cloud data security and storage security domains from the perspective of cloud data owners and service providers [35].

In the present day, we associate big data with vast databases with intricate and varied architecture. Such characteristics create obstacles when processing and storing the data to provide appropriate outcomes. The biggest disruption in the field of in-depth data analysis is security as well as privacy concerns. The modern techniques that emphasise big data, cloud computing, IoT, that is, Internet of Things, fog computing as well as, blockchain are our top priorities throughout this study. The provision of on-demand services to clients while minimizing costs is one of these, and cloud computing plays a part in it. Presently, the three main cloud providers involve Azure, AWS, and Google Cloud.

By acquiring services at the network's edges, fog computing provides fresh perspectives while expanding cloud computing systems. The Internet of Things implements this via working with many techniques that clears up the maze of coping with sophisticated technologies given their relevance in diverse application sectors. A dataset called the blockchain is used in a variety of areas involving payment systems and crypto currencies. This article focuses on basically providing a critical review and assessment of the topic within the framework of current sophisticated information systems. Here researchers discuss the issues raised by critics as well as the current dangers to the privacy of large-scale data systems. Researchers examined security breaches in cloud-based, blockchain-based, and Internet of Things (IoT) as well as fog based computing technologies. This study clearly explains the various threat behaviours and how they affect related computing technology. A thorough review of cloud-based innovations has been proposed by the authors, who have also covered their protection system as well as the security threats with regards to smart healthcare [36].

1.3.2 Security Risks, Issues, and Challenges

Although it creates security issues, cloud computing is a suitable solution for all size business firms. Due to businesses' greater reliability over the cloud, data-hungry hackers' attacks have turned it into a profitable opportunity. If businesses follow the proper protection mechanisms, businesses may safeguard themselves. Given the fierce competition for market share among household names such as Google, Amazon, and Microsoft, the rise in working remotely has expanded digital services carried through the Web;

cloud computing technology has evolved to one of the most crucial computing systems supporting both small as well as big organizations. It is understandable that cybercriminals would find this hyper-connected method of software delivery as well as resource sharing to be a tempting target given that half of all business data is currently maintained on the cloud (published in an article on statista.com: "Share of corporate data stored in the cloud in organizations worldwide from 2015 to 2022"). Subsequently companies are required to understand well about these risks and what's at stake, so that they are ready to follow preventive and defensive mechanisms to keep them safe from cyber attacks as well as possible security risks.

1.4 INTRODUCTION TO CLOUD COMPUTING SECURITY

Cloud computing may be defined as "a form of computing in which scalable and elastic IT-enabled capabilities are supplied as a service using internet technology," according to global research advisory firm Gartner.

When subscribing to a cloud computing provider like Microsoft Azure or Amazon Web Services, businesses can have instant computing power, access storage and more bandwidth as well as several different computing services and specific business applications. Subsequently there is an elimination of the need for companies to invest millions of dollars and spend weeks, months, or years in creating their applications, data centres, and services. According to Gartner, end-user expenditure for public cloud services is anticipated to climb by 20% globally to $332.3 billion in 2021 and $397.5 billion in 2022 (as per an article published in Gartner.com: "Gartner Forecasts Worldwide Public Cloud End-User Spending to Grow 23% in 2021").

Decreased IT expenses, the capacity to expand as well as swiftly introduce new features, the capability to massively increase performance in response to demanding spikes, and increased departmental cooperation are just a few of the many commercial advantages of cloud computing.

Three different service model categories are generally used to categorise cloud services:

- Software as a service (SaaS) gives customers access to programs.
- Platform-as-a-service (PaaS) gives programmers the tools as well as operating systems they required to create cloud-based apps.
- Infrastructure-as-a-service (IaaS) offers businesses server-based cloud infrastructure.

Pricing varies depending on different factors, involving the volume of bandwidth utilized, the number of clients (such as personnel accessing services), the apps utilized, the storage capacity needed, the uptime needed, and much more. All systems commonly charge via a subscription based approach.

1.5 SECURITY RISKS

Cloud computing offers many advantages, such as improved collaboration, greater access, more storage capabilities and mobility, and so on. Cloud computing, however, frequently poses potential risks. The most standard security concerns related to cloud computing are covered in the following:

1.5.1 Loss of Data

Loss of data is most prominent possible risk allied with cloud computing. It is also referred to as breach of privacy, loss of data, data theft that is, there are chances of data being stolen, destroyed, deleted, or making it unusable via some bad cyber applications, cyber criminals or through malicious application. When third parties have access to client personal information, then there is a possible threat of data being compromised, leaked, or mismanaged if data owners do not have the full control over the data management policies. There are chances when some portions of data are not available to data owners because a hard drive malfunctions, or outdated software, or data loss in cloud based systems.

1.5.2 Insecure APIs and Hacked Interfaces

The internet is completely necessary for cloud computing, hence, it's imperative to secure the interfaces especially application programming interfaces, that is, APIs which are utilised via outside customers. Typically cloud services are easily accessible via APIs. Fewer services with cloud computing are accessible to the normal public. These services have accessibility to third parties also, so there is a greater chance of damaging or compromising these through cybercriminals.

1.5.3 Breach of Data

The data of an organization is hacked by cybercriminals when confidential information is accessed, viewed, or taken via a third party in an unauthorized way (a process known as a "data breach").

1.5.4 Vendor Lock-In

Cloud computing involves one major security concern, that is, Vendor lock-in; when there is a shift of services of an organization from one to another, at this instance there might be some complications. Due to different platforms adopted by different vendors there might be a risk in shifting as well as the challenge of moving from one platform to a different one.

1.5.5 Complexity Increase Puts a Load on IT Employees

For the IT personnel, operating, migrating, or integrating the cloud services are complicated. To manage, maintain, as well as integrate data on the cloud, IT staff must include additional abilities and competencies.

1.5.6 Meltdown and Spectre

Spectre and meltdown vulnerabilities allow programs to watch and steal data that is currently being handled by computers. It is compatible with cloud computing platforms, mobile devices, and desktop computers. The memory of other active programs can be used to store the password as well as your personal data, including emails, photos, and business papers.

1.5.7 DoS (Denial-of-Service) Attack

Sometimes there is a huge traffic going to buffer a server, as a result of which denial of service, that is, DoS attack occurs. DoS attacks mainly make their targets organizations which are sizable such as media outlets, governments, banks, etc. Such DoS attackers demand huge money, kill a lot of time, money, and resources for processing the data so that lost information may be restored successfully.

1.5.8 Hijacking an Account

Account theft is a significant security problem in cloud computing. Account theft is a procedure by which attackers steal the data out of a user's or an organization's cloud accounts (such as email, bank account, and social media account). The hacked account is used by the hackers for illegal actions.

When it comes to technologies, very few are completely secure. Cloud computing technology has some security risks: as per Sophos, "The State of Cloud Security 2020" report, 70% IT administrators reported their organizations had suffered a public cloud security risk in the previous year, such as malware [37], stolen account details, and ransomware. These are a few of the main security risks:

1.5.8.1 Data Breaches and Leaks

Companies' confidential data, such as customer as well as intellectual property information, is often stored and handled by cloud computing providers. However, such data could be leaked, deleted, or held for ransom if the service provider has no proper security controls in place, is hacked, or experiences a system breakdown. Actually, respondents to the study say that their primary concern was data loss as well as leakage.

1.5.8.2 Vulnerable Online Apps

Vulnerabilities exist in Web-based applications which link organizations as well as their consumers to cloud services that data-hungry cybercriminals might take advantage of. Web apps may encounter issues with business logic, authentication management, and encryption [38, 39] setup flaws (published report "Web Application Security" on synopsys.com).

1.5.8.3 DDoS Attacks

DDoS attacks pose a major risk to cloud computing settings as they overwhelm a company's servers with fake queries for information. Long-lasting service outages brought on by a persistent DDoS attack may cause financial losses as well as business downtime.

1.5.8.4 Having Insufficient Visibility into Network Operations

While transferring data from this source to that source, there is also a transfer of managerial responsibility, that is, you also give the CSP, cloud service provider, the power to control certain aspects of it on your account. If you don't know exactly what you're doing, you risk losing perspective on your resources that would increase the demand for and service prices. Thus it's important to talk about the protocols in advance and make sure for maximum transparency is there during process of transfer.

1.5.8.5 Malware

Businesses moving 90% of their operations to the cloud are much susceptible to data theft. The primary security procedures have all been tried to be incorporated by cloud computing vendors to safeguard your personal information. But hackers have also advanced. They are accustomed to these recent technologies. Subsequently, hackers may now easily obtain private user data and evade more out of such regulations.

1.5.8.6 Compliance

The development of cloud computing is accelerating rapidly. Technology has helped businesses move outside offline systems more quickly, but it has also prompted crucial talks regarding compliance. The cloud computing service provider must therefore meet your personally identifiable information, that is, PII, data access, and storage utilizing the required privacy safeguards.

1.5.8.7 Data Loss

Among the top concerns about cloud-based security, information theft, deletion, and breach were mentioned in 64% of study participants. By giving the cloud service provider, or CSP, a portion of their authority, businesses also greatly increase the risk to their data. For example, there is a considerably higher chance that vital information about your firm could be compromised if the cloud computing service provider encounters a security flaw.

1.5.8.8 Inadequate Due Diligence

Understanding the actions that a business must take to migrate its data into the cloud is aided by operating guidelines. Firms typically underestimate the work that must be done to ensure a smooth transition process as well as the steps taken by the provider of cloud services to achieve the same.

1.5.8.9 Compliance Issues

Owing to data protection laws like the Health Insurance Portability and Accountability Act also termed as HIPAA and General Data Protection Regulation of Europe, termed as GDPR, enterprises in particular industries are required to maintain a tight lid on the information they gather. Companies could find themselves out of compliance and subject to financial penalties if a cloud service suffers an infringement that results in data loss or exposure.

1.5.8.10 Customer Distrust

A customer places a strong trust in a business organization with regard to their personal information; the customer does not consider the storage type or whether data is stored in a local repository or a cloud based storage. If by any means, the customer's information is leaked or lost, they will consider the business responsible and as a result the customer's trust will be broken and ultimately the business will suffer financial losses.

1.5.9 Possible Remedies: Preventive Techniques to Reduce and Manage Cloud Risks

In spite of these worries, businesses have a variety of options at their disposal to lower their cyber security threats and benefit from cloud computing. Some preventive measures that may be adapted are:

1.5.9.1 Always Backup Data

This adage holds true even in the cloud. Maintaining backups shouldn't be replaced by giving a third party access to your data. The best defenses for dangers including ransomware and data loss because of technological issues are thorough regular backups. Simple data migration from one platform to a different one can cause catastrophic data loss, as illustrated by MySpace's deletion of client data spanning longer than a decade (bbc.com article "MySpace admits losing 12 years' worth of music uploads").

1.5.9.2 Web App Pen Testing

One clever method to expose flaws in online apps—perhaps before the evil ones do—is to mimic a cyber attack (penetration testing) to evaluate where security breaches might lie. To find, address, and minimise bugs and software flaws, penetration testing needs to be carried out often.

1.5.9.3 Multifactor Authentication

It reduces the risks brought on by greater remote access via requiring two or even more credentials for verifying the identity of the user. For instance, registering into a web app can involve both a password and a code sent to the Smartphone of the client.

1.5.9.4 Geodiversity

Working with a cloud service provider that distributes data over servers located in various areas instead of just one. In case an individual data centre is targeted, it may help to prevent the information from being lost or stolen.

1.5.9.5 Examine Cloud Configurations

Do this frequently. Companies are susceptible to cyber attacks when cloud services are configured incorrectly, such as by mismanaging access permissions and exposing storage to the internet. The problem is made worse by the fact that a business is more vulnerable the more services it utilizes from various vendors.

Businesses and providers of cloud-based services must work together to ensure optimal security for cloud-based computing and the underlying protection of data. They can support the same in the following ways:

1.5.9.6 Risk Assessments

A risk evaluation approach includes analyzing your cloud infrastructure. It helps to comprehend how the protection measures that have been installed work and how well they are truly working. It enables teams to identify weaknesses and take appropriate action to remedy them.

1.5.9.7 User Access Controls

Since the cloud infrastructure is becoming more approachable, businesses must provide rigorous security controls for clients. Users must have security controls in order to stop intruders from disclosing important information. In order to safeguard the data against unauthorised users, just a limited number of individuals should have access to key functionalities.

1.5.9.8 Automation

Businesses must automate crucial tasks like vendor risk evaluations, real-time monitoring, and others. Despite of being slowed down by a plethora of unnecessary, repetitive chores, it would allow the IT staff to monitor crucial operations.

1.5.9.9 Continuous Monitoring

One of the crucial tasks of the present cloud environment is continuous assessment. One must bring in real-time evaluation to make sure your data is secure as the cloud becomes more open and fraudsters discover new methods to penetrate it.

1.5.10 Future of Cloud Computing and Its Challenges

A number of emerging technologies, including smart cities, 5G internet, the Internet of Things, that is, IoT, depends on cloud services for processing and storing more data. As a result, the cloud paradigm will have many more security risks because of the diversity of the new enterprises using the afore-mentioned technologies. At the moment, cloud computing includes every element, including networks, infrastructures as well as access controls. Without a clear understanding of the cloud architecture, security communities deal with issues including data duplication, a failure to recognize potential threats in a reasonable timeframe, a loss of control over data access as well as data security and a need to meet regulatory requirements.

We anticipate a rapid technological advancement in the computational demands catered by cloud computing models as cloud computing becomes a more ubiquitous component of our daily lives and digital computing infrastructure [40].

As per literature reviews available, there are a number of issues with cloud computing security unaddressed effectively. There are numerous unresolved problems to be addressed specifically, and the gaps in the existing answers will reveal the best directions for future studies. Research in the future may be carried out to reinstate the clients' trust and guarantee that they possess complete control over their information. To gain cloud users' trust, CSP capabilities must be enhanced, and data owners must have complete control over data accessibility, controlling, and management of the data. So that owners must be able to decide for a third party to access data when and in what manner and up to what extent whenever they get access to it [41].

We are discussing here about current concerns and potential directions for cyber security in the cloud computing system in this segment. Any investigator in the available literature focuses on a different security concern and handles the issues in their own way. Therefore, researchers discover multiple security fixes for a particular security concern. Different security mechanisms for the exact same problem may not always be practicable to execute. Therefore, the first unresolved problem is to develop a standard, highly integrated, and collaborative security solution that can satisfy all fundamental security needs in the context of cloud computing. Because many academics have given safety and confidentiality in cloud computing a lot of attention, there are still unresolved problems that require more work.

It is still a challenge to resolve various known and undiscovered dangers. Another significant issue is the necessity for appropriate authentication regulations as well as rules to ensure that only authorized individuals have access to sensitive data. In situations where integrity of data must always be guaranteed, it's essential to protect users' private information. A key component of cloud computing involves multi-tenancy, which allows efficiently using servers in the cloud data centre. In a multitenancy setting, various clients utilize the same program running on same hardware, same operating system, as well as using same data-storage mechanism. The improper implementation of multi-tenancy may result in the under using servers in a cloud data centre.

However, DDoS assaults might affect the multi-tenancy environment and stop further tenants from using computer resources. The efficient utilization of multi-tenancy is thus a significant challenge that necessitates careful consideration from cloud security researchers. By 2022, a market of 14.4 trillion dollars will exist thanks to Cisco's projection of 50 billion connected objects. As a result, the proliferation of IoT devices will unavoidably result in a massive volume of data that needs to be stored, processed, as well as widely accessible to end-users. IoT devices frequently have low processing speeds, making them unable to carry out complex calculations and store significant volumes of data [42].

So far, it appears that cloud computing is the greatest option for addressing the needs of IoT situations. Cloud of Things is an entirely new, ubiquitous computing model that was created as a result of the fusion of IoT with the cloud abbreviated as CoT. Consequently, for this new essential model, it is imperative that the problem of information security and different devices' accessibility to cloud data centres be overcome. Consumers may link any gadget to any data centre using CoT, an IoT product management platform. This modern CoT offers huge possibility for both customers and service providers, similar to what the internet is offering. However, there are clear issues and restrictions with the cloud system's reactivity, latency, as well as general processing and access capabilities in regard with IoT traffic data. The transfer of data for an IoT client as well as cloud computing has a slow reaction time, specifically for huge data quantities. Fog computing has been promoted recently as a possible new computing model for addressing the limitations related to CoT architecture. To address developing applications, reduce operational costs, and speed up application responsiveness, several leading telecom firms have started to develop a fog computing model. Such modern computing architecture demands cloud security through slower rate of data loss via support for latency-sensitive applications while safeguarding data transmitted across the IoT devices [43].

For storing, combining, and analyzing data gathered from medical equipment utilised in healthcare facilities, cloud computing is the recommended method in a system for healthcare monitoring. Because medical data is private, delicate, and stored in the cloud, there are significant security and privacy threats [44].

Here some of the main directions for future that needed to be resolved involve:

One of the important future directions in this sector that has to be addressed is how to securely store healthcare information on the cloud, implement privacy for healthcare data storage, build a system of access control which is more effective for the secure transfer of health-related data, efficiently communicate health data among many healthcare providers, preserve the accuracy of medical records, and securely protect patient information when in an urgent situation.

Another unresolved problem in the cloud infrastructure is determining who is a legitimate user as well as who is a malicious user. The majority of recent research has automated the detecting of outsider or insider attacks using artificial intelligence [45], machine learning, as well as deep learning. However, whoever will investigate this issue using a specific dataset, and many firms find it extremely challenging to adopt this. The answer to this problem will be essential for enabling quick organizational adoption. The question of how to effectively combine the various systems still needs to be answered.

1.5.11 Conclusions

Throughout this study the authors have given a brief overview about cloud computing, fog computing, and IoT. We have also discussed how modern advancements and dependency of users as well as businesses to cover-up most of things across the Web have posed many threats as well, but we can also not deny the ease of availability, and managing the different tasks of our daily lives via internet. Most business firms use cloud services for the good return in business. But we also came across various security risks, challenges which still need to be addressed and there is still a wider scope to further develop different preventive measures as well as security mechanism to protect consumer data, healthcare data, to prevent unauthorized access, loss of data, etc.

Businesses of all sizes may now expand and scale without needing to make significant financial investments thanks to cloud computing. Yet, because the cloud is public, they are also vulnerable to many types of cyber attacks. Companies can still profit from cloud services while limiting risks by being aware of these concerns and implementing the appropriate precautionary measures.

REFERENCES

[1] S. Z. Mohammadi and J. N. Navimipour, "Invalid cloud providers' identification using the support vector machine," *International Journal of Next-Generation Computing*, vol. 8, no. 1, 2017.

[2] S. Gupta, S. Rani, A. Dixit, and H. Dev, "Features exploration of distinct load balancing algorithms in cloud computing environment," *International Journal of Advanced Networking and Applications*, vol. 11, no. 1, pp. 4177–4183, 2019.

[3] P. Heinzlreiter, M. Krieger, and W. Hennerbichler, "Usage scenarios for a community cloud in education and research," in *Proceedings of the 1st International IBM Cloud Academy Conference*, pp. 1–9, Raleigh, NC, April 2012.

[4] D. Contractor and D. Patel, "Accountability in cloud computing by means of chain of trust," *International Journal on Network Security*, vol. 19, pp. 251–259, 2017.

[5] N. J. Navimipour, A. M. Rahmani, A. H. Navin, and M. Hosseinzadeh, "Job scheduling in the Expert Cloud based on genetic algorithms," *Kybernetes*, vol. 43, p. 12, 2014.

[6] W. Kong, Y. Lei, and J. Ma, "Data security and privacy information challenges in cloud computing," *International Journal of Computational Science and Engineering*, vol. 16, no. 3, pp. 215–218, 2018.

[7] S. Chenthara, K. Ahmed, H. Wang, and F. Whittaker, "Security and privacy-preserving challenges of e-health solutions in cloud computing," *IEEE Access*, vol. 7, Article ID 74382, 2019.

[8] A. Qasim, A. Sadiq, A. Kamaludin, and M. Al-Sharafi, "E-learning models: The effectiveness of the cloud-based E-learning model over the traditional E-learning model," in *Proceedings of the 2017 8th International Conference on Information Technology (ICIT)*. IEEE, May 2017.

[9] N. S. Aldahwan and M. S. Saleh, "Developing a framework for cost-benefit analysis of cloud computing adoption by higher education institutions in Saudi Arabia," in *Proceedings of the 2018 International Conference on Smart Computing and Electronic Enterprise (ICSCEE)*, pp. 1–9, Selangor, July 2018.

[10] H. Ding, X. Li, and C. Gong, "Trust model research in cloud computing environment," in *Proceedings of the 2015 International Symposium on Computers & Informatics*, Beijing, January 2015.

[11] D. Talia, "Clouds meet agents: Toward intelligent cloud services," *IEEE Internet Computing*, vol. 16, no. 2, pp. 78–81, 2012.

[12] S. Goyal, "Public vs. private vs. hybrid vs. community – cloud computing: A critical review," *International Journal of Computer Network and Information Security*, vol. 6, no. 3, pp. 20–29, 2014.

[13] C. C. Rao, M. Leelarani, and Y. R. Kumar, "Cloud: Computing services and deployment models," *International Journal of Engineering and Computer Science*, vol. 2, no. 12, pp. 3389–3392, 2013.

[14] G. Conway and E. Curry, "Managing cloud computing: A life cycle approach," in *Proceedings of the 2nd International Conference on Cloud Computing and Services Science Closer*, pp. 198–207, Porto, April 2012.

[15] V. Gonçalves and P. Ballon, "Adding value to the network: Mobile operators' experiments with software-as-a-service and platform-as-a-service models," *Telematics and Informatics*, vol. 28, no. 1, pp. 12–21, 2011.

[16] S. El Kafhali, I. El Mir, and M. Hanini, "Security threats, defense mechanisms, challenges, and future directions in cloud computing," *Archives of Computational Methods in Engineering*, vol. 29, no. 1, pp. 223–246, 2022.

[17] V. Singh and V. D. Kaushik, "Concepts of data mining and process mining," in *Process Mining Techniques for Pattern Recognition*, pp. 1–17. CRC Press, 2022.

[18] H. Raj, M. Kumar, P. Kumar, A. Singh, and O. P. Verma, "Issues and challenges related to privacy and security in healthcare using IoT, fog, and cloud computing," in *Advanced Healthcare Systems: Empowering Physicians with IoT-Enabled Technologies*, pp. 21–32. Wiley Online Library, 2022.

[19] E. Ismagilova, L. Hughes, N. P. Rana, and Y. K. Dwivedi, "Security, privacy and risks within smart cities: Literature review and development of a smart city interaction framework," *Information Systems Frontiers*, vol. 24, no. 2, pp. 393–414, 2022.

[20] M. Jangjou and M. K. Sohrabi, "A comprehensive survey on security challenges in different network layers in cloud computing," *Archives of Computational Methods in Engineering*, pp. 1–22, 2022.

[21] J. Chavan, R. Patil, S. Patil, V. Gutte, and S. Karande, "A survey on security threats in cloud computing service models," in *2022 6th International Conference on Intelligent Computing and Control Systems (ICICCS)*, pp. 574–580. IEEE, May 2022.

[22] N. S. Aldahwan and M. S. Ramzan, "Descriptive literature review and classification of community cloud computing research," *Scientific Programming*, vol. 29, pp. 1–12, 2022.

[23] M. Jangjou and M. K. Sohrabi, "A comprehensive survey on security challenges in different network layers in cloud computing," *Archives of Computational Methods in Engineering*, vol. 29, pp. 3587–3608, 2022. https://doi.org/10.1007/s11831-022-09708-9.

[24] H. E. Ghalbzouri and J. E. Bouhdidi, "Integrating business intelligence with cloud computing: State of the art and fundamental concepts," *Networking, Intelligent Systems and Security*, pp. 197–213, 2022.

[25] N. M. Ibrahim, D. Musleh, M. A. A. Khan, S. Chabani, and S. Dash, "Cloud-based smart grids: Opportunities and challenges," in *Biologically Inspired Techniques in Many Criteria Decision Making*, pp. 1–13. Springer, 2022.

[26] A. Karmakar, A. Raghuthaman, O. S. Kote, and N. Jayapandian, "Cloud computing application: Research challenges and opportunity," in *2022 International Conference on Sustainable Computing and Data Communication Systems (ICSCDS)*, pp. 1284–1289. IEEE, April 2022.

[27] P. Nayak, S. K. Mohapatra, and S. C. M. Sharma, "Privacy and security issues in IoT cloud convergence of smart health care," in *Connected e-Health*, pp. 439–455. Springer, 2022.

[28] H. K. Bella and S. Vasundra, "A study of security threats and attacks in cloud computing," in *2022 4th International Conference on Smart Systems and Inventive Technology (ICSSIT)*, pp. 658–666. IEEE, January 2022.

[29] N. Krishnaraj, K. Bellam, B. Sivakumar, and A. Daniel, "The future of cloud computing: Blockchain-based decentralized cloud/fog solutions–challenges, opportunities, and standards," *Blockchain Security in Cloud Computing*, pp. 207–226, 2022.

[30] M. T. Taghavifard and S. Majidian, "Identifying cloud computing risks based on firm's ambidexterity performance using fuzzy VIKOR technique," *Global Journal of Flexible Systems Management*, vol. 23, no. 1, pp. 113–133, 2022.

[31] F. K. Parast, C. Sindhav, S. Nikam, H. I. Yekta, K. B. Kent, and S. Hakak, "Cloud computing security: A survey of service-based models," *Computers & Security*, vol. 114, p. 102580, 2022.

[32] M. Gupta, L. Ahuja, and A. Seth, "A study on cloud environment: Confidentiality problems, security threats, and challenges," in *Soft Computing for Security Applications*, pp. 679–698. Springer, 2022.

[33] R. Khalid, K. Khaliq, M. I. Tariq, S. Tayyaba, M. A. Jaffar, and M. Arif, "Cloud computing security challenges and their solutions," in *Security and Privacy Trends in Cloud Computing and Big Data*, pp. 103–118. CRC Press, 2022.

[34] A. Vani, M. Naved, A. H. Fakih, A. N. Venkatesh, P. Vijayakumar, and P. R. Kshirsagar, "Supervise the data security and performance in cloud using artificial intelligence," in *AIP Conference Proceedings*, vol. 2393, no. 1, p. 020094. AIP Publishing LLC, 2022.

[35] M. S. Mushtaq, M. Y. Mushtaq, M. W. Iqbal, and S. A. Hussain, "Security, integrity, and privacy of cloud computing and big data," in *Security and Privacy Trends in Cloud Computing and Big Data*, pp. 19–51. CRC Press, 2022.

[36] K. Mishra, V. Bhattacharjee, S. Saket, and S. P. Mishra, "Cloud and big data security system's review principles: A decisive investigation," *Wireless Personal Communications*, 1–38, 2022.

[37] S. Rani, K. Tripathi, Y. Arora, and A. Kumar, "Analysis of anomaly detection of Malware using KNN," in *2022 2nd International Conference on Innovative Practices in Technology and Management (ICIPTM)*, vol. 2, pp. 774–779. IEEE, February 2022.

[38] V. Singh and V. Dubey, "A two level image security based on Arnold transform and chaotic logistic mapping," *International Journal of Advanced*

Research in Computer Science and Software Engineering, vol. 5, no. 2, pp. 883–887, 2015.

[39] V. Singh and V. Dubey, "An entropy based color image encryption based on Arnold transform and Pixel chaotic shuffling method," *International Journal of Advanced Research in Computer Science and Software Engineering*, vol. 5, no. 2, pp. 888–892, 2015.

[40] S. El Kafhali, I. El Mir, and M. Hanini, "Security threats, defense mechanisms, challenges, and future directions in cloud computing," *Archives of Computational Methods in Engineering*, vol. 29, no. 1, pp. 223–246, 2022.

[41] A. Singh and K. Chatterjee, "Cloud security issues and challenges: A survey," *Journal of Network and Computer Applications*, vol. 79, pp. 88–115, 2017.

[42] S. El Kafhali and K. Salah, "Efficient and dynamic scaling of fog nodes for IoT devices," *The Journal of Supercomputing*, vol. 73, no. 12, pp. 5261–5284, 2017.

[43] D. Zhang, F. Haider, M. St-Hilaire, and C. Makaya, "Model and algorithms for the planning of fog computing networks," *IEEE Internet of Things Journal*, vol. 6, no. 2, pp. 3873–3884, 2019.

[44] S. Chenthara, K. Ahmed, H. Wang, and F. Whittaker, "Security and privacy-preserving challenges of e-Health solutions in cloud computing," *IEEE Access*, vol. 7, pp. 74361–74382, 2019.

[45] P. Rajendra, M. Kumari, S. Rani, N. Dogra, R. Boadh, A. Kumar, and M. Dahiya, "Impact of artificial intelligence on civilization: Future perspectives," *Materials Today: Proceedings*, vol. 56, pp. 252–256, 2022.

Chapter 2

Security Aspects of Cloud, Fog, and Edge Computing

[1]*Ashish Kumbhare, [2]Ravi Kiran,*
and [3]Shashank Mane

[1]Faculty of Science and Technology, the ICFAI University, Raipur, C.G. 490042.
[2]Faculty of Science and Technology, the ICFAI University, Raipur, C.G. 490042.
[3]Department of Electronics and Communication, Shri Balaji Institute of
Information and Technology, Betul, M.P.

2.1 INTRODUCTION

Cloud computing (CC) has evolved into an acceptable alternative for providing an on-demand foundation for computation and storing massive amounts of data. CC is being used in a variety of fields, including education, accounting, production, and healthcare. Because more devices depend on CC, emerging technologies that utilize the advantages of CC while remaining a lightweight solution despite all of cloud's challenges are required to fit with the qualities of lightweight schemes like IoT systems. Although IoT devices can do some essential activities like sensing, regulating, and actuating, they are unable to carry out significant and complicated operations like managing sizable smart transport systems and intelligent healthcare procedures. Vehicle networks and aided medical applications are two examples of time sensitive IoT systems that may call for quick decisions in order to provide the optimum performance. Because such applications cannot manage network latency, sending information to cloud resources for computation may lead to a delay in making decisions in a time sensitive application (Chalapathi et al. 2021). Furthermore, CC is very complex for certain equipment to operate, and it doesn't help with some of the fundamental aspects of IoT such as geo-location and connectivity limitation. Fog computing (FC) and edge computing (EC) are two technological advances that can deliver CC advantages while also addressing the distinctive features of IoT applications. The desire to have a substantial amount of storage with effective virtualization has been an impelling cause for various companies, groups, and small firms for transitioning to cloud, edge, and fog frameworks from self-contained implementation. Whereas these technological advances enable the advancement and expansion of IoT systems, they also initiate numerous privacy and security concerns that could impact the implementation and use of IoT applications. When it comes to securing sensitive data like private information, the demand for computational intelligence transferring schemes is

DOI: 10.1201/9781003329947-2

growing quickly (Ranaweera 2021). Traditionally, cloud users have legal access to their private data. Notably, five distinct privacy and security features are brought up in whatsoever order: confidentiality, integrity, availability, accountability, and privacy preservation. We enumerate a few of the primary privacy and security issues of three methods, clarify how much each threat could impact them, and offer some preventive actions that might help alleviate or inhibit these security issues in order to attain a greater degree of safety, stability, and reliable performance. Whereas many threats on FC and EC are derived from cloud technology, numerous existing cloud-based solutions are unlikely to be impactful or might not work correctly because of the distinct characteristics of FC and EC. As a result, we will showcase the unique qualities of such threats with relation to FC and EC (Alhroob 2018).

2.1.1 An Overview of CC

Several more businesses infrastructures had also grown and expanded as a result of new developments in technology. CC is regarded as a special way to give businesses access to software. In particular over the Web, it employs a variety of elements, including both software and hardware to provide solutions. Initially, CC made it simple to obtain the varied information and applications offered (Parikh et al. 2019). CC enables optimal use of resources while maintaining scaling and adaptability. Other benefits include reduced energy usage and the ability for process management to be provided on demand, allowing clients to pay just for the assets they are using and connect directly from anywhere. From such an analysis, large, intermediate, and small businesses use cloud technology to protect or store critical cloud data, allowing them to access this data from anywhere in the globe by using the internet. The primary fusion that constitutes the CC structure is between service-oriented and event-driven configurations. Three distinct service models are offered by cloud technology: infrastructure as a service (IaaS), platform as a service (PaaS), and software as a service (SaaS) (Aljumah 2018).

2.1.2 Service Models for CC

2.1.2.1 IaaS

The IaaS represents the most extended form in which a provider of cloud services basically gives hosting and space as an online entity to one's clients via the cloud. Clients of such a service can utilize the infrastructure to configure their operating systems and software without being concerned about foundational infrastructure's operations and maintenance. Furthermore, because CC services are always on, clients can scale up or down their facilities without being required to purchase or keep updating their real devices.

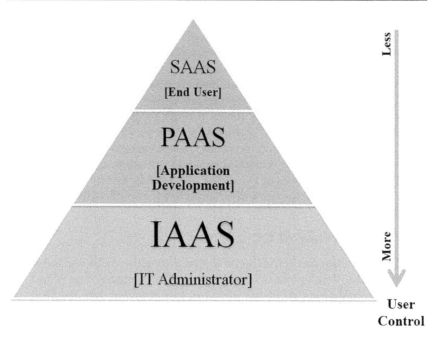

Figure 2.1 The control level for users for each service model.

Amazon's Ec2 is among the most well-known IaaS models (Aljumah 2018). Date warehousing and big data analytics are two examples of IaaS use cases. IaaS offers the following benefits:

- Regarded as the CC model with the most flexibility.
- Economical in terms of equipment buying based on usage.
- The entire infrastructure is completely under the client's control.
- A setting that is highly adaptable and expandable.

Since the customer is accountable for creating the infrastructure, there may be security risks that the customer isn't conscious of, making IaaS typically more concerning than the other two models. Furthermore, such models typically necessitate extra training for personnel in order to gain knowledge of how to successfully manage and control the facilities, which include extra responsibilities like modifications and backups for the system modules.

2.1.2.2 PaaS

This service model focuses on offering a platform for clients to implement, host, evaluate, and build software applications. In this model, a third-party provider grants the client internet connectivity to both hardware and software tools. PaaS liberates consumers from needing to install both software and hardware to create their implementation; additionally, it could offer extra computing power which is difficult to obtain by a specific user; rather, clients in this pay on a per-usage grounds for the tools. PaaS provides the following benefits:

- Low-cost and precise solution for app creation and deployment.
- Unlimited platform scalability.
- Business policy automation.
- Ease of mobility to hyper model.

Moreover, one of the issues about PaaS is vendor support, which occurs when distributors decide to alter the specifications or strategies in the long-term without providing consumers with transparent migration policies (Aljumah 2018). Furthermore, problems may occur once users of such a model attempt to combine and link stored data in off-premises clouds while utilizing a few components from existing IT systems.

2.1.2.3 SaaS

It is a popular service for CC model that several people utilize on a regular basis. Cloud application services are another name for this model. Applications are forwarded to users through the Web inside this concept, removing the requirement for the customer to configure or update such applications. Furthermore, the majority of applications immediately run through the internet explorer, providing an additional layer of comfort and flexibility to clients of this model. The following benefits are provided by SaaS:

- An economical solution for gaining access to various applications with no need to modify hardware.
- A wide range of services and solutions are offered to customers with a single click.
- It is not necessary to enhance the software because the customer will constantly have access to the latest version.
- Simplicity of use.

However, SaaS has raised issues, including a complete absence of assistance for interfacing for such software developed as a provider with different locally used programs by customers. Furthermore, because SaaS is usually offered as a universally applicable remedy, the user has limited customization options.

2.1.3 Fog Computing Overview

Unlike typical CC, FC, often referred as fogging, emphasizes on the decentralization of a computing structure, which is positioned in between equipment that generate the actual information and the cloud. The objective of FC is to reduce CC capabilities to the network's edge providing customers with faster services, such as telecommunication and software applications. This is useful in delivering cloud services for good mobility technology like the IoTs and vehicular ad-hoc networks. In FC, rather than syncing devices via sophisticated communications infrastructure, devices are often linked directly to its target. As a response, the connection will now have substantially reduced latency and higher service standards. Cisco Systems suggested the notion of FC. The FC technology wasn't really intended to substitute for CC; instead, it was designed to address the holes in CC's offerings (Ometov et al. 2021a). As per Cisco Systems, FC is a virtualized system that offers processing, storing, and networking capabilities to client units from CC data centers that are not particularly positioned at the network edge. Fog differs from cloud as it brings the end-user nearer to it in order to supply them with services and react to their requests in short time. In CC, computation, controlling, and stored information is transmitted to a cloud system, but in FC, both local and central data processing, storage, and network monitoring are matched. FC is described as a distributed system in which virtualized and non-virtualized end devices execute the majority of activities. It has certain properties with cloud, such as non-latency sensitive computing and the capacity to keep valuable data for an extended period of time by just being between consumers and the cloud (Guilloteau and Venkatesen 2013). The fundamental structure of FC is identical to that of CC; however, its lower levels incorporate specific components capable of detecting uncommon time responses quickly. Because of this property, FC is utilized to regulate and enhance health care departments, vehicle movement, parking systems, and many other things. FC is a distributed structure comprised of a sharp device with specific application solutions from an outside system. In other words, it empowers the devices to manage their alliances and duties in whatever manner they see fit. Essentially, FC is a focus layer located between both the cloud and the device that provides increased information processing, research, and capacity by minimizing the quantity of data transported to the cloud. FC allows for better management and a more pleasant customer satisfaction. It is essentially a collection of software and hardware systems capable of monitoring, controlling, and analyzing data with relatively low latency. Furthermore, FC cannot offer persistent storage. It lessens the burden on the cloud by eliminating unneeded data from its computing storage, hence reducing the cost (Cook et al. 2018). In terms of the location and use for which they are deployed, fog gadgets differ from cloud gadgets.

Some of the distinguishing characteristics are:

- If the device's installation objective is to customize end-user network services and to gather information, it is classified as a fog device; else, it is classified like a cloud device.

- The equipment is described as a fog device if it has minimal computing and sensory capabilities.
- FC has several characteristics, such as:
- Knowledge of the position of the edge.
- Extremely low latency.
- Support for mobility.
- Instantaneous services.
- Pleasant exchanges.
- Nature heterogeneous.
- Irreconcilability.

The majority of people today demand operating programs with large processing demands that exceed a portable device's computing power due to its slow information processing. Because application computation must be offloaded to adjacent cloud servers, there is a shortage of both computing capacity and energy (Xiao and Xiao 2013).

Offloading tasks resolves the problem of computation; however it is not practical for applications that need to be completed quickly. As a result, in these circumstances, the idea of FC is thought to be a good answer. However, there are several drawbacks to FC, like limited resources as contrasted to the cloud, which results in high latency, power consumption, bandwidth allocation, information management, and security threats.

2.1.4 Edge Computing Overview

In recent times, there has been a shift in computing trends that is driving cloud services to the network's edge. In other terms, computer processes and services are indeed being transferred from the network core towards the edge networks. This new technique is known as EC. In terms of processing position, EC differs from fog technology. A LAN serves as a gateway in a fog network, although electronic sensors like programmable automation controllers (PACs) execute computing tasks in an EC network. The purpose for the emergence of EC approach is to resolve the excessive latency and power usage services problems of CC and to provide minimal computational offloading solutions for resource constrained equipment and IoT applications (Henze et al. 2020). Furthermore, it offers the benefits of information caching and storage solutions, which assist in the control of excessive network traffic.

The following are the essential features of EC:

- Relatively low latency.
- Lower bandwidth limit.
- Deployment adaptability.
- Automation.

EC is the primary area that encompasses a variety of associated technology as sub-domains, including mobile cloud services, cloudlet, and multiple-access EC. Each of these domains are founded on the idea that computing resources need to be available at the network's edge, in which the real demand problem exists, and that results in the following (Nieuwenhuis 2018):

1. End users gain quick access to compute resources.
2. Significantly reducing the traffic pressure on the network core.

2.2 PRIVACY AND SECURITY OF COMPUTING MODELS

Privacy and security are intrinsically tied and have a symbiotic connection. Many scholars and organizations associate the two phrases with the ICT area. The impact of digitization on our daily lives has been enormous (Huttunen et al. 2019). Manufacturing giants are presently dealing with numerous computer concepts including massive processing and computation of big data. As a result, transferring this information through one source to another exposes them to risk and needed protection. In this chapter, we will describe security, privacy, vulnerabilities, remedies, and security methods, as well as look at some of the contrasts and potential connections between privacy and security (Heck et al. 2018).

2.2.1 Cloud-Related Aspects

Most wired networks as well as the concept of remotely saving data are heavily influenced by CC technology. One of the unusual requirements is for the cloud to guarantee that services are continuously offered, reliability is affirmed, and information is provided as required. A comparison of different computing models with different attributes has been shown in Table 2.1. As previously discussed, the significant risk for privacy and security of data is among the biggest reasons businesses and people are unwilling to accept the swift transition to a cloud model. Confidentiality, information security, hacking, and multi-tenancy are a few identified vulnerabilities of privacy and

Table 2.1 Comparison of several computing models

Attributes	Cloud Computing	Edge Computing	Fog Computing
Architecture	Centralized	Distributed	Distributed
Security	Centralized	Centralized	Mixed
Energy Consumption	High	Low	Medium
Latency	High	Low	Medium
Bandwidth Cost	High	Low	Low
Storage capacity and Computation	High	Very Limited	Limited
Scalability	Average	High	High

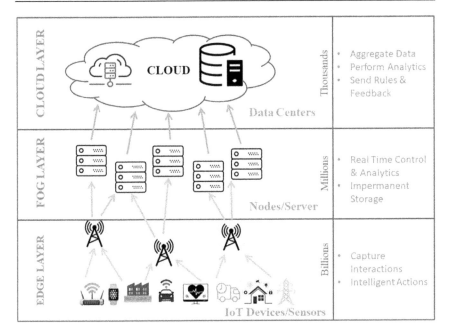

Figure 2.2 Architecture of edge, fog and cloud computing.

security in cloud technology. This chapter explores the numerous privacy and security concerns that exist with CC systems and makes some recommendations for risk management (Kaur et al. 2020).

Due to the variety of distributed cloud models that cloud users choose, depending on their individual requirements, the privacy and security risks associated with the cloud vary depending on the type of cloud infrastructure used as shown in Figure 2.2. The Cloud Security Alliance (CSA) lists data breaches, denial-of-service (DoS) attacks, and advanced persistent risks as key frequent threats (Alwarafy 2020).

This highlights the need of customizing an intrusion detection system (IDS) to proactively identify suspicious threats and prevent prospective network assaults. Additionally, the different events seen may be isolated in order to do network status analysis. Cloud-based services and resources are considered to face many forms of dangers from both within and outside intruders. Proper cloud platform security relies primarily on existing protection technologies with the several levels (Spatharakis et al. 2020).

2.2.1.1 Information Privacy and Security in the Cloud

Information security is an important consideration in managing cloud devices and keeping them operational. This could include data protection and recovery guidelines as well as cloud service centers, and information included in communications or transfers must be secured. In general, simple yet reliable techniques that provide a seamless means of understanding cloud service capability before they are implemented and methods that fit with cloud-based security characteristics throughout the developing stage is required. The deployment strategy is also influenced by the existence of cloud service providers (CSP) and cloud clients, as both parties are required to adhere to particular data security standards (Jadeja 2012). Service level negotiation, data traffic, and, most importantly, security of data will be discussed. To decrease or remove security flaws, cloud service providers must appropriately safeguard their clients' data hosted in the cloud. Encryption techniques have to be extremely powerful in order to ensure greater information security and to create authentication systems that track access to information. Data encryption must be used to implement access control to ensure that only the correctly designated personnel have access to the data (Gupta 2020).

The public cloud confronts increased privacy concerns, though these concerns vary greatly depending on the cloud model version. Some of the worries about the hazards include information dissemination, harmful use by an unauthorized individual, and client inability to regulate (Mebrek et al. 2017). Attackers can access confidential client records saved in the cloud by utilizing the hash codes of the files and a process employed in data duplication. Permissions, cloud systems, clients, and stored data are all seen as privacy threats. Understanding data privacy as well as other related privacy concepts can greatly aid in responding to identified danger problems. One significant barrier preventing some firms from going to the cloud is indeed the risk of exposing classified data due to data breach (Marbukh 2019).

User's privacy is frequently violated, either intentionally or unintentionally. Obtaining a user's sensitive information without their consent or authority is a serious violation of their privacy. Various trends, like information governance, privacy threats, data breaches, and other kinds of attacks, might arise (Gezer et al. 2017). Privacy leaks can be extremely detrimental, yet the following points can help to address privacy concerns:

- Trust: It is a violation of privacy to disclose a person's or organization's information. Trust is crucial in reducing or eradicating fear. There are many trust requirements that each client can agreed on, although in generally, they want to see low or no violations of privacy on an acceptable scale.
- Access control: Because cloud systems have so many flaws, an unauthorized person or group of people can gain access if they are not handled appropriately. Answering the questions are an excellent technique to deal with this.
- Data encryption must be powerful enough to preserve the privacy of the user's files. Data encryption flaws represent a severe threat to cloud privacy.

2.2.2 Edge-Related Aspects

Since the effectiveness of CC has declined significantly due to a variety of reasons, such as the increasing number of nodes, EC has given a substantial paradigm change. EC is regarded as a technical advance since it can handle software including its new shared computing capabilities and process information locally, on-demand, and without sending it to the cloud (Mäkitalo et al. 2020). Data processing near to users improves their perception of the user experience and speeds up reaction time. This is facilitated by the computing explicitly performed at the deployed equipment nodes (Sarkar 2016).

Several aspects and functions of our everyday routines are being replaced by fifth generation (5G) networks. EC is unquestionably at the center of the various developments in the 5G network, rendering it crucial for compact on resource-constrained equipment and their interactions. EC demonstrates a connection with diverse technology and numerous cross-connected networks. The interconnection of such edge supporting technologies expose them to the security issue that may affect equipment, technology, network, and most importantly, businesses. The hazards associated here should not be forgotten or ignored, which brings us to the issue of EC privacy and security (Mukherjee et al. 2017). Other security scenarios will arise with processing at the node of edge devices and the need for ongoing study effort for enhancements.

Despite significant privacy and security provided by the data processing at the nodes, edge's decentralized nature makes the likelihood of impending threats and assaults quite probable. EC, too, is exposed to security flaws and harmful infections via smart gadgets. The procedures for safeguarding and protecting data cannot be supported by the design of EC (Ometov et al. 2016). This signifies that the information is highly vulnerable and difficult to safeguard due to the sophistication of such an edge device at the network. Although EC technologies are expanding, their privacy and security are still being developed, that's why there aren't many study findings. Scholars and other researchers from across the world have been working tirelessly to conduct pertinent research and create remedies to enhance the privacy and security of edge technologies. For performing security tests, a variety of straightforward portable EC techniques were employed. A description of a comprehensive safety and defense strategy with suggestions from the research conducted was also made (Xiao et al. 2019). The security results from the edge do include a pertinent reference from a theoretical point of view. As earlier mentioned, there are four distinct elements to the recognized problems with EC privacy and security that are addressed in this study; information security, privacy protection, access control, and identity authentication (Kozyrev et al. 2018).

2.2.2.1 Edge Data Privacy and Security

The three main objectives and motivations for information security are integrity, secrecy, and threat detection. It helps in the development of a sustainable

EC system. Through outsourcing data with supervision, utilizing non-fixed storage, and delegating accountability, problems like data breach and data leakage are addressed; customers may handle data activities in a secure manner (Jiang et al. 2019). Currently, it is difficult to find studies on the privacy and security of EC because many researchers choose to concentrate primarily on cloud topologies or possibly fog paradigm. The main goal of data safety in edge systems is to create a common model with an efficient system in order to transport data safely and reduce the heavy load. This leads to the development of inexpensive architectures and extremely appropriate shared data security both for end customers and distant nodes (Dolui 2017).

Maintaining the trust associated and protecting client information is a top priority, particularly with the edge network. For instance, a building that has been digitalized and is equipped with a lot of IoT devices may be a potential target because of the vast amount of private data that it generates. So, ensuring that information processing takes place at the edge network or node of the home is a more respected strategy to safeguard consumers' privacy and earn their trust (Mäkitalo et al. 2019).

The following important edge-specific components should be taken into account in contrast to the already observed features. Note that in most cases, edge operation situations face the same cloud challenges:

- Confidentiality is usually treated carefully in the context of mobile users wishing to use the operations of mobile apps, so as a result, many customers find it hard to determine whether to use it. We highlight various problems in EC secrecy, demonstrating a very significant danger presented by service providers getting unrestricted access to secret data (Stojmenovic et al. 2016). This happens when data is transmitted via a dispersed or insecure connection and is subsequently collected and analyzed over the decentralized edge network. There are continuous breaches of data security. Fortunately, several recently developed technologies make it possible to limit access to project confidentially (Naha 2018).

- Identifying attacks: Edge devices, which is where the edge services are hosted, may help edge systems operate properly and provide the greatest amount of quality services. This guarantees that neither attack nor anomalies may enter the edge system overall. The edge node is vulnerable to attacks because of its hostile environment and insufficient security assurance. When attacks of one edge node are poorly handled and might potentially spread to some other edge node, the efficiency of an edge systems can be severely hampered (Ometov et al. 2021b). Finding a rapid fix might thus be challenging due to gravity of the risk which permeates the edge nodes. Finding the root cause of the issue would also involve additional expenditures, and even restoration may be slow. As a result, routine inspections must be carried out to find any past indications of impending or future assaults (Mahmood 2018).

In sharp contrast to other information protecting computer architectures currently in use, EC constantly causes a lot of concern. This is due to the difficulties, such as privacy-related edge data leaks. With such intertwined computing/cellular networks, edge data centers, applications, asset managers, organizations, as well as some customers might be the weak point that you cannot entirely trust (Qaim 2020). Regarding this, it is a responsibility that necessitates paying particular attention to safeguard customer privacy information.

- Privacy information security: Huge volumes of user data are obtained from software as well as other clients' machines at the edge nodes. After then, data is computed and examined. The EC nodes are reliable, but they still have a certain amount of risk. Confidential data, including a person's medical history, must be kept in strict confidence. To prevent leakage at the EC nodes, information privacy protection is therefore crucial (Qaim 2020).
- Identification privacy: When compared to CC, edge models still don't receive enough research focus to effectively safeguard consumer identities. Protection of identity privacy is a top priority for many businesses and even for individual customers. The model created by a third party is thought to still be vulnerable (Peng et al. 2016).
- Location privacy: A number of online programs and services offer location-based functionalities. A user must submit his geo-location as requested by the service provider in order to obtain access if users wish to take advantage of EC services. Data breaches through potential leaks is one of the more worrisome issues (Lin 2017). Various scholars provided some treatment plans for the problem of data leakage. Social media networks for mobile devices showed a progressive dispersion of geo-location privacy protection. Within a specific scope of social interactions, this model can identify site visitors with low levels of trust (Hu et al. 2017).

It does this by segmenting clients' data into separate storage systems according to their personalities and location (which is anonymous). The service provider can safely conceal consumer location data thanks to this division. The significance of this architecture is that even if an attacker is successful in breaching one of the storage facilities, such as a data geo-location, it won't constitute a serious threat because the client's identity isn't revealed (De Donno et al. 2019).

The following is a concise way to describe the central problems with EC. First, nodes of edge typically link to a large number of IoTs devices, each of which has a limited amount of resources and a variety of internal components. As a result, multiple routing protocols are used to distribute messages. This component variation could cause certain security problems (Chiang et al. 2016). It could result in a number of difficulties with access control in an IoT context. Key management in communications is another issue that raises additional security-related questions pertaining to EC. Despite the fact that EC can provide end-to-end connectivity among IoT devices using a variety of routing protocols, concerns remain over data confidentiality and integrity. To address these issues, a unique key management and distribution method may need to be created. The author provides a thorough examination of security issues in EC from five perspectives in a research paper (Bonomi et al. 2012): key management, access control, privacy protection, attack mitigation, and anomaly detection.

The following are some of the elements that can cause security and privacy problems in EC networks and jeopardize user data:

1. EC results in receiving a lot of sensitive data because edge nodes are located closer to users. This data can have grave repercussions if any of it is taken.
2. Compared to CC, EC has fewer network resources, which prevents it from supporting sophisticated encryption techniques.
3. An ever-evolving dynamic environment makes up the EC network. As a result, attackers can quickly integrate into the organization. Additionally, developing safety procedures for such a network environment is quite difficult.

The following are the EC attacks:

- Eavesdropping: Like a FC assault, an EC eavesdropper might conceal themselves and maliciously observe the activities on the channel in an effort to capture or monitor the secret data.
- Denial-of-service (DoS) Attacks: Similar to FC, a DoS attack enables a hacker to seize possession of a machine or connection and prohibits approved users from utilizing it by overloading the device with queries that cause network congestion (Khan 2016).
- Dispersed denial-of-service (DDoS) attack: This type of attack uses distributed resources, such as a cluster of infected edge devices, to disrupt the regular services offered by several servers. This attack takes place when an intruder transmits multiple packets via exploited distributed servers towards the targeted computer. As a result, the hardware resources of the victim are exhausted and are unable to handle any additional packets, making it impossible for the victim to timely respond to any legitimate requests (Anawar 2018).

- Data tampering attack: In this type of attack, the intruder can change the data that is stored or communicated through the communication channel.
- Service manipulation: This type of assault involves the adversary seizing control of the edge data center, which gives it the ability to alter or misrepresent the services.
- False data injection: This exploit involves the introduction of a fake code into the network that collects all the database's stored data and sends it to the intruder (Rani 2022).
- Physical assault: This assault takes place when physical safety of the edge infrastructure is shoddy or lax. Due to the widespread use of edge devices, physical attack will have an impact on the services in specific geographic locations.
- Rogue gateway: Similar to a MitM attack, a rogue gateway attack involves attackers injecting large amounts of traffic into the EC network architecture.

If the intruders have enough access rights to the edge data center, they can pretend to be the operator or falsify the services in EC. This gives the intruders the ability to attack the network in several ways, including MitM and DoS attacks (Lee 2012).

EC raises a number of privacy concerns, including:

- Weak security methods and algorithms for system defense that might make the network more open to intrusion by malevolent users, or the addition of other nodes to gather data in an illegal way.
- Risky device-to-device communications.
- Data backup and recovery that is challenging when the system goes down.
- There is no distinct pattern in the way the system receives and applies updates.
- Inadequate network visibility.
- Insufficient user-selected data collection.

The next chapter will present various defenses to deal with such assaults and lessen the danger they pose now that we have a solid grasp of the security and privacy concerns relating to both fog and EC.

2.2.3 Aspects Relating to Fog

Due to CC, many firms have seen significant transformations, particularly with the rapid increase in consumption of enormous data sets. The need for private services started to develop significantly at the same time. CC platforms provide a large number of well-centralized systems, however with significant drawbacks. Some people experience certain undesirable long and irregular delays and time-conscious services when using clouds and associated endpoints (Yi et al. 2015). When communication across network-connected devices and the data repository fails, there is a relevant high-risk. Possible privacy exposure is one potential violation here. The FC paradigm was established to help with this problem, and it helped Cloud-Edge—currently the most popular and well-respected computing service—improve computation, security, and privacy (Modi et al. 2013a).

Fog devices are seen as discrete, dispersed pieces of hardware, including gateways, routers, switches, and expertly installed conventional servers. Additionally, FC is widely regarded as a smart green platform with sustainability and excellent security benefits given the current necessity for massive emission reduction. The FC system is made up of numerous fog nodes (FNs), which are considered to be renewable. The geographical distribution of FNs may span numerous places. Because the several FNs cooperate through a carefully determined formula while operating separately, the load placed on the information center during computation is greatly reduced (Gupta 2019).

The middle layer's processing may be screened or separated by fog that sits between the endpoint and the cloud, potentially improving the QoS and lowering costs. As we will see in the following sub-section, FC was widely regarded as being in high demand to address the ever-growing IoT concerns. The ability of FC to cross-connect all digital equipment, wireless endpoints, and local devices made it the most practical strategy (Shubina 2020). Due to its interconnectedness, there is a risk of serious security and privacy breaches such the location of customer data disclosure, document leaks, and account theft. FC was introduced to extend cloud operations to the system's edge after initially being examined by Cisco. In terms of QoS, latency, and spatial distribution, FC is being taken into consideration as a local cloud alternative (Pearson 2010). FC, which is often regarded as a virtualized system, provides services including networking, storage, and, most critically, computation between the resource center and the customer, bringing the corresponding vulnerabilities with it (Mulazzani et al. 2011).

Every component of the EC system, according to the edge system, operates autonomously to ensure that data is processed locally rather than being sent to the cloud. On the other hand, FC nodes always decide whether to analyze data from diverse information sources or transfer it to the cloud after considering its resources. Some cloud services, such as infrastructure as a service (IaaS), software as a service (SaaS), and platform as a service (PaaS), that are not supported in edge structures can be expanded via FC (PaaS). While increasing connectivity and computational resources at the network's edge, FC is fully edge inclined but can be aided by FC (Di Vimercati 2007).

2.2.3.1 Fog Data Privacy and Security

Due to the fact that they use cloud, edge, and FC, these assaults typically pose a threat to both private and public enterprises. A threat intelligence platform (TIP) must be created in order to safeguard the architecture to some extent. Since information must be protected, data security is given top priority in the industrial sector (Li et al. 2016). To significantly reduce dangers and security attacks, intelligent machinery and sensor devices are used. The integration of cloud security frameworks into FC systems is impacted by the heterogeneity and geographic sharing characteristic. Confidentiality, authentication, availability, and information privacy are a few of the security issues that are taken into consideration (Tyagi 2016). Access to people and organizations can be created and tracked with the help of the frameworks provided. When we look at the medical industry, we can see that patient health histories contain sensitive data and that the fog architecture has a number of nodes that could be vulnerable. Unauthorized access to data during storage or transfer, unreliable insiders, and information distribution during systems are examples of these risks (Rusk 2014). Information from sensors of medical equipment is constantly transferred to the fog system by cable or wireless network. Targeting communication systems and sensors can result in tampering with patient personal data integrity and device accessibility. Due to the flaws found in wireless networks, some attacks such as DoS can be readily carried out. In general, fog presents difficulties akin to those with the edge while bridging them even further to the decentralized and distributed environment (Sun 2019).

The primary security risks of FC are as follows:

1. Forgery: This security risk type involves the attacker imitating another person's identity and actions in order to fool a safety system or other user by providing false data. It can also reduce network performance by consuming bandwidth, energy, and storage due to its bogus data packets (Ai et al. 2018).
2. Tampering: In this security breach, network intruders naughtily change the data that will be transmitted. Since the user's mobility and the transmission medium's wireless nature could cause a failure or delay in the data transmission, it is challenging to detect this attack.
3. Spam: The term "spam" describes undesired material generated by attackers, such as excess information and fraudulent data obtained from users. Spam causes the use of valuable network resources, privacy breaches, and deception (Moltchanov et al. 2018).
4. Sybil: Network intruders may occasionally create a false identity to influence FC's efficiency and performance as well as the nodes dependability. It's known as a Sybil attack. These false crowd-sensing reports are produced by the attackers, and they are absolutely unreliable.

Additionally, they have the ability to reveal the private data of an authorized user (França 2020).

5. Jamming: In this, network intruders produce a high amount of data packets to block the transmissions and use up more resources than necessary, denying legitimate users access to a dependable and effective transmission channel (Roman et al. 2018).

6. Eavesdropping: In this, the intruder secretly monitors the private data being transmitted by legitimate users. If the encryption method used over the sensitive data is ineffective, this attack is fairly common (Zissis 2012).

7. Denial-of-service (DoS): In this attack, attackers send false information to fog nodes, and these nodes are then inundated with a substantial amount of false inquiries, making them unavailable to legitimate users. Because the fog network has limited resources, such assaults degrade its performance by using network resources like bandwidth, batteries, time, etc. (Stojmenovic and Wen 2014).

8. Man in the Middle (MitM): In MitM attack, the intruder places themselves in the middle of two communicating nodes in order to listen in on and steal from legitimate users' useful communications while they are unaware of it because they believe that the data is being sent directly to the intended recipients. In this instance, the attacker creates a temporary situation by getting in the way of the communication parties (Bhat 2020).

9. Cooperation: In this kind of security assault, two or more parties work together to deceive and scam the legal users. These group members use a tactic to attack a group of cloud nodes, fog nodes, and IoT devices in order to amplify the impact of the attack.

10. Impersonation: In an impersonation attack, the intruder poses as a legitimate server in an effort to deceive the users by providing them with phony or harmful services, leading them to assume they are communicating with a genuine fog node or network. Within that technique, the hackers to take all private information from authorized user's machine (Khan et al. 2017a).

11. Virtual machine (VM) attack: A hacker surreptitiously seizes control of the hypervisor, which creates a virtual environment inside a VM, in a VM attack. A VM can be attacked in four different ways: From the outside, from the VM management, from the VM to the guest, and from the VM to the VM (Du et al. 2018).

12. Side-channel attack: In this type of attack, the device's cryptography is broken by learning more about the cryptographic algorithm that has been used.

The fog paradigm frequently encounters the primary concern of privacy protection of the individual as well as businesses, particularly when the fog nodes are placed close to the individuals and facilitate the collecting of critical data (Hou et al. 2020). Because of the decentralized structure of fog nodes, maintaining centralized monitoring is one of the biggest challenges. When such fog nodes aren't adequately protected, attackers can quickly access and steal crucial information during transmission. More real-world research is required to better comprehend privacy issues and invent fresh approaches to protect data privacy (Zeyu et al. 2020).

The exchange, collection, processing, and transmission of users' sensitive data through fog nodes is posing a severe threat to privacy, which is a key challenge for FC. When using network communication, every client request their information to be protected and confidential, however because of the high number of unauthorized users and hackers on the internet, protecting users' private information is quite difficult. Maintaining privacy is crucial from both the provider's and the user's points of view. The privacy of the user's information is the top issue because FC applications are processed on the user's device (Cao et al. 2020). There are six main components of privacy difficulties:

1. User privacy: Numerous IoT-capable gadgets are interconnected to the FC network via sensors or wireless networks. Critical information is generated by IoT devices and transmitted to fog nodes for analysis. Personal information, data from automated smart homes, health information, corporate information, etc. are all illustrations of critical information which with a weak security mechanism an attacker could steal (Zhang et al. 2018).
2. Identity privacy: Since each user must give the fog nodes their identity-related information to be verified, making a person's identity especially susceptible to being revealed.
3. Data privacy: A network attacker aiming to capture a user's private information obtained via transmission channel or relay nodes may gain access to the confidential data of that user. These details include the user's home address, political interests, and other personal information. For instance, the online voting process can jeopardize users' political preferences. It is crucial that such data be kept private (Liu et al. 2019).
4. Usage privacy: The manner in which a user consumes the network's services for FC is referred to as their usage privacy. An attacker can use this pattern to determine when a client is utilizing the connection for transferring data and when not. Based on this pattern, the intrusive party attacks the user's private data or the channel in an effort to make it appear "busy" to the legitimate user (Khalil et al. 2014).
5. Geo-location privacy: These days, every smartphone application requests access to the user's smartphone device's private information

like the photos, files, as well as the device's current or remembered location. Because of this, the user must give up their ability to remain anonymous when using the internet (Flueratoru et al. 2021). They are unaware, however, that maintaining the secrecy of their location is vital information that, if stolen by the attacker, can help them understand the user's trajectory. Therefore, a user's location privacy must always be protected.

6. Network privacy: Security and privacy threats constantly put wireless connections at danger, which is a very important problem. Furthermore, fog node management is expensive and difficult because they are located just at the network edge, wherein network settings are performed manually. As a result, privacy breaches are common. An encryption approach like Local Network could be highly beneficial in addressing this problem (Shubina et al. 2020).

2.3 ATTACKS ON FC AND EC AND THEIR DEFENSES

We will start with a detailed discussion of FC in this chapter before moving on to EC countermeasures.

2.3.1 Countermeasures for FC Attacks

As a result of its distinctive characteristics, FC is still in its infancy and must overcome many obstacles. Because it makes use of unused resources produced by user devices that are not properly scrutinized by any regulatory authority, privacy and security issues are brought up in the fog network (Wei et al. 2012). Since multiple devices are used in the processing of fog applications, secure and quick authentication procedures are now necessary.

The following are some of the methods suggested for reducing harmful assaults and privacy concerns:

- Advanced encryption methods: The problem of confidentiality could be with the aid of efficient encryption techniques because the attackers won't be able to decipher the intricate encryption algorithms. Nevertheless, when creating an encryption method, the creators should keep in mind that as technology develops, so do the systems and methods used by attackers (Li et al. 2015). Because they can decode any encryption method thanks to modern technology, they are always proactive of programmers.
- The decoy approach is a security method used to verify the information of a user who is practically accessible with in network. It substitutes false information for the genuine and gives it to the attackers. When a system security hole is created by an attacker, it discovers a

false data file instead of a genuine file (Wang et al. 2017a). The proposed method is referred to as the "decoy technique," and this file is known as the "decoy file." To provide increased security, the decoy files are created at the beginning. For system intruders, the system substitutes the actual data that is normally solely accessible to authorized individuals by default with a fake file (Shi et al. 2014).

- A method is suggested for maintaining privacy concerns during FC network utilizing the decoy strategy. This method is divided into two stages, with the first stage being the automatic provision of a fake data file to both verified and unverified users. Additionally, after successfully completing all security authentication challenges in the second stage, the authenticated client would be allowed a copy of the original file within the network (Chen et al. 2015a). When unusual movement is discovered in connection, the device instantly creates a decoy file using the decoy approach, which is then transmitted in the direction of the intrusion and appears to be the same as the original file. The spurious and false data is in the decoy file. While the attacker will be perplexed by the false information, the legitimate user will immediately recognize it (Chen et al. 2015b).

- Intrusion detection system (IDS): It is used in FC to identify and defend against a variety of attacks, including DoS, insider, port scanning, flooding, MitM, and hypervisor-related ones. A perimeter IDS system that can coordinate various IDS in the fog system is installed to secure it (Kumbhare 2014a). However, it can also pose a number of difficulties for ensuring that needs are met without delay. To counter MitM assaults in the fog network, intrusion detection and prevention method is suggested. This system is made up of IDS nodes that monitor the network at regular intervals and look for any anomalies that may be present. When a malicious node is found, the network isolates that node (Wang et al. 2017b).

- Authentication schemes: Using an authentication server, authentication allows users' identities to be confirmed by comparing their provided credentials to data stored in the database. This aids in defending against harmful entities' incursions. If a user is properly verified by the system to become a component of a networking infrastructure, the FC connection provides users with access to fog applications from fog architecture (Rimal et al. 2016). One of the major security issues is the possibility of network attackers harming the entire cloud, fog nodes, and user's device in the case of an insecure authentication mechanism.

- The idea of a blockchain was established for the safe use of Bitcoin as a crypto currency. The researchers eventually understood, though, that blockchain's exceptional security properties can also be utilized to secure networks for cloud and FC. Therefore, by using blockchain technology, the security of the fog environment may be improved. The following list of helpful blockchain features is provided with reference to FC (Aazam and Huh 2016):

- Decreases single point failure.
- Supports very safe encryption algorithms for network transactions.
- Able to efficiently track node status.
- Unchangeable technology.

Man-in-the-middle attacks, denial-of-service attacks, and data manipulation are just a few of the destructive attacks that blockchain technology can stop in a fog network.

2.3.2 EC Countermeasures

Since EC, as demonstrated, has unique qualities, numerous security methods utilized with CC services are incompatible with EC. A few recommended solutions that fit well with EC's special qualities are:

- Edge node security: To maintain effective safety protocols, the same degree of protection should be provided to every edge network nodes. If the security levels are varied, an attacker could compromise a node with a poor security algorithm, degrading the system. Identifying whether a node seems to have an inadequate safety barrier which allowed a security issue can be difficult for system administrators due to varied security levels (Mahmud 2018).
- Continuous monitoring: To keep a network secured against unauthorized clients, it is essential to continuously monitor all edge nodes and give users interactive network visibility.
- Appropriate encryption: New, cutting-edge encryption methods that are extremely difficult to decode is being proposed with the advancement of current technology. These methods include a secret key that is securely stored and sent only by the authorized sender and recipient. Genuine users can access the data and decrypt the algorithm thanks to this secret key (El-Sayed et al. 2017).
- Monitoring user behavior: This process involves keeping track of users' general behavior and observing, monitoring, and maintaining it such that any action which deviates from what is expected may be utilized to spot malicious individuals. The clients will therefore be notified of such odd behavior (Khan et al. 2017b).
- Data encryption advances: Data encryption advances are being given as a protection against security threats launched by attackers and intrusions. These techniques frequently make utilization of a private key which is accessible only to the receiver and the sender. This encryption

key is used to decipher the message that was delivered (Atlam et al. 2018). The data contained in the message could be taken if an intrusive party was successful in extracting these cryptographic keys from the transmission network's packets being sent and received.

- Data confidentiality: Numerous data confidentiality mechanisms are provided based on encryption techniques to address the various privacy difficulties brought on by unauthorized data operations, data loss, information leakage, privacy violations, etc., through network intruders (Ni et al. 2018). Some suggest Query Guard, a latency aware query optimization method, as a privacy-preserving solution. This method accomplishes two goals at once: First, it tackles the violation of privacy associated with distributed query execution, and it also optimizes searches for direct delivery. In terms of computing time and memory utilization, it performs better than traditional query optimization approaches (Modi et al. 2013).

Various more defense methods are suggested for edge networks, but sadly, the mobility, substantial percentage of edge nodes and the EC networks dynamic nature preclude the use of current means for ensuring privacy and security. However, when applied to EC, some mechanisms produce ineffective outcomes. Edge node privacy requires adaptive frameworks that can quickly select the best privacy strategy depending on the communication situation and involved edge nodes (Khorshed et al. 2012). As a result, there is still much to learn and think about in this field of communication.

2.4 CLOUD, FOG, AND EC IN THE FUTURE

With its capabilities, fog and EC technologies will completely transform the way wireless communication networks operate today. Furthermore, these technologies are expected to enhance the functionality and provision of other platforms, such as IoTs (Nenvani and Gupta 2016).

IoT technology has attracted a great deal of interest from both the academic and business worlds. In essence, it represents the impending era of "connectivity everywhere." By the end of 2020, it is predicted that more than 20 billion linked devices across various commercial organizations, industrial departments, and consumer-facing segments will be present. By 2025, there will be more than 21 billion connected gadgets, predicts the article (Ciurana 2009). The IoT is rapidly expanding as technology progresses, as a larger quantity of sensors linked to different devices in order to properly manage and store huge volumes of data collected on a daily basis. IoT applications need CC for processing. Furthermore, as the amount of IoT devices grows, so does the quantity of information they create, making it unfeasible for all IoT devices to depend on a single entity, like CC, to analyze such a vast volume of data (Ristenpart et al. 2009). They require a system that can operate and regulate a huge variety of sensors, controllers, equipment, clients, activities, and connections even while processing a big volume of information and services applications. Traditional CC is unable to address the problems with connectivity and time-sensitivity. In contrast, the IoTs have several applications where even a small delay can have significant effects, such as the discipline of telemedicine, hospitals, car-to-car communication, security divisions, and many more. FC is therefore thought to be a preferable option to use with the IoT platform (Naccache and Stern 1998).

The edge devices gather information from their assigned regions and deliver it to the nearest fog node for analysis and decision-making. FC has the advantage of managing IoT devices and resolving the processing issues with time-sensitive approach in CC. At the network's edge, fog nodes are present to provide high-quality services with no delay to edge users. This enables the provision of real-time processing, storage, and networking resources to users at the edge level (Hay et al. 2011). Waste disposal, smart signal timing systems, logistical control mechanisms, emergency services, and commercial sites are all suitable uses for the IoT. Wearable sensors and smart healthcare devices are the two most alluring applications of IoT. FC technology, which enables edge processing, offers a variety of capabilities in smart applications, including augmented and virtual reality, smart healthcare systems, smart transit systems, smart cities, smart homes, smart vehicles, and many more smart real-time applications. FC technology is commonly employed in the healthcare industry because the information recorded by healthcare devices is time-sensitive so requires rapid computation (Almtrf et al. 2019).

Cloud, edge, and fog ideas give a significant diverse volume of information that may be handled along a centralized or decentralized system. We concluded from the discussions in this work that a significant barrier in this ecosystem's heterogeneity is the security and privacy issues. Even if some of these flaws can be rapidly identified and fixed, data transit from one end to another creates many security and privacy concerns. Due to the ecosystem's complexity, solutions cannot be quickly distributed to user devices. IDS systems are important for many paradigms, though, some are thought to be successful at thwarting DoS or DDoS attacks. If higher computational power is required, IDS approaches may involve gateway equipment (Patel et al. 2020).

The most important security and privacy features of information systems are confidentiality, integrity, and availability. Data must be transferred and stored in a private, trustworthy, and open manner. Only those people and organizations who are the actual owners of the data can access it thanks to confidentiality. The primary network severely restricts access to data while it is being transferred between the various user layers and while it is being stored and processed in the cloud, edge, or fog paradigms (Kumbhare 2014b). Data secrecy can be attained by encrypting it. A notion of integrity called data correctness and consistency prevents information from being altered or changed. Data integrity checks can be performed using a few different ways. Access to the information is restricted to authorized individuals. According to set policies, availability therefore dictates that data must be accessible everywhere (Alrawais et al. 2017). Numerous tools, approaches, patterns, and mechanisms, including cryptography are applied to the various layers where data is exchanged and stored in order to meet these requirements. Overall, the cloud, edge, and fog paradigms have the same perspective on providing consumers with QoS, but each of them has a unique set of attributes that distinguishes it from the others (Grabosky 2015)

2.5 CONCLUSION AND FUTURE SCOPE

To offer consumers a range of on-demand service quality, cloud computing is continually developing. Cloud security is a serious worry, despite the fact that numerous people recognize the benefits that cloud computing offers. The internet of things (IoT) is a rapidly expanding industry. We will need to switch from outdated computer methods to more advanced ones as information and data-generating gadgets increase. When IoT device information is handled, fog and edge computing is beginning to take the place of conventional cloud computing. Yet when more data becomes available, we will need to develop new processing algorithms while emphasizing the security and privacy of user data.

Edge and fog computing should complement conventional cloud computing whenever feasible. There is still an opportunity to enhance in terms of latency and bandwidth requirements without jeopardizing system integrity. After being first configured in accordance with specifications, the system should operate on its own.

REFERENCES

Aazam, M.; Huh, E.N. Fog Computing: The Cloud-IoT/IoE Middleware Paradigm. IEEE Potentials 2016, 35, 40–44.

Ai, Y.; Peng, M.; Zhang, K. Edge Computing Technologies for Internet of Things: A Primer. Digit. Commun. Netw. 2018, 4, 77–86.

Alhroob, A.; Samawi, V.W. Privacy in Cloud Computing: Intelligent Approach. In Proceedings of the International Conference on High Performance Computing Simulation (HPCS), Orléans, 16–20 July 2018; pp. 1063–1065.

Aljumah, A.; Ahanger, T.A. Fog Computing and Security Issues: A Review. In Proceedings of the 7th International Conference on Computers Communications and Control (ICCCC), Oradea, 8–12 May 2018; pp. 237–239.

Almtrf, A.; Alagrash, Y.; Zohdy, M. Framework Modeling for User Privacy in Cloud Computing. In Proceedings of the 9th Annual Computing and Communication Workshop and Conference (CCWC), Las Vegas, NV, 7–9 January 2019; pp. 819–826.

Alrawais, A.; Alhothaily, A.; Hu, C.; Cheng, X. Fog Computing for the Internet of Things: Security and Privacy Issues. IEEE Internet Comput. 2017, 21, 34–42.

Alwarafy, A.; Al-Thelaya, K.A.; Abdallah, M.; Schneider, J.; Hamdi, M. A Survey on Security and Privacy Issues in Edge-Computing-Assisted Internet of Things. IEEE Internet Things J. 2020, 8, 4004–4022.

Anawar, M.R.; Wang, S.; Azam Zia, M.; Jadoon, A.K.; Akram, U.; Raza, S. Fog Computing: An Overview of Big IoT Data Analytics. Wirel. Commun. Mob. Comput. 2018, 2018, 7157192.

Atlam, H.F.; Walters, R.J.; Wills, G.B. Fog Computing and the Internet of Things: A Review. Big Data Cogn. Comput. 2018, 2, 10.

Bhat, S.A.; Sofi, I.B.; Chi, C.Y. Edge Computing and Its Convergence with Blockchain in 5G and Beyond: Security, Challenges, and Opportunities. IEEE Access 2020, 8, 205340–205373.

Bonomi, F.; Milito, R.; Zhu, J.; Addepalli, S. Fog Computing and Its Role in the Internet of Things. In Proceedings of the MCC Workshop on Mobile Cloud Computing, Helsinki, 17 August 2012; pp. 13–16.

Cao, K.; Liu, Y.; Meng, G.; Sun, Q. An Overview on Edge Computing Research. IEEE Access 2020, 8, 85714–85728.

Chalapathi, G.S.S.; Chamola, V.; Vaish, A.; Buyya, R. Industrial Internet of Things (IIoT) Applications of Edge and Fog Computing: A Review and Future Directions. In Fog/Edge Computing for Security, Privacy, and Applications; Springer: Cham, 2021; pp. 293–325.

Chen, S.; Irving, S.; Peng, L. Operational Cost Optimization for Cloud Computing Data Centers using Renewable Energy. IEEE Syst. J. 2015a, 10, 1447–1458.

Chen, X.; Jiao, L.; Li, W.; Fu, X. Efficient Multi-User Computation Offloading for Mobile-Edge Cloud Computing. IEEE/ACM Trans. Netw. 2015b, 24, 2795–2808.

Chiang, M.; Zhang, T. Fog and IoT: An Overview of Research Opportunities. IEEE Internet Things Journal, Dec. 2016, 3(6), 854–864. doi: 10.1109/JIOT.2016.2584538.

Ciurana, E. Developing with Google App Engine; Springer: New York, NY, 2009.

Cook, A.; Robinson, M.; Ferrag, M.A.; Maglaras, L.A.; He, Y.; Jones, K.; Janicke, H. Internet of Cloud: Security and Privacy Issues. In Cloud Computing for Optimization: Foundations, Applications, and Challenges; Springer: Berlin/Heidelberg, 2018; pp. 271–301.

De Donno, M.; Tange, K.; Dragoni, N. Foundations and Evolution of Modern Computing Paradigms: Cloud, IoT, Edge, and Fog. IEEE Access 2019, 7, 150936–150948.

Di Vimercati, S.D.C.; Foresti, S.; Jajodia, S.; Paraboschi, S.; Samarati, P. Over-Encryption: Management of Access Control Evolution on Outsourced Data.

In Proceedings of the 33rd International Conference on Very Large Data Bases, Vienna, 23–27 September 2007; pp. 123–134.

Dolui, K.; Datta, S.K. Comparison of Edge Computing Implementations: Fog Computing, Cloudlet and Mobile Edge Computing. In Proceedings of the Global Internet of Things Summit (GIoTS), Geneva, 6–9 June 2017; pp. 1–6.

Du, M.; Wang, K.; Chen, Y.; Wang, X.; Sun, Y. Big Data Privacy Preserving in Multi-Access Edge Computing for Heterogeneous Internet of Things. IEEE Commun. Mag. 2018, 56, 62–67.

El-Sayed, H.; Sankar, S.; Prasad, M.; Puthal, D.; Gupta, A.; Mohanty, M.; Lin, C.T. Edge of Things: The Big Picture on the Integration of Edge, IoT and the Cloud in a Distributed Computing Environment. IEEE Access 2017, 6, 1706–1717.

Flueratoru, L.; Shubina, V.; Niculescu, D.; Lohan, E.S. On the High Fluctuations of Received Signal Strength Measurements with BLE Signals for Contact Tracing and Proximity Detection. IEEE Sens. J. March 15, 2021, 2(6), 5086–5100.

França, R.P.; Iano, Y.; Monteiro, A.C.B.; Arthur, R. Lower Memory Consumption for Data Transmission in Smart Cloud Environments with CBEDE Methodology. In Smart Systems Design, Applications, and Challenges; IGI Global: Hershey, PA, 2020; pp. 216–237.

Gezer, V.; Um, J.; Ruskowski, M. An Extensible Edge Computing Architecture: Definition, Requirements and Enablers. In Proceedings of the UBICOMM, Barcelona, 12–16 November 2017.

Grabosky, P. Organized Cybercrime and National Security. In Cybercrime Risks and Responses; Springer: Berlin/Heidelberg, 2015; pp. 67–80.

Guilloteau, S.; Venkatesen, M. Privacy in Cloud Computing-ITU-T Technology Watch Report March 2012; International Telecommunication Union: Geneva, 2013.

Gupta, S.; Rani, S.; Batra, K. Maximal Security Issues and Threats Protection in Grid and Cloud Computing Environment. Int. J. Adv. Comput. Sci. Appl. 2020, 11(4), 4367–4373.

Gupta, S.; Rani, S.; Dixit, A.; Dev, H. Features Exploration of Distinct Load Balancing Algorithms in Cloud Computing Environment. Int. J. Adv. Netw. Appl. 2019, 11(1), 4177–4183.

Hay, B.; Nance, K.; Bishop, M. Storm Clouds Rising: Security Challenges for IaaS Cloud Computing. In Proceedings of the 44th Hawaii International Conference on System Sciences, Kauai, HI, 4–7 January 2011; pp. 1–7.

Heck, M.; Edinger, J.; Schaefer, D.; Becker, C. IoT Applications in Fog and Edge Computing: Where Are We and Where Are we Going? In Proceedings of the 2018 27th International Conference on Computer Communication and Networks (ICCCN), Hangzhou, 30 July–2 August 2018; pp. 1–6.

Henze, M.; Matzutt, R.; Hiller, J.; Erik, M.; Ziegeldorf, J.H.; van der Giet, J.; Wehrle, K. Complying with Data Handling Requirements in Cloud Storage Systems. IEEE Trans. Cloud Comput. 2020, 10(3), 1661–1664.

Hou, Y.; Garg, S.; Hui, L.; Jayakody, D.N.K.; Jin, R.; Hossain, M.S. A Data Security Enhanced Access Control Mechanism in Mobile Edge Computing. IEEE Access 2020, 8, 136119–136130.

Hu, P.; Dhelim, S.; Ning, H.; Qiu, T. Survey on Fog Computing: Architecture, Key Technologies, Applications and Open Issues. J. Netw. Comput. Appl. 2017, 98, 27–42.

Huttunen, J.; Jauhiainen, J.; Lehti, L.; Nylund, A.; Martikainen, M.; Lehner, O. Big Data, Cloud Computing and Data Science Applications in Finance and Accounting. ACRN Oxf. J. Financ. Risk Perspect. 2019, 8, 16–30.

Jadeja, Y.; Modi, K. Cloud Computing—Concepts, Architecture and Challenges. In Proceedings of the International Conference on Computing, Electronics and Electrical Technologies (ICCEET), Nagercoil, 21–22 March 2012; pp. 877–880.

Jiang, C.; Cheng, X.; Gao, H.; Zhou, X.; Wan, J. Toward Computation Offloading in Edge Computing: A Survey. IEEE Access 2019, 7, 131543–131558.

Kaur, J.; Agrawal, A.; Khan, R.A. Security Issues in Fog Environment: A Systematic Literature Review. Int. J. Wirel. Inf. Netw. 2020, 27, 467–483.

Khalil, I.; Khreishah, A.; Azeem, M. Consolidated Identity Management System for Secure Mobile Cloud Computing. Comput. Netw. 2014, 65, 99–110.

Khan, A.N.; Ali, M.; Khan, A.R.; Khan, F.G.; Khan, I.A.; Jadoon, W.; Shamshirband, S.; Chronopoulos, A.T. A Comparative Study and Workload Distribution Model for Re-encryption Schemes in a Mobile Cloud Computing Environment. Int. J. Commun. Syst. 2017a, 30, e3308.

Khan, S.; Parkinson, S.; Qin, Y. Fog Computing Security: A Review of Current Applications and Security Solutions. J. Cloud Comput. 2017b, 6, 1–22.

Khan, S.U. The Curious Case of Distributed Systems and Continuous Computing. IT Prof. 2016, 18, 4–7.

Khorshed, M.T.; Ali, A.S.; Wasimi, S.A. A Survey on Gaps, Threat Remediation Challenges and Some Thoughts for Proactive Attack Detection in Cloud Computing. Future Gener. Comput. Syst. 2012, 28, 833–851.

Kozyrev, D.; Ometov, A.; Moltchanov, D.; Rykov, V.; Efrosinin, D.; Milovanova, T.; Andreev, S.; Koucheryavy, Y. Mobility-Centric Analysis of Communication Offloading for Heterogeneous Internet of Things Devices. Wirel. Commun. Mob. Comput. 2018, 2018, 3761075.

Kumbhare, A. IDS Implementation in a Private Cloud. Int. J. Comput. Sci. Mob. Comput. 2014a, 3(6), 208–214.

Kumbhare, A. IDS: Survey on Intrusion Detection System in Cloud Computing. Int. J. Comput. Sci. Mob. Comput. 2014b, 3(4), 497–502.

Lee, K. Security Threats in Cloud Computing Environments. Int. J. Secur. Appl. 2012, 6, 25–32.

Li, H.; Shou, G.; Hu, Y.; Guo, Z. Mobile Edge Computing: Progress and Challenges. In Proceedings of the 2016 4th IEEE International Conference on Mobile Cloud Computing, Services, and Engineering (MobileCloud), Oxford, 29 March–1 April 2016; pp. 83–84.

Li, R.; Liu, A.X.; Wang, A.L.; Bruhadeshwar, B. Fast and Scalable Range Query Processing with Strong Privacy Protection for Cloud Computing. IEEE/ACM Trans. Netw. 2015, 24, 2305–2318.

Lin, J.; Yu, W.; Zhang, N.; Yang, X.; Zhang, H.; Zhao, W. A Survey on Internet of Things: Architecture, Enabling Technologies, Security and Privacy, and Applications. IEEE Internet Things J. 2017, 4, 1125–1142.

Liu, D.; Yan, Z.; Ding, W.; Atiquzzaman, M. A Survey on Secure Data Analytics in Edge Computing. IEEE Internet Things J. 2019, 6, 4946–4967.

Mahmood, Z.; Ramachandran, M. Fog Computing: Concepts, Principles and Related Paradigms. In Fog Computing; Springer International Publishing: Cham, 2018; pp. 3–21.

Mahmud, R.; Kotagiri, R.; Buyya, R. Fog Computing: A Taxonomy, Survey and Future Directions. In Internet of Everything; Springer: Berlin/Heidelberg, 2018; pp. 103–130.

Mäkitalo, N.; Aaltonen, T.; Raatikainen, M.; Ometov, A.; Andreev, S.; Koucheryavy, Y.; Mikkonen, T. Action-Oriented Programming Model: Collective Executions and Interactions in the Fog. J. Syst. Softw. 2019, 157, 110391.

Mäkitalo, N.; Flores-Martin, D.; Berrocal, J.; Garcia-Alonso, J.; Ihantola, P.; Ometov, A.; Murillo, J.M.; Mikkonen, T. The Internet of Bodies Needs a Human Data Model. IEEE Internet Comput. 2020, 24, 28–37.

Marbukh, V. Towards Fog Network Utility Maximization (FoNUM) for Managing Fog Computing Resources. In Proceedings of the 2019 IEEE International Conference on Fog Computing (ICFC), Prague, 24–26 June 2019; pp. 195–200.

Mebrek, A.; Merghem-Boulahia, L.; Esseghir, M. Efficient Green Solution for a Balanced Energy Consumption and Delay in the IoT-Fog-Cloud Computing. In Proceedings of the 2017 IEEE 16th International Symposium on Network Computing and Applications (NCA), Cambridge, MA, 30 October–1 November 2017; pp. 1–4.

Modi, C.; Patel, D.; Borisaniya, B.; Patel, A.; Rajarajan, M. A Survey on Security Issues and Solutions at Different Layers of Cloud Computing. J. Supercomput. 2013a, 63, 561–592.

Modi, C.; Patel, D.; Borisaniya, B.; Patel, H.; Patel, A.; Rajarajan, M. A Survey of Intrusion Detection Techniques in Cloud. J. Netw. Comput. Appl. 2013b, 36, 42–57.

Moltchanov, D.; Ometov, A.; Andreev, S.; Koucheryavy, Y. Upper Bound on Capacity of 5G mm Wave Cellular with Multi-Connectivity Capabilities. Electron. Lett. 2018, 54, 724–726.

Mukherjee, M.; Matam, R.; Shu, L.; Maglaras, L.; Ferrag, M.A.; Choudhury, N.; Kumar, V. Security and Privacy in Fog Computing: Challenges. IEEE Access 2017, 5, 19293–19304.

Mulazzani, M.; Schrittwieser, S.; Leithner, M.; Huber, M.; Weippl, E. Dark Clouds on the Horizon: Using Cloud Storage as Attack Vector and Online Slack Space. In Proceedings of the 20th USENIX Conference on Security, San Francisco, CA, 8–12 August 2011; pp. 1–11.

Naccache, D.; Stern, J. A New Public Key Cryptosystem Based on Higher Residues. In Proceedings of the 5th ACM Conference on Computer and Communications Security, San Francisco, CA, 2–5 November 1998; pp. 59–66.

Naha, R.K.; Garg, S.; Georgakopoulos, D.; Jayaraman, P.P.; Gao, L.; Xiang, Y.; Ranjan, R. Fog Computing: Survey of Trends, Architectures, Requirements, and Research Directions. IEEE Access 2018, 6, 47980–48009.

Nenvani, G.; Gupta, H. A Survey on Attack Detection on Cloud Using Supervised Learning Techniques. In Proceedings of the Symposium on Colossal Data Analysis and Networking (CDAN), Indore, 18–19 March 2016; pp. 1–5.

Ni, J.; Zhang, K.; Lin, X.; Shen, X. Securing Fog Computing for Internet of Things Applications: Challenges and Solutions. IEEE Commun. Surv. Tutor. 2018, 20, 601–628.

Nieuwenhuis, L.J.; Ehrenhard, M.L.; Prause, L. The Shift to Cloud Computing: The Impact of Disruptive Technology on the Enterprise Software Business Ecosystem. Technol. Forecast. Soc. Chang. 2018, 129, 308–313.

Ometov, A.; Chukhno, O.; Chukhno, N.; Nurmi, J.; Lohan, E.S. When Wearable Technology Meets Computing in Future Networks: A Road Ahead. In Proceedings of the 18th ACM International Conference on Computing Frontiers, Virtual Event, 11–13 May 2021a; pp. 185–190.

Ometov, A.; Olshannikova, E.; Masek, P.; Olsson, T.; Hosek, J.; Andreev, S.; Koucheryavy, Y. Dynamic Trust Associations Over Socially-Aware D2D Technology: A Practical Implementation Perspective. IEEE Access 2016, 4, 7692–7702.

Ometov, A.; Shubina, V.; Klus, L.; Skibińska, J.; Saafi, S.; Pascacio, P.; Flueratoru, L.; Gaibor, D.Q.; Chukhno, N.; Chukhno, O.; Ali, A.; A survey on wearable technology: History, state-of-the-art and current challenges. Computer Networks. 2021, 193, 108074.

Parikh, S.; Dave, D.; Patel, R.; Doshi, N. Security and Privacy Issues in Cloud, Fog and Edge Computing. Procedia Comput. Sci. 2019, 160, 734–739.

Patel, A.; Shah, N.; Ramoliya, D.; Nayak, A. A Detailed Review of Cloud Security: Issues, Threats Attacks. In Proceedings of the 4th International Conference on Electronics, Communication and Aerospace Technology (ICECA), Coimbatore, 5–7 November 2020; pp. 758–764.

Pearson, S.; Benameur, A. Privacy, Security and Trust Issues Arising from Cloud Computing. In Proceedings of the IEEE Second International Conference on Cloud Computing Technology and Science, Indianapolis, IN, 30 November–3 December 2010; pp. 693–702.

Peng, M.; Yan, S.; Zhang, K.; Wang, C. Fog-Computing-based Radio Access Networks: Issues and Challenges. IEEE Netw. 2016, 30, 46–53.

Qaim, W.B.; Ometov, A.; Molinaro, A.; Lener, I.; Campolo, C.; Lohan, E.S.; Nurmi, J. Towards Energy Efficiency in the Internet of Wearable Things: A Systematic Review. IEEE Access 2020, 8, 175412–175435.

Ranaweera, P.; Jurcut, A.D.; Liyanage, M. Survey on Multi-Access Edge Computing Security and Privacy. IEEE Commun. Surv. Tutor. 2021, 23, 1078–1124.

Rani, S.; Kumar, A.; Bagchi, A.; Yadav, S.; Kumar, S. RPL Based Routing Protocols for Load Balancing in IoT Network. In Journal of Physics: Conference Series, Volume 1950, International Conference on Mechatronics and Artificial Intelligence (ICMAI), Gurgaon, 27 February 2021. doi: 10.1088/1742–6596/1950/1/012073.

Rani, S.; Tripathi, K.; Arora, Y.; Kumar, A. Analysis of Anomaly detection of Malware using KNN. In 2022 2nd International Conference on Innovative Practices in Technology and Management (ICIPTM), Gautam Buddha Nagar, 2022; pp. 774–779. doi: 10.1109/ICIPTM54933.2022.9754044.

Rimal, B.P.; Maier, M. Workflow Scheduling in Multi-Tenant Cloud Computing Environments. IEEE Trans. Parallel Distrib. Syst. 2016, 28, 290–304.

Ristenpart, T.; Tromer, E.; Shacham, H.; Savage, S. Hey, You, Get Off of My Cloud: Exploring Information Leakage in Third-Party Compute Clouds. In Proceedings of the 16th ACM Conference on Computer and Communications Security, Chicago, IL, 9–13 November 2009; pp. 199–212.

Roman, R.; Lopez, J.; Mambo, M. Mobile Edge Computing, Fog et al.: A Survey and Analysis of Security Threats and Challenges. Future Gener. Comput. Syst. 2018, 78, 680–698.

Rusk, J.D. Trust and Decision Making in the Privacy Paradox? In Proceedings of the Southern Association for Information Systems Conference, Macon, GA, 21–22 March 2014.

Sarkar, S.; Misra, S. Theoretical Modelling of Fog Computing: A Green Computing Paradigm to Support IoT Applications. IET Netw. 2016, 5, 23–29.

Shi, W.; Zhang, L.; Wu, C.; Li, Z.; Lau, F.C. An Online Auction Framework for Dynamic Resource Provisioning in Cloud Computing. ACM Sigmetrics Perform. Eval. Rev. 2014, 42, 71–83.

Shubina, V.; Ometov, A.; Andreev, S.; Niculescu, D.; Lohan, E.S. Privacy versus Location Accuracy in OpportunisticWearable Networks. In Proceedings of the International Conference on Localization and GNSS (ICL-GNSS), Tampere, 2–4 June 2020; pp. 1–6.

Spatharakis, D.; Dimolitsas, I.; Dechouniotis, D.; Papathanail, G.; Fotoglou, I.; Papadimitriou, P.; Papavassiliou, S. A Scalable Edge Computing Architecture Enabling Smart Offloading for Location Based Services. Pervasive Mob. Comput. 2020, 67, 101217.

Stojmenovic, I.; Wen, S. The Fog Computing Paradigm: Scenarios and Security Issues. In Proceedings of the Federated Conference on Computer Science and Information Systems, Warsaw, 7–10 September 2014; pp. 1–8.

Stojmenovic, I.; Wen, S.; Huang, X.; Luan, H. An Overview of Fog Computing and Its Security Issues. Concurr. Comput. Pract. Exp. 2016, 28, 2991–3005.

Sun, P.J. Privacy Protection and Data Security in Cloud Computing: A Survey, Challenges, and Solutions. IEEE Access 2019, 7, 147420–147452.

Tyagi, A.K.; Niladhuri, S.; Priya, R. Never Trust Anyone: Trust-Privacy Trade-Offs in Vehicular Ad-Hoc Networks. J. Adv. Math. Comput. Sci. 2016, 19, 1–23.

Wang, K.; Du, M.; Yang, D.; Zhu, C.; Shen, J.; Zhang, Y. Game-Theory-based Active Defense for Intrusion Detection in Cyber-Physical Embedded Systems. ACM Trans. Embed. Comput. Syst. 2017a, 16, 1–21.

Wang, K.; Yuan, L.; Miyazaki, T.; Zeng, D.; Guo, S.; Sun, Y. Strategic Antieavesdropping Game for Physical Layer Security in Wireless Cooperative Networks. IEEE Trans. Veh. Technol. 2017b, 66, 9448–9457.

Wei, W.; Xu, F.; Li, Q. MobiShare: Flexible Privacy-Preserving Location Sharing in Mobile Online Social Networks. In Proceedings of the IEEE INFOCOM, Orlando, FL, 25–30 March 2012; pp. 2616–2620.

Xiao, Y.; Jia, Y.; Liu, C.; Cheng, X.; Yu, J.; Lv, W. Edge Computing Security: State of the Art and Challenges. Proc. IEEE 2019, 107, 1608–1631.

Xiao, Z.; Xiao, Y. Security and Privacy in Cloud Computing. IEEE Commun. Surv. Tutor. 2013, 15, 843–859.

Yi, S.; Qin, Z.; Li, Q. Security and Privacy Issues of Fog Computing: A Survey. In International Conference on Wireless Algorithms, Systems, and Applications; Springer: Berlin/Heidelberg, 2015; pp. 685–695.

Zeyu, H.; Geming, X.; Zhaohang, W.; Sen, Y. Survey on Edge Computing Security. In Proceedings of the International Conference on Big Data, Artificial Intelligence and Internet of Things Engineering (ICBAIE), Fuzhou, 12–14 June 2020; pp. 96–105.

Zhang, J.; Chen, B.; Zhao, Y.; Cheng, X.; Hu, F. Data Security and Privacy-Preserving in Edge Computing Paradigm: Survey and Open Issues. IEEE Access 2018, 6, 18209–18237.

Zissis, D.; Lekkas, D. Addressing Cloud Computing Security Issues. Future Gener. Comput. Syst. 2012, 28, 583–592.

Chapter 3

Security Aspects in Cloud Computing

[1]Archika Jain and [2]Devendra Somwanshi
[1]Dept. of Computer Engineering Swami Keshvanand Institute of Technology
Jaipur, India-302022
[2]Dept. of Electronics and Communication Poornima College of Engineering
Jaipur, India-302022

3.1 INTRODUCTION

One essential element is security for enabling privacy. This principle states that adequate security measures should be used to protect personal data against risks including loss or unauthorised access, use, alteration, destruction, or disclosure. The link between location and resources is altered by cloud computing, which alters the way we think about computing because cloud computing is a novel form of computing. There is a great deal on how to achieve security on every level (e.g., network, host, application, and data levels). As used in this study, the term "cloud" has its roots in network diagrams that showed the internet or different components of it as schematic clouds.

3.1.1 Cloud

The term "cloud computing" was created to describe what occurs when programmers and services are placed into the "cloud" of the internet. Where computer systems remotely share computing resources and applications; cloud computing has its roots; it did not just develop overnight. Today, the phrase "cloud computing" is more frequently used to refer to the large range of services and apps that are now made available over the internet cloud [1].

3.1.2 Cloud Computing Model

Online data or service access is the foundation of cloud computing. The internet can be used to put this into practice. Various ICT-enabled gadgets are connected in this concept using a variety of technical ideas. It is an assortment of parts that might be utilized to meet the software and hardware requirements for on-demand services. There are three different service models for cloud computing that each must meet a certain set of business requirements [2].

3.1.2.1 Software as a Service (SaaS)

On-demand software is another term for SaaS. It is software where the apps are hosted by a cloud service provider. Users must have access to the internet and a web browser in order to utilize these applications. The backbone of cloud computing is SaaS. It is sometimes referred to as the cloud computing interaction layer [3] since it allows users to communicate with the cloud. All cloud apps are available through this layer on a shared basis. SaaS may often be connected to other cloud tiers through the internet [3].

3.1.2.2 Platform as a Service (PaaS)

For the purpose of developing, testing, running, and managing applications, the PaaS cloud computing platform was developed. PaaS controls the intermediate layer of cloud computing. The SaaS and IaaS layers of a cloud can also be connected via this layer. For programmers or other professionals who are in charge of creating and building apps, there is a layer called PaaS. Every application utilized at the SaaS layer is created at the PaaS layer. It has programs like operating systems and programming languages, among others, which are necessary for creating applications [3].

3.1.2.3 Infrastructure as a Service (IaaS)

Hardware as a service (HaaS) is another name for IaaS. It is a computer infrastructure that is maintained online. IaaS adoption primarily benefits customers by sparing them the expense and inconvenience of having to

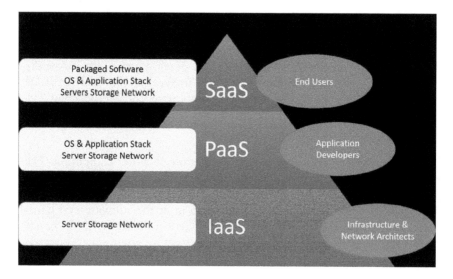

Figure 3.1 Cloud computing models [2].

purchase and maintain physical servers. The IaaS is the base layer of a cloud. It has every piece of hardware needed to create an application (Figure 3.1). It provides resources such as servers, storage discs, and other hardware, along with all the necessary networking tools, depending on the needs [3].

3.1.3 Types of Cloud Computing

Internet-based computing called "cloud computing" makes use of a shared pool of resources that are accessible over a wide network and may be deployed or released with little involvement from service providers (Figure 3.2).

3.1.3.1 Public Cloud

Everyone may use the public cloud, which uses a pay-per-usage model, to store and retrieve information through the internet. In a public cloud, the cloud service provider (CSP) manages and controls the computer resources [5].

3.1.3.2 Private Cloud

An internal or corporate cloud is another name for private cloud. Organizations use it to construct and operate their own data centers, either internally or through a third party. Open source technologies like Eucalyptus and Open stack can be used to deploy it [5].

3.1.3.3 Hybrid Cloud

Public and private clouds are combined to create hybrid clouds because services operating on public clouds may be accessed by anyone, while those running on private clouds can only be accessible by people within an organization. We can claim that hybrid clouds are only partially secure [5].

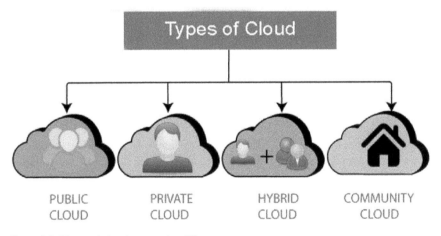

Figure 3.2 Types of cloud computing [4].

3.1.3.4 Community Cloud

In order to communicate information between an organization and a particular community, a collection of various organizations can access systems and services through a community cloud [5].

3.2 ASSESSMENT PROCEDURE

Every study should adopt the literature review process as its foundation.

3.2.1 Research Definition

Research is a process:

1. It is being done in accordance with a set of ideologies (approaches).
2. It employs strategies, methods, and processes that have been examined for reliability and validity.
3. It is intended to be impartial and unbiased.

3.2.2 Objectives of Research

1. Investigate or design a study to learn more about a phenomena or to acquire new perspectives on it.
2. To accurately portray the characteristics of a certain person, situation, or group-descriptive study.
3. To determine how frequently something occurs or how it is related to other things in diagnostic research.
4. To investigate if there is a causal relationship between two variables.

3.2.3 Issues

The maintenance of security and privacy in cloud computing is broken down into the next issue. Review and discussion of subtopics include the years 2009 through 2022.

- Security in cloud computing (76 Research Papers).

3.2.4 Review Outcome on Security in Cloud Computing

[Chun-Ting Huang et al. 2011] suggested many methods, such as certification, authorization, audit, and encryption, to guarantee cloud storage security. TPA generally used a homomorphic approach to audit or examine the integrated data in cloud storage. Each cloud node has a virtual machine monitor (VMM) host application that enables a single machine to handle numerous, identical execution environments [6]. [Gurudatt Kulkarni et al. 2012] provided a thorough review of the cloud computing security risks and difficulties, concentrating on the many forms of cloud computing and service delivery. The essential idea of protected cloud computing is presented in this work. It implies that cloud computing relies on encryption and decryption services that are distinct from storage services in order to improve data security in cloud computing [7]. [Birendra Goswami et al. 2012] presented a paradigm in which symmetric and asymmetric cryptographic techniques were used. In spite of the key size specified across the ring of integers, the suggested technique for public key cryptography using matrices is a three-stage secured procedure with constant complexity (fixed number of multiplications) [8]. [Dr. T. Kavitha et al. 2022] argues against cloud computing that use man-in-the-middle cryptography, cloud malware injection, side channel attacks, and authentication attacks, as well as potential fixes [9]. [Ching-Chiang Chen et al. 2019] provides a cloud computing security scenario and demonstrate a cloud computing security preventive technique, this study used system dynamics for information security policy. Finally, the simulation findings demonstrate that the Audit system may offer early breach prevention in the context of cloud computing for data centers and endpoint host sides [10]. [Doaa M. Bamasoud et al. 2021] provides the security of data in cloud computing is aided by a range of agents, such as file agents, encryption agents, and other types that are well suited and used to protect data [5]. [Anagha Markandey et al. 2018] provide that the goal of this study is to establish a comparable cloud storage security approach and to ensure data security for cloud storage [2]. By taking into account security concerns and user data on cloud storage, these methods are coupled with the results of current data to progress towards the most suitable security strategy, which is based on cloud storage system characteristics. The article will go into the finer points of information assurance techniques and procedures used globally to provide the highest level of information insurance by reducing risks and threats [2]. [Wang Xiaoyu et al. 2020] suggested a tree-based dynamic hash authentication system. The confidence in the empowerment management system is shown with the user dimension as the letter and the management technology as the side. Cloud storage security measures include a focus on data encryption technologies, from data, design, and devaluation [11]. [Harsh Gupta et al. 2019] gave the conclusion that the data stored in the cloud has to be secured and maintained immediately. The cloud service provider is doing everything for protecting and keeping this data [12].

3.3 COMMON FINDINGS ON SECURITY IN CLOUD COMPUTING

- By using a completely homomorphic encryption system, users of cloud computing may store and manipulate private data anywhere while also having their privacy protected [1].
- The remote server storage data has been authenticated by using the RSA-based hash function approach [10].

- The standard protocols and SSL have been utilised for cloud computing authentication [13].
- The virtualization method appears to be a key method for authorization in cloud computing. Virtual machines can also be utilized for security reasons. Some security solutions included Virtual Machine Monitors (VMM) and Virtual Private Networks (VPN) [7].
- There are several kinds of agents, such as the authentication agent, which handles user rights management, digital certificate issuance, and authentication. Similar to how file agents are employed to secure data. Encryption agents should choose the encryption algorithm [8].
- Identity management for security is an advanced authentication mechanism [14].
- For exchanging data in the cloud while maintaining secrecy and integrity, protocols like File Transfer Protocol Secure [FTPS], Hyper Text Transfer Protocol Secure [HTTPS], and Secure Copy Program [SCP] are helpful [15, 16].
- The authors examined the Hadoop Distributed File System (HDFS) for data security [17].
- Biometric authentication can be used in place of conventional passwords for security purposes [2].
- A possible option is to use service level agreements for security in cloud computing [18].
- Open Virtualization Format (OVF), ISO/IEC 27001/27002, and Information Technology Infrastructure Library (ITIL) have all been utilized as security management standards [7].
- The Third Party Auditor (TPA) and the Proofs of Irretrievability are two of the most often used methods for data integrity (PORs) [19].

3.4 ISSUE-WISE SOLUTION APPROACHES TO SECURITY IN CLOUD COMPUTING

- Researchers found that other common protocols, including those based on SSL, may be utilised to secure data in cloud computing [20].
- By using a completely homomorphic encryption system, users of cloud computing may store and manipulate private data anywhere while also having their privacy protected [1].
- The virtualization method appears to be a key method for authorization in cloud computing. Virtual machines can also be utilized for security reasons. Some security solutions included Virtual Machine Monitors (VMM) and Virtual Private Networks (VPN) [7].
- There are several kinds of agents, such as the authentication agent, which handles user rights management, digital certificate issuance, and

authentication. Similar to how file agents are employed to secure data, the encryption agent should choose the encryption algorithm [21].

- As a solution, the RSA-based hash function approach may be utilized to verify the storage data on remote servers [22].
- Identity management is an advanced authentication mechanism [14].

The following Table 3.1 contrasts the numerous approaches, tactics, and methodologies employed by various researchers as examined.

3.5 SECURITY THREATS IN CLOUD COMPUTING

From a security point of view, a cloud holds all of the user's sensitive and vital data so it has been said that security is absolutely essential. The security of the cloud must be ensured by the cloud provider. The cloud provider should be aware of all potential dangers and have all necessary precautions [12]. These security risks are ones that cloud providers need to be aware of. In Figure 3.3 various cloud computing threads are shown.

3.5.1 Data Loss

Sensitive data is being stored in ever-increasing amounts in the clouds, and it is possible for this data to be destroyed in a variety of ways, including through corruption, inadvertent deletion, and natural disasters like earthquakes and floods. The data of businesses, which is a vital asset for any firm, is also present in the cloud in addition to personal data. By storing several backups at data centers, this may be minimized [5, 12].

3.5.2 Data Breach

Any kind of data leak, including illegal access by outsiders or insiders of the data center. The sensitivity of the data determines the extent of the harm. The data may contain financial information, which might cause a great deal of harm. Large corporations like Microsoft have data centers that are so well guarded that entry requires both footprints and fingerprints as well as a valid justification. Armed guards are present in data centers run by companies like Microsoft to prevent unauthorized entry [12].

3.5.3 Data Location

There shouldn't be a single location where the entire cloud's data is kept. There should be adequate backups of the data at several places. The location of data shouldn't be made public; only higher authorities should know about it [5].

Table 3.1 Method of security in cloud computing

Technique	Approach/Methodology	Hardware/Software Used	Findings
Encryption and Decryption [23]	Anti-attack technology	Java Programming	Analysed the information security issues in its application
	Data security model	Java Programming	Presents a security module in cloud computing and introduces agent for the data protection
	Based on cloud computing service architecture	Java Programming	Key security considerations are highlighted
	Confidentiality, integrity and availability (CIA) security model	Jav Java Programming	Fin Finds out some security threats and their impact on security of data
	PKI technology	Java Programming	Designs a security framework of cloud computing platform
Homomorphic Encryption Mechanism [1]	PKI based cloud computing communication and privacy protection mechanisms	Java Programming	Stores and manipulates confidential data at any place
	Privacy protection system	Java Programming	Help users to control the storage and use of their sensitive information in the cloud
	Cipher text retrieval method	Java Programming	Data transmission between the cloud and the user safely
Virtualisation [13]	Virtual machine	Intel Core 2 processor running at 1.86 GHz	Protecting against DDOS, Trojan, Virus and Spam, etc., more effectively
	Hypervisor	Intel Core 2 processor running at 1.86 GHz	Supports redundant, self-recovering, highly scalable programming models
	VMM (Virtual Machine Monitor)	Intel Core 2 processor running at 1.86 GHz	Supports multiple, identical execution environments, in each cloud node
	VPN (Virtual Private Network)	Intel Core 2 processor running at 1.86 GHz	All the privacy information, encryption and decryption policies, data management and mapping organisation can be controlled

Category	Type	Tool	Description
Access Control Specifications [8]	RAS factor	Send Log Programming Language	Improves RAS parameters -reliability, availability and security
	Secure provenance scheme	Send Log Programming Language	Identifies top security concerns of cloud computing
Protocols [24]	File Transfer Protocol Secure [FTPS]	MATLAB	Useful for transferring data in the cloud to maintain confidentiality and integrity
	Hyper Text Transfer Protocol Secure [HTTPS]	MATLAB	Useful for transferring data in the cloud to maintain confidentiality and integrity
	Hadoop Distributed File System (HDFS)	MATLAB	Leads to data security requirement of cloud computing
Programming Languages [23]	Security Assertion Mark-up Language (SAML) standard	Notepad	Identity federation solution can be accomplished
	Extensible Access Control Mark-up Language (XACML)	Notepad	Controls access to cloud resources

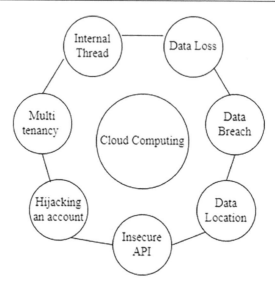

Figure 3.3 Cloud computing threads [25].

3.5.4 Insecure Application Programming Interfaces

Hackers and programmers may manipulate cloud services but thanks to application programming interfaces who secure our data, users shouldn't be forced to utilize poor APIs. APIs handle the deployment, management, and monitoring of cloud services [16]. Weak APIs may cause application configuration settings to change, sensitive data to leak, servers to become inoperable, etc. Accessing the cloud service APIs exclusively with encrypted keys that will authenticate the API user will help to lessen this hazard. The encrypted keys have to be kept on a safe piece of hardware [5, 12].

3.5.5 Hijacking an Account

This concern involves the disclosure of credentials to access cloud services, which would allow hackers to steal sensitive data, submit fraudulent information, and interfere with other people's transactions, potentially putting the user and the cloud service provider in legal hot water. All of the services and information that were previously available to authorized users are now available to hijackers [12].

3.5.6 Many Tenancies

Multiple renters sharing a variety of resources is known as multi tenancy [26]. Reduced costs are multi tenancy's main benefit.

3.5.7 Internal Threats

This is the threat that is particularly challenging to counter. This hazard comprises the insider employee altering, erasing, updating, or disclosing sensitive information. The cloud provider always ensures the reliability of all of his workers. This hazard may be diminished by doing background checks on the employee, granting just the access that is necessary to the person, and putting automation technologies in place to carry out all routine duties [18].

3.6 TECHNIQUES OF DATA SECURITY IN CLOUD COMPUTING

In Figure 3.4 various techniques of data security in cloud computing are shown.

3.6.1 Encryption and Decryption

The process of changing data from a readable format to a scrambled piece of information is known as data encryption—to prevent snoopers from viewing private data in transit. Any kind of network communication, including documents, files, messages, and messages themselves, can be encrypted. The hidden data is converted back into readable data during decryption [23].

3.6.2 Homomorphic Encryption Mechanism

Data is transformed into cipher text through homomorphic encryption so that it may be examined and used just like it would if it were still in its original format. Complex mathematical processes can be carried out on encrypted data using homomorphic encryptions without compromising the encryption [1].

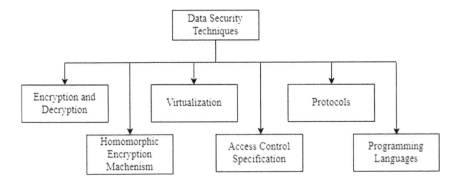

Figure 3.4 Data security techniques [2].

3.6.3 Virtualization

Making a virtual platform out of the server operating system and storage hardware is known as virtualization in cloud computing. The user will benefit from having access to several computers at once, and sharing a single physical instance of a resource or programme across numerous users is also made possible [13].

3.6.4 Access Control Specifications

Access control is a security technique that restricts who or what may use resources in a computing environment [8].

3.6.5 Protocols

In the context of cloud computing, there are several security concerns that require secure communication to be resolved. Transmission Control Protocol (TCP) and User Datagram Protocol (UDP) employ the Secure Transmission Cloud Protocol [24].

3.6.6 Programming Languages

Language-based security (LBS) is a class of approaches used in computer science to use the characteristics of programming languages to enhance the security of systems on a high-level. Due to its simplicity of use, PHP is a programming language that is frequently used for cloud computing and web development. So when it comes to automating websites and other tasks, it is well-liked [23].

3.7 CHALLENGES IN CLOUD COMPUTING

It is the supply of resources like data and storage in real-time and on demand. With the market valuation expanding quickly, one must be innovative in the IT business. Cloud development is shown to be advantageous for both large public and commercial corporations as well as small-scale firms since it reduces expenses. In light of this, we present to you today the most typical difficulties encountered while using cloud computing. Let's take a closer look at each of them individually in Figure 3.5.

3.7.1 Data Privacy and Security

When utilizing cloud computing, data security is a top issue. Important and confidential user or corporate data is saved in the cloud. Even though the cloud service provider promises data integrity, you are still in charge of user identification and authorization, identity management, data encryption, and

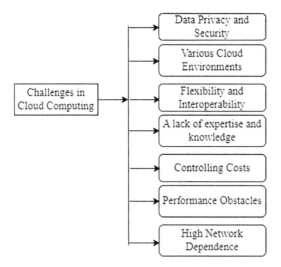

Figure 3.5 Challenges in cloud computing [27].

access control. Identity theft, data breaches, malware infections, and other security problems in the cloud reduce user confidence in your apps. This may lead to a potential loss of money, position, and reputation. Furthermore, the rapid transmission and receipt of large amounts of data required for cloud computing renders it susceptible to data breaches.

3.7.2 Various Cloud Environments

Enterprises now rely on numerous cloud service providers in addition to using a single cloud since there are more alternatives accessible to them. Most of these organizations employ hybrid cloud methods and close to 84% are dependent on several clouds. The infrastructure team frequently finds that managing this is impeded. Because of the variations between various cloud providers, the procedure usually ends up being quite complicated for the IT staff.

3.7.3 Flexibility and Interoperability

Applications built for one cloud and its application stack must be developed for the other cloud. Switching from one cloud service provider to another may be a time-consuming process for businesses. Due to the difficulties involved like switching cloud solutions, problems with handling data transfer, establishing security from the start and limiting flexibility the migrating from one cloud to another is not flexible.

3.7.4 A Lack of Expertise and Knowledge

Working with the cloud is often a very time-consuming process due to its complexity and high research requirement. It requires deep subject knowledge and competence. Despite the fact that the business has a large number of professionals, they need to continually improve their abilities. Salaries are particularly expensive in the field of cloud computing due to the significant supply and demand imbalance. Despite the large number of roles that remain unfilled, there are not enough skilled cloud engineers, developers, and specialists. Up skilling is therefore necessary to enable these individuals to actively comprehend, administer, and build cloud-based systems with the fewest problems and maximum level of dependability.

3.7.5 Controlling Costs

There are occasions when a company embracing cloud computing will incur significant fees, despite the fact that almost all cloud service providers use a "Pay-As-You-Go" model, which lowers the total cost of the resources used. When resources are not optimized, such as when servers are not being used to their full potential, hidden costs rise. If there are sudden spikes in use or poor application performance, the overall cost rises. The underuse of resources is one of the other main reasons for price increases.

3.7.6 Performance Obstacles

Since applications built for one cloud and its application stack must be developed for the other cloud, switching from one cloud service provider to another may be a time-consuming process for businesses. Ineffective load balancing may be the cause of this delay since the server is unable to divide incoming traffic effectively for the optimum user experience. Fault tolerance creates difficulties when it refers to the ability for operations to continue even when one or more of the components fail.

3.7.7 High Network Dependence

Cloud computing manages massive quantities of data flow to and from the servers because it uses real-time resource provisioning and a high-speed network. Even if these resources and data are dispersed over a network, they might still be susceptible in the event of low bandwidth or unexpected outages. Businesses must ensure that the internet bandwidth is high and there are no network outages even if they can lower the cost of their equipment since failing to do so might result in lost opportunities for income. Consequently, maintaining network capacity is quite expensive.

3.8 ADVANTAGES AND DISADVANTAGES OF CLOUD SECURITY

3.8.1 Advantages

3.8.1.1 A Quick Recovery

Applications and information may be recovered more quickly and accurately thanks to cloud computing. It is the most effective recovery plan with the least downtime.

3.8.1.2 Opening

Get to your data everywhere, at whatever point. By guaranteeing that your application is always accessible, a web cloud architecture boosts advantage and commerce capabilities. This takes into account the fundamental sharing and collaboration amongst clients in various places.

3.8.1.3 No Material is Needed

Everything will be supported by the cloud, negating the need for a physical storage community. In any case, it could warrant taking into account a support in the event of a disaster that seems to moderate down the performance of your corporation.

3.8.1.4 Preferred Position

Simple execution—cloud supporting enables a business to maintain comparable apps and trade forms without having to deal with specific back-end components. A cloud setup is readily and rapidly accessible to enterprises and is easily administered through the web.

3.8.1.5 With Cloud-Encouraging Businesses, Cost Per Head

Advancement overhead is maintained to a minimum, allowing firms to use more time and resources to advance the trade system because of the cloud's tremendous flexibility, businesses may add or remove resources in accordance with their needs. Organizational systems will evolve along with them as they produce.

3.8.2 Disadvantages

3.8.2.1 Problems with Bandwidth

Customers must organize accordingly and prevent from cramming numerous servers and capacity devices into a limited number of data centers for perfect operation.

3.8.2.2 Devoid of Excess

A cloud server is neither too robust nor exorbitant in any manner. Purchase an extra plan of action to protect yourself from being burnt because development might go catastrophically wrong. Despite the inconvenience, this is usually justifiable even though there may be an additional cost.

3.8.2.3 Data Transmission Capacity Problems

Customers should prepare ahead of time and avoid constructing a massive number of servers and capacity devices in a compact pattern of server farms for the best execution.

3.8.2.4 More Power

Your data and information is transferred with your businesses when you move them to the cloud. Organizations with internal IT staff will be required to resolve issues independently. In any event, Stratosphere Systems has a live helpline that is staffed around-the-clock and can address any issue immediately.

3.8.2.5 Lack of Redundancy

A cloud server is neither overkill nor supported. Stay away from getting burnt by having an excess arrangement because creativity might occasionally fail. Despite the fact that it adds further cost, it will typically be worthwhile.

3.9 STRENGTHS AND WEAKNESSES

Following a categorical analysis of 76 research publications, numerous strengths and shortcomings related to security in cloud computing have been identified and are discussed here.

3.9.1 Strengths

- The PKI (public key infrastructure) is well suited to provide security services, including data encryption, digital signatures, identification, as well as the necessary key and certificate management and other security services. Researchers have worked in the area of data security in cloud computing [23].
- The virtualization approach appears to be a vital technology in cloud computing, for the authorization process. The completely homomorphic encryption may secure the privacy of cloud computing users, store and alter secret data at any location [1].

- A variety of agents, including file agents, encryption agents, and other types that are well suited and employed to safeguard data, contribute to the security of data in cloud computing [5].
- The RSA-based hash function is particularly effective in authenticating the data stored on remote servers [22].
- The SSL and standard protocols used for authentication in cloud computing are very effective and well suited [28].
- Another answer to identity management is an advanced authentication mechanism [14].

3.9.2 Weaknesses

- When different methods for ensuring the security of data, such as RSA-based encryption, are used, the speed of data access and transfer dramatically decreases [22].
- Data must always be transmitted through a secure channel. HTTP is unsafe since it only sends plain text data. As a result, HTTPS is required since normal authentication mechanisms and SSL encryption are utilized throughout the HTTPS communication [14].
- The currently deployed additively homomorphic key agreement algorithm needs to be improved by more study.
- Authentication agents first verify the user's identity. Access to the data including the ability to read, write, and delete requires certification. If unauthorized users tricked the authentication agent, the key is handled by the encryption agent. If the key is stolen, it can be dangerous [1].
- The single point of failure in the hypervisor makes intrusion detection systems susceptible. All virtual machines are under the attacker's control if the hypervisor crashes or is taken over by an attacker [13].
- Fully homomorphic encryption schemes have significant computing issues and require more research [1].

3.10 FRAMEWORKS USED IN CLOUD COMPUTING

3.10.1 Public Key Infrastructure

PKI is a framework for enabling safe and trustworthy communication between various entities both inside and outside of the company. It comprises of security rules, communication protocols, processes, etc. PKI is constructed as a mix of symmetric and asymmetric encryption. The PKI, also known as the public key infrastructure, issues digital certificates. It helps to secure sensitive data by granting individuals and computer systems unique identities. It thereby ensures communication security. In order to ensure security, the public key infrastructure requires two keys: the public key and the private key [23].

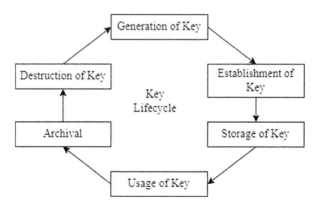

Figure 3.6 Key lifecycle [23].

3.10.1.1 Managing the Cryptosystem's Keys

Keys are what give a cryptosystem its security. We must thus have a reliable key management system in place. The following are the three primary aspects of key management:

- Data that has to be controlled through secure administration is a cryptographic key.
- It entails overseeing the main life cycle, which consists of the following and shown in Figure 3.6.
- Requirements of public key management:
  - **Protecting the private key:** Only the private key's owner is permitted to use it. Therefore, it should continue to be out of reach for anybody else.
  - **Making the public key secure:** Public keys are accessible to everyone and are in the public domain. It is challenging to determine whether a key is accurate and what it will be used for when there is this level of public accessibility. A public key's function must be clearly stated (Figure 3.7).

3.10.2 Virtualization

The idea of virtualized cloud computing is what drives the industry's primary motivation for embracing cloud computing. Although virtualization and multi-tenancy are cost-effective, they are not immune to threats and attacks. In many instances, the attacker used a coordinated attack to get access to the data and services. Due to many types of viruses present in the virtualization software used for virtualization services, the virtualized code may get corrupted or harmed. The primary function of virtualization technology is to give standard versions of apps to cloud users. If the next version of that application is published, the cloud provider must give those customers the most recent version, which is technically feasible since it is more expensive [13].

Figure 3.8 shows the virtualization in cloud computing in various aspects.

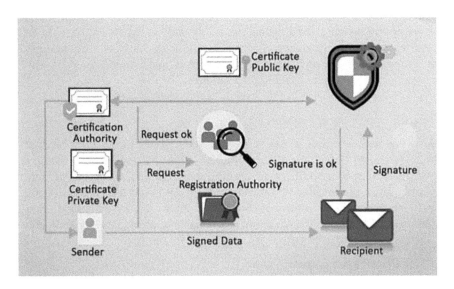

Figure 3.7 Public key infrastructure [23].

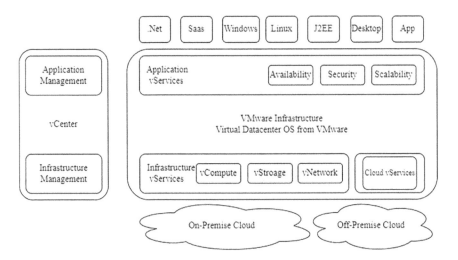

Figure 3.8 Virtualization in cloud computing [13].

3.10.2.1 Needs of Virtualization

The following list of five essential requirements for virtualization is provided in Figure 3.9.

3.10.2.1.1 Enhanced Performance

Currently, the end user system, or PC, is powerful enough to meet all of the users fundamental processing needs, as well as having a number of other features that are seldom utilized by the user. Most of their systems are equipped with the power to support a virtual machine manager and run virtual machines with acceptable performance.

3.10.2.1.2 Limited Use of Resources

Hardware and software resources are not being used to their full potential due to restricted utilization of the resources. Since all of the user's PCs are powerful enough to meet their typical computing requirements, many of them are often utilized and able to run nonstop for 24 hours a day. By utilizing these resources outside of business hours, IT infrastructure's efficiency might be improved. By using virtualization, it is feasible to create this environment.

3.10.2.1.3 Shortage of Space

Data centers are growing quickly due to the ongoing need for more capacity, whether it is in memory storage or computing power. Companies like Google, Microsoft, and Amazon create data centers to meet their specific demands

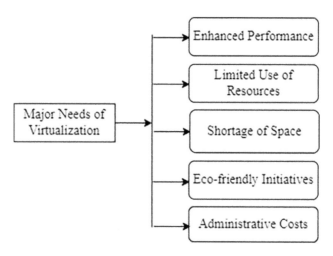

Figure 3.9 Needs of virtualization [13].

in order to grow their infrastructure. The majority of businesses are unable to afford to create another data center to handle more resource capacity. This contributes to the spread of a method known as server consolidation.

3.10.2.1.4 Eco-Friendly Initiatives

Currently, businesses are aggressively looking for ways to reduce the amount of electricity that their systems consume. Data centers are major energy users, and to keep them running well, they require a constant power source in addition to a lot of energy to keep them cool. As a result, server consolidation reduces the number of servers, which reduces the power and cooling effect. A sophisticated way of server consolidation may be offered through virtualization.

3.10.2.1.5 Administrative Costs

A considerable growth in administrative costs is also attributable to the rise in demand for capacity surplus, which results in more servers in a data center. Common system administration responsibilities include hardware monitoring, server setup and upgrades, replacing faulty hardware, monitoring server resources, and backups. These procedures need a lot of workers. As the number of servers increases, so do the administrative costs. With virtualization, fewer servers are needed to handle a given workload, which lowers the cost of administrative staff.

3.10.3 RSA Hash Function

Commonly employed for secure data transfer, public key cryptosystems are referred to as RSA. It makes use of paired keys, one of which is used to encrypt and the other to decode communications [22]. RSA based hash function is shown in Figure 3.10.

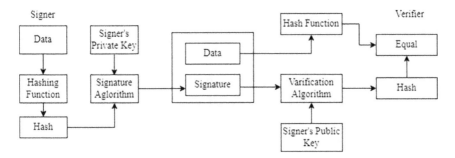

Figure 3.10 RSA based hash function [22].

Using RSA for hash:

- Create public and private RSA keys.
- Never store a private key; instead, discard it.
- Start by creating a hash with a length equal to the RSA encryption block size.
- Block each block, encrypt message using public key.
- Calculate the hash for each encrypted block of the message using the given algorithm (possibly a mix of +, xor, etc.).

3.11 SCOPE OF THE WORK

- It is possible to examine how quickly data is sent when different algorithms are used to protect security and privacy.
- To determine how encryption systems affect data, analysis can be done.
- To examine the details of the data.
- It is possible to work on highlighting the number and quality of data.

3.12 GAPS IN PUBLISHED RESEARCH

- Design a security framework of cloud computing platform.
- In Homomorphic encryption mechanism stores and manipulates confidential data at any place.
- In virtualization all the privacy information, encryption and decryption policies, data management, and mapping organization can be difficult to control.
- Improves RAS parameters like reliability, availability, and security in access control specifications technique.
- Difficult to transferring data in the cloud to maintain confidentiality and integrity.
- Leads to data security requirement of cloud computing.
- Cloud data might occasionally be extremely large and in a variety of forms so its security and privacy cannot always be preserved.
- Various cryptographic algorithms are utilized in cloud computing for security and privacy protection.

3.13 OBJECTIVE

- Utilize various techniques for maintaining the security and privacy of cloud data.
- Identify top security concerns of cloud computing.

- Framework has been designed for public key infrastructure, virtualization, and RSA based hash function.

3.14 CONCLUSION AND FUTURE SCOPE

A review of a total of 76 research publications in the area of security in cloud computing was done in order to analyse and identify existing challenges and the scope of work. After doing the assessment, I identified a number of problems that handled correctly and should be addressed in cloud computing. In this the security threads and handling techniques of those threads were found. Framework has been designed for public key infrastructure, virtualization, and RSA based hash function. These publications consider a variety of cloud computing issues that affect related cloud computing security. These methods and tactics aim to reduce inefficiencies and raise system dependability. In the future, explore different cryptography techniques to keep cloud data secure and private. Comparing and figuring out which of the already employed tactics is most successful as well as altering existing strategies to enhance the security and privacy preservation of cloud data.

REFERENCES

[1] Feng Zhao, Chao Li and Chun Feng Liu, "A Cloud Computing Security Solution Based on Fully Homomorphic Encryption," 16th International Conference on Advanced Communication Technology, vol. 4, pp. 485–488, 16–19 February 2014.
[2] A. Markandey, P. Dhamdhere and Y. Gajmal, "Data Access Security in Cloud Computing: A Review," 2018 International Conference on Computing, Power and Communication Technologies (GUCON), pp. 633–636, 2018. doi: 10.1109/GUCON.2018.8675033.
[3] M. Joshi, S. Budhani, N. Tewari and S. Prakash, "Analytical Review of Data Security in Cloud Computing," 2021 2nd International Conference on Intelligent Engineering and Management (ICIEM), pp. 362–366, 2021. doi: 10.1109/ICIEM51511.2021.9445355.
[4] A. Sun, G. Gao, T. Ji and X. Tu, "One Quantifiable Security Evaluation Model for Cloud Computing Platform," 2018 Sixth International Conference on Advanced Cloud and Big Data (CBD), pp. 197–201, 2018. doi: 10.1109/CBD.2018.00043.
[5] D.M. Bamasoud, A.S. Al-Dossary, N.M. Al-Harthy, R.A. Al-Shomrany, G.S. Alghamdi and R.O. Algahmdi, "Privacy and Security Issues in Cloud Computing: A Survey Paper," 2021 International Conference on Information Technology (ICIT), pp. 387–392, 2021. doi: 10.1109/ICIT52682.2021.9491632.
[6] Chun-Ting Huang, Zhongyuan Qin and C.-C. Jay Kuo, "Multimedia Storage Security in Cloud Computing: An Overview," 2011 IEEE 13th International Workshop on Multimedia Signal Processing, vol. 2, pp. 1–6, 2011. IEEE.

[7] Gurudatt Kulkarni, Jayant Gambhir, Tejswini Patil and Amruta Dongare, "A Security Aspects in Cloud Computing," 2012 IEEE International Conference on Computer Science and Automation Engineering, vol. 70, pp. 545–550, 2012. IEEE.

[8] Birendra Goswami and S.N. Singh, "Enhancing Security in Cloud Computing using Public Key Cryptography with Matrices," International Journal of Engineering Research and Applications (IJERA), vol. 2, pp. 339–344, 2012.

[9] T. Kavitha, S. Hemalatha, T.M. Saravanan, A.K. Singh, M.I. Alam and S. Warshi, "Survey on Cloud Computing Security and Scheduling," 2022 International Conference on Computer Communication and Informatics (ICCCI), pp. 1–4, 2022. doi: 10.1109/ICCCI54379.2022.9740932.

[10] C. Chen and C. Wang, "Constructing of Vulnerability Prevention Secure Model for the Cloud Computing," 2019 6th International Conference on Systems and Informatics (ICSAI), pp. 694–698, 2019. doi: 10.1109/ICSAI48974.2019.9010146.

[11] W. Xiaoyu and G. Zhengming, "Research and Development of Data Security Multidimensional Protection System in Cloud Computing Environment," 2020 International Conference on Advance in Ambient Computing and Intelligence (ICAACI), pp. 67–70, 2020. doi: 10.1109/ICAACI50733.2020.00019.

[12] H. Gupta and D. Kumar, "Security Threats in Cloud Computing," 2019 International Conference on Intelligent Computing and Control Systems (ICCS), pp. 1158–1162, 2019. doi: 10.1109/ICCS45141.2019.9065542.

[13] Rahul Dutta and B. Annappa, "Privacy and Trust in Cloud Database using Threshold-Based Secret Sharing," IEEE International Conference on Advances in Computing, Communications and Informatics (ICACCI), vol. 2, pp. 800–805, 2013.

[14] Syed Mujib Rahaman and Mohammad Farhatullah, "PccP: A Model for Preserving Cloud Computing Privacy," 2012 International Conference on Data Science & Engineering (ICDSE), vol. 3, pp. 166–170, 2013. IEEE.

[15] P. Syam Kumar, R. Subramanian and D. Thamizh Selvam, "An Efficient Distributed Verification Protocol for Data Storage Security in Cloud Computing," Second International Conference on Advanced Computing, Networking and Security, vol. 2, pp. 214–219, 2013.

[16] Pramod Kumar, Mahesh Bundele and Devendra Somwansi, "An Adaptive Approach for Load Balancing in Cloud Computing using MTB Load Balancing," 2018 3rd International Conference and Workshops on Recent Advances and Innovations in Engineering (ICRAIE). IEEE, 2018.

[17] D.A.G. Tadeo, S.F. John, A. Bhaumik, R. Neware, N. Yamsani and D. Kapila, "Empirical Analysis of Security Enabled Cloud Computing Strategy using Artificial Intelligence," 2021 International Conference on Computing Sciences (ICCS), pp. 83–85, 2021. doi: 10.1109/ICCS54944.2021.00024.

[18] S. Poonkodi, V. Kavitha and K. Suresh, "Providing a Secure Data Forwarding in Cloud Storage System using Threshold Proxy Re-encryption Scheme," International Conference on Information Systems and Computing (ICISC-2013), vol. 3, pp. 468–472, 2013.

[19] D. Jayalatchumy, P. Ramkumar and D. Kadhirvelu, "Preserving Privacy Through Data Control in a Cloud Computing Architecture using Discretion

Algorithm," IEEE Third International Conference on Emerging Trends in Engineering and Technology, vol. 1, pp. 456–460, 2009.

[20] P. Padma, R. Akshaya, H. Akshaya and R. Harini, "Perlustrate Study on Cloud Security and Vulnerabilities," 2021 4th International Conference on Computing and Communications Technologies (ICCCT), pp. 293–296, 2021. doi: 10.1109/ICCCT53315.2021.9711797.

[21] A. Gordon, "The Hybrid Cloud Security Professional," IEEE Cloud Computing, vol. 3, no. 1, pp. 82–86, 2016. doi: 10.1109/MCC.2016.21.

[22] M.B.H. Frej, J. Dichter and N. Gupta, "Comparison of Privacy-Preserving Models Based on a Third-Party Auditor in Cloud Computing," 2019 IEEE Cloud Summit, pp. 86–91, 2019. doi: 10.1109/CloudSummit47114.2019.00020.

[23] Leonardo A. Martucci, Albin Zuccato, Ben Smeets, Sheikh M. Habib and Thomas Johansson, "Privacy, Security and Trust in Cloud Computing the Perspective of the Telecommunication," 9th International Conference on Ubiquitous Intelligence and Computing and 9th International Conference on Autonomic and Trusted Computing, vol. 1, pp. 627–632, 2012.

[24] Aarti P. Pimpalkar and H.A. Hingoliwala, "A Secure Cloud Storage System with Secure Data Forwarding," International Journal of Scientific & Engineering Research, vol. 4, pp. 3002–3008, 2013.

[25] A. Varma, K. Saxena and S.K. Khatri, "Preventive Measures to Secure Issues in Cloud Computing," 2019 International Conference on Intelligent Computing and Control Systems (ICCS), pp. 504–508, 2019. doi: 10.1109/ICCS45141.2019.9065787.

[26] Manish H. Gourkhede and Deepti P. Theng, "Analysing Security and Privacy Management for Cloud Computing Environment," Fourth International Conference on Communication Systems and Network Technologies, vol. 4, pp. 677–680, 2014.

[27] H. Hourani and M. Abdallah, "Cloud Computing: Legal and Security Issues," 2018 8th International Conference on Computer Science and Information Technology (CSIT), pp. 13–16, 2018. doi: 10.1109/CSIT.2018.8486161.

[28] D.R. Bharadwaj, A. Bhattacharya and M. Chakkaravarthy, "Cloud Threat Defense – A Threat Protection and Security Compliance Solution," 2018 IEEE International Conference on Cloud Computing in Emerging Markets (CCEM), pp. 95–99, 2018. doi: 10.1109/CCEM.2018.00024.

Chapter 4

Cloud Storage Security Using Blockchain

Lipsa Das, Vimal Bibhu, Khushi Dadhich,
and Bhuvi Sharma
Amity University, Greater Noida, UP, India

4.1 INTRODUCTION

Due to the growing usability of information technology in industries, the internet of things (IoT), and the digitization of all enterprises, organizational activities, and initiatives, information has emerged as the most valuable resource for everybody. Data is one of the most useful things in the world right now.

The internet is currently the most popular means of data sharing on a global scale. Most businesses worldwide generate huge amounts of information through routine operations. There are 2.5 quintillion bytes of information generated daily, according to a Forbes article [1]. Over 90% of the world's total data production occurred in the past two years. This information must be kept someplace and ought to be simple to find. Because of the enormous growth of information, it is important to keep it in the cloud. Several cloud providers offer this service, enabling users to store and exchange data online. Most of the data that is currently accessible via the internet is highly centralized and is kept by a small number of technological firms that have the know-how and resources to construct gigantic data centres that can accommodate this vast amount of data. The security of the data is an issue with this method. For many businesses, the storage and rapid access to such vast amounts of data themselves becomes a major issue [2]. Additionally, because this information is kept in a centralized location, it is simple for an attacker to examine and alter the data if he gains access to the server. The security of consumer data is another issue with this strategy. Frequently, other parties will utilize this data for marketing and data research. Additionally, users frequently had to make payment for the full plan they chose even if they have only made usage of small portion of the storage portion because the cost associated with storing data in centralized servers is higher. As a result, the user is unable to pay only for the storage space that they actually using. Another problem is the system's ability to scale, as it is challenging to expand a centralized storage system to accommodate rising demand. Therefore, cloud companies have continually failed to make information 100% safe when it concerns privacy. The security protocol of cloud providers has

DOI: 10.1201/9781003329947-4

been endangered by data theft, data pirating, and cyber assaults. Even now, client data should be completely secure since it may contain sensitive information that should only be available to the author and a limited audience. Making this system safer is crucial in order to retain data privacy and trust in cloud providers. The existing computing system requires to be more dependable, secure, and always available in order to handle it. Hence, the current challenges in cloud storage despite its great development and potential can be summarized as follows.

4.1.1 Financial Loss Due to Security Issues

It is not believed to be a smart option to keep customers' private information in the cloud, despite the data's great potential value. "Sensitive information" in this context means user passwords, wallet encryption keys, private and confidential paperwork, documents comprising sensitive data, files of monetary operations, etc., whose theft or hacking could result in the systemic collapse of any person or business.

4.1.2 Cost to User

To download and upload data from the cloud, there are additional fees. If you attempt to access numerous files frequently, these costs can pile up quickly. You can access your app software more quickly thanks to cloud computing, and you can ignore spending your salary on expensive computer gear, software, management, and upkeep. But what is difficult—and costly—is setting up an organization's needs in third-party platforms. Another costly issue is the cost of moving data into a public cloud, particularly for small businesses or projects.

4.2 DATA LOSS AND PRIVACY ISSUES

Storing sensitive data exclusively on local machines or drives can occasionally be very discouraging since, if they are stolen, lost, or damaged in any other way, there is no way for the user to recover it. The plurality of cloud-based personal storage accounts also do not guaranty continuous availability of data, bear responsibility for calamitous rejection data loss, or offer data insurance. The terms and conditions of services like Dropbox, Box, Rapid-Share, Google Drive, Amazon Cloud Drive, MS OneDrive, etc., clearly indicate this. Therefore, relying solely on local storage or cloud storage for your data is not always secure or reliable.

The availability and security of the data is ensured by several cloud service providers and scattered data centres of the enterprise. The bulk of them, however, have provisions that provide the company access to edit, modify, view, erase, and analyze your information. This could be accomplished to give the customer the greatest experience possible, to create advertisements, to modify the information in certain ways to make money, or to use the data to fulfil their own purposes or conduct their own study. Information kept in a personal database has several access privileges granted to that company, making it occasionally unsafe.

Our topmost concern nowadays is privacy as our data is stored, managed, or handled by the unknown third-party vendor. You never know when and how your confidentiality of data is broken and is used for their benefit. Day by day, we hear about hacking, data breaches, broken authentication, and credentials, etc., this makes the user feel insecure for their data.

Blockchain technology offers a solution to the aforementioned challenge. Cloud users can increase trust and ensure data safety while outsourcing and getting facilities from the cloud by using blockchain, an innovative and growing technology. Blockchain can offer more advanced security compared to centralized database security. It continuously maintains a track list of files which are safeguarded and connected to the previous block/unit using a cryptographic hash algorithm [3]. A distributed ledger called a blockchain can track transactions and guard against manipulation. Typically, peer-to-peer networks are used to maintain blockchain, which is built to prevent unauthorized manipulation. Blockchain can offer security on par with central database data storage. The attacks and damages to data storage can be avoided from a management perspective.

Furthermore, when used in a field where data disclosure is necessary, the blockchain's openness attribute can enable transparency in data. Due to these advantages, it can be used in several contexts, such as the financial industry and IoT environments, and its uses are anticipated to grow [4, 5]. A lot of IT environments have adopted cloud computing because of its effectiveness and availability. Additionally, major security aspects have been explored in relation to cloud privacy and safety concerns [6].

4.3 BLOCKCHAIN TECHNOLOGY

A significant number of businesses have relocated their entire server centres to the cloud due to the new technological developments, which offer greater flexibility, load adjustment, excess, accessibility, and legitimacy. The key players in this rapidly increasing cloud ecosystem are Google, Microsoft, and Amazon, while other companies like Samsung and Apple have already started to contribute their own distributed storage resources to it. Public/pen cloud, private cloud, and hybrid/mix cloud are the various types of cloud storage provided by the cloud service provider is presented in Figure 4.1.

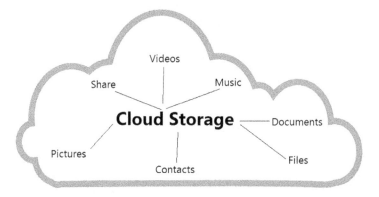

Figure 4.1 Data interred in cloud storage.

4.3.1 Structure of Blockchain

In Blockchain, a block typically comprises the important data, such as the timestamp, hash of the current and prior data, and other details. A block's [3, 7] structure is depicted in Figure 4.1.

- **Primary data:** Typically based on the services offered by the block, such as records of bank transactions, contacts, clearances, or data from the internet of things.
- **Hash:** Following transaction execution, it must be coded and broadcasted to other nodes. Because each node cell contains millions of transactional data also, the final hash to block header, blockchain uses the Merkle tree algorithm to minimize information transfer and resources of CPU.
- **Timestamp:** The time length of the block was generated.
- **Other information:** User-defined data, block signatures and nonce values are the main subtypes of other information [8].

4.3.2 Characteristics of Blockchain

Lately, blockchain technology has been in a spotlight! It is just not used as a backup network for cryptocurrencies like Bitcoin etc., but also, can be brought into applications in different sectors/areas because of its irresistibly stupendous characteristics. So, in this section we will discuss blockchain features:

- **Immutability:** The word "immutability" means the data that cannot be altered. Since Blockchain Technology follows decentralization system of data, ensuring that the blockchain features through a collection of nodes. There is the same copy of the transactions of every node, so if we need to add the new transaction or data, it needs a validation from each node. If it receives maximum of validations by nodes, then it can be added to the digital ledger. Once it is added up in the block-chain network, the information is immutable, that is, it is permanent. Therefore, making it corruption-free and unalterable; also ensuring transparency.

- **Consensus:** Consensus algorithms preserve the accuracy of the infor-mation stored on the blockchain and stores erroneous or misleading transactions from being broadcast to the network [9]. In order to guar-antee the integrity of transaction records, all nodes must concur by performing the common consensus algorithms. Before a transaction can be executed, each participant must first make an assertion to each other; only then will the transaction be considered valid. A consensus is the name given to this process [10, 11].
- **Data Decentralization:** The client can access the information because it is not centralized (decentralized), or controlled by a third party, under this technology. Since there are many nodes, it is decentralized. Or, to put it another way, the primary strength of blockchain is that there is no need for a centralized authority because every node maintains a report of all transaction information. This prevents the specific point of vulnerability from failing. With no centralized power and no service fees, the blockchain network relies on consensus algorithms to keep the data consistent. As a result, blockchain technology is the greatest option since it offers the highest level of transparency and is less sus-ceptible to harmful assaults. Additionally, it enables the legitimate user to have direct access or control.
- **Security:** No one can access, change the data in the network for their advantage as it is decentralized. Encryption and cryptography (a com-plicated mathematical algorithm) with decentralization makes the security system more enhanced as they act as a firewall for malicious attacks. Data in blockchain is cryptographically hashed, that is, the real nature of information is unrevealed. Every data block has unique hash id, if anyone tries to modify the information the changes (that is impossible) in hash id would also be reflected.
- **Distributed Ledgers:** Distributed ledger is the system used for transac-tion recording in various places at the same time. Generally, all transac-tion data and client information can be provided by public ledger easily.

The standard protocol used in this environment makes sure that every node receives every transaction and employs established criteria to organize the transaction into frames after execution. The blockchain is intended for sync-ing and sharing information over numerous networks.

But the case of the private ledger is little unique, by the name one can suggest that its totally private to one user but here many people can see what happens in ledger as the ledger is handled by the clients itself on the system. This computational power is distributed across the computers for a good result.

- **Anonymity and Confidentiality**: On the blockchain, everyone can communicate with a generated address. Members can examine the encoded transaction details, but the client's real information will be not revealed by the system.
- **Traceable**: Because each transaction on the blockchain is time-stamped and signed digitally, it is possible to trace each transaction back to a certain time and further identify the parties involved [12]. As a result, every block is inextricably linked to the one before it [13].

4.3.3 Existing Techniques of Blockchain for Cloud Storage

Details about the blockchain techniques chosen for this SLR are provided in this section. We organized the blockchain technologies used for cloud storage based on a few studies:

- CT: Cryptography technique.
- DDS: Data deduplication scheme.
- DIC: Data integrity checking technique.
- SET: Storage efficiency technique.
- BT: Bitcoin technology.
- BCS: Blockchain-based cloud storage.

The following acronyms are used in Figure 4.2, to denote the approaches chosen for this.

- SLR—Data auditing, fine-grained access control, and FAC VC is for verifiable computation.
- RDD—Reliable distributed deduplication.
- SDD—Secure data deduplication.

4.3.4 Blockchain-Based Cryptographic Technique for Cloud Storage Service

The system enables clients to distribute data substance to cloud hubs, transport information in encoded form, and employ cryptographic techniques to secure information accessibility [14].

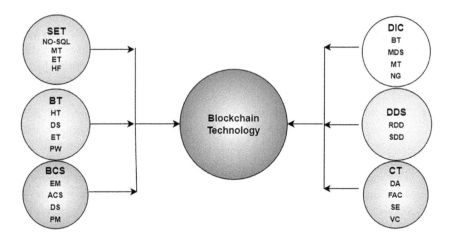

Figure 4.2 Overview of various blockchain method selected in study.

Source: [NG-Non-repudiation Guarantee; BT-Bitcoin Transaction; HF-Hyperledger Fabric; HT-Hash Technology; DS-Digital Signature; MT-Merkle Tree; ET-Ethereum Technology; Proof of Work or PW DS-Deletion Scheme; ACS-Access Control System; PM-Payment Method; Encryption scheme or ES.]

As seen in Figure 4.3, there are three components to the cryptographic storage structure.

- DP (Data processor): handling of data prior uploading to the cloud.
- DV (Data verifier): Validation of the cloud-stored data that has been damaged.
- TG (Token generator): The token generator creates a unique token for every user in order to save client documents to the cloud.

Figure 4.3 illustrates the following: (1) The Master "y" information processor sets the data before transmitting it to the cloud; (2) Master "x" needs the Master "y" permission's before scanning a keyword; (3) Master "y" generates a token for a keyword and sends it back to Master "x"; (4) Master "x" expects to receive the token and sends it to the cloud; and (5) The cloud uses the token to spot the suitable encrypted files and sends the resultant documents to Master "x". The data verifier of Master "y" is always able to vouch for the accuracy of the data.

4.3.5 Blockchain-Based Data Deduplication Scheme for Cloud Storage Service

Data deduplication is a technique to reduce redundant information and maximize cloud storage capacity. So to maximize storage area, this approach

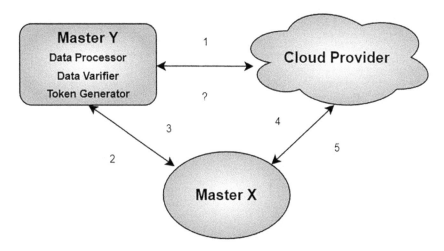

Figure 4.3 Cryptographic cloud storage architecture.

only stores one replica of the identical data. As a result, it can facilitate information efficiency and reduce the price of gadgets [15], but there is the possibility that the problem with data dependability will worsen. Deduplication is used to disperse the reports to several servers, and the data repository is tracked on the blockchain. Combining the blockchain method with the data deduplication scheme can protect system confidentiality and data integrity. Additionally, distributed storage systems can take advantage from it. CSP and the information owner should become nodes on the blockchain network to provide related services. To ensure data authenticity, every replication and transaction should be recorded in a blockchain [16]. Data unit, location, and disc placement is used to categorize the data deduplication technique [17].

The deduplication procedure has three types on the basis of where the information is processed: data unit deduplication, location deduplication, and disc placement deduplication. The deduplication categorization is shown in Figure 4.4. Two more subcategories of data unit deduplication are file-level and chunk-level deduplication. During file deduplication, the two files are compared using their unique hash values. If the hash values match, one copy is kept only. The file is separated into chunks of a fixed or variable length, and as part of deduplication at the chunk level, the duplicate content is then examined. Location-based deduplication methods fall under the categories of source and target deduplication. The target deduplication procedure is carried out after the person provides the reports and is refused the extra information. Deduplication is handled by the storage device without affecting client functioning. The deduplication process is not disclosed to users [18]. Prior to data transfer, the source deduplication stage is finished. The capacity of the

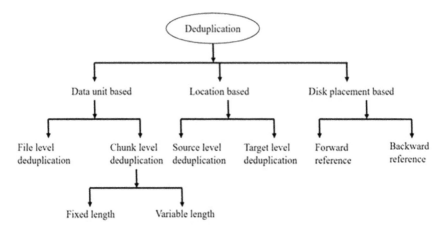

Figure 4.4 Classification of duplication [19].

network is benefited by this deduplication since it utilizes client resources. The other divisions of disk-level deduplication are forward reference deduplication and backward reference deduplication shown in Figure 4.4.

4.3.6 Blockchain-Based Data Integrity Checking Technique for Cloud Storage Service

The architecture for cloud storage which depends on the blockchain; their services enable the decentralized data integrity checks. Three elements are largely what the integrity checking method depends on. These three parties are the data consumer, the CSS (cloud storage service provider), and the blockchain. DIS expanded as "data integrity service" is blockchain-based architecture. When the DIS is required, nodes should initially launch the blockchain client [20]. Merkle trees are a tool that blockchain can employ to verify data integrity. The pre-processing stage and the validation stage make up this process.

- Pre-processing: The data are initially divided up into separate shards by the data consumer, and then the shards are utilized to build a hash Merkle tree. The consumer stores the hash tree's root after CSS and the hash Merkle tree is accepted by the user. The public Merkle trees and user data are published to CSS. The user receives the client's information location stored by CSS.
- Phase of verification: CSS chooses which shards to check after receiving a challenge number from the user. According to the challenge number and the shards, using the hash function, hash digest is calculated. The equivalent of CSS forward digest is a supporting statistic for the

blockchain. A new hash root is computed by the smart contract, and the hash roots are compared. Equality of hash roots determines the guarantee of data integrity. If they are not equal, then data integrity has suffered a decline. At last, the blockchain sends the client the validated output [21].

4.4 STORAGE EFFICIENCY TECHNIQUE FOR CLOUD-BASED DESIGN

The NoSQL database is the greatest option for storing data in the cloud given the increasing growth of cloud computing. Platforms such as MongoDB and Hadoop, Column-oriented DBs, Graph Databases, Document DBs, and key-value stores are used to store and manage NoSQL databases [22]. Data is saved on the cloud in plain text, making it a particularly inefficient method of data storage. This causes various issues in the cloud and increases the OS overhead while information is stored. The MapReduce method is used to manage massive amounts of data, although it is not appropriate for a RDBMS [23]. BigchainDB is a decentralized, expandable, masterless cloud database. It is effective storage for cloud, is added as a top layer of a NoSQL RethinkDB database. It uses a database as the foundation and offers features the same as blockchain, including hashed blocks, transactions, voting, and records unchangeability [24].

4.4.1 Redundant Array of Cloud Storage (RACS)

RACS is utilized for information distribution and network infrastructure protection. Among the customer and different information storage, RACS is conducted [25]. It demonstrated distributed parallel communication with many proxies. It can also be used on other intermediaries using similar vault configuration techniques. This tactic is mostly familiar with reducing the cost of switching suppliers and keeping a strategic distance from seller security. We put up with the disappointing suppliers. The system is simple and easy to understand. A single intermediate might easily become a bottleneck because every piece of data should pass through a RACS intermediary to be encoded or decoded [26]. Users can make use of a blockchain-based, secure cloud storage infrastructure [27] where files are divided into smaller pieces and erratically publish those pieces to a P2P network with unlimited storage.

4.4.2 Blockchain-Based Cloud Storage Access Control System

Blockchain technology could be applied to safeguard entry control for data gathered in a suspect cloud environment. The method is required in the unreliable environment of cloud storage to safeguard shared information. A technique which uses the attribute-based encryption scheme along with dynamic attributes for access privileges is provided by blockchain-based access control [28]. Blockchain maintains an unmodified track of all significant security occurrences, such as key generation, access control policy appointment, and termination [29].

In reference [30], entry control method is created based on blockchain. Procedures for identifying, authenticating, and authorizing are all included in access control. It establishes the level of accountability where client access can be monitored for a certain framework action. The newly developed framework enables users to access electronic health records (EHR) from common blockchain data pools after verifying their identity and cryptographic keys. Using identity-based validation, the client's authentication is completed prohibiting the malicious roles mimicry and adaptability, which enables companies to take part while preventing clients from exercising self-regulation. The creation of a smart contract-based entry control system is designed to be trustworthy, adaptable, and helpful to provide safe entry to sensitive data. The blockchain with smart contracts are taken into use by the role-based access control system known as the RBAC-SC expanded "smart contract-based role-based access control" to depict the trust relation which is important to RBAC and to carry out the challenge-response procedure execution validation, which would confirm the consumer's ownership of positions [31].

4.4.3 Blockchain-Enabled Payment System for Cloud

Due to the complexity of the current payment structure and the distributed environment of the transaction coordinators, safety attacks against it is expanding. A customer who expects to interchange cash will pay a yearly membership fee to obtain the card that is used to make purchases or access amenities. The banks of the buyer and the seller collaborate to clear the debt with the expectation that the buyer will use the bank-issued card to make purchases of goods and services. As more people use their mobile devices to make purchases of goods or services, a transaction must be made as simple as possible [32]. Regarding the advantages of implementing a client transaction as a P2P transaction using blockchain, the exchange is not only trustworthy and indisputable but also economical because no outside parties are involved. Additionally, a blockchain transaction could be completed rapidly, but a traditional transaction across a border might take longer because of the physical distance. As all important data is processed within the central server, typical, centrally controlled transactions are defenceless against major data leakage during database maintenance. On the other hand, it is extremely challenging to attack blockchain-based transactions because all necessary information is transmitted, and a striker would have to hack and

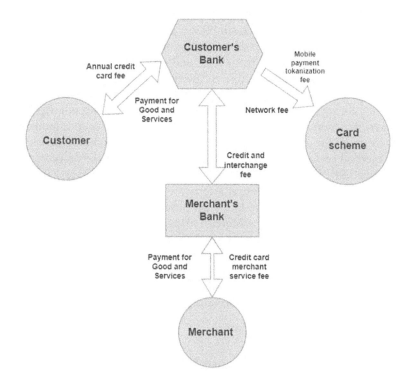

Figure 4.5 Model for process of payment system [19].

alter 51% of the shared P2P. An alluring business model for cloud computing is outsourcing services, which typically entail internet security and payment issues. Wide-ranging cloud services may be greatly hampered by customer and outsourcing provider mistrust. However, several recent payment methods only consider outsourcing providers and depending on a reliable third party. A digital payment system which is blockchain-based is required for outsourcing cloud amenities to ensure a secure and equitable payment service without the involvement of a reliable third party [33]. The payment process system based on the non-blockchain based cloud framework is shown in Figure 4.5.

4.4.4 Blockchain-Based Cloud Storage Data Deletion Scheme

To alleviate the administrative burden of saving, updating, and removing data, the cloud server keeps the end-user data. As a result, the security function must be used when removing, stashing, and modifying cloud information. Various research projects [34] have recently been carried out to safely erase the required information. However, the "one-bit-return" protocol approach can be used to represent the majority of the currently existing techniques: The data is deleted from the cloud server, and the one-bit result is reversed. Because they are unable to check the results, the information owners must have faith in the outcome. As a result, the cancellation strategy built on the blockchain can improve delete operation transparency. Regardless of how maliciously the cloud server acts, the information administrator may examine the cancellation outcome. By using blockchain, the secure deletion method can also get public confirmation without the assistance of a third party [34]. Even though wiping the information securely has been discussed, apparently the suggested strategy still has two key limitations. The vast majority of overwriting-based proposed designs are unable to provide verification. Since they are unable to assess the effects of data deletion, the framework for handling the data must be accepted by the owner of the information in such protocols. Despite some schemes confirming, they need to include a reliable third party. The proposed conventions are ineffective for real-world applications, which is one of the other inherent restrictions. It is important for creating safe data cancellation schemes to delete information properly and perpetually [35].

4.4.5 Blockchain-Based Bitcoin Technology for Cloud Storage

Digital currency referred as Bitcoin is supported by a P2P payment system that was created using open-source software. Bitcoin is a type of virtual currency that is established and transferred through cryptographic connections [36]. As it provided a method for P2P transactions without the need for intermediary agencies like banks, Bitcoin sparked a revolution. The cryptographic methods used by the highly secure and advanced P2P procedures used by bitcoin, which is reliant on the blockchain, are the cornerstones of the democratically supported and dispersed public archives of transactional events. Bitcoin makes sure that user data relating to identity is kept anonymous while validating transactions and maintaining a permanent record [37–39]. Considering this, using blockchain or comparable digital currency technologies eliminates the need for intermediaries or for clients to confide in one another; instead, confidence is demonstrated within the decentralized network architecture itself.

4.4.6 Searching Process in Blockchain-Based Cloud Storage

Traditional cloud storage relies only on large storage suppliers who act as trustworthy intermediaries for data transit and storage. This model depicts a variety of problems, such as difficult access to information, high operational costs, and information security. A framework that impacts blockchain technology has been provided in a number of research in order to provide safe dispersed data storage and the service of keyword searches. The architecture enables customers to send information in an encrypted format, moves data content to cloud servers, and uses cryptographic techniques to ensure information accessibility [39]. Additionally, it allows the information administrator to permit authorization for other people to conduct searches on the data and the technology offers secret keyword scanning over encrypted collection of information [40].

4.4.7 Auditing Scheme in Blockchain-Based Cloud Storage

A growing number of businesses and individuals are sharing and storing information on unreliable clouds as a result of the cloud computing industry's rapid advancement. As a result, the auditing of shared information has gained significant attention in cloud storage and is now a hot topic. In an open audit or social audit sharable cloud storage data protocol, Merkle AVL tree (RB-MHT) based on rank and blockchain are implemented to accomplish privacy protection and batches auditing to retain the security of the modified blockchain records. The public key for the group manager is the fundamental requirement for the TPA to validate the information evidence. Additionally, the community manager is not permitted to make discretionary changes to the altered records. The suggested plan is secure and efficient, according to the performance evaluation.

Reference [41] put out a clever and decentralized public auditing schemes for cloud storage. In the structural model, the TPA was removed by incorporating the blockchain architecture within the strategy. The entirely decentralized development improves stability and dependability. Along with the smart contract, they also created an automatic auditing protocol that can regularly verify the accuracy of the information in the cloud rather than the data holder. As a result, this guarantees that the information holder is relieved of the responsibility of ongoing validation. Because every single automated contract is carried out and recorded by each and every node in the system, the audit outcomes are unmodifiable.

4.5 SECURITY AND PRIVACY ISSUES IN BLOCKCHAIN-BASED CLOUD STORAGE

Blockchain eliminated the need for a server to disallow association with the central authority, allowing transactions by users who collectively kept exchange papers and approved transactions using P2P network technology. The blockchain utilizes peer networks and peer resource computation within a shared architecture. To increase blockchain security, specialized estimates like proof of work (PoW) and proof of storage (PoS) were executed. Despite this, security of blockchain is constantly increasing, issues have been taken into account, and there are several safety evaluations. A burglar might try several different methods to access the client's equipment or mobile phone's personal keys. To protect the personal key, research is being done on using a safe token or safely storing it. The writers of reference [42] discuss the development of blockchain technology and associated technologies and examined the research trends to find additional research fields. For contemporary issues, the application of blockchain in cloud computing surroundings should be taken into consideration. Blockchain still causes several problems, including transaction security, wallets, and programming, and multiple investigations have been made to find solutions. The client information should be totally wiped when the software is deactivated and client data confidentiality should be guaranteed while using blockchain in a cloud computing environment. If the user's information is not destroyed but is still marginally present in the data, it can be deduced from the other data. Given the settings in which significant huge quantity of information is exchanged, efficiency evaluations are also necessary in addition to protection.

4.5.1 Encryption Methods Used in Blockchain-Based Cloud Storage

As a result of the simplicity and low cost of cloud computing, an enhancement for consumers and businesses is outsourcing and providing venues for third parties to store their data indefinitely and computational capabilities. It is crucial to encrypt the information before it is outsourced to the cloud because client data confidentiality cannot be guaranteed by cloud servers. However, the immediate use of traditional encryption improvements prevents clients from being searchable, which results in a bad client experience. Accessible encoding improvements are made in two delegate settings, comprising the settings for symmetric keys and public keys, to secure this search service [43].

4.5.2 Blockchain Technology for Off-Chain Cloud Storage

For blockchain-based solutions, modern organizations have managed data as on-chain or off-chain storage structures. This might be used as data storage in either a private or open blockchain system. Off-chain merely indicates that anything is not on a public database, which does not imply that it is "not at the ledger." Off-chain management makes sure the material is not accessible to the public, just as any corporation might not keep it in a publicly accessible repository [44]. Off-chain transfers are extremely valuable since they have increased security and are not hampered by transactional speed limits. Traditional on-chain transactions are exceedingly slow because each transfer must first be approved by each peer in the network before it can be marked as complete. An off-chain transfer, however, does not require all peers to wait until the transfer has been validated before classifying it as successful or finished.

Off-chain platforms are more secure since they are not connected to the public internet; in fact, they are quite near to the level of security that might be attained by placing a server or piece of software on the intranet as opposed to the internet. Many participants check transfers as part of the on-chain transaction, and for that transaction to be successful, the validation signatures of all participants must exactly match. While each exchange's specifics are made available for review on the public blockchain to prevent modification or rollback, this process could take longer than with off-chain transactions. As participants have the option to use an off-chain method, it is also extremely likely that the payment fees will be high [45, 46].

Off-chain transactions deal with "values outside of the Blockchain which can be concluded via different methods," according to an IBM article [18]. The transfer must be approved by both parties before a third party may confirm the deal. Since it is not advised to store non-transactional data in the main blockchain database, such as photos, contracts, PDFs, and confidential information, off-chain or side DB space is needed. The off-chain object will generate a hash or signature, and that is what is stored in the blockchain database. The specific object is kept either on-site, in a near-cloud storage network, or in the cloud. It's anticipated that off-chain data storage needs would exceed blockchain storage needs. Without the higher on-chain transaction costs, any form of off-chain transaction happens rather quickly [47, 48].

4.6 CONCLUSION

Blockchain is emerging technology in the area of information technology. Its frameworks are based on the distributed digital ledger system which gives the storage of data in distributed fashion. The properties of blockchain such as temper-proof and immutability provide the security by means of non-modifiable and irreversible records management. Cloud storage is a third-party solution to store the users' and businesses' data having the services like storage as a service by inclusion of redundant array of inexpensive disk and other mediums. This third-party solution of the cloud service in the case of storage as a service has many different categories of security and privacy issues of data and information pertaining to the users and businesses. This paper addresses all the issues related to cloud-based security and privacy of users' and business' data and their solution by inclusion of blockchain technology with it. Further, blockchain technology changes the storage criteria and stores the transactional data in the chain of block which is irreversible and immutable, so that it is not possible to alter the stored data and information once block is added under the cloud storage based on the blockchain technology. The systems such as payment processes, other business transactions are placed under a block of the blockchain under the cloud environment to make them irreversible and immutable forever. Blockchain also has the Advanced Encryption Standard (AES), 256 bit to encrypt the block data which is one way that it is not possible to reverse the data by any means. When this is deployed over the cloud then cloud storage system becomes immutable and irreversible and thus the security and privacy of users' data and business' information get robust security and privacy from any type of adversaries. The auditing of the data with blockchain based data storage in the cloud environment is easy as it stores the data transaction and date time wise. Therefore, instant auditing and management of audit trails supports the security professionals to get the usability and accessibility identities to the data and information related to users and businesses.

REFERENCES

[1] B. Marr, "How Much Data Do We Create Every Day? The Mind-Blowing Stats Everyone Should Read," *Forbes*, 2018.

[2] Gurudatt Kulkarni, Rani Waghmare, Rajnikant Palwe, Vidya Waykule, Hemant Bankar, and Kundlik Koli, "Cloud Storage Architecture," in IEEE 7th International Conference on Telecommunication Systems, Services, and Applications (TSSA), 2012. https://en.wikipedia.org/wiki/Blockchain.

[3] A. Beikverdi and S. JooSeok, "Trend of Centralization in Bitcoin's Distributed Network," in Proceedings of the 2015 16th IEEE/ACIS International Conference on Software Engineering, Artificial Intelligence, Networking and Parallel/Distributed Computing (SNPD), Takamatsu, 2015.

[4] S. Huh, C. Sangrae, and K. Soohyung, "Managing IoT Devices using Blockchain Platform," in Proceedings of the 2017 19th International Conference on Advanced Communication Technology (ICACT), Bongpyeong, 2017.

[5] S. Singh, Y.-S. Jeong, and J.H. Park, "A Survey on Cloud Computing Security: Issues, Threats, and Solutions," J. Netw. Comput. Appl. 2016; 75: 200–222.

[6] J. Bonneau, A. Miller, J. Clark, A. Narayanan, J.A. Kroll, and Felten E.W. Sok, "Research Perspectives and Challenges for Bitcoin and Cryptocurrencies," in Proceedings of the 2015 IEEE Symposium on Security and Privacy (SP), San Jose, CA, 2015.

[7] Antonopoulos, A. M. *Mastering Bitcoin: unlocking digital cryptocurrencies.* "O'Reilly Media, Inc." 2014.

[8] Zibin Zheng, Shaoan Xie, Hongning Dai, Xiangping Chen, and Huaimin Wang, "An Overview of Blockchain Technology: Architecture, Consensus, and Future Trends," in Proceedings of the IEEE International Congress on Big Data (BigData'17), pp. 557–564, 2017. https://doi.org/10.1109/BigDataCongress.2017.85

[9] J.H. Mosakheil, "Security Threats Classification in Blockchains. Culminating Projects in Information Assurance," 2018. Retrieved from https://repository. stcloudstate.edu/msia_etds/48.

[10] Lakshmi Siva Sankar, M. Sindhu, and M. Sethumadhavan, "Survey of Consensus Protocols on Blockchain Applications," in Proceedings of the 4th IEEE International Conference on Advanced Computing and Communication Systems (ICACCS'17), 2017. https://doi.org/10.1109/ICACCS.2017.8014672

[11] Ao Lei, Haitham Cruickshank, Yue Cao, Philip Asuquo, Chibueze P. Anyigor Ogah, and Zhili Sun, "Blockchainbased Dynamic Key Management for Heterogeneous Intelligent Transportation Systems," IEEE Internet Things J. 2017; 4(6): 1832–1843. https://doi.org/10.1109/JIOT.2017.2740569

[12] Chinmay A. Vyas and Munindra Lunagaria, "Security Concerns and Issues for Bitcoin," in Proceedings of the National Conference cum Workshop on Bioinformatics and Computational Biology (NCWBCB'14), 2014.

[13] Hoang Giang Do and Wee Keong Ng, "Blockchain-Based System for Secure Data Storage with Private Keyword Search," in Proceedings of the IEEE World Congress on Services (SERVICES'17), pp. 90–93, 2017. https://doi. org/10.1109/SERVICES.2017.23

[14] Jingyi Li, Jigang Wu, Long Chen, and Jiaxing Li, "Deduplication with Blockchain for Secure Cloud Storage," in Proceedings of the CCF Conference on Big Data, pp. 558–570, 2018. Springer. https://doi.org/10.1007/ 978-981-13-2922-7_36

[15] Xiao-Long Liu, Ruey-Kai Sheu, Shyan-Ming Yuan, and Yu-Ning Wang, "A File-Deduplicated Private Cloud Storage Service with CDMI Standard," Comput. Stand. Interfaces 2016; 44: 18–27. https://doi.org/10.1016/ j.csi.2015.09.010

[16] S. Supriya and S. Mythili, "Study on Data Deduplication in Cloud Computing," Int. J. Adv. Res. Comput. Sci. 2017; 8: 8. https://doi.org/10.26483/ ijarcs.v8i8.4689

[17] Bin Liu, Xiao Liang Yu, Shiping Chen, Xiwei Xu, and Liming Zhu, "Blockchain Based Data Integrity Service Framework for IoT Data," in Proceedings of the IEEE International Conference on Web Services (ICWS'17), pp. 468–475, 2017. https://doi.org/10.1109/ICWS.2017.54

[18] Xiaolong Liu, Riqing Chen, Yu-Wen Chen, and Shyan-Ming Yuan, "Off-Chain Data Fetching Architecture for Ethereum Smart Contract," in Proceedings of the International Conference on Cloud Computing, Big Data and Blockchain (ICCBB'18), pp. 1–4, 2018. https://doi.org/10.1109/ ICCBB.2018.8756348

[19] P. Sharma, R. Jindal, and M. D. Borah, "Blockchain Technology for Cloud Storage," ACM Comput. Surv. 2021; 53(4): 1–32. https://doi. org/10.1145/3403954.

[20] Dongdong Yue, Ruixuan Li, Yan Zhang, Wenlong Tian, and Chengyi Peng, "Blockchain Based Data Integrity Verification in P2P Cloud Storage," in Proceedings of the IEEE 24th International Conference on Parallel and Distributed Systems (ICPADS'18), pp. 561–568, 2018. https://doi.org/10.1109/ PADSW.2018.8644863

[21] Deka Ganesh Chandra, Ravi Prakash, and Swati Lamdharia, "A Study on Cloud Database," in Proceedings of the 4th IEEE International Conference

on Computational Intelligence and Communication Networks (CICN'12), pp. 513–519, 2012. https://doi.org/10.1109/CICN.2012.35

[22] Vandana Bhatia and Ajay Jangra, "SETiNS: Storage Efficiency Techniques in No-SQL Database for Cloud Based Design," in Proceedings of the IEEE International Conference on Advances in Engineering and Technology Research (ICAETR'14), 2014. https://doi.org/10.1109/ICAETR.2014.7012839

[23] Josef Gattermayer and Pavel Tvrdik, "Blockchain-Based Multi-Level Scoring System for P2P Clusters," in Proceedings of the 46th International Conference on Parallel Processing Workshops (ICPPW'17), pp. 301–308, 2017. https://doi.org/10. 1109/ICPPW.2017.50

[24] Hussam Abu-Libdeh, Lonnie Princehouse, and Hakim Weatherspoon, "RACS: A Case for Cloud Storage Diversity," in Proceedings of the 1st ACM Symposium on Cloud Computing, 2010. https://doi.org/10.1145/1807128.1807165

[25] Ambarish Kumar Patel, "Cloud Storage and Its Secure Techniques," Int. J. Engineer. Sci. 2017; 7: 6603.

[26] Jiaxing Li, Jigang Wu, and Long Chen, "Block-Secure: Blockchain Based Scheme for Secure P2P Cloud Storage," Inf. Sci. 2018; 465: 219–231. https://doi.org/10.1016/j.ins.2018.06.071

[27] Ilya Sukhodolskiy and Sergey Zapechnikov, "A Blockchain-Based Access Control System for Cloud Storage," in Proceedings of the IEEE Conference of Russian Young Researchers in Electrical and Electronic Engineering (EIConRus'18), pp. 1575–1578, 2018. https://doi.org/10.1109/EIConRus.2018.8317400

[28] Qi Xia, Emmanuel Sifah, Abla Smahi, Sandro Amofa, and Xiaosong Zhang, "BBDS: Blockchain-Based Data Sharing for Electronic Medical Records in Cloud Environments," Information 2017; 8(2): 44. https://doi.org/10.3390/info8020044

[29] S. Gupta, S. Rani, and A. Dixit, "Recent Trends in Automation-A Study of RPA Development Tools," in 2019 3rd International Conference on Recent Developments in Control, Automation & Power Engineering (RDCAPE), pp. 159–163, October 2019. https://doi.org/10.1109/RDCAPE47089.2019.8979084.

[30] Jason Paul Cruz, Yuichi Kaji, and Naoto Yanai, "RBAC-SC: Role-Based Access Control using Smart Contract," IEEE Access 2018; 6: 12240–12251. https://doi.org/10.1109/ACCESS.2018.2812844

[31] Ittay Eyal, Adem E. Gencer, Emin G. Sirer, and Robbert Van Renesse, "Bitcoin-ng: A Scalable Blockchain Protocol," in Proceedings of the 13th USENIX Symposium on Networked Systems Design and Implementation (NSDI'16), pp. 45–59, 2016.

[32] Christopher Natoli and Vincent Gramoli, "The Blockchain Anomaly," in Proceedings of the IEEE 15th International Symposium on Network Computing and Applications (NCA'16), pp. 310–317, 2016. https://doi.org/10.1109/NCA.2016.7778635.

[33] Yinghui Zhang, Robert H. Deng, Ximeng Liu, and Dong Zhen, "Blockchain Based Robust and Efficient Fair Payment for Outsourcing Services in Cloud Computing," Inf. Sci. 2018; 462: 262–277. https://doi.org/10.1016/j.ins.2018.06.018

[34] S. Pavithra, S. Ramya, and S. Prathibha, "A Survey on Cloud Security Issues and Blockchains," in Proceedings of the 3rd International Conference on Computing and Communication Technologies (ICCCT'19), pp. 136–140, 2019. https://doi.org/10.1109/ICCCT2.2019.8824891

[35] G. Arora, P. L. Pavani, R. Kohli, and V. Bibhu, "Multimodal Biometrics for Improvised Security," in 2016 International Conference on Innovation and Challenges in Cyber Security (ICICCS-INBUSH), pp. 1–5, 2016. doi: 10.1109/ICICCS.2016.7542312.

[36] Changsang Yang, Xiaofeng Chen, and Yang Xiang, "Blockchain-Based Publicly Verifiable Data Deletion Scheme for Cloud Storage," J. Netw. Comput. Appl. 2018; 103: 185–193. https://doi.org/10.1016/j.jnca.2017.11.011

[37] Pasquale Giungato, Roberto Rana, Angela Tarabella, and Caterina Tricase, "Current Trends in Sustainability of Bitcoins and Related Blockchain Technology," Sustainability 2017; 9(12): 2214. https://doi.org/10.3390/su9122214

[38] Mahdi H. Miraz and Maaruf Ali, "Applications of Blockchain Technology Beyond Cryptocurrency," Int. Assoc. Educ. Res. 2018; 2(1): 1–6. https://doi.org/10.33166/AETiC.2018.01.001

[39] Huige Li, Haibo Tian, and Jiejie He, "Blockchain-Based Searchable Symmetric Encryption Scheme," Comput. Electr. Eng. 2018; 73: 32–45. https://doi.org/10.1016/j.compeleceng.2018.10.015

[40] S. Salagrama, Y. S. Boyapati, and V. Bibhu, "Security and Privacy of Critical Data in Ad Hoc Network Deployed Over Running Vehicles," in 2022 3rd International Conference on Intelligent Engineering and Management (ICIEM), pp. 411–414, 2022. doi: 10.1109/ICIEM54221.2022.9853172.

[41] Han Wang, Xu An Wang, Shuai Xiao, and Zichen Zhou, "Blockchain-Based Public Auditing Scheme for Shared Data," in Proceedings of the International Conference on Innovative Mobile and Internet Services in Ubiquitous Computing. Springer, Cham, pp. 197–206, 2019. https://doi.org/10.1007/978-3-030-22263-5_19

[42] Hiayang Yu and Zhen Yang, "Decentralized and Smart Public Auditing for Cloud Storage," in Proceedings of the IEEE 9th International Conference on Software Engineering and Service Science (ICSESS'18), pp. 491–494, 2018. IEEE. https://doi.org/10.1109/ICSESS.2018.8663780

[43] V. Bibhu, A. Kumar, B.P. Lohani, and P.K. Kushwaha, "Robust Secured Framework for Online Business Transactions Over Public Network," in 2021 2nd International Conference on Intelligent Engineering and Management (ICIEM), pp. 555–560, 2021. https://doi.org/10.1109/ICIEM51511.2021.9445380.

[44] Jin Ho Park and Jong Hyuk Park, "Blockchain Security in Cloud Computing: Use Cases, Challenges and Solutions," Symmetry 2017; 9(8): 1–13. https://doi.org/10.3390/sym9080164

[45] Yinghui Zhang, Robert H. Deng, Jiangang Shu, Kan Yang, and Dong Zheng, "TKSE: Trustworthy Keyword Search Over Encrypted Data with Two-Side Verifiability via Blockchain," IEEE Access 2018; 6: 31077–31087. https://doi.org/10.1109/ACCESS.2018.2844400

[46] Jacob Eberhardt and Stefan Tai, On or Off the Blockchain? Insights on Off-Chaining Computation and Data," in Service-Oriented and Cloud

Computing (ESOCC'17), F. De Paoli, S. Schulte, and Johnsen E. Broch (Eds.). Lecture Notes in Computer Science, Vol. 10465. Springer, Cham, 2017. https://doi.org/3-15. 10.1007/978–3-319–67262–5_1.

[47] S. Rani, A. Kumar, A. Bagchi, S. Yadav, and S. Kumar, "RPL Based Routing Protocols for Load Balancing in IoT Network," J. Phys. Conf. Ser. 2021; 1950(1): 012073. https://doi.org/10.1088/1742-6596/1950/1/012073

[48] G. Kalra, et al., "Study of Fuzzy Expert Systems Towards Prediction and Detection of Fraud Case in Health Care Insurance," Mater. Today Proc. 2022; 56: 477–480. https://doi.org/10.1016/j.matpr.2022.02.157

Chapter 5

Machine Learning and Deep Learning Models for Data Privacy and Security

K. Aditya Shastry
Nitte Meenakshi Institute of Technology, Bengaluru-560064, India

5.1 INTRODUCTION

The capability to regulate how much private details concerning oneself is exchanged with or conveyed to others is known as data privacy. One's name, address, phone number, or offline or online activities are examples of personal data. Several internet consumers desire to regulate or limit specific sorts of personal data collecting, much as someone might want to keep specific individuals out of a private discussion. Over time, as online activity has grown, so has the significance of privacy protection. To deliver solutions, webpages, software, and social media sites frequently must gather and preserve private user information. Nevertheless, certain systems and apps could go beyond what consumers had anticipated in terms of data gathering and utilization, giving users less protection than they had anticipated. Several sites and apps might not put enough protections in place for the information they gather, which could lead to a data leak that breaches consumer privacy [1].

Data security is the technique of preventing electronic data from being accessed by unauthorized parties, being corrupted, or being stolen at any point in its lifetime. It is a notion that covers all facets of information security, including managerial and access controls, logical security of software programs, and physical security of storage and hardware equipment. Administrative guidelines and policies are also included. Comprehensive data security measures, when executed correctly, protect against insider attacks and user mistakes that continue to be among the major causes of privacy violations in the modern era. It also safeguards an organisation's data resources from cybercrime activity. Implementing tools and technology that improve the firm's transparency into where its crucial information is kept and how it is utilised is a key component of data security. These solutions ought to be capable of safeguarding sensitive documents via cryptography, anonymization, and erasure, as well as automate monitoring to speed up inspections and ensure compliance with legal needs [2].

Despite being distinct, data privacy and data security both require safeguarding information. Limiting the availability of information in stern, binary ways is part of data security. A data security policy might specify, for instance, that no one else besides a person debugging a repository problem is permitted to read client transaction information at any given time. By doing this, you lower your risk of experiencing a data security breach. On the contrary, data privacy requires making more nuanced, intentional choices over who has access to particular types of information [3].

Machine learning (ML) is being used more frequently for a wide range of tasks, including film recommendation and intrusion detection. Some ML systems need information on specific persons. For ML algorithms to identify patterns and generate predictions from them, such personal information is uploaded to centralized sites in readable form. The issue extends beyond the risks posed by these enterprises' exposure to internal or external threat if the organizations hosting these sets of data are breached. Additionally, even though the material was anonymized, or if the information and the ML models were unavailable and only the testing results were disclosed, it is still possible to learn extra details about the personal sets of data [4].

Deep learning algorithms are more capable of detecting sophisticated threats since they are not dependent on memory of well-known characteristics and typical attack behaviours. Rather, they become familiar with the system and can see odd behaviour that could be a sign of malicious software or individuals. Deep learning is exhibiting superior performances on modern security devices. Each small-, medium-, and large-scale company is currently dealing with a very serious issue; day after day, many novel malware and virus risks are being produced, and sophisticated attackers are exploiting resource gaps to target powerful financial and government sectors. Even though there are numerous security solutions, security research is still underway. By identifying intrusion attempts, eradicating viruses, discovering weaknesses, and safeguarding the computer, deep learning has opened up fresh perspectives in data privacy and security [5].

This chapter is organized as: Sections 5.2 and 5.3 discuss the different ML and DL techniques being utilized for maintaining data privacy and security respectively. Section 5.4 discusses the case studies where ML and DL is applied for ensuring data privacy and security. Section 5.5 gives the summary of the research challenges faced by ML and DL developers in the domain of data privacy and security. The chapter ends with the conclusion followed by references.

5.2 MACHINE LEARNING TECHNIQUES FOR DATA PRIVACY AND SECURITY

This section discusses some of the ML techniques used for ensuring data privacy and security.

The knowledge gap between the machine learning and privacy communities needs to be resolved for privacy issues to be addressed appropriately in today's ML systems. Three separate responsibilities are available throughout every ML work, including categorization, prediction, etc.: The source part (information owners or collaborators), the computational side, and the outcomes party [6]. In these platforms, the owners (shareholders) of the information transmit their information to the computational side, which then carries out the necessary machine learning tasks and sends the outcomes to the results group. Such a solution may be an ML model that the entity that received the findings can employ to test additional samples. In other situations, the computation group may preserve the ML model, do the assessment of fresh instances provided by the results side, and then provide the findings of the tests to the results group. When one entity fulfils all three tasks, confidentiality is automatically maintained; nevertheless, whenever such duties are split between two or more organizations, privacy preserving techniques are required.

It is typical for the same organisation to serve as both the responsible party for the computations and the entities receiving the findings, and this organiation is usually distinct from the involved parties. In reality, with the quantities of information gathered every day from individuals all over the world, data owners may not be conscious of how their information is being utilized (or exploited), and in many situations, might not be conscious that certain kinds of information is being gathered. As can be observed from Figure 5.1, there are various degrees of dangers based on the privacy violations related to the data sharing procedure.

Private information would be transmitted to the computing entity, presumably over a secured network, if the information owners are different from the computation entity. Nevertheless, it would probably be stored in the computation central server(s) in its unaltered state, without being encoded or otherwise altered. This poses the greatest concern because both insiders and outsiders could attack the confidential information. Raw data or features derived from the original data may be used to preserve these confidential details. Obviously, because the information is ready to be handled in any possible way, retaining it in its raw form offers a bigger hazard.

- *Reconstruction attacks:*

These pose a risk even when only the attributes (retrieved from the original information) are sent to and retained in the computation party server(s). The attacker's objective in this instance is to recreate the original sensitive information utilizing their understanding of the extracted features. Whitebox accessibility to the ML model is essential for reconstruction attempts, meaning the extracted features in the system should be recognized. Whenever the extracted features utilized during the ML training stage are not removed after creating the appropriate ML model, similar threats might be viable. Several ML techniques like "support vector machine" and "k-nearest

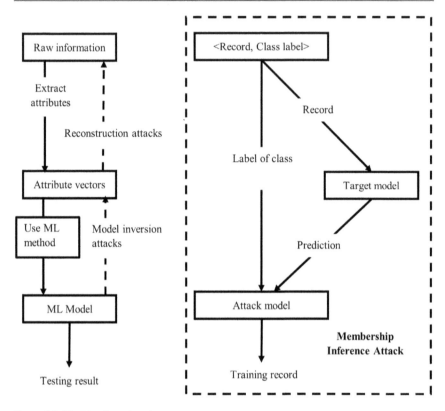

Figure 5.1 Machine learning threats.

neighbors" store feature vectors within the models themselves. Effective reconstruction threats case studies involve biometric reconstruction [7] where a biometric template (original data) might be recreated from a small blueprint (characteristics), and mobile phone haptic motion reconstruction [8] where touch occurrences (original data) might be recreated from gesture attributes like speed and pressure. In both instances, a verification framework security issue (resulting from failure to safeguard the sensitive information in its feature form) led to a confidentiality risk (induced by failure to safeguard the sensitive information in its feature shape), which in turn led to a failure to protect the confidentiality of the involved parties (just as hackers might obtain access to the information owners' gadgets). Some reconstruction hacks may explicitly expose private information, such as geolocation or birthdate, but the goal of these incidents was to trick an ML system into believing the rebuilt actual data belonged to a specific data holder. ML models that contain explicit feature vectors (like SVM, for example) must be disregarded or, if employed, shouldn't be given to the entity receiving the findings. To avoid synthesizing feature maps, safeguards against modelling inverted assaults must be in effect.

- *Inversion attacks on models:*

Some machine learning (ML) algorithms, such as regression analysis or neural nets, build models without explicitly storing feature maps. As a result, the intruder's understanding would only include White box accessibility, an ML model without any previously saved extracted features, or just solutions supplied whenever the results entity provides new testing data (black box access). By exploiting the feedback from that ML algorithm, the intruder's goal in this case is to produce feature maps that mirror the ones used to build an ML model. These attacks make use of the trust data (like probabilities or SVM selection score) that is returned in reply to test data provided by the results entity. Such attacks create an aggregate that reflects a particular class, so they pose the greatest harm to confidentiality when that category is one specific person, as in facial recognition. It ought to be emphasized that the model inversion attack demonstrated in the work [9] includes restoration in the same stage. This was the situation as their case's characteristics mirrored the original data (face images). The outputs must be restricted, and the outcomes side should only be provided entry through a black box, reducing the intelligence of the black box hacker. For instance, the attack success rate dropped when classification methods only provided the anticipated class labels [8] or adjusted confidence levels [9]. Accumulating the results of analyzing many records could go one stage ahead [8], however this strategy wouldn't work for all scenarios.

- *Hacks using membership inference:*

Unlike membership inference attacks, model inversion attacks do not really generate a specimen from the training dataset or deduce whether a specimen was in the training dataset obtained from the results of the ML model. Membership inference threats seek to ascertain if the specimen was a component of the training set used it to create the ML model (the adversary's goal) provided a ML algorithm and a specimen (the adversary's knowledge). An attacker might employ this approach to determine whether such a specific person's records were used to build an ML model linked to a particular ailment. These attacks take use of the variances between predictions made by the ML model for data comprising the training dataset against ones excluded. In order to detect if a data was in the training dataset or not, the work [10] examined these strategies and developed intrusion algorithms that accept a pattern's right label and the target ML model prediction as inputs. Model inversion attack, statistics-based synthesis, and noisy real data were the three strategies used to produce the information used to build these intrusion systems. Intrusions employing such designs solely needed a black box entity, even though developing the threat methodologies used a black or white box approach. Restricting the outcome to the class label constituted the most successful protection strategy, according to the work [10], even if it was insufficient to entirely stop the threat. Other mitigation strategies that were attempted included regularisation and coarse accuracy of predictions matrices.

- *De-anonymization (Re-identification):*

Eliminating personal identifiers from information prior to release to the community may appear to be a logical method for safeguarding people's privacy. In fact, several businesses tried to preserve the security of their consumers just by making anonymized information available, as was the situation with the secret movie ratings provided by Netflix to help competitors for its one million dollar award create more effective recommendation system (for movies). Notwithstanding the privacy protection, researchers were able to determine the Netflix recordings of known individuals using this information and additional info from IMDB, and they were also able to determine the individuals' perceived ideological preferences [11]. This instance shows that anonymization cannot consistently safeguard confidentiality in the presence of potent enemies.

5.2.1 ML for Information Privacy

Several privacy-enhancing methods focused on enabling several input sources to jointly build machine learning models avoiding disclosing their personal information in its raw state. The major methods used for this were selectively personal data leak or encryption algorithms (perturbation techniques). Differential privacy is particularly good at stopping threats that use membership inference. Ultimately, as mentioned previously, restricting the predicted values outcome may reduce the effectiveness of design reversal and membership inference threats (e.g., class labels only).

Data encryption techniques may be employed to execute ML training/testing on encrypted files whenever a specific ML application needs information from various input partners. Several of these solutions required data owners to contribute their encrypted information to the computing server in increasing the productivity, resulting in problem simplification to a protected two- or three-party computing environment. These methods possess the benefit of not needing the source entities to be live, in addition to the high productivity.

The majority of these methods deal with the situation where data is horizontally divided, and each data holder has gathered the same set of characteristics for various data objects. One such instance is face recognition, where any user who wants a machine learning model created for her appearance could provide numerous attribute maps taken from their own images. Every data owner in these situations extracts the identical set of characteristics. The following are the most popular cryptography methods for PPML:

- *Homomorphic cryptography:*

Computing on encrypted files is largely owing to whole homomorphic encryption, which allows for basic operations like multiplication and addition to serve as the building blocks for more complicated arbitrary functions. Additive homomorphic cryptographic algorithms were employed in PPML methods owing to the high expenses linked with constantly rebuilding the encrypted message (refreshing the cypher text due to the cumulative distortion). These systems only provide multiplication by a plaintext and addition actions on cipher text. Paillier encryption algorithm is a well-known illustration. To increase the capabilities of additive encryption algorithms, methods were created to allow the evaluation of two encoded scores as well as stable multiplication and decoding processes. This was primarily accomplished by "blinding" the cypher text by encrypting a random number and adding it to the encoded value that needed to be safeguarded. To improve the effectiveness of applying incremental homomorphic encryption, information packaging methods were created to allow more than one simple text element to be encoded by the same cypher text. Certain PPML methods used these strategies to build effective and safe PPML platforms, like the collaborative filtering system suggested by the researchers in [12] that made utilization of all the above methods. In this approach, information contributors protect their information using the public key of a privacy service provider (PSP), but they send the encrypted information to the PSP instead of decrypting it (SP). Whilst SP offers storage and computing services with the goal of creating private suggestions for its clients, the PSP offers security and computing solutions (the data owners). The SP and the PSP cannot collaborate for the network to be safe. As they offer different products, it makes sense that the SP and the PSP might be two separate businesses; as a result, the non-collusion premise is tenable. The SP and PSP are the calculation entities in this method, whilst data owners serve as both the input and outcomes entities.

- *Garbled circuits:*

Alice can transform the function into a garbled circuit and deliver this circuit together with her garbled input, presuming a two dual-entity scenario in which Alice and Bob desire to receive the outcome of a product calculated on their individual inputs. Despite Alice being aware of Bob's personal information, Alice gives Bob the jumbled form of it. Bob may now use the circuit's jumbled output with his jumbled source to get the desired outcome. Certain PPML methods coupled circuits with incremental homomorphic encryption. A PP ridge regression system was discussed in [13] that included both approaches. An assessor sums the encoded portions provided by various stakeholders to produce encoded intermediate results. Such files are protected using the public key of the crypto service provider CSP and incremental encryption algorithm. The assessor likewise receives the distorted form of the interim values from the CSP. The CSP then generates a distorted circuitry and transmits it to the assessor. The assessor could continue with building the required ML model(s) utilizing the jumbled circuitry and its jumbled data. Certain PPML techniques (testing phase as opposed to training/testing stages) focused solely on the classification task. The work [14] developed encryption construction blocks that resulted in the creation of the three well-known categorization algorithms hyperplane decision, Naive Bayes, and decision trees. The idea was to make it possible to test additional samples whilst also safeguarding the submitted data and the ML models.

- *Secret sharing:*

For each party owning a "share" of the secret, secret sharing is a technique for information sharing between many individuals. Copies by themselves are useless, but when aggregated, they may be used to rebuild the hidden value. Using threshold secure communication, just "t" of the "shares"—where "t" is the threshold—are necessary to reconstruct the hidden information. Various input sources can create "shares" of their personal information in a single configuration and transmit these shareholdings to a collection of quasi compute processors. Every server might use the "shares" it received to calculate a "partial outcome". After receiving such partial results, a results party (or a proxy) can then combine them to determine the complete outcome. To persuade digital assets that the calculation providers would not coordinate, special focus is given towards where these servers are situated as well as which parties manage them. This is because these calculation servers have comparable capabilities (excluding SP and PSP, which were discussed above). Secret sharing techniques may be more effective overall than other cryptography techniques, which led to the development of multiple business solutions that use secret sharing. As an illustration, the Cybernetica programme ShareMind was utilised to create a PCA calculation confidentiality solution by modifying the massively parallel PCA computing approach to the secret sharing concept [15].

- *Secure processors:*

Intel SGX processors are used in privacy-preserving computations, even though they were intended designed to protect confidential information from unauthorized access by malicious programs at greater permission levels. Ohrimenko et al. [16] development of an information machine learning algorithm for SGX-based neural networks, SVM, k-means clustering, decision trees, and matrix factorization. To complete one of the aforementioned ML activities, many data owners must cooperate, and the computational party must conduct the ML task on an SGX-enabled data centre. Each of the information centres equipment and software, save the computation-related SGX-processors, is under the authority of an attacker. Every data owner in this technique creates a secure connection with the enclaves (which contains the code and data), authenticates oneself, checks the accuracy of the ML program on the internet, and safely transfers its sensitive information to the enclave. Following the transfer of all the information, the private processor operates the machine learning task, and the result is communicated to the recipients of the findings via private, authorized connections.

5.3 DL TECHNIQUES FOR DATA PRIVACY AND SECURITY

Even while applying machine learning methods to address system security concerns is not a novel concept, lately the quickly developing deep learning technology has sparked a significant amount of curiosity in guaranteeing data privacy and security [17, 18]. A few of the DL strategies for data privacy and security are discussed in this section.

5.3.1 Deep Belief Networks (DBN)

Deep belief networks were first introduced in a pioneering study by Hinton [19]. They belong to a type of DNN that consists of layers upon layers of hidden nodes linked only to themselves and not to the components in other layers. DBNs are developed without supervision. They are usually trained by separately changing the weights within every hidden unit to recreate the input.

5.3.2 Deep Autoencoders

Unsupervised neural networks that use autoencoders take a matrix as input and attempt to correlate the result with the same column. One could produce a greater or lower dimensional representation of the information by taking the input, altering the dimensions, and rebuilding the input. Since they acquire the skill of condensed information encoding via unsupervised learning, these kinds of neural networks are very flexible [18]. They can also be taught one layer at a time which lowers the amount of processing power needed to create a powerful model. The net is utilized to encode the data when the hidden layers are less dimensional than that of the input and output layers (Figure 5.2). (i.e., feature compression).

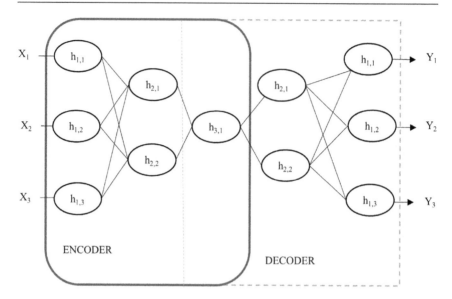

Figure 5.2 Architecture of deep autoencoder.

By training an autoencoder to rebuild the source from a distorted form of the data, known as a denoising autoencoder, an autoencoder can be developed to eliminate distortion and become more resilient. It has been demonstrated that this method is more reliable and generalizable than standard autoencoders [18].

5.3.3 Restricted Boltzmann Machines

The fundamental units of DBNs are restricted Boltzmann machines (RBMs), which are two-layer, bipartite, undirected graphical models (information can travel in both ways instead of just one) [20]. RBMs are unsupervised and may be learnt single layer at a time, just as autoencoders. The input layer forms the top layer, while the hidden layer is the bottom layer (Figure 5.3).

There aren't any intra-layer links (that is, interconnections across units within a single layer), yet each input layer unit is linked to each hidden layer component.

5.3.4 Recurrent Neural Networks (RNN)

It increases the capacity of a traditional neural network, as depicted in Figure 5.4 that can only process input sequences of fixed length. The outcome of the hidden neurons are used as supplementary input for the following element as the RNN examines inputs one component at a time. The

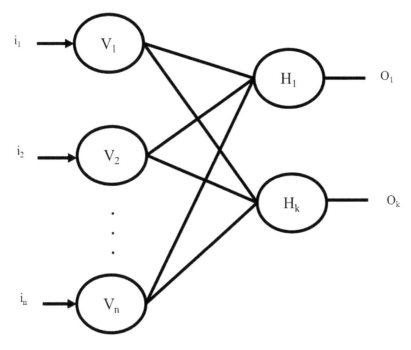

Figure 5.3 RBM architecture.

RNNs can thus handle both time series issues and linguistic and speech issues. Figure 5.4 depicts the RNN's design.

Due to the ease with which the grades might disappear or burst, RNNs are generally more challenging to operate [21]. Nevertheless, a range of RNNs that are simpler to train have been developed via improvements in learning and design [22, 23]. RNNs have thus demonstrated effectiveness in a variety of time-series prediction applications, including voice recognition, image captioning, language processing, and next-word-in-sentence forecasting [24, 25]. An RNN's hidden layers can keep track of the previous events in the series in a "state vector," or internal storage. Depending on the kind of RNN unit that is utilized, the size of this "storage" can be changed. Having larger storage, the RNN is better able to comprehend long-term associations. The introduction of the long short-term memory (LSTM) modules [26] enables RNNs to handle issues that call for long-term memories. A component of LSTM units known as a memory cell stores data and links to itself during the following time step. New input is added to the storage cell's contents, and a forget gate adjusts the weights of older and newer data based on the situation. The gated recurrent unit (GRU) is another RNN unit created for long memory [27]. Similarly, to LSTM modules, GRUs are made to have fewer features, which makes training them simpler.

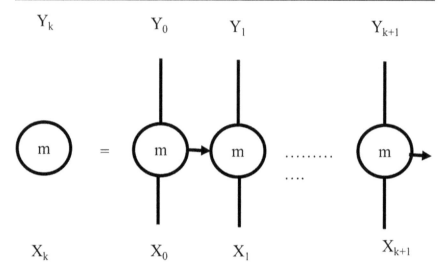

Figure 5.4 RNN architecture.

5.3.5 Convolutional Neural Networks (CNN)

An artificial neural network designed to process input from arrays is a convolutional neural network (CNN) [28]. A colour or monochrome graphic, which consists of a two-dimensional (2D) collection of cells, serves as an illustration of a source. CNNs are frequently used to analyse acoustic spectrograms and 2D picture matrices. They are widely utilized for three-dimensional (3D) arrays as well. They are increasingly used with one-dimensional (1D) arrays of signals, though less frequently. CNNs are utilized in situations in which there is spatial or temporal ordering, irrespective of complexity.

The three diverse types of layers make up the structure of a CNN are convolutional layers, average pooling, and categorization levels as shown in Figure 5.5. The foundation of the CNN is its convolutional layers. The input vector, which is defined by the weights, is a convolution kernel that is given to the initial input, one tiny window at a time. Following the application of such filtration to the full source, the output goes through a non-linearity, commonly a ReLU, and is referred to as an attribute map. These convolution kernels, which take their name from the theoretical convolution procedure, save space by using the same kernel throughout the image sequence while accounting for close physical or spatial correlations inside the information.

By using a particular function, like the maximum, to non-overlapping sections of the convolution layer, pooling levels are utilized to carry out non-linear down sampling. Max pooling also reduces the computational

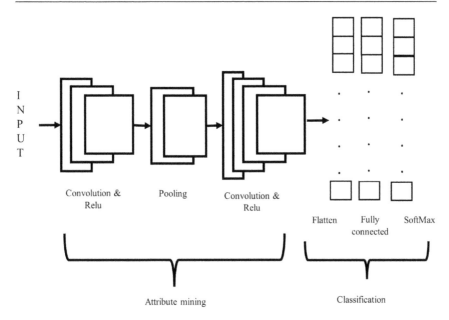

Figure 5.5 CNN architecture.

complexity, which reduces generalization error in in addition to decreasing the feature space and the storage needed. Typically, these levels are intermittently added across convolution layers and supplied into a fully linked, conventional DNN.

5.3.6 Generative Adversarial Networks (GAN)

In unsupervised machine learning, generative adversarial networks (GANs), which are depicted in Figure 5.6, are a sort of neural network design where two neural networks fight against one another in a zero-sum competition to outwit one another. Two networks were created by Goodfellow et al. [29]; one serves as a creator and the other is a discriminator. When information is fed into the synthesizer, it produces output data with exactly the very same properties as actual data. When genuine information and generator information is supplied, the differentiator attempts to determine if the source is genuine or false. After training is complete, the synthesizer can produce fresh data which cannot be distinguished from actual information.

Since its creation, GANs have demonstrated a wide range of applications, particularly for images. Applications involve caption creation [30, 31], optical flow estimates [32], and image restoration [33]. Deep convolution generative adversarial network (DCGAN), an accessible, pre-trained GAN for image generation, is available on Facebook [32].

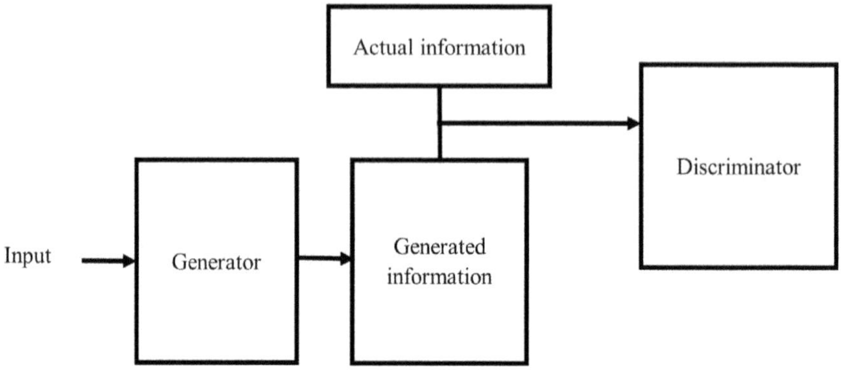

Figure 5.6 GAN architecture.

5.3.7 Recursive Neural Networks

Recursive neural networks are neural networks that iteratively assign a weight set to a stream of data. In these nets, a node's outcome is utilized as the input for the subsequent stages. The first two inputs are originally combined and sent into the system. The outcome from that is then sent into the succeeding stage's source. This kind of approach has been applied to a variety of image segmentation and natural language processing problems [34].

5.4 CASE STUDIES OF ML AND DL FOR DATA PRIVACY AND SECURITY

This section discusses some of the case studies/use cases of how ML and DL are being currently used to maintain data privacy and security in the real world.

- *Utilizing ML/DL to prevent SMS fraud:*

Numerous workers than ever before are operating from home because of the outbreak. Workers and university students use texts to communicate and remain informed about tasks. Hackers are hacking and defrauding users via SMS, World Wide Web messaging apps like WhatsApp, and Telegram underneath the guise of "COVID-19." The MTD system, or mobile threat defense system, is employed in this machine learning application case. Here the ML models have been trained to distinguish between authentic Covid-19 informative signals and attackers. Diverse destinations are protected, including smartphones, laptops, PCs, and others. The unified endpoint management (UEM) application protects them. SMSs and content apps benefit greatly from UEM. Here, the model has been trained using a variety of samples to find hazards amid genuine communications [35].

- *Employing ML/DL to secure cellular access points:*

Regarding portable devices, machine learning is already widely used. Software for privacy protection, software upgrades, and malware detection currently employ ML, whether they are for Android or iOS. Google already employs machine learning for mobile device protection. ML is used to protect networking, machines, and even security testing products themselves from intrusions. Pioneer in the security industry Wandera employs ML algorithms. In the commercial portable devices of the multiple businesses, they discovered 500 malware variants. Personalized, AI-powered help is available through Apple's Siri, Google Assistant, and Amazon's Alexa. They have important duties related to applying ML to secure vocal style instructions. Additionally, to distinguish the tone of the real owner from a hacker's command DL is being used [36].

- *Applying ML/DL to Strengthen Human Analysis and Prevent Human Inconsistencies:*

Without a question, machine learning and artificial intelligence outperform people in finding flaws and avoid committing mistakes. Data utilization rose quickly, which led to the introduction of ML/DL in cybersecurity. Identifying and assessing any dangers was like looking for a needle in a haystack for people. MIT recently unveiled a system dubbed AI2. These "needles in the haystack" were discovered by analysts with the aid of a flexible ML/DL security technology. From the trillions of acts undertaken in a single day, the technology was able to filter out every suspicious attack. The risk rate was decreased by AI2 by 85%. Analysts now frequently use vulnerability assessment tools to identify any threat [37].

- *Utilizing ML/DL for intrusion detection systems and antivirus technology:*

Modern antivirus programmes employ ML/DL models that have been regularly trained to recognize dangers. From the basis of cognitive acts, they improve. Systems used in ML/DL are built to alert users when something unusual happens. Antivirus software powered by machine learning uses anomaly detection to monitor behavioural responses. Upgrades to the viral signatures are necessary for periodic antivirus programs. However, intelligent antivirus solutions are improved with ML algorithms from start and do not require signed malware. A cybersecurity instance of ML/DL is the antivirus program. Whenever harmful documents are accessed, ML/DL in cybersecurity can identify the type of infection. The latest and most potent antiviral software has developed trillions of different malware samples that are analysed [38].

- *Monitoring emails with ML/DL:*

Several firms are aware of the significance of mail protection. Technology for risk monitoring and assessment that uses ML/DL can speed up the detection of intrusions and improve detection performance over a period. Modern surveillance systems may now find malicious software or viruses without the email being opened. Additionally, the trends are compared with regular emails using the NLP technology to look for attempts at spoofing in emails. Utilizing anomalous software to detect, companies may determine if an email, writer, or attachment is part of a phishing scam or hack. Therefore, one of the applications of ML in cybersecurity is email surveillance [39].

- *Employing ML/DL to combat spammers:*

Several firms are aware of the significance of email protection. Technology for risk monitoring and assessment that uses ML/DL can speed up the detection of intrusions and improve detection performance over a period. Modern surveillance systems may now find malicious software or viruses without the email being opened. Additionally, the trends are compared with regular emails using the NLP technology to look for attempts at spoofing in emails. Utilizing anomalous software to detect, companies may determine if an email, writer, or attachment is part of a phishing scam or hack. Therefore, one of the applications of ML in cybersecurity is email surveillance [40].

- *Network threat identification utilizing ML/DL:*

For any organisation, network security is of the highest significance. It can be difficult to comprehend the many configurations of the network security infrastructure, even for a lot of cybersecurity professionals. It is not a laughing matter given the volume of information entering and leaving the system. Alongside information analysis, website maintenance, and network activity detection, the improved ML-based computer security system will trace all calls and information flowing in and leaving out to spot any erratic informational anomalies in the system. Through using anomaly tracking technology, a broad range of apps could analyse connections. It is employed to notify administrative officials about information anomalies, such as historical cyberattacks [41].

- *Mitigating AI-based threats with ML/DL:*

Attackers are advancing with AI and ML/DL just like security researchers. Therefore, companies need to build ML/DL algorithms to spot assaults carried out by other AI algorithms. For instance, ML/DL can be used by attackers to find vulnerabilities in security systems and networks. Intelligent malware and synthetic attackers have been created by other attackers to make threats unique and tailored to the unique circumstances of the targets. Companies all over the globe have seen malware and intrusions like Notpetya and Wanna-Cry in recent times. High-level AI/ML was used in the creation of both [42].

- *Technologies for detecting and preventing intrusions (IDS/IPS):*

Such technologies inform users and stop unauthorized access the services by malware detection. They are typically identified by well-known fingerprints and commonly exploited formats. This is helpful in defending off risks including information leaks. Typically, ML/DL algorithms handled this job. The system generated several false positives because of these techniques, which made the task of security personnel laborious and added to their already excessive exhaustion. Through more technique for determining the traffic, lowering the number of erroneous notifications, and assisting security people in differentiating between malicious and lawful internet activity, DL, convolutional neural networks, and RNNs can be used to develop intelligent ID/IP mechanisms. The "next-generation firewall (NGFW)," "Web application firewall (WAF)," and "user entity and behaviour analytics (UEBA)" are noteworthy approaches [43].

- *Malware management:*

A signature-based detection technique is used by conventional malware technologies like common firewalls to find spyware. The business maintains a repository of existing risks that are regularly updated to include brand new dangers that have appeared recently. Although this method is effective against basic attacks, it fails to counter increasingly sophisticated attacks. DL algorithms are more capable of detecting sophisticated attacks since they are not dependent on memory of well-known signatures and typical attack behaviours. Rather, they become familiar with the computer and can see odd behaviour that could be a sign of malicious software or individuals [44].

- *Identification of spam and social engineering:*

A deep learning method called natural language processing (NLP) can assist organizations in quickly identifying and dealing with malicious Web as well as other kinds of social engineering. NLP uses numerous predictive methods and natural modes of communication and linguistic trends to identify and prevent spam. Google employs DL to find spam that Gmail filters over-looked. In recent times, Google added ML/DL technologies to several of its services. The search engine giant frequently uses AI, from Reactive Batteries in Android Pie to the most current Shadow Art online app. Google has enhanced the spam filters in Gmail by incorporating ML/DL. The Mountain View based firm claims that the new safeguards stop an estimated 100 million spam communications per day. That is not at all an enormous amount when you think about the scope of Gmail. This equates to around one email being censored per 15 people among 1.5 billion subscribers Nevertheless, Google asserts that it currently filters out more than 99.9% of spam, spoofing, and malware emails; therefore, locating an additional 100 million spam messages is no easy task. TensorFlow, a ML/DL framework developed by the business, was employed to prevent spamming groups that are challenging to identify. This includes communication with attached images, emails with concealed information, and emails from recently established sites that attempt to cloak a small number of fraudulent emails from inside legitimate users. Additionally, TensorFlow enables Gmail to customise its spammers for every person, since not each person views nearly identical emails as spam [45].

- *Monitoring of usage patterns:*

An essential security practice for any firm is monitoring and analysing user activity and behaviour. Because it gets beyond security measures and frequently will not really trigger any warnings or alarms, it is significantly harder to spot than regular harmful operations targeting systems. For instance, internal threats arise when employees utilize existing authorized access for nefarious purposes rather than breaking into the network from elsewhere, making numerous computer defence systems worthless in the face of these attacks. One effective defence against these attacks is user and entity behaviour analytics (UEBA). After some initial learning, it can pick up on typical employee patterns of behaviour and identify abnormal activity that may be an inside intrusion, like logging into the system at strange hours. For such activities, the UEBA will raise alarms alerting the administration of a possible attack [46].

Table 5.1 lists some of the additional case studies that use ML and DL to preserve data security and privacy along with a brief overview of each.

5.5 RESEARCH CHALLENGES FOR DL AND ML IN DATA PRIVACY AND SECURITY

From the viewpoint of a security professional, we present a list of pertinent issues and concerns for ML/DL research in this section.

- *Impact evaluation of changes in policy:*

Table 5.1 ML/DL Case studies for data security and privacy

Use case	Description
Malware identification	Spyware information which is obtained on ML is used by cybersecurity company Deep Instinct from Tel Aviv. Instead of relying on viral signatures or other criteria, this Israeli business develops potent neural networks which understand infection behaviours directly from the original coding of the infection. A new paradigm occurs when we examine a software for malware characteristics. We go from an elevated, sentient description of ransomware to a reduced, machine-based representation based on subtle virus elements that are practically impossible to detect for human analysts.
Security of information stored in cloud	Information in Amazon's S3 storage is protected by Amazon Macie, a machine learning algorithm. The system dynamically examines all efforts to retrieve personal information and highlights several abnormalities, such as odd connection attempts, the downloading of sizable piles of information, or the movement of information to an unforeseen region. Additionally, Macie categorizes the information vulnerability using a variety of information attributes, file content, and source code. The software then performs routine security screening for the most sensitive information employing data sensitivity ratings and notifies proprietors in the event of data intrusions or if the material was unintentionally made public. In comparison to past methods, Amazon's new security architecture for privacy laws is more flexible and adaptable.
Information Security: ML and Behavioural Transformation	MasterCard unveiled its Decision Intelligence technology, which uses machine learning to assess a transaction's integrity. The technology underlying the DL looks at a particular cardholder's account usage over time to identify regular and irregular purchasing behaviour. To measure the behavioural conformance and rate a transaction's riskiness, it makes use of information including consumer value segmentation, geography, retailer, personal devices, period of day, as well as the kind of item purchased [47].

Regulations could be linked to the privacy and security aspects of the enterprise and are subject to modification on a routine basis in an enterprise setting. Utilizing the experience of human analysts, the effectiveness of these regulations on the industrial setting is evaluated. If the company has implemented ML/DL as a privacy and security measure, all changes to policies must be incorporated in the training and implementation of the ML/DL methodology. Currently, no research has been done as to how variable rules will affect ML/DL applications that are already in use. Consequently, a crucial development would be the predicted influence study of legislation changes on DL-based security and privacy mechanisms [48].

- *Formulating a new regulation/policy:*

Guidelines and rulesets outline the privacy and security objectives of the organization. These regulations and set of rules are reflected in the tagging of specific items in the training information set in current DL. The choice is to create a novel training set based on the fresh rules and reskill the DL algorithm, if indeed the policy shifts after installation of a DL-based solution. Expenses in terms of effectiveness as well as maintenance could be attributed to creating the training data collection and retraining. The goal is to reduce this expense and implement changes in policy that are as close to established security products as possible, such as firewalls, access controls, and intrusion detection systems.

- *Getting DL ready to handle the "future":*

The world of privacy and cybersecurity is continuously changing. DL needs to be adaptable and capable of picking up fresh trends even after distribution in order to handle this transition. Additionally, the background knowledge that a specific occurrence of DL has acquired is significant and being able to transmit it to different occurrences (for instance, across different organizations) will significantly increase the preparedness of the overall security industry. Making lifelong learning a key component of DL approaches may be a viable future direction [49].

- *Individual/group learning:*

Learning alone has advantages and disadvantages. The good news is that the organization's unique behaviour gets profiled. Nevertheless, it also implies that they will not be able to identify it until they suffer an internet breach. If one member of the partnership suffers a cyberattack, the other members of the partnership might partake in its profiling thanks to collaborative learning. This could potentially hasten the improvement of security defences against novel and previously undiscovered assaults [50]. There are various new difficulties brought on by cooperative learning, such as:

- Cooperation centred on expertise: Must algorithms in cooperative learning share their expertise or just the actual data from the off-profile observation? Also, it necessitates a mechanism for different DL implementations to share previous knowledge.
- Cooperation based on raw data: Distributing original data seems straightforward since every example may apply its very own process of learning to it. Nevertheless, this might expose confidential information and breach confidentiality laws. It is necessary to devise effective and robust anonymization strategies for basic record keeping interaction.

Using this anonymization approach, classified information must be protected for security and privacy even while retaining enough properties to make it usable for training new DL examples.

- *Inducing deep learning to forget:*

It is better to have the DL de-profile a few of the items out of its knowledge base under several circumstances. For instance, a) the identification of harmful material in the training set of data that must now be re-labelled as harmful, b) the removal of antagonistic instances from the DL knowledge, and c) the exercise of RtR or the right to be forgotten under GDPR by a customer or client. In these circumstances, DL methods must "forget" about specific entries. The best way to accomplish this appears to be up for debate, but it will be crucial in the future as security concerns among the general public rise and attackers effectively train DL systems using hostile instances [51, 52].

5.6 CONCLUSION

As more and more DL and ML are incorporated into our daily lives, security and privacy concerns increase. Numerous studies on the security and privacy-preserving challenges and their solutions for DL and ML have been conducted recently. Consequently, security and privacy become very essential issues that cannot be ignored, just like with other technologies. This chapter provides a thorough overview of the various ML and DL strategies used to preserve data security and privacy. DBN, deep autoencoders, RBM, RNN, CNN, GAN, and recursive neural networks are a few of the DL techniques that were covered in-depth. Additionally, several case studies that actively employed DL and ML approaches were discussed. It was noted that DL and ML algorithms are being utilized for identifying SMS scams, protecting mobile endpoints, preventing human error, identifying malware, monitoring emails, avoiding bot attacks, discovering intrusions, protecting cloud data, and analysing user activity. A synopsis of the research obstacles that ML and DL technologies face in the areas of data security and privacy was covered.

REFERENCES

1. S. Riaz, A. H. Khan, M. Haroon, S. Latif and S. Bhatti. 2020. Big Data Security and Privacy: Current Challenges and Future Research perspective in Cloud Environment. International Conference on Information Management and Technology 977–982.
2. P. Goel, R. Patel, D. Garg and A. Ganatra. 2021. A Review on Big Data: Privacy and Security Challenges. 3rd International Conference on Signal Processing and Communication (ICPSC) 705–709.

3. P. S. Chauhan and N. Kshetri. 2021. State of the Practice in Data Privacy and Security. Computer 54(8):125–132.
4. M. Al-Rubaie and J. M. Chang. 2019. Privacy-Preserving Machine Learning: Threats and Solutions. IEEE Security & Privacy 17(2):49–58.
5. Tariq, M. I., Memon, N. A., Ahmed, S., Tayyaba, S., Mushtaq, M. T., Mian, N. A., Imran, M. and Ashraf, M. W., 2020. A review of deep learning security and privacy defensive techniques. Mobile Information Systems, 2020, pp. 1–18. Review Article | Open Access Volume 2020 | Article ID 6535834 | https://doi.org/10.1155/2020/6535834
6. I. H. Sarker, A. S. M. Kayes, S. Badsha, H. Alqahtani, P. Watters and A. Ng. 2020. Cybersecurity Data Science: An Overview from Machine Learning Perspective. Journal of Big Data 7:1–29.
7. M.-S. Lacharité, B. Minaud and K. G. Paterson. 2018. Improved Reconstruction Attacks on Encrypted Data using Range Query Leakage. 2018 IEEE Symposium on Security and Privacy (SP) 297–314.
8. Mohammad Al-Rubaie and J. Morris Chang. 2016. Reconstruction Attacks against Mobile-Based Continuous Authentication Systems in the Cloud. IEEE Transactions on Information Forensics and Security 11(12):2648–2663.
9. S. Hidano, T. Murakami, S. Katsumata, S. Kiyomoto and G. Hanaoka. 2017. Model Inversion Attacks for Prediction Systems: Without Knowledge of Non-Sensitive Attributes. 15th Annual Conference on Privacy, Security and Trust (PST) 115–11509.
10. Reza Shokri, Marco Stronati, Congzheng Song and Vitaly Shmatikov. 2017. Membership Inference Attacks against Machine Learning Models. IEEE Symposium on Security and Privacy (SP) 3–18.
11. J. Zhang, L. Fu, X. Wang and S. Lu. 2020. De-anonymization of Social Networks: The Power of Collectiveness. IEEE Conference on Computer Communications 89–98.
12. Y. Ke, M.-Q. Zhang, J. Liu, T.-T. Su and X.-Y. Yang. 2020. Fully Homomorphic Encryption Encapsulated Difference Expansion for Reversible Data Hiding in Encrypted Domain. IEEE Transactions on Circuits and Systems for Video Technology 30(8):2353–2365.
13. Yi-Ruei Chen, Amir Rezapour and Wen-Guey Tzeng. 2018. Privacy-Preserving Ridge Regression on Distributed Data. Information Sciences 451–452:34–49.
14. X. Sun, P. Zhang, J. K. Liu, J. Yu and W. Xie. 2020. Private Machine Learning Classification Based on Fully Homomorphic Encryption. IEEE Transactions on Emerging Topics in Computing 8(2):352–364.
15. D. Bogdanov, L. Kamm, S. Laur and V. Sokk. 2018. Implementation and Evaluation of an Algorithm for Cryptographically Private Principal Component Analysis on Genomic Data. IEEE/ACM Transactions on Computational Biology and Bioinformatics 15(5):1427–1432.
16. O. Ohrimenko, F. Schuster, C. Fournet, A. Mehta, S. Nowozin, K. Vaswani and M. Costa. 2016. Oblivious Multi-Party Machine Learning on Trusted Processors. 25th USENIX Security Symposium (USENIX Security 16) 619–636.
17. Y. H. Choi, P. Liu, Z. Shang, H. Wang, Z. Wang, L. Zhang, J. Zhou and Q. Zou. 2020. Using Deep Learning to Solve Computer Security Challenges: A Survey. Cybersecurity 3:1–15.

18. D. S. Berman, A. L. Buczak, J. S. Chavis and C. L. Corbett. 2019. A Survey of Deep Learning Methods for Cyber Security. Information 10(4):1–35.
19. G. Hinton, S. Osindero and Y. W. Teh. 2006. A Fast-Learning Algorithm for Deep Belief Nets. Neural Computing 18:1527–1554.
20. A. Skabar. 2019. Restricted Boltzmann Machines: An Eigen Centrality-Based Approach. International Joint Conference on Neural Networks (IJCNN) 1–8.
21. M. Kaur and A. Mohta. 2019. A Review of Deep Learning with Recurrent Neural Network. International Conference on Smart Systems and Inventive Technology (ICSSIT) 460–465.
22. G. Van Houdt, C. Mosquera and G. Nápoles. 2020. A Review on the Long Short-Term Memory Model. Artificial Intelligence Review 53:5929–5955.
23. Song Xianduo, Wang Xin, Song Yuyuan, Zuo Xianglin and Wang Ying. 2022. Hierarchical Recurrent Neural Networks for Graph Generation. Information Sciences 589:250–264.
24. I. Sutskever, O. Vinyals and Q. V. Le. 2014. Sequence to Sequence Learning with Neural Networks. Advances in Neural Information Processing Systems, 3104–3112. MIT Press: Cambridge, MA.
25. A. Thanda and S. M. Venkatesan 2017. Audio Visual Speech Recognition using Deep Recurrent Neural Networks. In: F. Schwenker, S. Scherer (eds) Multimodal Pattern Recognition of Social Signals in Human-Computer-Interaction. MPRSS 2016. Lecture Notes in Computer Science, vol 10183. Springer, Cham.
26. B. B. Sahoo, R. Jha, A. Singh and D. Kumar. 2019. Long Short-Term Memory (LSTM) Recurrent Neural Network for Low-Flow Hydrological Time Series Forecasting. Acta Geophysica 67:1471–1481.
27. Kyunghyun Cho, Bart van Merrienboer and Çaglar Gü. 2014. Learning Phrase Representations using RNN Encoder-Decoder for Statistical Machine Translation. EMNLP 1724–1734.
28. Sakshi Indolia, Anil Kumar Goswami, S. P. Mishra and Pooja Asopa. 2018. Conceptual Understanding of Convolutional Neural Network: A Deep Learning Approach. Procedia Computer Science 132:679–688.
29. Goodfellow, Ian, Jean Pouget-Abadie, Mehdi Mirza, Bing Xu, David Warde-Farley, Sherjil Ozair, Aaron Courville, and Yoshua Bengio. "Generative adversarial nets." Advances in neural information processing systems 27 (2014).
30. Scott Reed, Zeynep Akata, Xinchen Yan, Lajanugen Logeswaran, Bernt Schiele and Honglak Lee. 2016. Generative Adversarial Text to Image Synthesis. 33rd International Conference on Machine Learning, PMLR 48:1060–1069.
31. M. Mehralian and B. Karasfi. 2018. RDCGAN: Unsupervised Representation Learning with Regularized Deep Convolutional Generative Adversarial Networks. 9th Conference on Artificial Intelligence and Robotics and 2nd Asia-Pacific International Symposium 31–38.
32. C. Ledig, L. Theis, F. Huszár, J. Caballero, A. Cunningham, A. Acosta, A. Aitken, A. Tejani, J. Totz, Z. Wang and W. Shi. 2017. Photo-Realistic Single Image Super-Resolution Using a Generative Adversarial Network. IEEE Conference on Computer Vision and Pattern Recognition (CVPR) 105–114.
33. X. Zhang, R. Jiang, T. Wang and J. Wang. 2021. Recursive Neural Network for Video Deblurring. IEEE Transactions on Circuits and Systems for Video Technology 31(8):3025–3036.

34. S. Mishra, D. Soni and D. Smish. 2021. SMS: A System to Detect Smishing SMS. Neural Computing and Applications 1–18.
35. C. Gupta, I. Johri, K. Srinivasan, Y. C. Hu, S. M. Qaisar and K. Y. Huang. 2022. A Systematic Review on Machine Learning and Deep Learning Models for Electronic Information Security in Mobile Networks. Sensors (Basel) 22(5):1–34.
36. M. Ponti and A. Seredko. 2022. Human-Machine-Learning Integration and Task Allocation in Citizen Science. Humanities and Social Sciences Communications 9:1–15.
37. H. Liu and B. Lang. 2019. Machine Learning and Deep Learning Methods for Intrusion Detection Systems: A Survey. Applied Sciences 9(20):1–28.
38. Zeeshan Bin Siddique, Mudassar Ali Khan, Ikram Ud Din, Ahmad Almogren, Irfan Mohiuddin and Shah Nazir. 2021. Machine Learning-Based Detection of Spam Emails. Scientific Programming 2021:1–11.
39. F. Hossain, M. N. Uddin and R. K. Halder. 2021. Analysis of Optimized Machine Learning and Deep Learning Techniques for Spam Detection. IEEE International IOT, Electronics and Mechatronics Conference (IEMTRONICS) 1–7.
40. A. Halbouni, T. S. Gunawan, M. H. Habaebi, M. Halbouni, M. Kartiwi and R. Ahmad. 2022. Machine Learning and Deep Learning Approaches for CyberSecurity: A Review. IEEE Access 10:19572–19585.
41. N. Akhtar and A. Mian. 2018. Threat of Adversarial Attacks on Deep Learning in Computer Vision: A Survey. IEEE Access 6:14410–14430.
42. Lirim Ashiku and Cihan Dagli. 2021. Network Intrusion Detection System using Deep Learning. Procedia Computer Science 185:239–247.
43. R. Patil and W. Deng. 2020. Malware Analysis using Machine Learning and Deep Learning Techniques. SoutheastCon 1–7.
44. Merton Lansley, Francois Mouton, Stelios Kapetanakis and Nikolaos Polatidis. 2020. SEADer++: Social Engineering Attack Detection in Online Environments using Machine Learning. Journal of Information and Telecommunication 4(3):346–362.
45. S. Dash, A. K. Luhach, N. Chilamkurti, S. Baek and Y. Nam. 2019. A Neuro-Fuzzy Approach for User Behaviour Classification and Prediction. Journal of Cloud Computing 8:1–15.
46. Daniel Gibert, Carles Mateu and Jordi Planes. 2020. The Rise of Machine Learning for Detection and Classification of Malware: Research Developments, Trends, and Challenges. Journal of Network and Computer Applications 153:1–22.
47. Ali Nassif, Manar Abu Talib, Q. Nasir, Halah Albadani and Fatima Albab. 2021. Machine Learning for Cloud Security: A Systematic Review. IEEE Access 9:20717–20735.
48. S. A. Salloum, M. Alshurideh, A. Elnagar and K. Shaalan. 2020. Machine Learning and Deep Learning Techniques for Cybersecurity: A Review. In: A. E. Hassanien, A. Azar, T. Gaber, D. Oliva, F. Tolba (eds) International Conference on Artificial Intelligence and Computer Vision (AICV2020). Advances in Intelligent Systems and Computing 1153:50–57.

49. J. A. Meister, R. N. Akram and K. Markantonakis. 2019. Deep Learning Application in Security and Privacy – Theory and Practice: A Position Paper. In: O. Blazy, C. Yeun (eds) Information Security Theory and Practice. Lecture Notes in Computer Science, Springer, vol. 11469, 1–17.
50. G. Xu, H. Li, H. Ren, K. Yang and R. H. Deng. 2019. Data Security Issues in Deep Learning: Attacks, Countermeasures, and Opportunities. IEEE Communications Magazine 57(11):116–122.
51. F. Khalid, M. A. Hanif, S. Rehman and M. Shafique. 2018. Security for Machine Learning-Based Systems: Attacks and Challenges During Training and Inference. International Conference on Frontiers of Information Technology (FIT) 327–332.
52. I. H. Sarker 2021. Machine Learning: Algorithms, Real-World Applications and Research Directions. SN Computer Science 2:1–21.

Chapter 6

Cyber Physical System and Enabling Technologies

Opportunity, Challenges, and Applications

Gunpreet Singh Walia, Divakar Kumar,
Jai Sanger, and Subrata Sahana
Computer Science and Engineering, School of Engineering and Technology,
Sharda University, Greater Noida-201308

6.1 INTRODUCTION

Currently, numerous enterprise sectors are looking to catch up with the big data era, namely handling a couple of information sources, in specific formats, and specific velocities. With the internet of things (IoT) proliferation, businesses could have their enterprize processes complemented with sensors that produce information contributing to tracking their processes [1]. Considering the life of these hardware capabilities, a few technologies to address all of the information that is continuously being produced is required, consisting of Spark 1, Druid 2, or Storm 3, which might be of foremost relevance for processing, aggregating, or reading streaming information in actual time [2]. Besides the technology that has to deal with the streaming information, a few technologies for big data warehousing (e.g., Hive4) may be relevant to supplement the streaming information analysis. Considering these technologies, the device's scalability concerning information processing and garage is guaranteed. However, processing (CEP) and rule-primarily based technology (e.g., Drools5) are known in this context to permit the processing of various sorts of occasions, locating styles among them and the use of policies for that, reflecting the enterprise requirements recognized within the context of every organization [2]. The integration of these concepts and technology is already stated in a few recognized works. However, it isn't taken into consideration that they may be complemented with machine learning (ML) strategies designed to permit the device to make predictions or tips in the use of pre-decided ML fashions over situations that arrive on the device.

In addition, no other topic mentions the importance of an entire and modern visualization for tracking this type of structure, which is being taken into consideration in these topics [3]. In this context, the purpose of this doctoral thesis supervised via Professors Maribel Y as mina Santos and Carlos Costa is the concept of a logical and technological device structure that offers to

128

DOI: 10.1201/9781003329947-6

businesses the functionality of the use of all their situational information in actual-time fashion.

Consider:

1. Enterprize necessities that ought to be effortlessly integrated into the device.
2. Effective methods of doing predictions and tips to show everyday operations.
3. Device self-control and tracking to save you uncontrolled increase of the device.

As may be located in Section 6.2, the idealized device structure addressing the stated factors are no longer recognized within the literature review, one reason why this overview discusses the concept of a CEP device for the big data era. This report is split as follows: Section 6.2 offers the state-of-the-art, Section 6.3 mentions the anticipated contributions, Section 6.4 dissects the study methodology, Section 6.5 highlights the proposed method and cutting-edge consequences, and, Section 6.6 summarizes the disadvantages.

6.2 BRIEF SUMMARY OF CYBER-PHYSICAL SYSTEMS

A cyber-physical device (CPS) is a PC device wherein a mechanism is managed or monitored via way of PC-primarily based algorithms. In cyber-physical structures, physical and software program additives are deeply intertwined, capable of performing on one-of-a-kind spatial and temporal scales, showcase more than one behavioural modalities, and highlights some of the key characteristics that make them unique and challenging to design and manage [1].

CPS includes transdisciplinary approaches, merging principles of cybernetics, mechatronics, layout, and procedure technology [2, 4]. The procedure management is regularly known as embedded structures. In embedded structures, the emphasis tends to be extra on the computational elements and much less on a severe hyperlink among the computational and physical elements. CPS is likewise much like the internet of things (IoT), sharing the identical primary structure, nevertheless, CPS offers a better mixture and coordination among physical and computational elements [5].

Examples of CPS encompass clever grid, self-sufficient vehicle structures, scientific tracking, commercial management structures, robotics structures, and automated pilot avionics [6]. Precursors of cyber-physical structures may be observed in regions as varied as aerospace, automotive, chemical processes, civil infrastructure, strength, healthcare, manufacturing, transportation, entertainment, and client appliances.

6.3 METHODS AND MATERIALS

A CEP device may be defined as a device that analyzes occasions via specific perspectives like sample matching or inference. In these processes, the device can filter and mix the applicable information, complementing it with outside information [1, 2]. CEP structures as being a project for the data stream management systems, thinking about that except processing the information in actual-time, it's miles vital to do so over it [4–6]. This challenge commenced within the 90's and provided the functionality of figuring that could automatically extract temporal and causal relationships among events from large collections of text documents. However, the cutting-edge quantity of information calls for upgrades to this idea, adapting it to big data environments. In this context, and reading the prevailing architectures that goal to combine the CEP and big data concepts, the visual artworks created by artists is use of the diagnosed Lambda and Kappa architectures because the base for the concept of BIDCEP, a structure that integrates CEP and big data streaming concepts [7]. Applicable factor stated by the authors is the relevance of the IoT idea, which ought to be taken into consideration as an enabler for descriptive, predictive, and prescriptive analytics, even though it isn't substantive wherein those aspects are taken into consideration within the proposed structure. Another structure is highlighted within the FERRARI challenge context [8], with a prototype for real-time CEP that manner vast quantities of information in a dispensed way. These architectures proportion a few principles, consisting of the additives chargeable for the relationship to the information sources, the additives related to the processing and the additives associated with the information of consumers.

The major issues that ought to be taken into consideration within the improvement of a big data CEP [9, 10] device is stated through [3] parallelism, elasticity, multi-question, and dispensed resources.

However, the authors additionally point out that, even though there are a few works that try and cope with these issues, the combination of CEP and big data technology is still something drastically unexplored.

Nevertheless, integrating CEP in big data contexts, a few works [11–13] emphasize the relevance of mixing big data, CEP, and IoT to aid the manufacturing enterprize via cyber-physical systems (CPSs) (Figures 6.1 and 6.2).

The visual artworks of [11] propose a framework for a manufacturing CPS that considers the physical world (e.g., manufacturing centres and shop-ground resources), the cyber world (e.g., simulation and prediction fashions), and the interface among these worlds (e.g., sensor networks and dependent and unstructured information). In this case, the CEP device is a part within the cyber world, chargeable for processing occasions and go back consequences in real-time that should offer operational visibility and recognition for the producing device. The authors discover using occasion

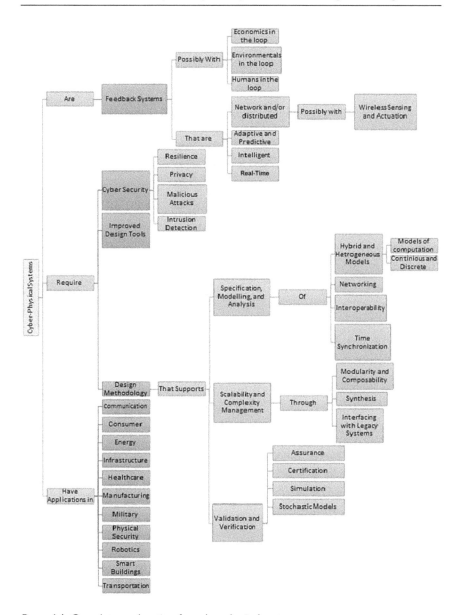

Figure 6.1 Complete explanation for cyber-physical system.

primarily based predictions for production making plans and control [12]. In this case, sensors established within the production plant are the information source for the CEP device that, combining the events with past information, will offer the opportunity of accomplishing the primarily

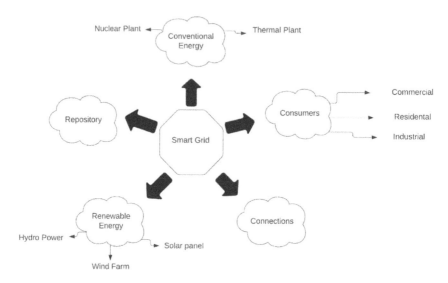

Figure 6.2 Energy management in cyber-physical system.

based prediction for manufacturing making plans and control. The visual artworks [13] propose a framework that may be carried out to reveal the influence of a CPS via using IoT information. This framework offers a publish-subscribe messaging system that gets the information for additional identity of significant events in a rule primarily based CEP System (strolling in a dispensed way). The processing consequences are posted within the self-recovery mechanism and predictive preservation for the execution of the moves formerly defined [9].

6.4 WHAT IS THE DISTINCTION BETWEEN THE INTERNET OF THINGS (IOT) AND CYBER-PHYSICAL-SYSTEMS (CPS)?

The Internet of Things (IoT) is indeed a concept that revolves around connecting various objects and machines to the internet, allowing them to communicate and share data with each other and with centralized systems. At the same time as cyber-physical-systems (CPS) is the combination of computation, networking, and physical procedure.

6.4.1 Advantages

Many reasons make CPS very useful, certainly considered one among them is: Without essential adjustments to its unique configuration, it's retaining excessive reliability in open, evolving, and unsure environments so that the device can maintain performance even within the presence of failures.

6.5 OPTIMIZATION OF SMART GRIDS IN A CYBER-PHYSICAL-SYSTEM APPROACH

It appears you are discussing the key functionalities required to enhance cyber-physical systems (CPS) in the context of Smart Grids (SGs). Cyber-physical systems combine digital, computational elements with physical components to monitor and control various processes. In the case of Smart Grids, these systems play a crucial role in ensuring efficient and reliable energy distribution. Let's break down the six key functionalities you mentioned:

1. *Fault Tolerance and Easy Repair*: The system should be designed to detect and respond to faults swiftly. This means that when a malfunction or fault occurs in any part of the system, it should be identified promptly. Additionally, the system should facilitate easy and timely repairs or replacements, minimizing downtime and ensuring uninterrupted service.
2. *High Predictability*: Predictability in a CPS is essential, especially in critical applications like Smart Grids. This involves the ability to forecast and anticipate system behavior accurately. For instance, predicting power demand or potential equipment failures can help in proactive management and resource allocation.
3. *High Sustainability with Self-Recovery and Adaptation*: Sustainability in this context refers to the system's ability to maintain functionality over time. Self-recovery mechanisms can help the system automatically recover from faults or disturbances without human intervention. Furthermore, the system should be adaptive, capable of adjusting to changing environmental conditions and demands efficiently.
4. *High Security*: Ensuring the security of the Smart Grid CPS is paramount. It's crucial to have robust cybersecurity measures in place to protect against unauthorized access, data breaches, and cyberattacks. This includes encryption, access control, intrusion detection systems, and more.
5. *High Interoperability*: Interoperability is essential for effective communication and collaboration among various components within the Smart Grid system. It ensures that different devices and systems can work together seamlessly, sharing data and services as needed. Standards and protocols play a critical role in achieving high interoperability.

6. *Effective Communication*: Effective communication is at the core of a successful Smart Grid CPS. It enables real-time data exchange, control, and coordination among different components. This can include communication between sensors, control systems, and end-users.

6.5.1 Smart Grid

A smart grid is indeed an advanced and modernized electrical grid system that relies heavily on data acquisition, evaluation, and decision-making processes for improved efficiency, reliability, and sustainability. In the smart grid, many conventional components use cyber-physical systems. They are used within the generation, transmission, and distribution and, additionally, within the purchaser side. In a power generation, it's going to manage the relationship of the community with the operational elements. CPS monitors the situations and handles the steadiness of transmission and distribution networks that join end-customers to the smart grid. It offers a two-manner communique and management among the energy grid and clients. Medical CPS: Wireless sensor networks gather the diagnostic data, display the fitness and drug management of patients. The integration of computing and management mechanisms to the vital scientific data communicated offers an essential prerequisite to self-reliant scientific cyber-physical systems.

6.6 DISADVANTAGES

The potential disadvantages of advancing technology, specifically in the context of cyber-physical systems (CPS). Let's explore these concerns:

1. Unemployment.
2. Unpredictability.
3. Computers gaining self-awareness.

6.7 APPLICATION OF CPS

The most visible use of computers is for human consumption. We use them to write emails, browse websites, type documents, do financial analysis, watch videos on YouTube and check news feeds on Facebook. However, the vast majority of the computers being used are much less visible. These computer systems are called embedded systems and the systems they interact with, together become cyber-physical systems (Figure 6.3).

This article will provide a new and very crucial angle on embedded system design, especially those who want to design embedded control, processing, and intelligence for physical systems (robots, drones, machines, physical

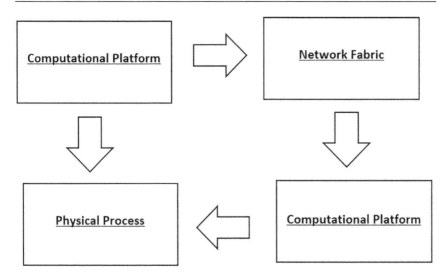

Figure 6.3 Physical computational process.

process), etc. It is expected that the reader has some basic understanding of computer systems, communication protocols, software/hardware, etc.

6.8 THE ENGINEERING CHALLENGES

The principal challenge in designing embedded systems stem from their inter-action with the physical processes [1]. In cyber-physical systems, computers and networks control and monitor the physical processes. Thus, their design must require a joint understanding of the computational and physical parts. A highly parallel nature of the physical process must be controlled with an inherently sequential nature of computers.

Let's take an example of an automotive airbag system where a highly physical event (the deployment of the airbag seconds before the event of a crash) is controlled with an electronic control unit (an embedded con-trol system). Figure 6.4 below shows a typical airbag system architecture of most modern cars, where a radar system detects the minimum distance (along with approaching speed) and the ECU deploys the airbag a hun-dredth or a thousandth of a second before the passenger hits their head on the dashboard.

In most control system applications, the goal is to get real-world data into some sort of algorithm. Before software technology (a consequence of microprocessor technology advancement) became mature, such applica-tions were made using analogue circuits or custom hardware logic. Today, the majority of the applications in the embedded world are implemented in

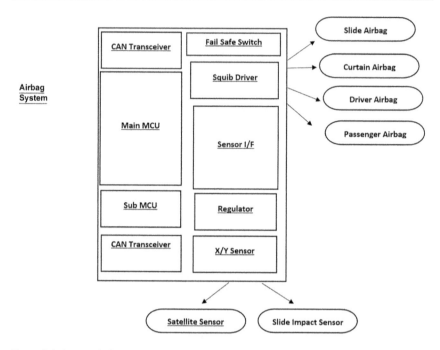

Figure 6.4 A typical electronic airbag deployment system.

software, allowing more abstraction, simplifying development and reducing design iterations.

What needs to be understood here is how a single measurement (radar data point) makes its way into the embedded computer system and the algorithm. We also need to look into the key actors which play a pivotal role in bringing the sensor data into the algorithm and then sending a signal to the actuator for deployment. The key players are shown in Figure 6.5. Here, the radar sensor must get conditioned (amplified, filtered), digitized via analogue-to-digital converter and travel on a data bus via some sort of a digital protocol (SPI, I2C), etc. Then a memory transfer must take place (FIFO, memory-mapped register access), etc. The delays caused by these players can be grouped into three major categories:

1. Signal conditioning and analog-to-digital conversion: Turing a physical signal (change in voltage or current) into a digital representation.
2. Hardware Communication: Taking data off of the ADC and bringing it into the software. This includes bus speed, latency, etc.
3. Software: Memory transfer needed such as DMA, processing interrupts and copying data in the algorithm. It also includes algorithm-specific delays such as compute time (arithmetic operations).

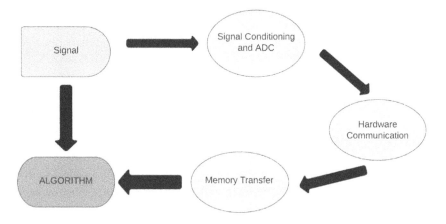

Figure 6.5 Memory processing and transfers in ADC.

All the above players contribute to the delays, which might not seem much to a normal eye. But in cyber-physical systems, physical processes are dependent on complex interactions of variables and hence demand timely interaction and communication from the cyber and physical parts.

6.9 RESEARCH METHODOLOGY

This layout or technique inspired technology [14] studies technique with the aim of extending the limits of human or organizational talents via the introduction of new and modern artifacts, in this case, offering an answer for companies pursuing (near) real-time choices and automatic movements primarily based on big data streams and CPSs. This context [14] offers a fixed recommendation to behaviour layout technology studies in information systems:

1. Endorse an artifacts to deal with an organizational problem.
2. Apprehend the relevance of the problem that is being solved.
3. Examine the utility, high-satisfactory and efficiency of the proposed artifacts.
4. Offer clean and verifiable studies contributions.
5. Follow rigorous techniques at the artifacts improvement and evaluation.
6. Don't Forget the Layout of the Artifact as a Seek Procedure Utilizing Available Methods to Fulfill the Goals and Fulfill the Constraints: This recommendation emphasizes the importance of carefully designing the artifact, considering available methods and approaches to achieve the intended goals and address constraints effectively.

7. Present the Research to Technology Practitioners and Researchers, as well as Management-Oriented Audiences: Disseminating the research is crucial. It should be presented not only to fellow researchers but also to technology practitioners and management-oriented audiences.

Therefore, the broadly diagnosed design science research methodology for information systems [15] is used in this doctoral thesis, thinking about an objective-centred technique for the designing of a logical and technological device structure that ought to meet the subsequent goals:

1. Handle big data produced via numerous assets outside and inside the companies (e.g., records from manufacturing lines, cars, citizens, and smartphones, amongst others).
   a) Consider numerous viable records assets and their interface differences, to layout a device that guarantees that new records assets may be without problems added.
   b) Consider the volume, range and pace of the records that might arrive on the system, for you to outline its scalability, multi-query, parallelism and disbursed asset characteristics.
2. Consider the commercial enterprize necessities and signs described via companies, besides the records itself.
3. To establish a process for handling records within specific timeframes to meet the needs of multiple decision-makers while organizations presenting inputs concerning the latency for the one-of-a-kind device use cases, as this may be used to assess the timeliness of the automatic movements brought about via the device.
4. Provide predictions and guidelines for the organization's day-by-day activities; design and examine a suitable device structure to effectively combine predictive and prescriptive ML into streaming data or event processing systems to achieve high throughput and low-latency predictions or prescriptions.
5. Autonomously execute suitable movements to keep away from substantial troubles for the organization (e.g., forestall a manufacturing machine). Design and examine the maximum suitable manner to speak with outside systems, executing computerized movements immediately associated with the commercial enterprise necessities (rules) and signs described via the organization.
6. Consider the relevance of self-control and tracking, stopping the uncontrolled increase of the device with the regular tracking and visualization of what occurred within the device (e.g., Which manufacturers are introducing extra records into the device? What is the maximum brought about movements?). Designing a tracking device and a visualization platform to monitor strategic endpoints and

provide user-friendly analysis of device status involves multiple steps and considerations (e.g., immersive and drill-down visualization, digital or augmented reality). Considering these goals, a few metrics have been recognized as relevant for the device evaluation: scalability and complexity whilst integrating new records assets, manufacturers and clients in the context of devices, their production or usage rates, the number of rules, movements, and ML models involved, response times of ML models, and the effectiveness of analysis available in a monitoring platform. These metrics may be evaluated thinking about the companies' necessities and the use of baselines and recommendations recognized within the literature review (e.g., throughput, latency, and scalability benchmarks). The effects of a primary iteration (after completing the second one of the four years of the doctoral program) at the design and development section of the study methodology is supplied in Section 6.5 implemented the first, second, third, and fifth goals in a real-world prototype at Bosch Car Multimedia Portugal but it still requires a rigorous evaluation.

6.10 RESULTS ANALYSIS

This section presents the first iteration of the design and development phase of the research methodology explained in Section 6.4, using a proof of concept based on the active lot release application from Bosch Car Multimedia Portugal as a demonstration case. Taking into consideration the organization's needs and the gap found in the literature review, a system architecture is being proposed to fill these needs. This system named Intelligent Event Broker aims to represent a big data-oriented CEP system that combines a collection of software components and data engineering decisions, integrated to ensure their usefulness, efficiency, and harmonious functioning, to process the events that arrive in the system. The proposed architecture for the Intelligent Event Broker (Figure. 6.1) considers a vast number of components for dealing with the volume, variety, and velocity of the data:

1. Source Systems: The system architecture should be prepared to receive data from several sources: relational, NoSQL or NewSQL databases, IoT gateways or (Web) servers, and even components of the Hadoop ecosystem, such as Hive Tables or HDFS files.
2. Producers: To ensure that all the Source Systems identified in one can be integrated into the system, regardless of their communication interfaces, the producers' component is proposed to standardize the collection of events entering the system. Kafka (a distributed streaming platform) is proposed for the deployment of this component.

3. Broker Beans: The events collected in the Source Systems by the Kafka producers are serialized into the form of classes that define the several business entities existing in the system—Broker Beans.

4. Brokers: Events serialized into Broker Beans, can be published by the producers a Kafka topic that is stored in a cluster of Kafka Brokers.

5. Event Processor: Events are subscribed by the event processor (Kafka Consumers that are embedded into Spark Applications) that is always waiting for processing the events arriving at the system, regardless of their frequency.

6. Complementary Data: In addition to the events published in the topics, the *event the processor* can use complementary data from the source systems, if useful for the event processing, providing additional and relevant information.

7. Rules Engine: Includes the defined rules that represent the business requirements (with strategical, tactical, or operational rules). This work is usually associated with a data engineer who creates the rules that represent the business needs. Here Drools is used to store the rules that will be then translated by the event processor, using a custom-made integration of Spark and Drools, based on previously explored paths by the technical community [16].

8. Triggers: Connectors to the destination systems, execute the actions previously defined for the rules when the condition is evaluated as being true.

9. Destination Systems: the results of processing the events can be sent to, for example, IoT gateways that can activate an actuator, text or e-mail messages, or even transactional or analytical applications.

10. Predictors and Recommenders: The concept of *a lake of ML models,* which are trained beforehand, is proposed in this system architecture as being of major relevance. Allow the application of those ML models to the data that is being processed, providing the capability to predict occurrences or recommend actions based on the events that are arriving at the system.

11. Event Aggregator: Stores the raw event data (events that arrived at the system) or processed event data (the events processing result, such as results from the predictors and recommenders component) used to calculate the KPIs relevant to the business. This component is supported by Druid, a columnar storage system useful for aggregating event data at ingestion time [17, 18].

12. Mapping and Drill-down System: Allows the constant monitoring of the Intelligent Event Broker and includes:
    a) Graph Database: Stores the relevant metadata of the Intelligent Event Broker, allowing the exploration of the flows of the events in the Intelligent Event Broker.

b) Web Visualization Platform: Provides an interactive and immersive visualization regarding the Intelligent Event Broker metadata, stored in the graph database, taking into account the various implementation contexts of the system.

Currently, a demonstration case was implemented using data from the Bosch Car Multimedia Portugal plant [19]. This data comes from its ALR System that supports the quality control used in the manufacturing and packaging processes. This system is based on rules that are applied to the products contained in lots before they are shipped to customers. The ALR system provides a stream of events that contain information about the quality control process being considered at this point, the lot identification, its packaging date, the production line, and the status (Valid or Invalid lot).

Therefore, for this demonstration case, one operational rule and two tactical rules were defined, as well as their triggers that are activated if the result for the rule condition is true. Considering these two types of rules, two types of dashboards were created on the analytical application, one oriented for operational analysis and the other one oriented for a more tactical point of view [19].

6.11 CONCLUSION AND FUTURE SCOPE

In general-purpose computing, the time it takes to perform a task is a measure of its performance, not correctness. In cyber-physical systems, however, the time it takes to produce a valid result is a measure of its correctness. In the case of an airbag system, if the control system is unable to give a valid signal to the squib driver in time, the output will be catastrophic because of an ongoing parallel process (car approaching at high speed). This result will be catastrophic and hence, incorrect. So, the design of embedded systems requires a framework, architecture, design process, modelling, and implementation in a way that considers the joint understanding of both physical and computed parts. At this time, a first version of the system was already implemented with the Bosch Car Multimedia Portugal demonstration case, where the first, second, third and fifth objectives discussed in Section 6.4 were fulfilled. With this prototype, a CEP system in big data contexts that reveal its adequacy to the problem and contains several components already developed (e.g., data producers and consumers, rules and triggers with the business requirements, an event aggregator and an analytical application as a destination system) is presented to practitioners and researchers.

Cyber-physical structures (CPS) will remodel how people have interacted with and manage the physical world. Correct low-cost and flexible deployment of CPS can best be made viable via essential advances in technology, engineering, and education. CPS technology ought to be scalable throughout time and area and ought to cope with more than one timescales, uncertainty, privacy concerns, and protection issues. A new CPS technology will outline new mathematical foundations with formalisms to specify, analyze, affirm, and validate structures that display and manage physical items and entities. Cyber-physical sensing structures and inexperienced communications positioned a brand new emphasis on the venture of strength control for Wi-Fi communications and want the usage of strength-harvesting technology.

Without any questions, CPS may be taken into consideration as a crucial step within the improvement of producing structures. Whether this step might seem because of the fourth commercial revolution can be determined via the approaching generations, however certainly, this may manifest without probability.

REFERENCES

[1] Leavitt, N.: Complex-Event Processing Poised for Growth. Computer. 42, 17–20 (2009). doi:10.1109/MC.2009.109
[2] Luckham, D.C.: Rapide: A Language and Toolset for Simulation of Distributed Systems by Partial Orderings of Events. Stanford University (1996).
[3] Flouris, I., Giatrakos, N., Deligiannakis, A., Garofalakis, M., Kamp, M., Mock, M.: Issues in Complex Event Processing: Status and Prospects in the Big Data Era. Journal of Systems and Software. 127, 217–236 (2017). doi: 10.1016/j.jss.2016.06.011
[4] Chakravarthy, S., Qingchun, J.: Stream Data Processing: A Quality-of-Service Perspective: Modeling, Scheduling, Load Shedding, and Complex Event Processing. Springer (2009).
[5] Luckham, D.C., Vera, J.: An Event-Based Architecture Definition Language. IEEE Transactions on Software Engineering. 21, 717–734 (1995). doi:10.1109/32.464548
[6] Cugola, G., Margara, A.: Processing Flows of Information: From Data Stream to Complex Event Processing. ACM Computing Surveys. 44(15), 62 (2012). doi:10.1145/2187671.2187677
[7] Hadar, E.: BIDCEP: A Vision of Big Data Complex Event Processing for Near Real-Time Data Streaming Position Paper – A Practitioner View. In: CEUR Workshop Proceedings (2016).
[8] Flouris, I., Manikaki, V., Giatrakos, N., Deligiannakis, A., Garofalakis, M., Mock, M., Bothe, S., Skarbovsky, I., Fournier, F., Stajcer, M., Krizan, T., Yom-Tov, J., Curin, T.: FERARI: A Prototype for Complex Event Processing Over Streaming Multi-Cloud Platforms. In: Proceedings of the 2016 International Conference on Management of Data, pp. 2093–2096. ACM, New York, NY (2016).

[9] Costa, C., Santos, M.Y.: Evaluating Several Design Patterns and Trends in Big Data Warehousing Systems. In: Krogstie, J. and Reijers, H.A. (eds.) Advanced Information Systems Engineering, pp. 459–473. Springer International Publishing (2018).

[10] Tawsif, K., Hossen, J., Emerson Raja, J., Jesmeen, M.Z.H., Arif, E.M.H.: A Review on Complex Event Processing Systems for Big Data. In: 2018 Fourth International Conference on Information Retrieval and Knowledge Management (CAMP), Kota Kinabalu (2018).

[11] Babiceanu, R.F., Seker, R.: Manufacturing Cyber-Physical Systems Enabled by Complex Event Processing and Big Data Environments: A Framework for Development. In: Service Orientation in Holonic and Multi-Agent Manufacturing, Studies in Computational Intelligence, pp. 165–173. Springer International Publishing (2015).

[12] Krumeich, J., Jacobi, S., Werth, D., Loos, P.: Big Data Analytics for Predictive Manufacturing Control – A Case Study from Process Industry. In: 2014 IEEE International Congress on Big Data, pp. 530–537 (2014).

[13] Dundar, B., Astekin, M., Aktas, M.S.: A Big Data Processing Framework for Self-Healing Internet of Things Applications. In: 12th International Conference on Semantics, Knowledge and Grids (SKG), pp. 62–68, Beijing (2016)

[14] Hevner, A.R., March, S.T., Park, J., Ram, S.: Design Science in Information Systems Research. MIS Quarterly. 28, 75–105 (2004).

[15] Peffers, K., Tuunanen, T., Rothenberger, M.A., Chatterjee, S.: A Design Science Research Methodology for Information Systems Research. Journal of Management Information Systems. 24, 45–77 (2007). doi:10.2753/MIS0742-1222240302

[16] Ganta, M.: How-to: Build a Complex Event Processing App on Apache Spark and Drools. https://blog.cloudera.com/blog/2015/11/how-to-build-a-complex-event-processing-app-on apache-spark-and-drools/10

[17] Yang, F., Tschetter, E., Léauté, X., Ray, N., Merlino, G., Ganguli, D.: Druid: A Real-Time Analytical Data Store. In: Proceedings of the 2014 ACM SIGMOD International Conference on Management of Data, pp. 157–168. ACM, Utah (2014).

[18] Correia, J., Santos, M.Y., Costa, C., Andrade, C.: Fast Online Analytical Processing for Big Data Warehousing. Presented at the International Conference on Intelligent Systems, Madeira Island, September (2018).

[19] Andrade, C., Correia, J., Costa, C., Santos, M.Y.: Intelligent Event Broker: A Complex Event Processing System in Big Data Contexts. In: AMCIS 2019 Proceedings. Cancun (2019). Manuscript Accepted for Publication.

Chapter 7

Unveiling the Impact of Blockchain and Cryptocurrency on the Indian Economy

Exploring Modern Transaction Methods

¹Lipsa Das, ¹Pooja Singh, ¹Dev Bahubal,
²Sangeeta Rani, and ³Ajay Kumar
¹Amity University, Greater Noida, UP, India
²Department of Computer Science and Engineering, World College of
Technology and Management, Gurgaon, India
³Associate Professor, Department of Mechanical Engineering, School of
Engineering and Technology, JECRC University, Jaipur, Rajasthan, India

7.1 INTRODUCTION

Blockchain technology and cryptocurrencies are changing the way people do business throughout the world. Blockchain technology's decentralised and secure nature has the potential to alter a variety of industries, including banking, healthcare, and supply chain management. Cryptocurrencies, on the other hand, provide a viable alternative to existing fiat currencies, with the potential to broaden financial inclusion and lower transaction costs.

In recent years, India has emerged as one of the fastest-growing markets for blockchain and cryptocurrency adoption. However, the country's regulatory landscape has been uncertain, leading to a lack of clarity and direction for market participants. This has resulted in a divide among policymakers, with some pushing for a blanket ban on cryptocurrencies, while others advocate for their regulation.

The purpose of this paper is to examine the influence of blockchain technology and cryptocurrencies on the Indian economy and transaction style. It will present an overview of the existing regulatory framework and its implications for the growth of India's blockchain and cryptocurrency industries. The analysis will also look at the possible advantages and hazards of blockchain and cryptocurrency adoption, such as enhanced financial inclusion and efficiency, as well as potential concerns like fraud and money laundering.

This paper will present a complete assessment of the influence of blockchain and cryptocurrencies on the Indian economy and transaction style through an in-depth research of industry trends, government legislation, and case studies. This report's findings will be valuable for policymakers, market

DOI: 10.1201/9781003329947-7

actors, and anybody interested in learning more about the possibilities of blockchain and cryptocurrencies in India.

7.2 LITERATURE REVIEW

Wajde Baiod et al. [1], blockchain technology use has grown dramatically over the years, with numerous enterprises and industrial communities realising its potential to provide new possibilities and benefits. According to Wajde Baiod et al. [1], the decentralised, distributed, and trustless nature of blockchain technology has made it a unique and superior technology, providing businesses that adopt it with increased efficiency, lower costs, enhanced integrity and transparency, better security, and improved traceability. While the financial and banking industry has been the major area of application for blockchain, recent trials and suggested uses in other disciplines have highlighted blockchain's promise in a variety of industries. Wajde Baiod et al. [1] present an outline of blockchain technology in their article, outlining major design aspects, characteristics, and advantages. The authors also discuss prominent consensus protocols and blockchain system taxonomy. Moreover, the study examines blockchain-based applications in banking, insurance, supply chain management, energy, advertising and media, real estate, and healthcare. The research intends to investigate the major difficulties in these businesses, as well as blockchain solutions and application cases. The report cites three primary blockchain technology limitations: scalability, security, and regulation. These difficulties may have an influence on the implementation and acceptance of blockchain technology in several sectors. Scalability difficulties, for example, might lead to sluggish transaction processing, while security flaws could lead to data leaks and hackers. Additionally, regulatory uncertainty may stymie blockchain technology development in a variety of businesses. Finally, Wajde Baiod et al. [1] offered a thorough examination of blockchain technology, stressing its primary advantages and disadvantages. The paper's emphasis on blockchain-based applications across several areas gives insights into blockchain's potential in numerous businesses. The identification of the three major constraints of blockchain technology in the study serves as a starting point for future research in overcoming these difficulties in order to improve blockchain technology adoption.

Watanabe et al. [2] proposed the concept of the "Blockchain Contract" which is a decentralised method of executing contracts using blockchain technology. The authors highlighted that the traditional method of executing contracts is often cumbersome and requires intermediaries. The introduction of the blockchain contract enables an efficient method of contract execution using smart contracts that run automatically when preset circumstances are satisfied. The authors' research illustrates how the blockchain contract uses blockchain technology to offer total unanimity. The consensus technique is accomplished through the use of dispersed network nodes that validate transactions and contracts. Moreover, the implementation of blockchain technology assures that transactions are safe, transparent, and tamper-proof, which is crucial in contract execution. Watanabe et al. [2] investigated the possibility of applying blockchain contracts in a variety of industries, including banking, real estate, and supply chain management, in their study. The writers also investigated the blockchain contract's potential benefits, such as lower transaction costs, improved security, and transparency. They also emphasised the difficulties in executing the blockchain contract, such as scalability and regulatory issues. Watanabe et al.'s [2] research sheds light on the possibility of the blockchain contract. The authors' idea for a decentralised contract execution approach based on blockchain technology has the potential to revolutionise contract execution across sectors. The implementation of smart contracts in blockchain contracts guarantees that contract execution is transparent, safe, and automated, hence decreasing the need for manual intervention. However, the scalability and regulatory challenges associated with the blockchain contract must be addressed before widespread adoption in different fields. In conclusion, the study by Watanabe et al. (2015) provides a valuable contribution to the literature on blockchain technology. The proposal of the blockchain contract is a significant development in the execution of contracts, and its potential benefits could be significant in various industries. However, addressing the scalability and regulatory challenges will be critical in ensuring the widespread adoption of the blockchain contract.

Mukhopadhyay et al. [3] did a review of cryptocurrency systems and presented an overview of several cryptocurrencies such as Bitcoin, Litecoin, Ripple, and Ethereum. The authors highlighted the common characteristics of these cryptocurrencies, such as decentralisation, anonymity, and security. The study by Mukhopadhyay et al. [3] also provided insights into the technical aspects of cryptocurrency systems, such as blockchain technology, mining, and digital wallets. The authors evaluated the advantages and limitations of these systems, including transaction speed, scalability, and regulatory challenges. One of the key findings of the study was that the use of cryptocurrencies is growing rapidly, and their adoption is no longer limited to tech-savvy individuals. According to the authors, governments and corporations are also investigating the possibilities of cryptocurrencies and blockchain technology, with various initiatives and pilot projects being established throughout the world. Overall, Mukhopadhyay et al. [3] present a thorough examination of the many characteristics of cryptocurrency systems. The authors' evaluation of the advantages and limitations of these systems is essential in understanding the potential of cryptocurrencies in various industries. The rapid growth and adoption of cryptocurrencies suggest that they have the potential to revolutionise traditional financial systems. However, addressing the scalability and regulatory challenges associated with cryptocurrencies will be crucial in ensuring their widespread adoption.

Zheng et al. [4] offered an overview of blockchain technology, including its design, consensus, and future prospects. The writers emphasised blockchain's essential characteristics, such as decentralisation, immutability, and transparency. They also talked about the many forms of blockchain architecture, such as public, private, and consortium blockchains. Zheng et al. [4] conducted an evaluation of the different consensus algorithms utilised in blockchain systems, such as proof of work (PoW), proof of stake (PoS), and delegated proof of stake (DPoS). The authors analysed the benefits and drawbacks of each consensus method, as well as how they affect the scalability, security, and energy efficiency of blockchain systems. The research also shed light on the potential uses of blockchain technology outside of the financial industry, such as healthcare, supply chain management, and energy. The writers examined the difficulties and prospects of blockchain adoption in different industries. Overall, Zheng et al. [4] give a thorough introduction of blockchain technology. The authors' assessment of the various forms of blockchain architecture and consensus algorithms is critical for understanding the potential of blockchain systems. The report also discusses the possible uses of blockchain technology outside of the financial industry, as well as the problems connected with its implementation. According to the study's future trends, blockchain technology is projected to play a key role in numerous industries and change old business methods.

Hassani et al. [5] explored the intersection between cryptocurrency and big data. The writers stated that bitcoin has been a trendy issue during the previous decade, attracting worldwide investments worth trillions of dollars. They also emphasised the Bitcoin technology and network's distinct design, which has characterised its global efficiency, flexibility, and data-demanding qualities. The study looked at the connection between Bitcoin and big data, two essential concepts in today's digitalised society. The authors conducted a thorough examination of the most current applications and developments since 2016, with the goal of presenting a comprehensive overview of the links between big data and cryptocurrency. The authors identified several key areas where big data and cryptocurrency intersect, including data analytics, security, and scalability. They also highlighted the potential of big data in improving the efficiency and security of cryptocurrency transactions. Overall, the study provides insights into the potential of big data and cryptocurrency, as well as highlighting the challenges and limitations of the technologies. The authors conclude by calling for further research into the intersection of these two areas to fully realise their potential.

Wanga et al. [6], blockchain technology has been intensively investigated in numerous businesses in recent years. The intellectual property (IP) sector has gotten a lot of attention because of its distinctive qualities and prospective advantages. Wanga et al. [6] present an overview of academic research and business uses of blockchain technology in intellectual property. The study emphasises the potential of blockchain technology to address several concerns confronting the IP business, such as copyright, patents, and trademarks. The authors also give many case studies on the usage of blockchain in IP protection, such as digital art protection and the establishment of an IP marketplace. Furthermore, the authors propose a new approach for blockchain research and development in the field of intellectual property, namely the use of blockchain to construct a decentralised autonomous organisation (DAO) for IP administration. This strategy would entail the development of a blockchain-based platform that enables the decentralised, transparent, and safe administration of intellectual property assets. Overall, the study adds to the body of knowledge on blockchain technology, particularly in the context of the intellectual property market.

Ante [7] conducted a literature assessment on the academic basis, present trends, and projected research paths in the field of blockchain technology from the viewpoints of business and economics. Using factor analysis, the review assessed 9672 references from 467 articles in these disciplines and found five key research strands. According to the assessment, research on market efficiency and economics, asset pricing and valuation, and the concepts and applications of blockchain technology and transactions are rather mature, with a concentration on cryptocurrencies. Nevertheless, research on the concepts and applications of blockchain technology and transactions is still in its early stages and is mostly concerned with cryptocurrencies. The review also employed social network analysis to map the interrelationships between these research strands. The results show that blockchain technology is now a worldwide phenomenon and that the business and economics literature has caught up with computer science. This literature review discusses prospective future study areas and gives full knowledge of the present status of research in the business and economics domains linked to blockchain technology.

Wang et al. [8] used the Web of Science Core Collection database to conduct a bibliometric study to investigate the research status of blockchain-related articles as well as the development and evolution of this developing subject. The study looked at 2451 papers published between 2013 and 2019 and took into account factors like annual publication and citation trends, author distribution, popular research themes, country and institution collaboration, top papers, prominent publication venues, supportive funding agencies, and developing research trends. According to the findings, the number of blockchain publications continues to rise, and the focus of blockchain-related research has switched from Bitcoin, cryptocurrencies, and blockchain to smart contracts and the internet of things. The report also identified the top blockchain researchers, nations, and institutions, as well as the top publication venues and funding sources. Overall, the report gives a thorough review of the present status of blockchain research, emphasising new patterns and future research paths in this quickly growing field.

Alghamdi and Almuhammadi [9], blockchain technology has grown in popularity in recent years, with bitcoin being the most well-known use. But, with the introduction of quantum computers, the security of blockchain technology is being called into doubt. Alghamdi and Almuhammadi investigate the prospects of blockchain technology in the age of quantum computing in their study. The authors suggest that blockchain technology is immune to quantum computing threats and may stay safe even when quantum computers are widely adopted. The authors provide a comprehensive review of the literature on the topic of quantum computing and blockchain technology, examining the current state of research and highlighting potential future research directions. They identify the current limitations of blockchain technology and suggest that new approaches to key generation, signature schemes, and consensus algorithms will be required in the future. Overall, the study presents a thorough examination of the issues that blockchain technology will face in the age of quantum computing, as well as potential solutions. According to the authors, the development of new cryptographic protocols that can withstand quantum assaults is vital to the future of blockchain technology.

Shakya et al. [10], the scope of blockchain-based cryptocurrency in India was investigated. The paper aimed to investigate the present status of cryptocurrencies in India, legal and regulatory aspects of cryptocurrency, and the benefits of using blockchain-based cryptocurrencies in the country. The study employed a literature review approach to collect data from relevant sources. The findings suggest that despite a lack of clarity in the regulatory framework and skepticism among Indian policymakers, the demand for cryptocurrencies is rapidly increasing in the country. The authors also discussed the advantages of using blockchain-based cryptocurrency, such as improved transparency, reduced transaction costs, and decentralised systems. Furthermore, the paper proposed some recommendations, such as developing a suitable legal and regulatory framework, increasing awareness among the public and policymakers, and improving the technical infrastructure for better cryptocurrency adoption. Overall, the paper provides a thorough examination of the Indian cryptocurrency sector as well as insights into the possible uses of blockchain technology in the country.

Guild [11] examines the potential of financial technology (fintech) to improve access to financial services and pioneer new financial practices when supported by appropriate policies and regulatory frameworks. This has particular significance for financial inclusion and sustainable economic growth. Peer-to-peer lending platforms in China and digital currency transfer services in Kenya and India are two examples of fintech advancements that have the potential to assist hundreds of millions of people who now do not have access to financial services. According to the study, effective regulatory oversight is critical for the spread of financial inclusion through technological innovation. The article advocates for a responsive regulatory strategy, rather than an unduly interventionist one, as the optimal foundation for promoting financial inclusion through fintech by evaluating differing degrees of success in the uptake of fintech services in Kenya, India, and China. The report emphasises the need of supporting government policies and regulatory frameworks for the acceptance and spread of fintech services. It also emphasises the need of regulatory oversight in ensuring the financial system's safety and stability while encouraging innovation and competition in the industry. The paper provides valuable insights for policymakers, regulators, and industry stakeholders in their efforts to promote financial inclusion and sustainable economic growth through fintech.

The article by Raj and Upadhyay [12] explore the potential influence of fintech on the financial services business and financial inclusion in India. Fintech is defined as financial innovation enabled by technology that can result in new business models, apps, procedures, or products that have a significant influence on financial markets and institutions. According to the authors, fintech companies can increase competition and accelerate financial inclusion in India by introducing new business models, applications, and innovations that reduce costs and improve access to financial services for underserved groups such as those in low-income, rural, and other underserved sectors. The article underlines that the great majority of micro-units in India are still unconnected with the traditional credit system, and that cooperation between banks and fintech companies may assist this group, as well as small enterprises. The authors suggest that the success of fintech in India will depend on a regulatory framework that fosters collaboration between banks and fintech companies and ensures data privacy and customer protection concerns are addressed. The authors argue that a suitable regulatory and supervisory framework is required to foster fintech growth and guarantee that it continues to aid in the acceleration of financial inclusion in India. The report also underlines the need of an environment that encourages collaboration between banks and fintech firms, and calls for the necessity for banks and fintech firms to collaborate for mutual benefit.

Kaur et al. [13] cover India's growing cashless economy and the use of different digital payment methods such as IMPS, RTGS, NEFT, eWallets, Aadhar Pay, debit cards, and UPI. They emphasise the importance of digitisation in satisfying both short- and long-term business and technological goals, such as better customer satisfaction, faster output, and operational efficiency. The Indian government's 'Digital India Campaign' is viewed as a crucial step towards boosting self-reliance and sustainable development. The writers also cover the rise of numerous fintech startups, including Paytm, BillDesk, PhonePe, PolicyBazaar, and RazorPay, which have become industry unicorns. The study emphasises the potential benefits of digitisation, such as enhanced financial inclusion and access to financial services for low-income persons and those living in rural regions. According to the authors, the transition to a cashless economy has substantial consequences for the economy's growth and development, and the digitization of financial services is projected to play an important part in India's economic future. The study does, however, address the issues connected with digitisation, such as concerns about data privacy and security, as well as the need for effective regulatory control to manage these risks. Overall, the paper presents an in-depth examination of the history of financial services in India, as well as the rising significance of digitisation in supporting economic growth and financial inclusion.

Jakhiya et al. [14], the usage of mobile payments have increased dramatically in India over the years, notably since the National Payment Corporation of India launched the Immediate Payment Service (IMPS). The commercialisation of mobile money and the development of 'smart gadgets,' such as smartphones, smartwatches, smart cards, and bill payment devices, have accelerated this trend. Moreover, voice-enabled internet of things (IoT) devices have sped up the payment process, resulting in a dramatic shift in the shopping experience and retail business. The Indian government's Digital India initiative has been critical in transitioning the country into a digital society and knowledge economy. The integration of artificial intelligence (AI) and smart solutions, which have decreased fraud in high-risk mobile payments and enhanced peer-to-peer payment systems, have also supported the expansion of mobile payments. Additionally, the widespread availability of mobile phones and gadgets have resulted in a considerable shift in customer behaviour towards mobile commerce. The COVID-19 pandemic has expedited digital payment uptake in India, with the government and RBI advocating the use of digital payment systems as a safeguard against the virus. The purpose of this study is to investigate the growth and effect of mobile payments in India, with a particular emphasis on the impact of the COVID-19 epidemic on the digital payments market.

N. Kshetri [15] highlights the significance of digital payments in the banking and financial industries, which have been supported and encouraged by governments and financial institutions globally for over two decades. The article focuses on India's digital transformation, where the country has made significant progress in adopting digital payments and moving towards a cashless economy. Despite India's large and diverse population struggling with poverty and illiteracy, the authors commend the government's rigor and drive to drive digitisation, especially in the financial sector, with the help of Aadhaar, a unique identifier. To understand India's progress towards a cashless future, the article uses a technology adoption model. The writers address the significance of digital transformation in the Indian economy and how it has the potential to overhaul the country's financial sector. Overall, the article emphasises the need for India to continue its efforts to create a cashless digital economy and highlights the importance of digital payments in achieving this goal.

Kashyap and Beyadwal [16] discuss the rise of digital currency and its impact on consumer behavior. According to the authors, digital money is an intangible element that is employed in a variety of applications and systems, such as online social games, virtual worlds, and distributed systems. The study aims to investigate customers' attitudes towards the future of digital currencies, examining the certainty of customers regarding the management of digital currencies in an era where their use cannot be controlled and directed. Additionally, the study evaluates the spread of digital currency to provide a pragmatic perspective. The article provides a comprehensive review of cryptocurrencies, including their history, types, operations, advantages, and disadvantages, as well as challenges and opportunities. The authors also analyse the legal status of Bitcoin in India. The study highlights the potential benefits of digital currency, such as increased financial inclusion and reduced transaction costs, but also identifies risks and challenges associated with this new form of currency, such as security and regulatory concerns. Overall, Kashyap and Beyadwal [16] provide an insightful and informative review of digital currency, its impact on consumer behavior, and the legal status of Bitcoin in India.

Kumar and Swathy [17], the rise of cryptocurrencies and Bitcoin has been a highly debated topic in the financial industry for several years. Cryptocurrencies are digital or virtual currencies that use cryptography for security. They have contributed to extraordinary developments in the financial markets, both positively and negatively. The notion of cryptocurrencies may be tough to grasp, but it is simple to implement. Bitcoin, which was founded in the aftermath of the 2008 global financial crisis, was intended to function independently of governments, central banks, and financial institutions. Regulators have struggled to find ways to handle it, resulting in some countries banning it or making it illegal, while others remain wary and seek to tax and regulate its operations. This article attempts to study various aspects of cryptocurrencies, including their history, types, activities, advantages and disadvantages, challenges, and opportunities. It also examines the legal status of Bitcoin in India. Despite its challenges, cryptocurrencies continue to attract a significant number of users due to their potential for decentralisation and anonymity, among other factors. However, the lack of regulations and concerns about their use in illegal activities remain significant barriers to their widespread adoption.

Parab and Nitnaware [18] study focuses on assessing the role and impact of Bitcoin in India. With India's growing technology sector, the use and ownership of Bitcoin has been increasing. The research will look into the function of Bitcoin in the Indian economy and if it is a blessing or a curse. The paper analyses the impact of Bitcoin in India through exploratory research. It investigates the many elements that drive Bitcoin adoption, including awareness, trust, and government laws. It also investigates the use of Bitcoin in India, including its benefits and risks. The study finds that Bitcoin's adoption in India is growing, but it is still in its early stages. The lack of awareness and trust in Bitcoin is a significant challenge, along with the lack of clear regulations from the government. However, the study also identifies several benefits of Bitcoin, such as lower transaction fees and faster transactions. Overall, the study suggests that Bitcoin's impact in India is still uncertain, and it cannot be determined whether it is a boon or a curse. Further research is needed to completely comprehend Bitcoin's significance in India and its potential economic effect.

Agrawal et al. [19] discussed the concept of cryptocurrency, a digital currency that relies on a decentralised system called blockchain to prevent fraudulent transactions. Cryptocurrency blockchain technology is supposed to be difficult to hack, and each block on the chain holds a record of several transactions. To record transactions, the system employs an unchangeable cryptographic signature known as a hash. To change the blockchain, a hacker would have to change each block in the chain, which is always changing, making it more secure. The writers stressed the significance of blockchain technology in assuring the cryptocurrency system's security and integrity. With the growing use and popularity of cryptocurrencies, it is vital to keep safe and trustworthy transaction records. The paper offered an outline of how blockchain technology works and its function in avoiding fraudulent digital currency transactions. The authors' research demonstrates how blockchain technology has the potential to transform the way we record and verify transactions, resulting in a more secure and efficient financial system. The study of the authors shows how blockchain technology has the potential to alter the way we record and verify transactions, resulting in a more secure and efficient financial system.

The usage of cryptocurrencies have sparked controversy and intrigue throughout the world [20]. Bitcoin is a type of digital money that is not backed by a government or other central authority. It uses encryption techniques to secure and verify transactions, making it a decentralised system. Bitcoin is one of the most well-known examples of cryptocurrency, with limited usage in India. Despite the advantages of cryptocurrencies, such as the ability to perform transactions freely and without any restrictions, there are some challenges. The security of digital coins remains a concern, as they are not as secure as many people think. Another challenge is the problem of currency fluctuations, which can create uncertainty. Furthermore, there is no validating organisation to determine the number of bitcoins produced and keep documentation of the quantity, making it a decentralised network controlled by the owners with strict rules to protect their boundaries of operation. As India moves towards the digital era, there is much to learn about this new age of technology, some of which may create stress and anxiety. Nevertheless, it is expected that virtual digital currencies will continue to gain popularity.

In their recent study, More and Aslekar [21] highlight the challenges faced in the digitisation of agriculture in developing countries and rural regions.

The key barriers, according to the authors, are low levels of e-literacy and digital skills, insufficient technological infrastructure, expensive technology prices, a poor regulatory environment, and restricted access to services. The study underlines the importance of data analytics (DA), the internet of things (IoT), and fintech in improving agricultural operational efficiency and productivity. According to the authors, contemporary IoT technologies that combine radio frequency identification, cloud computing, and end-user applications are critical for future improvements. Furthermore, the authors note that fintech and IoT in agriculture can help identify farming patterns and make specialised judgments. The paper highlights the need for improved accessibility of production techniques, gadgets, and software gear. The study also emphasises the significant benefits of digital technology for smallholder farmers and rural businesses in accessing the market, loans, and high-quality farm supplies, thereby increasing crop productivity. Lastly, the authors believe that having access to digital technology allows them to tap into workforce skills, have access to support services, and form strategic alliances in areas such as training, finance, and legal services.

Wang et al. [22] presented a parallel healthcare system (PHS) architecture that uses artificial healthcare systems, computational experiments, and parallel execution to improve diagnostic and treatment efficacy. The PHS model combines patient situations, diagnosis, and treatment procedures, with artificial healthcare systems analysing and evaluating alternative therapy regimens. Parallel execution enables decision-making support and real-time optimisation in both real-world and simulated healthcare operations. Moreover, the authors combine blockchain technology with the PHS by developing a consortium blockchain that allows patients, hospitals, health bureaus, and healthcare communities to share healthcare data, examine medical records, and audit services. Lastly, the authors show a parallel gout detection and treatment system prototype as an illustration of the blockchain-powered PHS framework's use and efficiency. The suggested framework intends to improve diagnostic and treatment efficacy in the healthcare system by using modern technologies and parallel execution to optimise decision-making and improve patient care quality.

Ziyi Li et al. [23] discuss the potential of blockchain technology for addressing issues in educational credentialing. The authors present an abstract credentialing process based on the Australian tertiary education sector and identify six challenges faced by the industry. They also propose five critical characteristics of excellent credential infrastructure. The paper suggests a tiered framework for examining seven blockchain-based education efforts, as well as insights into why these solutions have not yet been broadly adopted. The authors conclude with recommendations for future development of blockchain-based education applications. While there is growing interest in the use of blockchain for educational credentialing, current attempts have not achieved worldwide acceptance. The authors propose a blockchain-based solution for credentialing, which could improve transparency, security, and trust in the educational system. However, there are challenges that need to be addressed, such as the need for a standard and interoperable infrastructure, the involvement of multiple stakeholders, and the establishment of trust among them. The tiered methodology proposed in the study could help in evaluating the effectiveness of blockchain-based education initiatives. The authors' observations may be valuable in the creation of future blockchain-based education systems.

Hamouda et al. [24] present a novel approach for energy trading in interconnected microgrids (IMGs). IMGs are a promising future grid construction, providing independence and resilience in energy exchangeability with neighboring microgrids. An interconnected market between separate microgrids participating through an energy management system (EMS) agent is a major need for the development of such a linked structure. Each agent is self-benefit-driven (SBD), which means it only operates in the best interests of its own network. To improve these benefits, energy trading has been introduced. The authors provide a unique utility function for each microgrid that considers the microgrid's multiple purposes while importing versus exporting. Each microgrid benefits from import and/or export benefits under the utility definition. A centralised Nash bargaining mechanism for global energy trade is presented to secure fair settlements through a single agency. The proposed technique is based on an upgraded blockchain, which increases platform security and transparency. Numerous case studies are used to show the efficacy of the suggested method. Overall, the paper proposes a unique paradigm for IMG energy trading that takes the self-benefit-driven character of microgrid agents into consideration, guaranteeing a fair and transparent energy trading system.

7.3 METHODOLOGY

This study analyses the impact of blockchain technology and cryptocurrency on Indian economy and on styles of transaction, we will be studying the literature review comprehensively to develop the relation between blockchain and cryptocurrency with Indian economy. Also a historical pathway is introduced in the paper to lay the entry of these technologies. The impacts of these technologies on various sectors of economy in India is studied and how it is beneficial for businesses in India is suggested. Also, this study is based on the theoretical secondary data which is recognised from various sources like the Indian Ministry of Commerce and Finance, Reserve Bank of India, World Bank data, and other research generals.

7.4 INDIA'S CRYPTOCURRENCY JOURNEY

The Bitcoin journey in India has been turbulent, with many ups and downs along the road. While cryptocurrency is still a new idea in India, it has the potential to revolutionise the country's economy and the way transactions are carried out [25, 26].

1. **The early days**

   The early days of cryptocurrency in India were marked by excitement and curiosity. Bitcoin, the first and most well-known cryptocurrency, was introduced in 2009, and by 2013, it had started gaining popularity in India. At the time, many Indians were looking for alternative investment options, and Bitcoin appeared to be a promising opportunity.

   In 2013, Unocoin, one of the first Bitcoin exchanges in India, was launched. The exchange allowed users to buy and sell Bitcoin in Indian rupees, making it easier for Indians to invest in the cryptocurrency.

2. **Government reaction**

   When Bitcoin and other cryptocurrencies gained traction in India, the authorities began to take note. The Reserve Bank of India (RBI) issued a warning in 2013 regarding the hazards of investing in cryptocurrencies.

   The government appointed a committee in 2017 to investigate the impact of cryptocurrencies on the Indian economy. The committee suggested that cryptocurrencies be outlawed in India due to worries about money laundering and other illegal activity. The RBI issued a circular in 2018 instructing all regulated organisations to discontinue providing services to cryptocurrency exchanges and other businesses dealing with cryptocurrencies. The circular basically put an end to the cryptocurrency business in India, as exchanges were unable to function without access to banking services.

3. **Legal challenges and court battles**

   The RBI's circular led to a legal battle between the cryptocurrency industry and the government. Several cryptocurrency exchanges challenged the circular in court, arguing that it was unconstitutional and violated their rights to conduct business.

   In 2020, the Supreme Court of India ruled in favor of the cryptocurrency industry, overturning the RBI's circular. The ruling was a significant victory for the cryptocurrency industry, as it cleared the way for exchanges to resume operations.

4. **Status and the road ahead**

   Following the Supreme Court's ruling, the cryptocurrency industry in India has started to recover. Several exchanges have resumed operations, and there has been renewed interest in investing in cryptocurrencies.

   However, the road ahead for the cryptocurrency industry in India is still uncertain. While the Supreme Court's ruling was a significant victory, there is still no regulatory framework for the industry, and the government has not yet made its stance on cryptocurrencies clear.

The government launched the Cryptocurrency and Regulation of Official Digital Currency Bill in January 2021, with the goal of outlawing all private cryptocurrencies in India and creating a framework for the establishment of a digital currency issued by the RBI.

The measure has not yet been signed into law, and its destiny remains unknown. If enacted, it would be a severe blow to India's cryptocurrency economy, virtually outlawing all private coins.

Notwithstanding the uncertainties, cryptocurrencies have a big potential in India. India is a big prospective market for cryptocurrencies, with a population of over 1.3 billion people. As the country embraces new technology and grows more connected, cryptocurrencies are expected to play a growing role.

To summarise, the Bitcoin journey in India has been a rollercoaster ride, with several problems and impediments along the way. While the future of cryptocurrencies in India remains unknown, the technology's potential to revolutionise the country's economy is too great to ignore.

7.5 INDIA'S BLOCKCHAIN TECHNOLOGY JOURNEY

The journey of blockchain technology in India has been a fascinating one. While blockchain technology is still in its nascent stage in India, it has the potential to transform several industries and change the way transactions are conducted in the country [27].

1. **The early days**
   The early days of blockchain technology in India were characterised by experimentation and exploration. Several blockchain-based startups emerged in India, each trying to explore the potential of blockchain technology in different industries.

   One of the first blockchain-based startups in India was Auxesis, which was founded in 2014. The company focused on using blockchain technology to build decentralised applications and smart contracts. Another early player in the blockchain space was Primechain Technologies, which focused on providing blockchain-based solutions for the financial industry.
2. **The emergence of government support**
   Although blockchain technology was still in its early stages in India, the government began to express its support for it. The government established the Blockchain Committee of India in 2016 to investigate the possibilities of blockchain technology and to provide a regulatory framework for the business.

In 2017, the government launched the India Chain initiative, which was aimed at building a blockchain-based infrastructure for the country. The initiative was part of the government's broader Digital India campaign and was aimed at using blockchain technology to transform several industries, including finance, healthcare, and education.

3. **Adoption by the financial industry**

The banking sector was among the first in India to adopt blockchain technology. In 2016, many Indian banks, including ICICI Bank, HDFC Bank, and Axis Bank, began investigating the possibilities of blockchain technology.

In 2017, the State Bank of India (SBI), one of India's major banks, announced its participation in the Blockchain Consortium of India, an organisation dedicated to researching the possibilities of blockchain technology in the financial industry. The SBI began experimenting with blockchain technology for trade financing as well, and in 2018, it reported the successful completion of its first blockchain-based transaction.

The National Payments Corporation of India (NPCI) said in 2019 that it was investigating the possibilities of blockchain technology for its Unified Payments Interface digital payments network (UPI). The NPCI also unveiled Vajra, a blockchain-based platform focused at safeguarding digital transactions.

4. **Adoption by other industries**

While the banking industry was one of the first in India to adopt blockchain technology, other businesses have begun to explore the technology's possibilities. For example, the healthcare industry has begun to investigate the possibility of blockchain technology for storing and exchanging medical records.

The government has also begun to investigate the possibilities of blockchain technology in a variety of businesses. The government said in 2018 that it was investigating the possibility of blockchain technology for land registration, and in 2019, it unveiled IndiaStack, a blockchain-based platform aiming at offering a safe and decentralised platform for storing and exchanging personal data.

7.5.1 Challenges and the Road Ahead

While the growth of blockchain technology in India has been encouraging, there are still a number of issues that must be solved. One of the most significant difficulties is a lack of understanding about blockchain technology in India. While various businesses have begun to investigate the technology's possibilities, there is still a dearth of understanding about how the technology works and what its potential is.

Another issue is the absence of an industry regulatory structure. While the government has initiated various programmes to investigate the possibilities of blockchain technology, it remains unclear how the technology will be regulated.

Notwithstanding these obstacles, the future of blockchain technology in India is bright. The technology has the ability to disrupt various sectors and change the way business is done in the country. With government backing and growing understanding of the technology's potential, blockchain technology is poised to play a key part in the future of India's economy.

7.6 IMPACT OF BLOCKCHAIN TECHNOLOGY AND CRYPTOCURRENCY ON THE INDIAN ECONOMY

7.6.1 The Economic Effects of Blockchain Technology in India

Blockchain technology and cryptocurrencies have had a big influence on the Indian economy. India boasts the world's second-largest population and one of the fastest-growing economies. In numerous aspects, the use of blockchain technology and cryptocurrency has the potential to alter the Indian economy [28].

- **To begin with,** blockchain technology has the potential to decrease corruption and promote transparency in the government sector. The Indian government has already adopted various blockchain-based projects, such as the Indian Customs Single Window project, which aims to streamline the trading process and minimise corruption at customs. The application of blockchain technology in government procedures can help eliminate corruption and increase transparency.
- **Secondly,** cryptocurrencies can help increase financial inclusion in India. A large number of Indians are unbanked or underbanked, which means they do not have access to basic financial services. Cryptocurrencies can offer an alternative to traditional banking systems and enable individuals to participate in the economy without the need for a bank account. This can be particularly beneficial for people in rural areas or those who are unable to access traditional banking services.
- **Finally,** the usage of blockchain technology can assist lower transaction costs in India. Cross-border transactions are currently expensive due to the involvement of middlemen such as banks and payment gateways. Blockchain technology can eliminate the need for intermediaries, lowering transaction costs.

Blockchain technology has the ability to alter many sectors and has already begun to have an influence on the Indian economy in a variety of ways. The following are some of the ways blockchain technology has influenced the Indian economy:

1. **Improved transparency and efficiency in supply chain management**
   Supply chain management is one of the key applications of blockchain technology in India. It is now feasible to follow the transit of goods from the manufacturer to the final customer in a transparent and efficient manner using blockchain. This has not only helped to reduce cases of fraud and counterfeiting, but it has also enhanced the supply chain's general efficiency.
2. **Increased security in financial transactions**
   Blockchain technology has also helped in increasing the security of financial transactions in India. With the help of blockchain, it is now possible to conduct financial transactions in a decentralised and secure manner, without the need for intermediaries such as banks. This has not only made financial transactions faster and more efficient but has also reduced the instances of fraud and cyber-attacks.
3. **Reduction in operational costs**
   The reduction in operating expenses is another big consequence of blockchain technology on the Indian economy. Blockchain technology has helped some firms in India reduce operating expenses by removing intermediaries and automating various operations.

7.6.2 The Effect of Cryptocurrencies on the Indian Economy

The impact of cryptocurrency on the Indian economy has been significant, and it has already started to change the way people conduct transactions in India. Some of the ways in which cryptocurrency has impacted the Indian economy are [29, 30]:

1. **Increased financial inclusion**
   Increased financial inclusion is one of the most significant effects of Bitcoin on the Indian economy. Those who do not have access to regular banking services may now perform financial transactions with the aid of cryptocurrencies. This has not only boosted financial inclusion, but it has also helped to reduce fraud and theft.
2. **Increased investment opportunities**
   Cryptocurrency has also created several investment opportunities for people in India. With the help of cryptocurrency, people can now invest in digital assets and participate in initial coin offerings (ICOs). This has not only created new investment opportunities but has also provided a new asset class for people to diversify their investment portfolios.

3. **Reduction in transaction costs**
   Another significant impact of cryptocurrency on the Indian economy is the reduction in transaction costs. With the help of cryptocurrency, it is now possible to conduct transactions in a decentralised and secure manner, without the need for intermediaries such as banks. This has not only made transactions faster and more efficient but has also reduced the transaction costs for people in India.

7.6.3 Impact on Different Sectors of the Economy

The influence of blockchain technology and cryptocurrencies is visible not only in the broader economy, but also in several sectors of the economy.

1. **Banking and Finance**
   One of the industries that can profit the most from blockchain technology and cryptocurrencies is banking and finance. Blockchain technology can help cut transaction costs and time while also improving financial transaction security. Cryptocurrencies can make cross-border payments faster and cheaper, making international transactions more accessible and economical.
2. **Healthcare**
   Blockchain technology can help the healthcare industry in a variety of ways. Blockchain can help maintain a secure and decentralised database of medical records that can be accessed by healthcare providers with the patient's consent. This can help reduce the risk of medical identity theft and enable faster and more accurate diagnosis and treatment.
3. **Supply Chain Management**
   Blockchain technology can assist boost openness and accountability in supply chain management. Blockchain technology may be used to maintain a decentralised and immutable database of supply chain information, such as raw material origin, transit details, and product information. This can assist decrease the risk of fraud and increase product traceability.
4. **Real Estate**
   The adoption of blockchain technology for property transactions can improve the real estate industry. Blockchain technology has the potential to facilitate safe and transparent property transactions, such as the sale and transfer of property ownership. This can assist in lowering the danger of fraud as well as the time and expense of real estate transactions.

7.7 ADVANTAGES OF BLOCKCHAIN TECHNOLOGY AND CRYPTOCURRENCY FOR THE INDIAN ECONOMY

Blockchain technology and cryptocurrency is becoming increasingly popular in various industries across the globe. These technologies have immense potential to revolutionise the Indian economy by offering several advantages. Some of the benefits of blockchain technology and cryptocurrencies to the Indian economy are [31]:

1. **Decentralised System**
   The decentralised system provided by blockchain technology and Bitcoin is one of the most significant advantages. This decentralised approach eliminates the need for a central authority and lets users to transfer payments directly to one another. The elimination of middlemen in financial transactions makes the process more efficient, cost-effective, and faster. This can help reduce corruption and fraud, which is prevalent in centralised systems, making the Indian economy more secure.

2. **Improved Payment Systems**
   Blockchain technology and cryptocurrency offer a more efficient and cost-effective payment system. With the traditional payment systems in India, there is often a delay in funds transfer, high transaction fees, and security issues. Blockchain technology and cryptocurrency address these issues by facilitating quick, secure, and low-cost payments. This is especially beneficial for small businesses and entrepreneurs who can save a significant amount of money on transaction fees.

3. **Increased Transparency**
   Another advantage of blockchain technology and cryptocurrency is increased transparency. Because blockchain technology employs a distributed ledger system, every transaction is accessible to all network users. Every transaction is recorded and validated as a result, making the system more transparent and trustworthy. Transparency can help eliminate corruption and boost confidence in the Indian economy.

4. **Reduced Transaction Costs**
   Traditional payment systems have high transaction costs, which can make it difficult for small businesses and entrepreneurs to succeed. Blockchain technology and cryptocurrency offer a more cost-effective payment system, with significantly lower transaction fees. This can help businesses save money, making them more profitable, and allowing them to invest in other areas of their business.

5. **Improved Record-Keeping**
   Blockchain technology provides an immutable and tamper-proof record-keeping system. This means that every transaction is recorded and verified, ensuring that the data is accurate and reliable. This can assist to minimise fraud risk and promote openness in the Indian economy.

6. **Enhanced Security**
   Blockchain technology and cryptocurrency offer enhanced security. Because there is no single point of failure with blockchain technology, it is more secure than centralised systems. Furthermore, cryptocurrencies

are kept in digital wallets that are protected by cryptographic keys, making it impossible for hackers to steal the cash. Increased security can serve to boost trust in the Indian economy, attracting more investment, and propelling the country forward.

In conclusion, blockchain technology and cryptocurrency has several advantages that can benefit the Indian economy. These technologies can offer a more cost-effective, efficient, and secure payment system, increased transparency, improved record-keeping, and enhanced security. By leveraging these advantages, India can further promote economic growth, attract investment, and increase entrepreneurship opportunities.

7.8 REGULATORY FRAMEWORK AND POLICY INITIATIVES FOR BLOCKCHAIN AND CRYPTOCURRENCIES IN INDIA

The Indian government has recognised the importance of blockchain technology and cryptocurrencies and has taken various measures to regulate and promote their use in the country. The Reserve Bank of India (RBI) and the Securities and Exchange Board of India (SEBI) largely oversee the regulatory environment for cryptocurrencies in India (SEBI) [32, 33].

1. The RBI issued a circular in April 2018 barring banks and financial institutions from providing services to individuals or companies dealing with virtual currency. The crypto sector and stakeholders were outraged by this action, prompting a legal challenge in the Supreme Court. The Supreme Court removed the prohibition in March 2020, ruling that the RBI's circular was unconstitutional and infringed the basic freedom to engage in any trade or enterprise.
2. At that time, the Indian government has been working to develop a regulatory framework that balances innovation and investor protection. The Ministry of Finance established a committee in 2019 to investigate the possibilities of blockchain technology and cryptocurrencies and give suggestions for their implementation. The committee advocated for the creation of a legal framework for cryptocurrencies, claiming that they had the potential to become a significant asset class.
3. The Supreme Court overturned the prohibition on cryptocurrencies in March 2020, and the government has subsequently taken numerous efforts to regulate their usage. The Ministry of Finance has proposed the Cryptocurrency and Regulation of Official Digital Currency Bill, 2021, to govern cryptocurrencies in India. The law proposes a prohibition on all private cryptocurrencies and the establishment of a framework for the development of an official digital currency issued by the RBI. The measure is now being debated in parliament.

4. In addition to the legislative framework, the Indian government has promoted the adoption of blockchain technology through several programmes. In 2018, the policy think tank, NITI Aayog, published a paper on the potential of blockchain technology for the Indian economy. The research advocated for the development of a blockchain infrastructure to facilitate safe and transparent transactions, particularly in land registration, supply chain management, and identity management.

5. The Indian government has been investigating the application of blockchain technology in a variety of industries, including banking, healthcare, and education. The National Health Authority (NHA) launched the NDHM blockchain-based system in 2020 to provide citizens with a secure and interoperable health data platform. The Indian School Certificate Examination (ISCE) board has also begun to use blockchain technology to give pupils with secure and tamper-proof certificates.

Finally, the Indian government has realised the promise of blockchain technology and cryptocurrencies and has implemented a variety of policies to regulate and encourage their usage in the country. The legislative environment for cryptocurrencies is still growing, and the proposed measure is anticipated to clarify their use. The government's measures to encourage the use of blockchain technology in many areas are likely to benefit the Indian economy.

7.9 BENEFITS TO BUSINESSES

In recent years, blockchain technology and cryptocurrency has gained widespread attention and adoption, with many businesses around the world exploring ways to leverage these technologies to gain a competitive edge. India, in particular, is an exciting market for businesses looking to tap into the potential of these new technologies, as the country has a rapidly growing economy and a large, tech-savvy population.

Benefits of blockchain technology for businesses:

1. **Increased security:** Blockchain technology is built on a decentralised, secure ledger system that makes it virtually impossible for data to be tampered with or hacked. This can provide businesses with increased security when it comes to sensitive financial transactions, and can help protect against fraud and cyber-attacks.

2. **Improved efficiency:** Blockchain technology can streamline many business processes, such as supply chain management and financial transactions, by removing intermediaries and reducing the time and cost involved in these processes. This can lead to increased efficiency and lower costs for businesses.

3. **Increased transparency:** Blockchain technology provides an unprecedented level of transparency, making it easy for businesses to track their transactions and see the entire history of a transaction. This can help businesses make more informed decisions and can increase trust and accountability in the business.

Benefits of cryptocurrency for businesses:

1. **Lower transaction fees:** Cryptocurrency transactions typically come with lower transaction fees compared to traditional fiat currency transactions, as they can bypass intermediaries and are processed directly between two parties. This can help businesses save money and increase their bottom line.
2. **Increased accessibility:** Cryptocurrency can be used by anyone with an internet connection, making it a global, accessible currency that can be used by businesses to reach a wider audience. This can open up new markets and revenue streams for businesses.
3. **Faster transactions:** Cryptocurrency transactions are processed in real-time and can be completed within minutes, compared to traditional fiat currency transactions that can take several days. This can help businesses improve their cash flow and make quicker, more informed decisions.

To summarise, blockchain technology and cryptocurrencies have the potential to drastically change the Indian business environment and offer businesses with a competitive advantage. Businesses may improve their security, efficiency, transparency, and accessibility by embracing these technologies, allowing them to expand and flourish in today's fast-paced, global market.

7.10 STYLES OF TRANSACTIONS

7.10.1 Evolution in India

India has a rich history of various styles of transactions, from bartering to the use of precious metals as currency. The British introduction of paper currency in the nineteenth century signalled the commencement of modern-day transaction procedures in India. The Reserve Bank of India (RBI) was created in 1935 and was given responsibility for issuing and administering the Indian rupee.

Over time, traditional banking services such as cheques, demand drafts, and wire transfers became prevalent in India. The introduction of credit and debit cards in the 1980s and 1990s revolutionised the Indian payment system, making it more convenient and secure. In recent years, digital payment methods such as internet banking, mobile wallets, and Unified Payment Interface (UPI) have become increasingly popular.

The National Payments Corporation of India (NPCI) established the UPI system in 2016 and it has since become the primary way of digital payment in India. UPI enables consumers to transfer money between bank accounts quickly by utilising a virtual payment address or cellphone number. It has also made it possible to integrate several payment systems into a single platform, making it easier for consumers to access and utilise various payment methods.

7.11 IMPACT ON TRANSACTIONS IN INDIA

The rise of blockchain technology and cryptocurrencies has the potential to transform India's transaction ecosystem. Blockchain technology offers a decentralised and secure way to verify and store transactions, eliminating the need for intermediaries like banks and financial institutions. Cryptocurrencies like Bitcoin, Ethereum, and Ripple can be used to make transactions securely and quickly, without the need for traditional payment methods.

Nevertheless, adoption of blockchain technology and cryptocurrency has been gradual in India, with the Reserve Bank of India voicing worries about the security and regulation of such transactions. The RBI barred banks and financial organisations from trading in cryptocurrencies in 2018, thereby restricting their use in India.

Yet, several Indian firms are investigating the use of blockchain technology to enhance transactional processes. Tata Consultancy Services, for example, has created a blockchain-based platform for trade finance transactions. Quartz is a platform that promises to simplify commercial transactions by providing a safe and transparent means to share trade papers.

1. **Improved Security:** One of the most important effects of blockchain technology and cryptocurrencies on modern-day transaction methods on the Indian subcontinent is increased transaction security. Blockchain technology is built on cryptographic principles, which make it virtually impossible for hackers to tamper with the data stored on the block-chain. Cryptocurrency transactions are also secured using advanced cryptographic techniques, which make them more secure than traditional methods of payment.

2. **Increased Efficiency:** Blockchain technology and cryptocurrency has also increased the efficiency of modern-day transactions in the Indian subcontinent. Transactions on a blockchain can be completed in real-time, which eliminates the need for intermediaries such as banks or financial institutions. Bitcoin transactions are also speedier and more efficient than traditional payment methods, which might take several days.

3. **Financial Inclusion:** Another significant impact of blockchain technology and cryptocurrency on modern-day styles of transactions in the Indian subcontinent is the potential for financial inclusion. Since cryptocurrency transactions may be completed by anybody with an internet connection, those who do not have access to traditional financial institutions can participate in the global economy.
4. **Reduced Transaction Costs:** Blockchain technology and cryptocurrency has also led to a reduction in transaction costs. A network of nodes validates transactions on a blockchain, eliminating the need for intermediaries like as banks or financial organisations. This reduces the transaction costs associated with traditional methods of payment, which often include fees charged by intermediaries.
5. **Challenges and Limitations:** Despite the potential benefits of blockchain technology and cryptocurrencies, a number of problems and restrictions remain. One of the most significant issues is a lack of regulatory clarity, which has created anxiety among firms and investors. The existing blockchain infrastructure may not be able to manage the amount of transactions necessary to operate a global economy.

In conclusion, blockchain technology and cryptocurrency has had a significant impact on modern-day styles of transactions in the Indian subcontinent. These technologies have improved the security, efficiency, and inclusivity of financial transactions, while also reducing transaction costs. However, significant obstacles and limits must yet be addressed, notably in the areas of regulatory clarity and scalability.

Notwithstanding these obstacles, it is apparent that blockchain technology and cryptocurrencies have the potential to transform the way we conduct financial transactions in India and elsewhere. Advances in technology and evolving customer requirements have fueled the growth of transaction systems in India. Use of digital payment systems such as UPI has made transactions easier for consumers and cleared the door for the integration of blockchain technology and cryptocurrencies in India.

While blockchain technology and cryptocurrencies are still in their early stages in India, they have the potential to alter the transactional landscape. It is crucial for policymakers to address concerns related to security and regulation to enable the seamless integration of these technologies in India's transaction systems.

7.12 CHALLENGES

Blockchain technology and cryptocurrency has emerged as disruptive technologies that can potentially transform various industries, including finance, supply chain, and healthcare. However, these technologies face several challenges in the Indian economy, which could limit their widespread adoption. In this research, we will look at the issues that blockchain technology and cryptocurrencies are facing in the Indian economy [34]. While blockchain technology and cryptocurrencies have had a huge influence on the Indian economy and several industries, there are some difficulties that must be solved.

As blockchain technology is being utilised in a variety of businesses, cryptocurrency has evolved as a digital asset that can be swapped decentralisedly. India is no exception to this transformation, and the introduction of blockchain technology and cryptocurrency has had a tremendous influence on its economy and transaction practises.

The influence of blockchain technology and cryptocurrencies is a vivid illustration of how the world is presently experiencing a technological revolution.

1. **Regulatory challenges:** One of the primary challenges that blockchain technology and cryptocurrency face in the Indian economy is regulatory challenges. The Reserve Bank of India (RBI) has banned banks and financial institutions from dealing in cryptocurrencies. Moreover, the government is yet to come up with clear regulations on cryptocurrencies, which has created a regulatory vacuum in the country. The absence of a regulatory framework has discouraged many investors from investing in cryptocurrencies, limiting the growth potential of this market.

2. **Security concerns:** Blockchain technology is widely regarded as secure, and it uses cryptography to protect data. However, there have been instances of security breaches in the past, and it is important to ensure that the blockchain networks are secure. In the case of cryptocurrencies, the exchanges that facilitate the buying and selling of cryptocurrencies are vulnerable to hacking attacks, and several exchanges have been hacked in the past. These security concerns have led to a lack of trust among investors and has limited the growth of the cryptocurrency market.

3. **Lack of awareness and education:** Another significant challenge that blockchain technology and cryptocurrency face in the Indian economy is the lack of awareness and education about these technologies. Many people in India are still unaware of blockchain technology and cryptocurrency and do not understand the benefits that these technologies can offer. Because of this lack of understanding, these technologies have not been widely adopted, and it is critical to educate the public about the potential benefits of blockchain technology and cryptocurrencies.

4. **Lack of infrastructure:** To operate the network, blockchain technology needs a substantial amount of computer power, which might be an issue in the Indian economy. Many parts of the country still lack the

necessary infrastructure to support blockchain networks, which can limit the growth potential of these technologies. Similarly, there is a lack of cryptocurrency exchanges in the country, which makes it difficult for people to buy and sell cryptocurrencies.

5. **Volatility:** Cryptocurrencies are notorious for their volatility, which can be a problem for investors. The value of cryptocurrencies can fluctuate rapidly, and this makes it difficult for investors to make informed decisions about their investments. This volatility can also lead to a lack of trust in cryptocurrencies and limit their adoption in the Indian economy.

6. **Integration with existing systems:** Integrating blockchain technology and cryptocurrency with existing systems can be a significant challenge in the Indian economy. Many existing systems in the country are based on traditional technology, and it can be difficult to integrate blockchain technology with these systems. Similarly, many financial institutions in the country still rely on traditional banking systems, which can make it difficult for them to adopt cryptocurrency.

In conclusion, blockchain technology and cryptocurrency has the potential to transform various industries, including finance, and supply chain. However, these technologies face several challenges in the Indian economy, including regulatory challenges, security concerns, lack of awareness and education, lack of infrastructure, volatility, and integration with existing systems. It is important for the Indian government and businesses to address these challenges to ensure the widespread adoption of blockchain technology and cryptocurrency in the country.

7.13 SUGGESTIONS

1. **Educating the Public:** Given that blockchain and cryptocurrency are relatively new technologies, there is a need for increased public education and awareness. This could be achieved through workshops, seminars, and other forms of education aimed at both the general public and business owners. Informing people on the potential benefits and hazards of blockchain and cryptocurrencies might aid in their adoption.

2. **Government Regulations:** The Reserve Bank of India (RBI) has issued multiple cautions concerning the usage of blockchain and cryptocurrencies by the Indian government. However, there is a need for clear regulatory frameworks that would provide legal certainty and security for businesses and individuals. The government should collaborate with industry experts and stakeholders to develop appropriate regulations that balance innovation with investor protection.

3. **Promoting Innovation:** The government should encourage research and development in blockchain and cryptocurrency by providing funding, tax incentives, and other forms of support. This would help to promote innovation in the industry and increase India's competitiveness in the global market. Encouraging the development of blockchain and cryptocurrency start-ups and investing in blockchain-based projects could help to create jobs and boost economic growth.

4. **Collaboration:** Cooperation among stakeholders such as the government, corporations, and academic institutions is essential for the effective adoption and implementation of blockchain and cryptocurrencies in India. A collaborative approach could help to address issues such as lack of technical expertise, infrastructure, and regulatory uncertainty. It could also help to create partnerships and collaborations that would foster innovation and growth in the industry.

5. **Bridging the Digital Divide:** Lastly, in order for blockchain and cryptocurrencies to have a meaningful influence on the Indian economy, the digital gap must be addressed. The government should invest in digital infrastructure, including internet connectivity, to enable more people to access and use blockchain and cryptocurrency. Promoting financial inclusion through blockchain and cryptocurrency could help to boost economic growth and improve living standards in India.

In conclusion, the adoption and implementation of blockchain and cryptocurrency in the Indian economy present a range of challenges and opportunities. However, with appropriate regulations, public education, collaboration, and innovation, blockchain and cryptocurrency could have a positive impact on the Indian economy and the lives of its citizens.

7.14 WAYS FORWARD

Moving forward, there are several steps that can be taken to better understand the impact of blockchain and cryptocurrency on the Indian economy and style of transactions.

1. **Firstly,** more thorough and trustworthy data on the use of cryptocurrencies and blockchain technologies in India is required. This may be accomplished by conducting surveys and interviews with organisations and individuals that use these technologies on a regular basis. Additionally, regulatory bodies in India can work with industry stakeholders to develop reporting standards and frameworks that help to track the use of these technologies.

2. **Secondly,** there is a need to improve awareness and education around blockchain and cryptocurrency in India. This can be done through

government-led initiatives and programs that aim to educate individuals and businesses on the benefits and risks associated with these
technologies. Additionally, industry stakeholders can work together to
create more accessible and user-friendly platforms for buying, selling,
and trading cryptocurrencies.

3. **Thirdly,** there is a need for the Indian government to provide more
regulatory clarity and guidance on the use of blockchain and cryptocurrency. This can be achieved by working with industry stakeholders
and experts to develop comprehensive and flexible regulatory frameworks that balance innovation and consumer protection. Additionally,
the government can consider providing tax incentives and other forms
of support to encourage the growth and adoption of these technologies
in India.

4. **Fourthly,** there is a need for more research and development on the use
of blockchain and cryptocurrency in specific sectors of the Indian economy, such as agriculture, healthcare, and logistics. This can be achieved
by funding academic and industry research projects that explore the
potential use cases of these technologies in different sectors. This will
help to identify new opportunities for innovation and growth in the
Indian economy.

Finally, various actions may be made to better comprehend and exploit
the potential of blockchain and cryptocurrencies in the Indian economy. By
improving data collection, increasing awareness and education, providing
regulatory clarity and guidance, and funding research and development,
India can position itself as a leader in the global blockchain and cryptocurrency market.

7.15 CONCLUSION

In recent years, blockchain technology and cryptocurrency has gained significant traction globally, including in India. The potential of these technologies to revolutionise the way transactions are conducted has sparked much
interest and debate. In this paper, we looked at the influence of blockchain
and cryptocurrencies on the Indian economy and transaction style.

The capacity of blockchain technology to provide a secure and tamper-
proof platform for digital transactions is one of the most important implications of blockchain technology on the Indian economy. The decentralised
nature of blockchain technology means that transactions can be conducted
without the need for intermediaries, reducing transaction costs and increasing transparency. This has the potential to revolutionise the way businesses
operate in India and has already shown significant benefits in the banking
and finance sectors.

The emergence of cryptocurrencies, on the other hand, have had a more mixed impact on the Indian economy. While some have embraced cryptocurrencies as a new investment opportunity, others remain cautious due to concerns about volatility and the lack of government regulation. The Central Bank of India is likewise concerned about the hazards presented by cryptocurrencies and has taken efforts to control their usage.

Another impact of blockchain and cryptocurrency on the Indian economy has been their potential to promote financial inclusion. With a significant portion of India's population still unbanked, the ability to conduct digital transactions using blockchain technology and cryptocurrency has the potential to provide greater financial access to many. This is especially true in rural regions where traditional financial services are scarce.

In terms of transaction speed and efficiency, blockchain technology and cryptocurrencies outperform traditional techniques. Businesses may save time and money by doing transactions virtually quickly. This has been especially helpful in the supply chain and logistics industries, where the introduction of blockchain technology has resulted in increased transparency and traceability.

In conclusion, blockchain technology and cryptocurrency has the potential to revolutionise the Indian economy and the style of transactions. While there are still concerns and uncertainties surrounding their use, the benefits they offer in terms of security, transparency, efficiency, and financial inclusion cannot be ignored. It would be interesting to observe how these technologies impact the future of the Indian economy and transaction style as they grow and achieve greater use.

REFERENCES

1. Wajde Baiod, Janet Light and Aniket Mahanti, "Blockchain Technology and Its Applications Across Multiple Domains: A Survey," Journal of International Technology and Information Management, 2021, 29(4), Article 4. doi: https://doi.org/10.58729/1941-6679.1482
2. T. Watanabe, S. Fujimura, T. Nakajima and K. Nakamura, "Blockchain Contract: Securing a Virtual Asset with a Decentralized Method," Proceedings of the 2015 ACM Sixth International Conference on Future Energy Systems, 2015, pp. 1–7.
3. S. Mukhopadhyay, B. Sikdar and N. Ganguly, "A Survey on Cryptocurrency," International Journal of Computer Applications, 2016, 145(11), 1–6.
4. Z. Zheng, S. Xie, H. Dai, X. Chen and H. Wang, "An Overview of Blockchain Technology: Architecture, Consensus, and Future Trends," 2017 IEEE International Congress on Big Data (BigData Congress), 2017, pp. 557–564. IEEE, doi: 10.1109/BigDataCongress.2017.85
5. H. Hassani, X. Huang and E. Silva, "Cryptocurrency and Big Data: An Interdisciplinary Approach," Journal of Big Data, 2018, 5(1), 1–22.

6. Y. Wanga, X. Bai and Q. Luo, "Blockchain Technology and Its Applications in the Intellectual Property Field," Journal of Intellectual Property Rights, 2019, 24(1), 13–24.
7. L. Ante, "Blockchain Technology from a Business and Economics Perspective: A Literature Review," Business Horizons, 2020, 63(3), 335–347, doi: 10.1016/j.bushor.2019.12.002
8. Q. Wang, Y. Liu, X. Huang and W. Liu, "Bibliometric Analysis of Blockchain Research: A Web of Science-Based Exploration," Journal of Cleaner Production, 2021, 315, 128231, doi: 10.1016/j.jclepro.2021.128231
9. S. Alghamdi and S. Almuhammadi, "The Future of Cryptocurrency Blockchains in the Quantum Era," 2021 IEEE International Conference on Blockchain (Blockchain), 2021, pp. 544–551, doi: 10.1109/Blockchain53845.2021.00082.
10. R. Shakya, K. Bhandari, S. Shrestha and S. Shakya, "Exploring the Scope of Blockchain-Based Cryptocurrency in India," International Journal of Advanced Science and Technology, 2021, 30(3), 2512–2522.
11. J. Guild, "FinTech and Financial Inclusion: A Framework for Regulatory Response," Hastings Business Law Journal, 2017, 13(2), 157–182.
12. R. K. Raj and A. Upadhyay, "Financial Technology (Fintech) and Financial Inclusion in India," Journal of Financial Services Research, 2020, 57(3), 299–322.
13. R. Kaur, H. Kaur and A. Dhir, "Digitalization of Financial Services in India: Implications for Financial Inclusion and Economic Growth," Journal of Public Affairs, 2021, e2668.
14. M. Jakhiya, A. Bhatt and R. Tripathi, "Mobile Payments in India: Growth, Innovation and the Role of AI," In R. Tripathi, S. Mishra, R. Kapoor and J. Gao (Eds.), Intelligent Systems Design and Applications (pp. 479–486). Springer International Publishing, 2020.
15. Kshetri, Nir. "1 Blockchain's Roles in Meeting Key Supply Chain Management Objectives," International Journal of Information Management, 2018, 39(2018), 80–89.
16. M. Kashyap and V. Beyadwal, "Digital Currency: Consumer Behaviour and Legal Status in India," Journal of Advanced Research in Dynamical and Control Systems, 2019, 11(Special Issue 4), 217–224.
17. A. Kumar and P. Swathy, "Cryptocurrencies: A Review of the Literature and Its Legal Status in India," International Journal of Engineering and Advanced Technology (IJEAT), 2019, 9(1), 5101–5109.
18. Leenata J. Parab and Prashant P. Nitnaware, "Investigating Existence of Cryptocurrency Over Traditional Investment in India-A Comparative study," International Journal of All Research Education and Scientific Methods (IJARESM), 2022, 10(1), ISSN: 2455-6211.
19. A. Agrawal, N. Yadav and K. Kumawat, "An Overview of Cryptocurrency: A Decentralized Digital Currency," 2020 11th International Conference on Computing, Communication and Networking Technologies (ICCCNT), IEEE, 2020, pp. 1–6.
20. S. Kashyap and K. Chand, "Cryptocurrency: A Study of Its Advantages and Disadvantages," International Journal of Engineering and Technology, 2018, 7(2.34), 25–28.

21. R. More and R. Aslekar, "Challenges and Opportunities of Digitization in Agriculture: A Review," Agricultural Water Management, 2022, 255, 107132.
22. S. Wang, Y. Zhang, C. Li, P. Li and X. Wang, "A Parallel Healthcare System Framework Using Blockchain-Based Consortium Blockchain for Secure Storage and Medical Data Sharing," Journal of Medical Systems, 2018, 42(7), 121, doi: 10.1007/s10916-018-0973-5.
23. Z. Ziyi Li, L. Liu, Y. Zhou and J. Zhang, "Blockchain-Based Education Credentialing: Challenges, Solutions, and Future Directions," Educational Technology Research and Development, 2022, 13(2), 1–25.
24. N. Hamouda, M. Nassar and M. M. Salama, "Blockchain-Based Interconnected Microgrid Energy Trading with Self-Benefit-Driven Agents," IEEE Transactions on Industrial Informatics, 2021, 17(8), 5645–5656, doi: 10.1109/TII.2021.3064645.
25. Shukla, Varun, Manoj Kumar Misra, and Atul Chaturvedi, "Journey of Cryptocurrency in India in View of Financial Budget 2022–23," arXiv preprint arXiv:2203.12606 (2022).
26. Arora, Gaurav, "RBI and the Indian Crypto Industry," Available at SSRN 3733291 (2020).
27. Kumar Bhardwaj, Amit, Arunesh Garg and Yuvraj Gajpal, "Determinants of Blockchain Technology Adoption in Supply Chains by Small and Medium Enterprises (SMEs) in India," Mathematical Problems in Engineering, 2021, 2021, 1–14.
28. G. Sankaranarayanan and Kamal Kumar Rajagopalan, "Usage of Blockchain Technology in Banking Sector and Its Implication on Indian Economy," Alochana Chakra Journal, 2020, 9(5), 7383–7389.
29. Arvind Kumar Singh and Karan Veer Singh, "Cryptocurrency in India-Its Effect and Future on Economy with Special Reference to Bitcoin, International Journal of Research in Economics and Social Sciences (ILJRESS), 2018, 8(3), 115–126.
30. Abhinav Pal, Chandan Kumar Tiwari and Aastha Behl, "Blockchain Technology in Financial Services: A Comprehensive Review of the Literature," Journal of Global Operations and Strategic Sourcing, 2021, 14(1), 61–80.
31. Malaika, Rana. "Economic Opportunities for Digital India-Centralizing it the Decentralized Way," IJCSPUB-International Journal of Current Science (IJCSPUB), 2022, 12(4), 930–940.
32. Soujaatyaa Roy, "The Impact of Blockchain Technology on Financial Regulations and Legal Frameworks," Available at SSRN 4521762, 2023.
33. Devkant Kala and Dhani Shanker Chaubey, "Cryptocurrency Adoption and Continuance Intention Among Indians: Moderating Role of Perceived Government Control," Digital Policy, Regulation and Governance, 2023, 25(3), 288–304.
34. Diego Valdeolmillos, Yeray Mezquita, Alfonso González-Briones, Javier Prieto and Juan Manuel Corchado, "Blockchain Technology: A Review of the Current Challenges of Cryptocurrency," In Blockchain and Applications: International Congress, pp. 153–160. Springer International Publishing, 2020.

Chapter 8

Analysis of Covid-19 Second Wave in India and Prediction Using Machine Learning Models

K. Ghousiya Begum

School of Electrical & Electronics Engineering, SASTRA University,
Thanjavur 613 401, India

8.1 INTRODUCTION

Supervised machine learning (ML) finds its application in solving many intricate real-time tasks such as patient sickness prediction, medical diagnosis, climate modeling, natural language processing (NLP), autonomous vehicle (AV), business applications, robotic applications, and speech and image processing. Artificial intelligence (AI) were also used in anomaly detection and has more impact on our society (Rani et al. 2022; Rajendra et al. 2022). Unlike conventional algorithms, ML algorithms learn by themselves using the trial-and-error method and following the programming instructions (Rustam et al. 2020). The other most significant area where ML can be applied is in forecasting (Talkhi et al. 2021), where the course of actions is predicted in areas like disease prognosis, weather forecasting, and stock market forecasting. The appropriate models which suit this application are the neural network and regression models and these are used to predict the patient's condition in the future if they have a specific disease (Nilashi et al. 2017). Many research works have been undergone to forecast the various diseases using ML techniques (Verma et al. 2019) namely, prediction of breast cancer (Gupta and Garg 2020), coronary artery disease (Gárate-Escamila et al. 2020), lung infections (Bharati et al. 2020), and cardiovascular disease (Faiayaz Waris and Koteeswaran 2021). Recently, there is also research works executed to forecast Covid-19 confirmed cases, outbreaks, and early response (Petropoulos et al. 2022; Jain et al. 2021; Sharma and Nigam 2020; Sujath et al. 2020; Mohan et al. 2021; Senapati et al. 2021; Achterberg et al. 2020) which help in making decisions quickly to manage these diseases effectually. The changes in the predictability of susceptible-infected-removed (SIR) model using ML models have been discussed in (Kondapalli et al. 2022). The regression models were developed to predict the total number of discharges and death predictions of each state in India and Union territories (Meenu Gupta Rachna Jain 2021). The SARS-CoV-2 (named Covid-19 by WHO) is a threat to mankind, leading to a severe respiratory disorder, multi-organ failure, and finally death within a

DOI: 10.1201/9781003329947-8

very short period. In the second wave of Covid-19, the confirmed cases and death rates are more and the most stimulating feature is that the mutant virus spreads rapidly compared to the first wave as the infected person is asymptomatic. The second wave is a big challenge to the healthcare system and the hospitals are struggling to cope with the increasing demand for critical drugs and oxygen supplies, as infected cases are rising day by day. Moreover, this second wave seems to have more impact on young people between 21 to 40 years of age as it is virulent and dangerous. Within a week of getting infected, the patients ended up with severe lung infections and they required constant oxygen supply. During post-recovery, the patients infected by this mutated strain of the virus were also having some side effects. The second wave gives a warning sign to India and its spread is not uniform in all states. But still, due to the lockdown in May and June 2021, the rate of decline of cases seems to be faster in the second wave compared to the first wave as reported in BBC news. Even though the SUTRA model and other research work envisage that daily infected case rates would continue to decline asymptotically in July, they cannot be overlooked (Kavitha et al. 2021).

The existing literature studies deal with the forecasting of only confirmed cases and deaths, or prediction based on specific B-cells datasets using ensemble techniques, or forecasting using complex models like ARIMA, Holt-Winters, SIR, MLP, Vector Autoregression or LSTM models where the prediction is done for a limited period (Panda 2020; Sujath et al. 2020). A large dataset is needed for precise prediction. Most of this has been done to determine the trend of the first wave of Covid-19 and that, too, related to countries like China, Netherlands, Turkey and Nigeria (Busari and Samson 2022). So, to forecast the current scenario of the second wave of Covid-19 infected cases in India, an attempt has been made to design a simple forecasting scheme for the COVID-19 trend using a large dataset (around 15 months). The prediction is done for the number of active cases, cured cases, death cases, and confirmed cases in India. This forecasting task has been accounted for as a regression problem in this current research. So, the work is based on supervised ML regression models namely, multiple linear regression (LR) as it is effective in forecasting the infected cases of the corona, cured cases, and death (Kondapalli et al. 2022; Mojjada et al. 2020). The responses or outputs are the sequences of training samples with the values shifted by a one-time step. Here, the model forecasts the values of future time steps. At every time step of the input sequence, the ML model studies to forecast the value of the next time step. Other supervised ML models such as DTR and SVM are considered for comparison purposes. The learning models are trained using the analytics of the Covid-19 patient dataset of India. Before training, the data must be pre-processed and divided into two sets: the training set (75% records) and the testing set (25% records) which is used for forecasting. The performance of the applied model is validated in terms of cost functions or measures like mean absolute error (MAE), mean square error (MSE), R-squared score (R^2 score), and root mean square error (RMSE). The paper is framed using six sections. Section 8.1 is the introduction; section 8.2 explicates the exploration and explanation of the dataset considered in this work, the ML methods applied, and the various cost functions required to estimate the performance of models, and section 8.3 displays the results and summarizes the manuscripts and section 8.4 concludes the study.

8.2 MATERIALS AND METHODS

This section explicates the data description, the ML models deployed in forecasting the required information and the performance metrics to assess the deployed models.

8.2.1 Data Analysis and Exploration

The analytics of the second wave of the Covid-19 dataset of India pertaining to the number of patients belonging to confirmed cases, cured cases, death, and active cases have been taken from the Worldometer site. Worldometer's Covid-19 data is reliable and used by Johns Hopkins CSSE, The New York Times, Business Insider, Financial Times and many others. The complete.xlsx file of India and state-wise report consisting of the date and the exact numbers of patients belonging to different categories have been considered.

The dataset has the above information from 12 March 2020 to 05 June 2021. Here, the active cases are the number of recovered cases and deaths subtracted from the number of confirmed cases. The active case can be either a "confirmed case" or a "probable case" that is, the possibility of being currently infected. Figure 8.1 displays the ten most affected states in India due to the second wave of Covid-19 taken from the Government of India portal and numbers displayed in Table 8.1.

To analyze and forecast the related trend of the second wave of Covid-19, the following steps (Figure 8.2) are involved: 1) Collection of datasets from Worldometer or any other repositories, 2) Pre-processing, training, and testing of collected sample datasets, 3) Apply, train, and select a suitable model to forecast the second wave of Covid-19 data trends, 4) Validate the performance of the model, 5) Forecast the final second wave of Covid-19 data trends. The following has been shown as a flowchart in Figure 8.3. The dataset plays a decisive role in the exact prediction of the second wave of Covid-19 cases. The first and second wave datasets of India from 12 March 2020 up to 05 June 2021 are used for plotting the graphs. Figure 8.3 shows the number of patients belonging to the different cases in India during the second

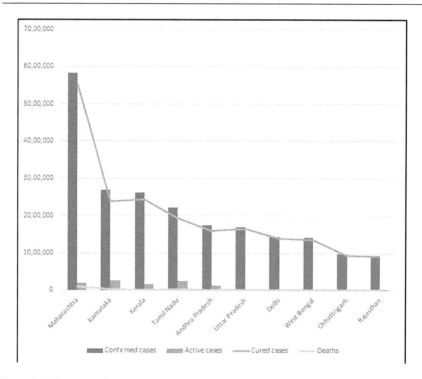

Figure 8.1 Ten most affected state-wise reports as on 6 June 2021.

Table 8.1 State-wise reports of different cases

States	Confirmed cases	Active cases	Cured cases	Deaths
Maharashtra	58,19,224	1,90,878	55,28,834	99,512
Karnataka	26,83,314	2,68,296	23,83,758	31,260
Kerala	26,18,410	1,68,049	24,40,642	9,719
Tamil Nadu	22,16,812	2,57,463	19,32,778	26,571
Andhra Pradesh	17,49,363	1,28,108	16,09,879	11,376
Uttar Pradesh	16,97,352	19,438	16,56,763	21,151
Delhi	14,28,863	6,731	13,97,575	24,557
West Bengal	14,19,130	44,441	13,58,537	16,152
Chhattisgarh	9,79,576	24,895	9,41,489	13,192
Rajasthan	9,45,442	21,550	9,15,261	8,631

wave of Covid-19. From the the figures, the confirmed cases are cumulative but at the same time the active cases of Covid-19 are declining may be due to the lockdown. Further, the prediction can be done for the forthcoming days using different ML algorithms.

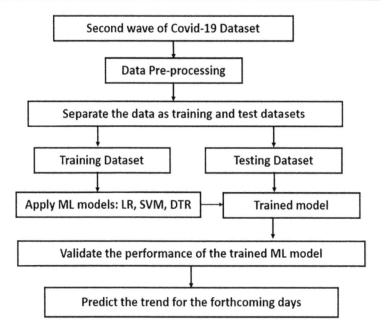

Figure 8.2 Steps for prediction.

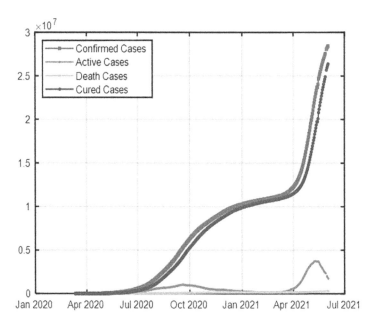

Figure 8.3 Number of infected cases in India due from the first to the second wave of Covid-19.

8.2.2 Forecasting Using Supervised ML Models

8.2.2.1 Multiple Linear Regression (LR)

There are various ML techniques to predict a target (y) with the help of the values of one or more predictors (x). This is done by separating the data as training and testing data in which these models use the mathematical equation to describe (y) as a function of (x). One of the ML techniques that estimate its performance for a continuous value of the target attribute (based on the relationship with other attributes) is regression analysis used for predictive modeling [9]. It also estimates how one dependent/target (y) variable is related to many independent/input (x) variables. The applications include—stock market index, weather forecasting, health diagnosis and many more. Depending on the number of input variables, one can classify regression as simple linear regression or a multiple regression model.

The equation based on beta estimates is as follows,

$$y = \beta_o + \beta_1 x_1 + \beta_2 x_2 + ... + b\beta_n x_n \tag{1}$$

Where, β_0 is the intercept and β_1, β_2 are the coefficients, y is the dependent variable, x_1, $x_1 ....x_n$ are independent variables and n indicates the number of observations.

Equation 1 can be written as,

$$y = \beta_0 + \beta_1 x + \xi \tag{2}$$

$$E(y) = \beta_0 + \beta_1 x \tag{3}$$

This error term which is a linear term for error regression considers the variability between x and y. The objective is to determine the optimal values for β_0 and β_1 to get the best fit (regression) line. Generally, the actual and the predicted values should be close and the difference should be minimum and represented as,

$$\text{MSE} = \text{Minimize } \frac{1}{n}\sum_{i=1}^{n}(y_{pred} - y_i)^2 \tag{4}$$

Where MSE is mean square error which is the cost function, n is the collective data points, y_{pred} is the predicted value and y_i is the actual value. Here, other performance metrics are also considered.

8.2.2.2 Support Vector Machine (SVM)

Another supervised ML model is SVM which performs nonlinear classification of data and implicitly maps the inputs into higher dimensional space.

SVM can be used for classification, regression, and outlier detection and is less susceptible to overfitting compared to other methods. SVM uses a hyperplane that decides the boundary of N-dimensional space. Based on dimensions it is called a line or plane or hyperplane. Hyperplanes decide the boundaries to classify the data points. The ones which are closer to the hyperplane are support vectors based on which the orientation and position of the hyperplane change. The equation of the line is written as:

$$y = ax + b \tag{5}$$

where, x and y are selected as features and named as x_1, x_1............x_n. The hyperplane equation is written as:

$$W^T X = 0 \tag{6}$$

SVM works on the supposition whose function is written as:

$$b(x_i) = \begin{cases} +1 \ \ if \ w.x + b \geq 0 \\ -1 \ \ if \ w.x + b < 0 \end{cases} \tag{7}$$

The margin of the hyperplane is computed as per the following equation,

$$\left[\frac{1}{n} \sum\nolimits_{i=1}^{n} \max\left(0, 1 - y_i \left(w.x_i - b\right)\right) \right] + \lambda \parallel w \parallel^2 \tag{8}$$

8.2.2.3 Decision Tree Regressor (DTR)

A decision tree is one of the frequently used techniques, applied in many domains to solve classification as well as regression tasks. The decision tree regressor involves a recursive partition process where the data points are divided at each node based on the chosen criterion. The path from the root node leading to the leaf node is used for the prediction. It handles tabular data with numerical features or categorical features and captures the non-linear interaction between the inputs (features) and the target. If there are a huge number of separate decision trees operating as an ensemble, we do call it a random forest that averages the prediction of each tree.

8.2.3 Performance Metrics

The performance and accuracy of ML models are assessed based on the metrics—mean absolute error (MAE), R^2 scores, mean squared error (MSE) and root mean squared error (RMSE).

8.2.3.1 MAE

The future prediction of the second wave of Covid-19 cases in India is displayed as graphs showing observed (actual) cases versus predictive cases. The MAE is a mean of the difference between the actual data points and predicted data points, determined as:

$$MAE = \frac{1}{n}\sum_{i=1}^{n}\left|y_i - y_{pred}\right| \qquad (9)$$

It is calculated by averaging the error that resulted from each sampled dataset written as,

$$MAE = \frac{\left|error_1\right| + \left|error_2\right|\dots\dots + \left|error_n\right|}{n} \qquad (10)$$

8.2.3.2 MSE

MSE is another way to estimate the performance of the developed model which is calculated by averaging the squares of the errors obtained between the actual and predicted data points. In other words, it squares the regression line data points. The equation for MSE is,

$$MSE = \frac{1}{n}\sum_{i=1}^{n}\left|y_i - y_{pred}\right|^2 \qquad (11)$$

8.2.3.3 RMSE

This is one of the most commonly used metrics or cost functions used to evaluate the quality of predictions. It is the square root of the mean square value

$$RMSE = \sqrt{\frac{1}{n}\sum_{i=1}^{n}\left|y_i - y_{pred}\right|^2} \qquad (12)$$

The three above-mentioned metrics values should be small and the lower the values, the closer will be the model to the actual data.

8.2.3.4 R² Score

The R^2 score is a performance measure that tells the efficacy of the ML models deployed for specific applications and measures how well the model fits the data. It shows the amount of variance in the dependent variable that is predictable from the independent variable(s) and the fitness of the trained models. It varies between 0% and 100% (zero to one). The high R^2 value signifies the reliability of the model learned. So, if the score value is one it indicates the dependent and independent variables are perfectly correlated, (with no variance) and the ideal value should be one. In contrast, the lower value shows a low correlation level and the regression model is not reliable. It is expressed as,

$$R^2 = 1 - \frac{SS_{RES}}{SS_{TOTAL}} = 1 - \frac{\Sigma(y_i - y_{pred})^2}{\Sigma(y_i - \overline{y}_i)^2} \qquad (13)$$

where,
SS_{RES} is the residual sum of squared errors of the regression model
SS_{TOTAL} is the total sum of squared errors
$\overline{y}$ is the mean value of y_i

8.3 RESULTS

The main subject of this work is to forecast the status and number of individuals affected in the second wave of Covid-19. The exact data of the confirmed, active, cured, and death cases in India have been divided into two sets: To train the model and to test the model. Here, 443 data points are considered of which 75 % (333) of data points are taken as training datasets (observed data points) and the remaining 25% (110) are taken as test datasets (forecast) to make possible predictions. Using the training datasets, the models are trained and the test datasets are used to forecast the remaining trend. In this study to predict the patient status and numbers in the second wave of the Covid-19 outbreak, three ML models namely, SVM, LR (multiple), and DTR. The number of infections registered each day, the number of confirmed cases, deaths, and the numeral of recovered (cured) cases for about 443 days are accounted and accordingly, the numbers can be predicted for the forthcoming days. The results during training and testing are shown in Figures 8.6–8.11. Figure 8.4a displays the graph during training using ML models, in which LR proves to be the best fit (hence LR is used). Here, for training, the first 333 numbers of confirmed cases are taken (days from 12 March 2020 to 11 February 2021). The remaining 110 confirmed cases (days from 12 February 2021 to 05 June 2021) are taken as a test dataset. The same has been followed for the remaining cases. Figure 8.4b displays the predicted cases using LR. Figure 8.4c shows the performance evaluation between the observed cases (actual) and predicted cases (forecast). The comparison is done among the three ML models namely, LR, SVM, and DTR, and the predicted results are displayed as graphs in Figure 8.5a-c.

Figure 8.5 proves the efficacy of LR to be the best fit between the true and predicted cases. To validate the performance numerically, the model's performance is evaluated using R^2, MSE, MAE, and RMSE. The values of MSE, MAE and RMSE are lower for LR and the value is the expected one (0.99) as shown in Table 8.2. But for DTR and SVM the error values are larger

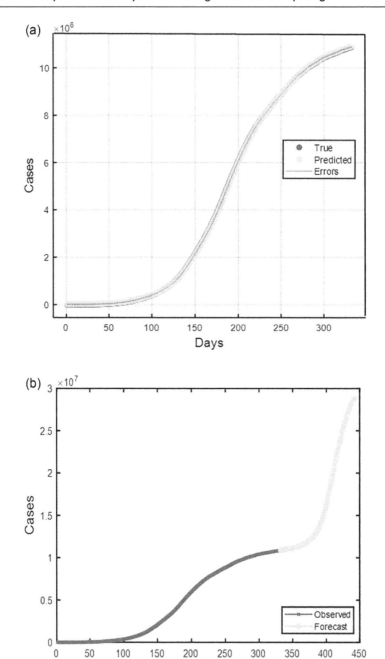

Figure 8.4 a) Confirmed cases vs multiple linear regression model during training, b) Testing the model and forecasting, c) Performance evaluation using test data points.

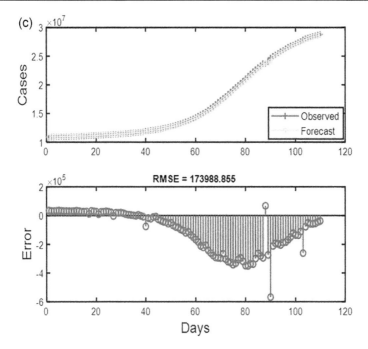

Figure 8.4 (Continued)

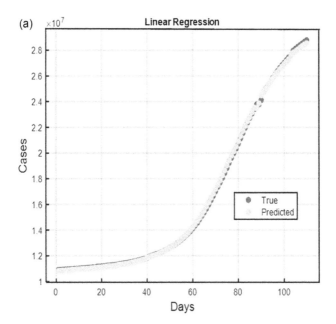

Figure 8.5 Comparison of prediction results using a) LR, b) DTR, and c) SVM.

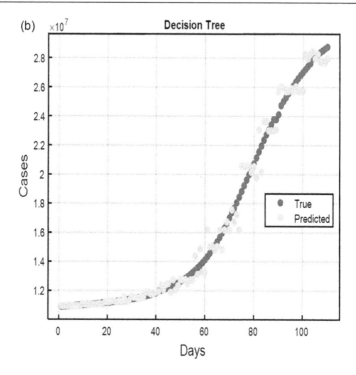

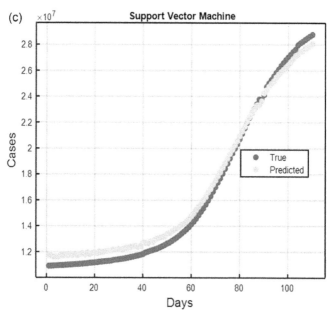

Figure 8.5 (Continued)

Table 8.2 Results of confirmed cases using ML models

	Training				Testing			
Model	R^2 Score	MSE	MAE	RMSE	R^2 Score	MSE	MAE	RMSE
LR	1.00	739100000	23146	27186	1.00	30272000678	124800	173988
SVM	0.98	254870000000	470570	504850	0.98	401111000000	596670	633340
DTR	0.98	19375000000	92120	139190	0.98	448220000000	444190	669500

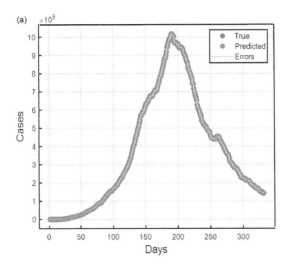

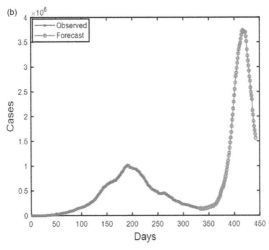

Figure 8.6 a) Active cases vs multiple linear regression model during training, b) Testing the model and forecasting, c) Performance evaluation using test data points.

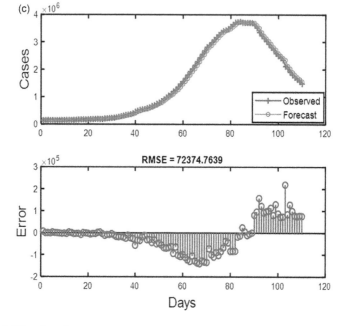

Figure 8.6 (Continued)

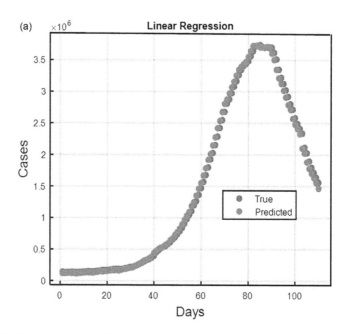

Figure 8.7 Comparison of prediction results using a) LR, b) DTR, and c) SVM.

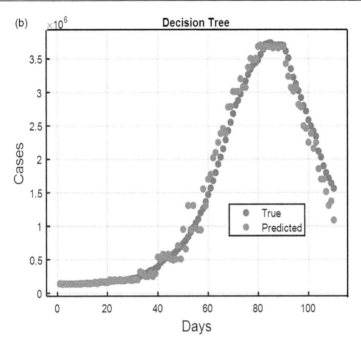

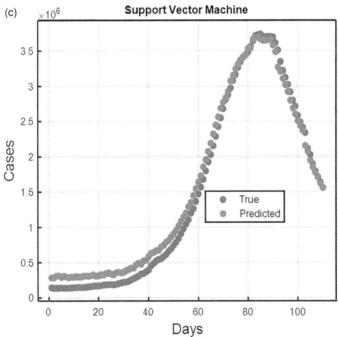

Figure 8.7 (Continued)

Table 8.3 Results of active cases using ML models

	Training				Testing			
Model	R^2 Score	MSE	MAE	RMSE	R^2 Score	MSE	MAE	RMSE
LR	1.00	68223000	5982.6	8259.7	1.00	5238100453	53778	72374
SVM	0.98	597800000	21861	24450	0.98	18756000000	125470	136950
DTR	0.98	244610000	11075	15640	0.98	29747000000	120480	172470

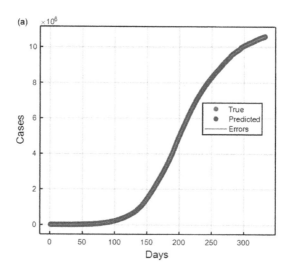

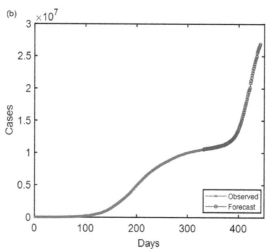

Figure 8.8 a) Cured cases versus multiple linear regression model during training, b) Testing the model and forecasting, c) Performance evaluation using test data points.

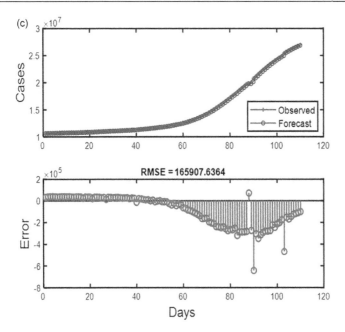

Figure 8.8 (Continued)

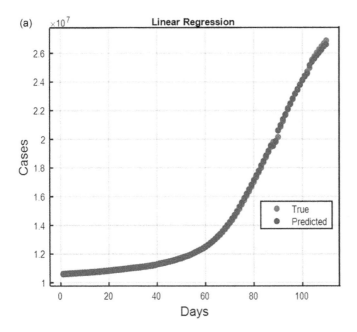

Figure 8.9 Comparison of prediction results using a) LR, b) DTR, and c) SVM.

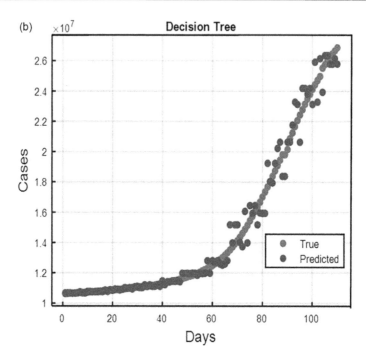

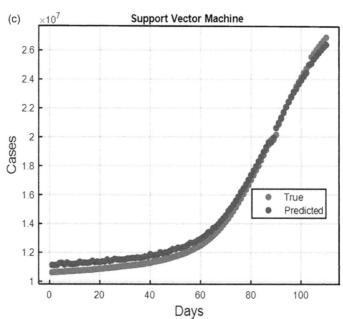

Figure 8.9 (Continued)

Table 8.4 Results of recovered cases using ML models

	Training				Testing			
Model	R^2 Score	MSE	MAE	RMSE	R^2 Score	MSE	MAE	RMSE
LR	0.99	710740000	22851	26660	1.00	27525343812	115650	165907
SVM	0.98	232570707600	449450	482260	0.99	194340000720	416990	440850
DTR	0.98	20147000000	92090	141940	0.98	452090056000	438760	672370

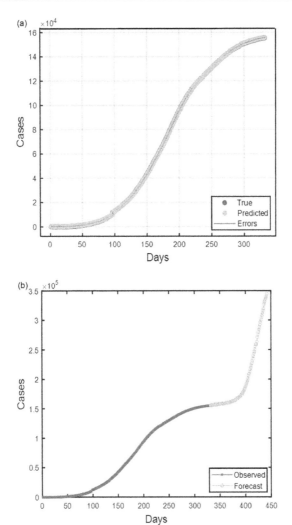

Figure 8.10 a) Death cases vs multiple linear regression model during training, b) Testing the model and forecasting, c) Performance evaluation using test data points.

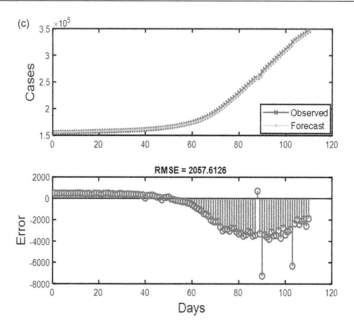

Figure 8.10 (Continued)

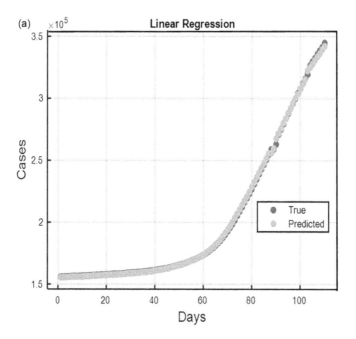

Figure 8.11 Comparison of prediction results using a) LR, b) DTR, and c) SVM.

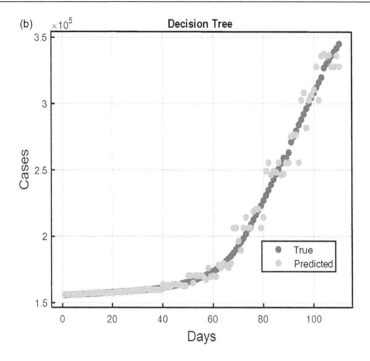

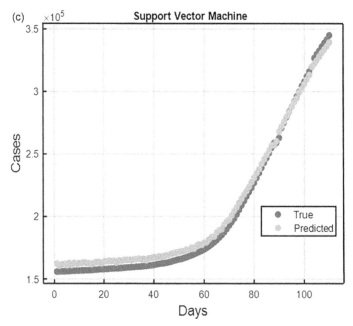

Figure 8.11 (Continued)

Table 8.5 Results of death cases using ML models

	Training				Testing			
Model	R^2 Score	MSE	MAE	RMSE	R^2 Score	MSE	MAE	RMSE
LR	0.99	13310	304.21	365.12	1.00	4233800	1465.6	2057.6
SVM	0.98	50370000	6576.3	7097.2	0.987	26194000	4828.6	5118.1
DTR	0.99	4234600	1431.7	2057.8	0.98	52138000	4363.7	7220.7

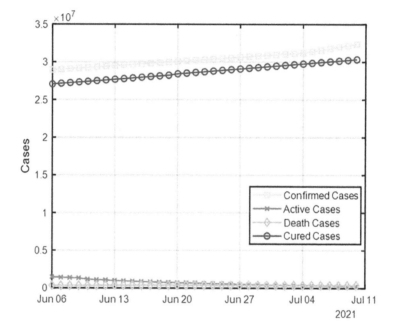

Figure 8.12 Prediction for the next 35 days using LR model.

and the R^2 value is less, hence, LR proves to be a good fit for predicting the confirmed cases of the second wave of Covid-19 infected patients.

Similarly, Figures 8.6a-c display the result for active cases and the comparison among the ML model is executed to display the predicted results in Figures 8.7a-c. Table 8.3 shows the numerical results of active cases evaluated using performance metrics (cost function), in which LR is the best fit. Figures 8.8a-c and Figures 8.9a-c are for cured cases. Figures 8.10a-c and Figures 8.11a-c is to forecast the number of deaths wherein, the LR model again proves to be the best fit and the results are tabulated for active, cured and death cases in Tables 8.3–8.5. In all the cases SVM model shows poor performance and the DTR model seems to be a moderate fit.

With this LR model, the trend of the second wave of the Covid-19 scenario can be predicted for the forthcoming days as shown in Figure 8.12. Here, the prediction for the next 35 days is done from 6 June to 10 July 2021. Thus, this framework analyzes the dataset containing real data of Covid-19 infected patients in India during the first and second waves using ML algorithms to predict the trends it will follow in the forthcoming days. The analysis made in this manuscript proves (from the figures and graphs plotted using the dataset), that multiple linear regression (LR) accomplishes its job of prediction in a better way compared to other models. The other algorithms have been effective in assessing and verifying diverse cases to some extent. The number of active cases is declining and there is a surge in the number of confirmed cases and death cases. But at the same time, the number of recovered cases is also increasing. And with the increase in the number of vaccinated cases, there will be a decrease in the infected and death cases in the future. In general, it is assumed that the current scenario of the model prediction is right and will guide us to comprehend the future.

8.4 CONCLUSIONS

In this manuscript, the dataset of Covid-19 infected patients from 12 March 2020 to 5 June 2021 is considered to analyze the trend of the second wave in India. In this study, three ML models have been implemented—LR, SVM, and DTR to analyze and predict the second wave of the Covid-19 trend. The forecasts made by the LR are very close to the actual values providing a high value of R^2 score with good predictions for all four cases namely, confirmed, active, recovered, and death cases during training as well as testing. It is obvious from the prediction made by this ML model that there is a rapid rise in the confirmed cases along with death cases and the active cases are decreasing, which may be due to the lockdown enforced by the government. An optimistic sign is that the cured cases are also increasing and people are thereby, recovering from the second wave of Covid-19. The good news is that with the number of vaccinated cases increasing, it is expected that this second wave will get subdued and the third wave can be postponed. Consequently, this study concludes that the LR model is the most appropriate model for predicting the Covid second wave trend. The reduction in cases depends only on people and how far they abide by the rules and regulations framed by the Government of India. Although the vaccines are available throughout India and people have started taking vaccines but still, the experts tell that the only possible and effective way to safeguard from the second wave of Covid-19 is by wearing a mask, maintaining social distancing, self-isolation if symptoms are seen, and quarantining the infected patients. Thus, in this work, the predictions are made related to various cases using three ML models in which the LR technique proves to be superior.

REFERENCES

Achterberg, M.A., Prasse, B., Ma, L., Trajanovski, S., Kitsak, M., and Van Mieghem, P., 2022. Comparing the accuracy of several network-based COVID-19 prediction algorithms. *International Journal of Forecasting*, 38 (2), 489–504.

Bharati, S., Podder, P., and Mondal, M.R.H., 2020. Hybrid deep learning for detecting lung diseases from X-ray images. *Informatics in Medicine Unlocked*, 20, 100391.

Busari, S.I., and Samson, T.K., 2022. Modelling and forecasting new cases of Covid-19 in Nigeria: Comparison of regression, ARIMA and machine learning models. *Scientific African*, 18, e01404.

Faiayaz Waris, S., and Koteeswaran, S., 2021. Heart disease early prediction using a novel machine learning method called improved K-means neighbor classifier in python. *Materials Today: Proceedings*.

Gárate-Escamila, A.K., Hajjam El Hassani, A., and Andrès, E., 2020. Classification models for heart disease prediction using feature selection and PCA. *Informatics in Medicine Unlocked*, 19, 100330.

Gupta, P., and Garg, S., 2020. Breast cancer prediction using varying parameters of machine learning models. *Procedia Computer Science*, 171, 593–601.

Jain, N., Jhunthra, S., Garg, H., Gupta, V., Mohan, S., Ahmadian, A., Salahshour, S., and Ferrara, M., 2021. Prediction modelling of COVID using machine learning methods from B-cell dataset. *Results in Physics*, 21, 103813.

Kavitha, C., Gowrisankar, A., and Banerjee, S., 2021. The second and third waves in India: When will the pandemic be culminated? *The European Physical Journal Plus*, 136 (5), 1–12.

Kondapalli, A.R., Koganti, H., Challagundla, S.K., Guntaka, C.S.R., and Biswas, S., 2022. Machine learning predictions of COVID-19 second wave end-times in Indian states. *Indian Journal of Physics*, 96 (8), 2547–2555.

Meenu Gupta Rachna Jain, S., 2021. AI-enabled COVID-19 outbreak analysis and prediction: Indian States *vs.* Union Territories. *Computers, Materials \& Continua*, 67 (1), 933–950.

Mohan, S., John, A., Abugabah, A., Adimoolam, M., Kumar Singh, S., Kashif Bashir, A., and Sanzogni, L., 2021. An approach to forecast impact of Covid-19 using supervised machine learning model. *Software – Practice and Experience*, 1–17.

Nilashi, M., Bin Ibrahim, O., Ahmadi, H., and Shahmoradi, L., 2017. An analytical method for diseases prediction using machine learning techniques. *Computers & Chemical Engineering*, 106, 212–223.

Panda, M., 2020. Application of ARIMA and Holt-Winters forecasting model to predict the spreading of COVID-19 for India and its states. *medRxiv*, 2020-07.

Petropoulos, F., Makridakis, S., and Stylianou, N., 2022. COVID-19: Forecasting confirmed cases and deaths with a simple time series model. *International Journal of Forecasting*, 38 (2), 439–452.

Rajendra, P., Kumari, M., Rani, S., Dogra, N., Boadh, R., Kumar, A., and Dahiya, M., 2022. Impact of artificial intelligence on civilization: Future perspectives. *Materials Today: Proceedings*, 56, 252–256.

Rani, S., Tripathi, K., Arora, Y., and Kumar, A., 2022. Analysis of Anomaly detection of Malware using KNN. In: *2022 2nd International Conference on Innovative Practices in Technology and Management (ICIPTM)*. 774–779.

Rustam, F., Reshi, A.A., Mehmood, A., Ullah, S., On, B.-W., Aslam, W., and Choi, G.S., 2020. COVID-19 future forecasting using supervised machine learning models. *IEEE Access*, 8, 101489–101499.

Senapati, A., Nag, A., Mondal, A., and Maji, S., 2021. A novel framework for COVID-19 case prediction through piecewise regression in India. *International Journal of Information Technology (Singapore)*, 13 (1), 41–48.

Sharma, V.K., and Nigam, U., 2020. Modeling and forecasting of COVID-19 growth curve in India. *Transactions of the Indian National Academy of Engineering*, 5 (4), 697–710.

Sujath, R., Chatterjee, J.M., and Hassanien, A.E., 2020. A machine learning forecasting model for COVID-19 pandemic in India. *Stochastic Environmental Research and Risk Assessment*, 34 (7), 959–972.

Talkhi, N., Akhavan Fatemi, N., Ataei, Z., and Jabbari Nooghabi, M., 2021. Modeling and forecasting number of confirmed and death caused COVID-19 in IRAN: A comparison of time series forecasting methods. *Biomedical Signal Processing and Control*, 66, 102494.

Verma, A.K., Pal, S., and Kumar, S., 2019. Comparison of skin disease prediction by feature selection using ensemble data mining techniques. *Informatics in Medicine Unlocked*, 16, 100202.

Chapter 9

Prediction of Chronic Kidney Disease Using BIRCH Algorithm in Machine Learning

¹Saranya K. and ²Deepa C.

¹Department of Artificial Intelligence and Data Science, KIT-Kalaignarkarunanidhi Institute of Technology, Coimbatore, Tamil Nadu, India

9.1 INTRODUCTION

CKD is caused by a variety of factors, including lifestyle and environmental issues, which can lead to a variety of serious health problems, including anaemia, electrolyte disturbances, hypertension, and an increased risk of developing cardiovascular disease [1]. According to the study, the annual global death rate from CKD increased by 90% between 1990 and 2013 [2]. Analytic studies about CKD shows that it is the thirteenth most common cause of death. This alarming statistic shows the drastic rise in CKD-related deaths over the past two decades, revealing that more research is needed to be done to combat this life-threatening condition. At least 2.4 million people per year pass away from kidney-related diseases, based on the report from the 2019 World Kidney Day [3]. The severity of these diseases can be reduced through early detection and prediction [4]. Data analysis in the healthcare sector is challenging due to the volume and complexity of the generated data. Most of the time, doctors have a challenging dilemma when it comes to physically identifying ailments. To diagnose CKD, blood and urine tests can be used. One of the imaging methods that can be used to diagnose kidney abnormalities is ultrasound imaging. Kidney abnormalities can include things like changes in the shape, position, or swelling of a limb, as well as formation of stones, cysts, blocked urinary tract, congenital anomalies, and cancerous cells. Since kidney stones have low contrast and speckle noise, detecting them using ultrasound imaging is a very difficult task. High blood pressure and diabetes are the two main causes of chronic renal disease [5, 6]. Early detection and successful treatment can help to lessen and stop the progression of CKD symptoms. To address this challenge, medical practitioners and researchers are leveraging machine learning technologies to make sense of the data and identify patterns associated with CKD [7]. In data classification and regression, machine learning is extremely important. Applications of machine learning are used to forecast CKD from various data sets [8]. This approach aims to create and validate CKD prediction models. The primary objective will be to first assess kidney

DOI: 10.1201/9781003329947-9

failure, which indicates the requirement for kidney dialysis or kidney transplantation [9]. These models also show the patient how to lead a healthy lifestyle, assist the doctor in determining the risk and severity of the disease, and provide guidance on how to continue the treatment in the future. Using ANN and mining techniques, it may be possible to spot patterns in data collection, and the occurrence of specific diseases that could be harmful in the future may be predicted [10].

9.2 RELATED WORK

Various researchers are particularly interested in the detection of chronic kidney disease. In order to create a reliable and accurate prediction system, they employed various classification algorithms. Chen et al. [4] developed an Adaptive Hybridised Deep Convolutional Neural Networks for the categorisation of tissue features with high accuracy to predict CKD. Internet of medical things (IoMT) platforms are further used to test the effectiveness of various deep learning techniques. Maurya et al. [5] highlighted that a suitable dietary plan should be provided to CKD patients based on an analysis of test results using a machine learning algorithm. Focusing on the blood potassium level, diet recommendations are made to restrict the progression of CKD. Gupta et al. [6] collected a multitude of feature combinations and transferred them into the machine learning algorithms. On the basis of the chosen features, the algorithms were deployed, and their results were compared. Ekanayake and Herath [8] used clinical data, combined data preprocessing, a missing data handling technique, filtering, and characteristic selection to make CKD predictions. They also highlighted how the random forest and additional tree classifiers produced results with maximum accuracy and negligible bias towards the specified attributes. Emon et al. [11] evaluated the performance of eight different machine learning classifiers and concluded that random forest has the greatest ROC value and achieves 99% accuracy. Raju et al. [12] used random forest and extra gradient boosting techniques to analyse and forecast CKD. It displayed an exceptional level of classification accuracy from the provided dataset.

Aljaaf et al. [13] did an experimental analysis using four classifiers based on machine learning that produced favourable outcomes in the diagnosis of kidney ailments. Gudeti et al. [14] did a performance analysis of the K-nearest neighbor (KNN), logistic regression (LR), and support vector machine (SVM) algorithms. Within the confined parameters of a medical scenario, they demonstrated that the SVM algorithm predicts CKD more accurately than LR and KNN. Elkholy et al. [15] chose a modified deep belief network (DBN) as the classification algorithm, using categorical cross-entropy as the loss function and softmaz as the activation function. This approach reduced the progression of kidney damage and demonstrated 98.5% accuracy in the early prediction of CKD. In order to efficiently predict CKD, Hasan et al. [16] chose seven machine learning methods depending on their correctness and false negative error. Results indicated that the ensemble machine learning approach could diagnose CKD with 99.17% accuracy and zero false negatives. Stella and Vasanthi Kumari [17] validated the use of SVM, random forest, and KNN in CKD prediction. Additionally, the accuracy criteria of ML classifiers were used to analyse their performance. Pitolli et al. [18] evaluated the performance of several algorithms, including DBSCAN, K-means, Mini-Batch K-means, EM, CURE, and BRICH. BRICH outperformed other algorithms and made the most accurate identification of the malware family. Haan et al. [19] classified CKD using six machine learning models: EANet, CCT, Swin transformers, VGG16, Resnet, and Inception V3. With an accuracy of 99.30 %, Swin Transformer scored the best of all of them in terms of accuracy. Chu et al. [20] illustrated through comparative analysis, employing the K-means algorithm, that the speed of cluster analysis of automatic identification system (AIS) ship data points in the spark cluster is significantly better than non-big platforms, which in turn improves the effectiveness of data processing. The malware was identified by using the KNN algorithm. This analysis of the anomaly, significantly helps to classify and detect the malware [21]. Hui et al. [22] demonstrated the comparative analysis of algorithms using evaluation indicators to show their performance; this is so effective in identifying the algorithm with great efficiency. Pitolli et al. [18] identified malware using a variety of clustering algorithms, and it was demonstrated that the BRICH method produced the most significant outcomes in the efficient and precise detection of malware families.

9.3 METHODOLOGY

BRICH, an unsupervised machine learning technique, is employed in this study to conduct hierarchical clustering over a particularly huge dataset. The following flowchart illustrates the proposed method of this study (Figure 9.1).

9.3.1 Phase I: Loading the Data into Memory

Starting with the initial threshold, in this phase, the data are examined and points are added to the tree. When it runs out of memory before finishing the scanning process, it boosts the threshold level and regenerates a new, reduced CF tree by re-adding the leaf values from the previous tree. It then picks up where it left off with the scanning of the data. Outliers are removed by rebuilding the tree.

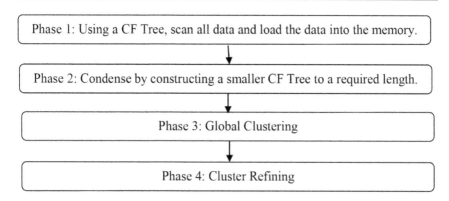

Figure 9.1 Proposed method.

9.3.2 Phase II: Condense

In this level, the initial CF tree's leaf entries are scanned, with more outliers being removed and crowded sub-clusters being combined into larger ones.

9.3.3 Phase III: Global Clustering

All leaf entries are grouped together using a global (or semi-global) algorithm. The subclusters that are denoted by their CF vectors are subjected directly to the agglomerative hierarchical clustering algorithm.

9.3.4 Phase IV: Cluster Refining

Inaccuracies are fixed, and the clusters are further refined by running the data again. The phase III cluster centroids are used as seeds to relocate the data points to the closest seed in order to create the new clusters. During this phase, outliers are eliminated. The CKD data collected from Kaggle datasets is clustered using the hierarchical clustering approach [19]. The hierarchical clustering technique begins with single point clusters and considers each point in the database to be a cluster. The given Figures 9.2–9.5 depict datasets that are clustered based on the closest points, and this process is repeated till only one cluster is left. The distance matrix $(O(n^2))$ time is used to perform the cluster computation.

With the use of the CF tree (Figure 9.6) and matching pattern method in BRICH, expected findings are refined and clustered using the normal and CKD datasets from the Kaggle datasets [19]. A triple is a key characteristic feature of the CF tree, which represents a group of objects (N, LS, SS). There is a cluster comprising data points of N-dimension. X_i represents data points where i ranges from one to N. N denotes the number of data points.

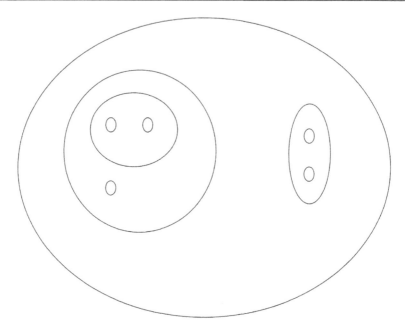

Figure 9.2 Hierarchical clustering.

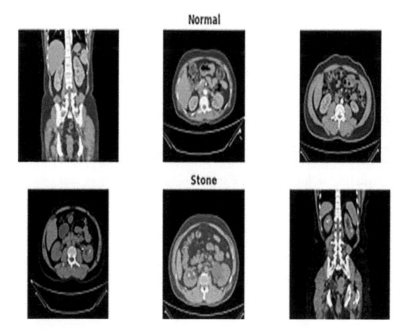

Figure 9.3 Normal kidney and kidney with stone.

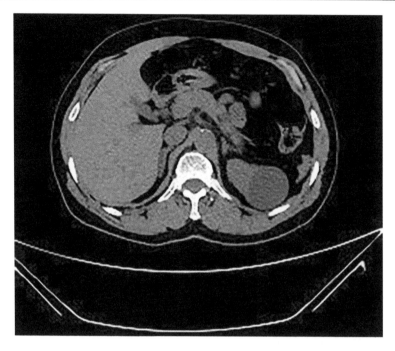

Figure 9.4 Kidney cyst.

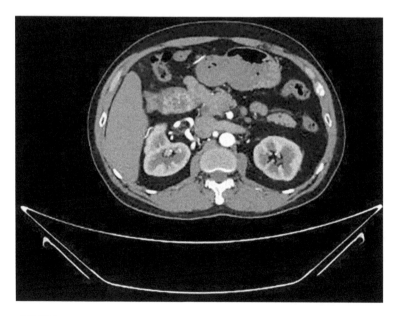

Figure 9.5 Kidney tumor.

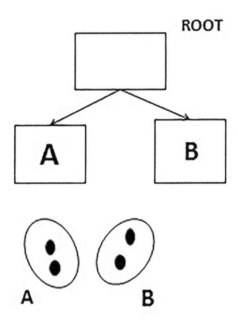

Figure 9.6 CF tree with two nodes.

LS indicates linear sum of N data points. SS represents the sum of the squares of N data points. A height balanced tree, CF has two parameters, balancing factor (B), threshold (T).

Elements of the kind [CFi, child$_i$] are present in each non-leaf node, with a maximum of B elements. Here child$_i$ represents a pointer to its ith child node, and CF$_i$ depicts the CF of this child's subcluster. A cluster composed of all the subclusters indicated by its entries is termed a "non-leaf" node. At most, L entries can be found in a leaf node, each of which is of the form [CF], in which i ranges from one to L. For effective scans, it has previous and next pointers, which are used to group all leaf nodes. Following a threshold value of T, leaf node entries should meet the threshold condition. The diameter must be lower than the threshold value T. This is shown in the following Figure 9.7–9.9.

9.3.5 Matching Based Measures (I)

A purity measure [23] is applied to the obtained result to determine the purity of clustered data. The purity of cluster C$_i$ is defined in Equation 1.

$$\text{Purity}_i = \frac{1}{ni} max_{j=1}^{k} \{nij\} \tag{1}$$

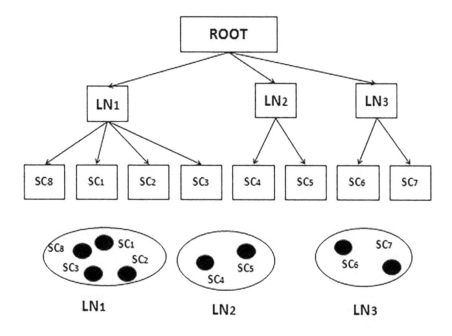

Figure 9.7 A leaf node's branching factor shouldn't be greater than three.

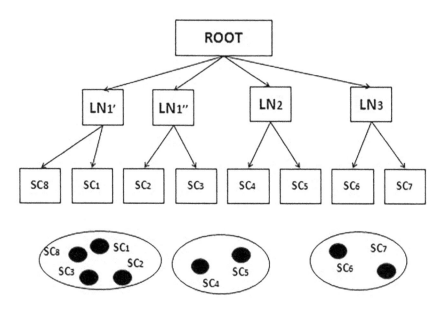

Figure 9.8 Branching factor of a leaf node greater than three split LN1 as LN1 and LN2.

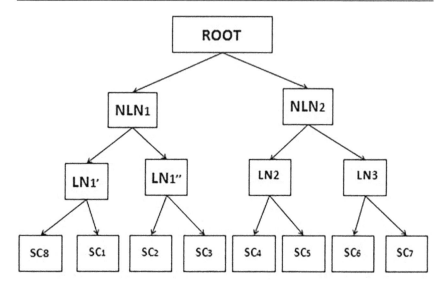

Figure 9.9 A non-leaf node's branching factor cannot be more than three, and split root height has risen by one.

Total purity of clustering C is defined in the Equation 2.

$$\text{Purity} = \sum\nolimits_{i=1}^{r} \frac{ni}{n} \qquad (2)$$

The clustering is perfect when r = k and purity = 1. If the number of clusters produced is similar to its ground truth, then purity is calculated using Equation 3.

$$\text{Purity}_i = \frac{1}{n} \sum\nolimits_{i=0}^{r} max_{j=1}^{k} \left\{ n_{ij} \right\} \qquad (3)$$

For the given data sets, the results obtained are matched, and the purity is measured through matching based measures.

Here we used the BRICH algorithm, whose input images are taken from Kaggle datasets and loaded as inputs. The data sets are scanned only once, and then they are condensed into desirable lengths to build the CF tree. The CKD images are clustered. After clustering, it is then refined. To check the purity of the clustered data sets, we introduce the concept of matching-based measures. The normal kidney image is compared with the CKD images obtained after clustering, and then it ensures the purity of clustering which is shown in Figure 9.10.

DBSCAN [18] is an algorithm that is based on density. This scan is effective for large spatial datasets and is capable of identifying arbitrary

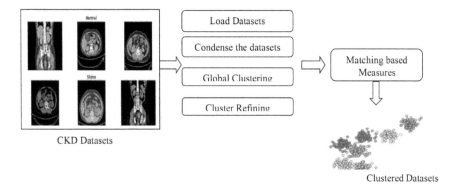

Figure 9.10 Clustering data sets using BRICH algorithm.

shaped clusters. The method analyses search data point's neighbourhoods inside the dataset to find clusters. Hierarchical algorithm [18] is divided into agglomerative and divisive hierarchical algorithms. A bottom-up approach called "agglomerative hierarchical clustering" starts with each and every instance in a single separate cluster. The closest pair of clusters is then repeatedly merged using a different method until all the data is arranged in one cluster. Clusters, on the other hand, are divided by the dividing hierarchical clustering until only singletons of distinct points remain.

A popular clustering approach is the K-means algorithm. The core principle is to iteratively determine a division scheme for K clusters, with the mean of these K clusters serving as a representation for the associated types of data. The lowest is the overall error. The minimal error sum of squares criterion serves as the foundation of the K-means algorithm.

9.3.6 Parameter Selection

To evaluate the performance of the algorithms, the parameters of each algorithm are optimised here. K is the parameter in the K-means algorithm and also represents the K-nearest neighbors. To adopt an integer value for K, it is taken from the range of three to 50. If the value of K is less than the lower limit of three, then it will result in an error. For an upper limit of 50 with an increasing K value, the neighbouring points also gradually increase. After considering clustering and space-cost timing, a K value between one and three was chosen [21].

DBSCAN requires two parameters: ∈ (eps) and minimum number of points required to form a dense region (minPts), and the maximum number of points. The default value of minPts in this chapter's image data evaluation is four, since the data set is two-dimensional.

Table 9.1 Comparison of BRICH with DBSCAN, hierarchical and K-means

Algorithm	K	ARI_M	AMI_M	FMI_M	ARI_A	AMI_A	FMI_A
BIRCH	NO	0.947±0	0.616±0	0.616±0	0.819±0	0.727±0	0.851±0
DBSCAN	NO	0.911±0	0.515±0	0.927±0	0.865±0	0.606±0	0.891±0
HIRARCHICAL	NO	0.949±0	0.606±0	0.957±0	0.891±0	0.739±0	0.91±0
K-MEANS	YES	0.644±0,104	0.535±0,008	0.698±0,008	0.738±0,046	0.625±0,025	0.792±0,035

The hierarchical cluster algorithm uses 'n' as the parameter to define the number of clusters. It uses affinity to measure the distance between the neighbouring points.

9.3.7 Comparative Analysis

The comparison of BRICH with DBSCAN, hierarchical, and K-means clustering is shown in Table 9.1.

The above table is a comparison of the BRICH algorithm with other clustering algorithms for the identification of the CKD dataset. The comparison result shows BRICH produces significant clustering.

In Figure 9.11, it decomposes the given input image into multiple subband images known as Low-Low (LL), Low-High (LH), High-Low (HL), and High-High (HH). This helps to retrieve clear information about the image. To measure the homogeneousness of the image, the gray scale level co-occurrence matrix (GLCM) is used, and that is represented in Figure 9.11b. It is suitable to measure and detect the disorder in the texture image. In the resultant co-occurrence matrix (CCM), the matching-based measure N(i, j) corresponds to the total number of pixels with values of i and j in the input image that occurred in defined spatial relationships. It measures the local variation, texture of shadow depth, and hidden parts in the GLCM.

Based on the maximum matching pattern (Figure 9.12), the input images are compared with the given normal CKD image. The pixel value's purity is analysed using a matching based measure. The image with high purity is considered to be normal CKD. The image with low purity is considered as abnormal CKD. In the input image, the pixels' values are matched with normal CKD pixel values, and if it has a low purity, it is considered to have an abnormal texture, after which it is popped out as shown in Figure 9.13.

9.4 CONCLUSION

Using the BRICH technique, we significantly clustered and detected the CKD data from the provided input image data sets in this chapter. To

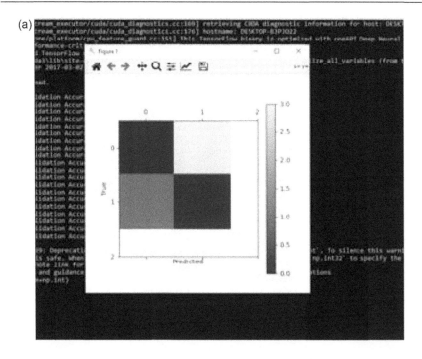

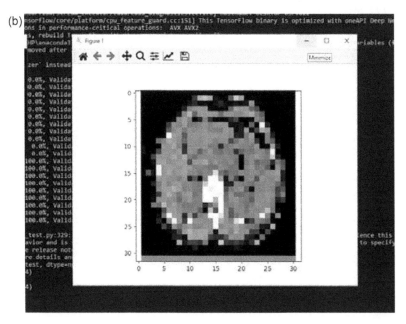

Figure 9.11 a) Discrete wavelet transformation of CKD; b) Grayscale level—co-occurrence matrix.

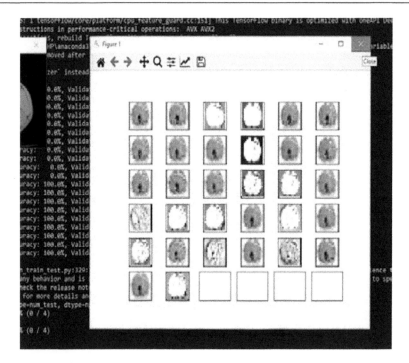

Figure 9.12 Maximum matching pattern.

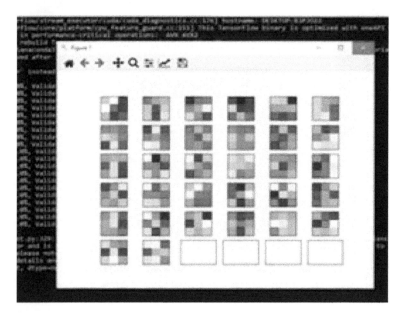

Figure 9.13 Pop out of the abnormal texture.

ensure the cluster's purity with the appropriate ground truth values, match-based methods were used. Cluster results obtained using BRICH, K-means, DBSCAN, and hierarchical cluster algorithms were compared using AMI, ARI, and FMI evaluation indicators, which can automatically reflect the performance of each algorithm. The results obtained showed that the BRICH clustering algorithm was more suitable than K-means, DBSCAN, and hierarchical cluster algorithms for cluster purity analysis with regard to the input image data sets. Furthermore, BRICH allows more flexibility and scalability compared to other algorithms, as the number of clusters can be adjusted dynamically without affecting the overall time complexity. It exhibits exceptional performance in clustering CKD data with great accuracy and execution speed. The BRICH algorithm outperforms traditional clustering algorithms in both accuracy and speed, making it an excellent choice for given image data sets.

9.5 FUTURE ENHANCEMENT

In this chapter, we compared the performance of various algorithms and observed that the BRICH algorithm is effective at accurately clustering the data. But here, we demonstrated a limited set of image data sets. In the future, we will augment with a large set of sample data sets to uncover additional parameters important in detecting CKD at an early stage.

REFERENCES

1. George C; Mogueo A; Okpechi I; Echouffo-Tcheugui JB; Kengne AP. "Chronic kidney disease in low-income to middle-income countries: The case for increased screening." BMJ Glob Heal. 2017; 2(2):1–10.
2. Radhakrishnan J; Mohan S. "KI reports and world kidney day." Kidney Int Rep. 2017; 2(2):125–126.
3. Ethiopia: kidney disease. https://www.worldlifeexpectancy.com/ethiopia-kidney-disease. Accessed 7 February 2020.
4. Chen G; Ding C; Li Y; Hu X; Li X; Ren L; Ding X; Tian P; Xue W. "Prediction of chronic kidney disease using adaptive hybridized deep convolutional neural network on the Internet of medical things platform." IEEE Access. 2020; 9.
5. Maurya A; Wable R; Shinde R; John S; Jadhav R; Dakshayani R. "Chronic kidney disease prediction and recommendation of suitable diet plan by using machine learning." International Conference on Nascent Technologies in Engineering, 2019.
6. Gupta R; Koli N; Mahor N; Tejashri N. "Performance analysis of machine learning classifier for predicting chronic kidney disease." International Conference for Emerging Technology, 2020.

7. Aljaaf AJ. "Early prediction of chronic kidney disease using machine learning supported by predictive analytics." Proceedings of the IEEE Congress on Evolutionary Computation (CEC), Wellington, 2018.

8. Ekanayake IU; Herath D. "Chronic kidney disease prediction using machine learning Methods." Moratuwa Proceeding, Engineering Research Conference, 2020.

9. Nishanth A; Thiruvaran T. "Identifying important attributes for early detection of chronic kidney disease." IEEE Rev. Biomed. Eng. 2018; 11:208–216.

10. Ogunleye A; Wang Q-G. "XGBoost model for chronic kidney disease diagnosis." IEEE/ACM Trans. Comput. Biol. Bioinform. 2020; 17:2131–2140.

11. Emon U; Imran M; Islam R; Keya MS; Zannat R. "Performance analysis of chronic kidney disease through machine learning approaches." 6th International Conference on Inventive Computation Technologies, 2021.

12. Ganapathi Raju NV, Prasanna Lakshmi K, Gayathri Praharshitha K, Likhitha C. "Prediction of chronic kidney disease (CKD) using Data Science." International Conference on Intelligent Computing and Control Systems (ICCS), 2019.

13. Aljaaf AJ; Al-Jumeily D; Haglan HM; Alloghani M; Baker T; Hussain AJ; Mustafina J. "Early prediction of chronic kidney disease using machine learning supported by predictive analytics." IEEE Congress on Evolutionary Computation (CEC), 2018.

14. Gudeti B; Mishra S; Malik S; Fernandez TF; Tyagi AK; Kumari S. "A novel approach to predict chronic kidney disease using machine learning algorithms." Fourth International Conference on Electronics, Communication and Aerospace Technology (ICECA), 2020.

15. Elkholy SMM; Rezk A; El Fetoh Saleh AA. "Early prediction of chronic kidney disease using deep belief network." IEEE Access. 2021.

16. Hasan Z; Khan RR; Rifat W; Dipu DS; Islam MN; Sarker IH. "Development of a predictive analytic system for chronic kidney disease using ensemble-based machine learning." International Scientific Conference on Information Technology and Management Science of Riga Technical University (ITMS), 2021.

17. Stella A; Vasanthi Kumari P. "Forecasting of chronic kidney disease and analysis of the classifiers using ML based classification approaches." International Conference on Advancements in Electrical, Electronics, Communication, Computing and Automation (ICAECA), 2021.

18. Pitolli G; Aniello L; Laurenza G; Querzoni L; Baldoni R. "Malware family identification with Birch algorithm." International Carnahan Conference on Security Technology (ICCST), 2017.

19. Islam MN; Haan M; Hossain M; Alam M; Rabiul G; Uddin MZ; Soylu A. "A vision transformer and explainable transfer learning models for auto detection of kidney cyst, stone and tumor from CT-radiography." Sci. Rep. 2022; 12(1):1–4.

20. Chu X; Lei J; Liu X; Wang Z. "K MEANS algorithm clustering for massive AIS data based on the spark platform." 5th International Conference on Control, Robotics and Cybernetics, 2020.

21. Rani S; Tripathi K; Arora Y; Kumar A. "Analysis of anomaly detection of Malware using KNN." 2nd International Conference on Innovative Practices in Technology and Management, 2022.
22. Zhuang H; Cui J; Liu T; Wang H. A Physical Model Inspired Density Peak Clustering. Torrens University Australia, 2020.
23. Manning CD; Raghavan P; Schütze H. Introduction to Information Retrieval. Cambridge University Press, 2008.

Chapter 10

Machine Learning Based Prediction of Social Media Performance Metrics Using Facebook Data

[1]K. Karthick, [2]Aruna S. K., and [3]Ravivarman S.

[1]Department of Electrical and Electronics Engineering, GMR Institute of
Technology, Rajam, Andhra Pradesh, India
[2]Department of Computer Science and Engineering, School of Engineering and
Technology, CHRIST (Deemed to be University), Bangalore, Karnataka, India
[3]Professor, Department of Electrical and Electronics Engineering, Vardhaman
College of Engineering, Shamshabad, Hyderabad, Telangana, India

10.1 INTRODUCTION

Participation in social media online websites have gained in popularity
in recent years, and today's teenagers and young people are growing up
immersed in social media platforms that emphasise user-generated information and user interactions, such as Facebook and Twitter [1]. Visitors can
communicate freely among themselves on digital platforms, which provides
marketers with several options for connecting with and engaging customers.
Social media is utilised by millions around the world and has quickly emerged
as one of the platforms that define our day. As of March 31, 2019, [2] Facebook, for instance, claimed 2.38 billion monthly active users and 1.56 billion
daily active users. It is necessary to evaluate digital media's growth from the
perspectives of customer behaviour and marketing since it has evolved into an
essential marketing and communications medium for businesses, companies,
and institutions of all kinds, including the political sphere [3]. Social media
has evolved into the primary platform for many people to access a wide range
of data, share material and elements of their life with one another, and know
about the rest of the world, making it culturally significant [4].

Organisations may attain their business objective at a low cost by utilising the internet and social media promotion. Over 50 million businesses
have Facebook pages, and over than 88% use Twitter for marketing [5].
Social media as well as other digital platforms were also frequently used to
promote public services and election campaigns. Websites and applications
are created by content producers in order to publish their material and gain
as many viewers as possible [6]. Greater readers equal greater influence and
cash from advertising. As more content websites fight for visibility through

DOI: 10.1201/9781003329947-10

their social media profiles, acquiring large amounts of traffic through social media is becoming more difficult. Some social media sites have created methods for ranking content in order to improve the user experience. For example, Facebook employs "meaningful engagement" to assess if a post from a Facebook account should reach a certain person [7].

Social media are platforms and service allow humans to rapidly, effectively, and in real-time sort through different bits of information. Most big- and medium-sized firms are always concerned about customer feedback on products and services. Social media is a common source of information about a company's customer perceptions. Most firms use a variety of methods and approaches to determine their consumers' impressions of their services and products [8]. However, tying data from social media about customer sentiments to co-related aspects of an organisation such as productivity, profitability, financial performance, and economics is not always straightforward [9]. ML plays a vital role in prediction and classification problems [10–12]. A regression analysis using ML is frequently used for one of two reasons: forecasting the value of the dependent variable for those who know something about the explanatory components, or assessing the effect of an explanatory variable on the dependent variable.

Marketing executives use social media to increase corporate revenue and gain a competitive advantage. Simultaneously, they must choose the optimum strategy for implementing and exploiting digital interactive communication technology. A great deal of study has been conducted on consumer behaviour in the setting of technology and social media, as well as the implications for practitioners. Management studies, on the other hand, are significantly less prevalent in the field and tend to concentrate on conceptual questions of how internet technologies effect organisations, as well as arguing for boosting value and return on investment via evaluation. Despite its importance, little study has been undertaken on the difficulties that managers face when engaging in social media activities.

In this work, ML algorithms have been applied to predict social media performance measures using the Facebook metrics dataset. To forecast social media performance measures, ML regression methods such as LightGBM, random forest, AdaBoost and XGBoost regressor were used in this model. Also, the performance of the model has been analysed with regression evaluation metrics.

10.2 RELATED WORKS

The associated studies are concerned with the performance of social media in terms of scenario analysis and visualisation tools for accessible black box mining procedures used to make sound judgments. They employ a variety of learning techniques to create a data-driven framework that learns an unknown underlying function that translates multiple inputs to a single output target. Then, they can decide if the model makes sense to experts in the field and if it shows information that could be useful.

Nti et al. [13] studied the association between academic accomplishment and a social networking site's usage rate, type of use, and level of exposure. A simple sampling strategy was used to sample 550 people; an effort was made to address the literature's various opinions on social media use and academic achievement. Furthermore, using a predictive framework based on the ML algorithms decision tree (DT) and random forest (RF), they projected the students' grade point average.

Andy et al. [14] developed a cardiovascular risk prediction system using social media data. They received Facebook status updates for all consenting patients up to five years prior to study enrolment. Patients were found who had no previous record of coronary artery disease, an atherosclerotic cardiovascular disease rating in the electronic medical data, and over 200 words in the Facebook postings. Based on these people's Facebook remarks, they used a ML algorithm to generate ten-year atherosclerotic risk of cardiovascular disease ratings. Using an ML model, a psycholinguistic lexicon, grammatical analysis, and words rate, they investigated whether language from posts alone could predict changes in risk ratings and the identification of certain words with danger categories.

Kongar et al. [15] use ML and data investigation to observe Twitter tweets, Twitter analytics, and company financial indicators to get insights on important messaging types on social media networks (DEA). Several DEA models are used to examine numerous input data sets and generate an efficiency score for the selected brands, while automated ML is used to classify tweets from selected US furniture retail stores. Based on the survey's findings, the study analyses the significance of the results for small and large firm digital marketers at the corporate level.

Because this information affects investor behaviour, Khan et al. [16] claim that equity markets may be anticipated using ML algorithms based on social network and economic news. They used ML algorithms on social network and economic news statistics to investigate the impact of social platform and business news information on share market prediction performance over a 10-day interval. The datasets are subjected to feature selection and spam tweet reduction in order to improve prediction quality and effectiveness. Additionally, they conducted tests to determine which financial markets are challenging to forecast as well as those that are impacted by social media and economic news. They compared the findings of many approaches in order to find a consistent classifier.

According to Salminen et al. [17], ML has a promising opportunity for automatically identifying clients' pain points, which are specific problems identified by customers that the organisation can address. The unstructured material spread through social media, on the other hand, makes identification difficult. As a result, the researchers tested and evaluated the efficiency of several ML techniques for recognising pain points for improved customer insights in order to assist businesses in gaining deeper insights into their customers' pain points. The data collection consists of 4.2 million user-generated tweets separated into five categories and directed towards 20 international organisations. Neural networks provide the greatest overall pain point identification accuracy among the studied models, at 85%. It has been demonstrated that using RoBERTa, 100 samples with SYNONYM augmentation is the most efficient way to distinguish between five distinct pain locations. This work advances ML research in academic marketing by building and assessing ML models for natural language-based content identification and categorisation. The authors advise organisations to use pain point profiling, a technique for classifying discovered pain point signals, in order to gain a deeper understanding of their clients' issues.

The proliferation of COVID-19, according to Rustam et al. [18], has created extensive health problems. Social media platforms are increasingly being used to spread news and ideas. To allocate resources effectively and economically, the situation must be accurately assessed. In this study, they use supervised machine learning to analyse sentiment in COVID-19 tweets. Being able to identify COVID-19 behaviours in tweets would help decision-makers deal with the current pandemic more intelligently. The dataset was used with permission from IEEE Data Port. An internal crawler that makes use of the Tweepy library is used to gather tweets. The TextBlob module is used to extract sentiments after pre-processing the dataset to clean it. By evaluating the effectiveness of several ML classifiers, this research advances our understanding of the subject. This collection is obtained by concatenating the bag-of-words with the keyword 'inverse document frequency'. Favourable, neutral, or unfavourable tweets are categorised. The findings demonstrate that additional tree classifiers beat all other models when utilising the concatenated feature set. We advise, reaching an accuracy rate of 0.93. The LSTM classifiers are not as accurate as ML classifiers.

According to the findings of multiple studies, researchers employed ML algorithms to create emotional analyses or regression models. The same method, however, may not provide the same accuracy across all datasets. As a result, selecting the ML approach best matched to the given dataset is crucial. In this article, the social media performance has been predicted based on the total interactions on Facebook brand's page. The following section describes the methodology of the proposed prediction model.

10.3 METHODOLOGY

10.3.1 Data

The first stage in creating a predictive model using ML is to collect data. The Facebook metrics dataset that is adopted from UCI ML repository [19, 20]. It is explained in terms of forecasting social media performance indicators

Table 10.1 Dataset features and their descriptions

S No	Feature	Description
1	Lifetime post total reach	The total number of unique viewers for a post on a page.
2	Lifetime post total impressions	Impressions measure how frequently a post from a page is shown, whether or not the post is clicked.
3	Lifetime engaged users	The quantity of distinct people that made any clicks in anywhere in a post.
4	Lifetime post consumers	The quantity of user clicks on each given post's content.
5	Lifetime post consumptions	The number of clicks on the post.
6	Lifetime post impressions by people who have liked a page	Total amount of impressions generated solely by those who have liked a page.
7	Lifetime post reach by people who like a page	The number of unique users that viewed a post on a page because they liked it.
8	Lifetime people who have liked a page and engaged with a post	The total number of unique users that liked a page and clicked anywhere in a post.
9	Comments	Total number of comments of the page.
10	Like	Total number of likes of the page.
11	Share	Total number of shares of the page.
12	Total interactions	Total sum of likes, comments and shares.

and assessing the influence on brand creation using a data mining technique. All posts produced between 01 January and 31 December 2014, were put on the Facebook page of a well-known cosmetic firm. This dataset contains 500 instances with 19 attributes. A typical data mining approach involves steps such as data comprehension, data preparation, modelling, and evaluation. The features in the dataset can be used to assess the performance of posts. As a result, any of the traits can be utilised to anticipate. It should be noted that the 'page total likes' feature is not tied to any specific post, but rather to the overall success of the page. As a result, we included it as an input feature because it may change the impact of posting each post. So, the method involved modelling each of the twelve post-performance-related variables to find out which ones could be predicted better. Table 10.1 describes the 12 important attributes of the dataset. The 'total interaction' attribute will be considered as the target variable and others are considered as independent variable in the proposed prediction model.

10.3.2 Data Preprocessing

Many existing industrial and research datasets contain missing values. They appear for a variety of reasons, including incorrect measurements and manual data input techniques. The deletion of rows or columns with null values is one method of dealing with missing values. Many off-the-shelf ML techniques, including artificial neural network models, are incapable of directly dealing with missing information. If any of the attributes have a missing value, the entire instance in the dataset is discarded. After eliminating them, 495 instances were used to build the model. The model has been developed with 80:20 data split where 80% of the 495 instances have been used for training and 20% of the instances have been used for testing. The performance of the model has been evaluated with test set.

10.3.3 Exploratory Data Analysis (EDA)

A thorough knowledge of the various data types is necessary for feature engineering for ML models and EDA. Some variables' data types must be converted in order to make acceptable visual encoding choices in data visualisation and storytelling. In terms of ML, most data can be divided into four categories: numerical data, categorical data, time-series data, and text data [20]. Figure 10.1 shows the count of posts like link, photo, status, and video. In this dataset most of the posts are in the form of photos. The 'Type' attribute has been converted into integer type by assigning the numerical values for the objects photo, status, link, and video as 1, 2, 3, and 4 respectively.

Figure 10.2 shows the distribution of likes per post Vs frequency. Here, frequency talks about the number of likes for every distribution on a scale

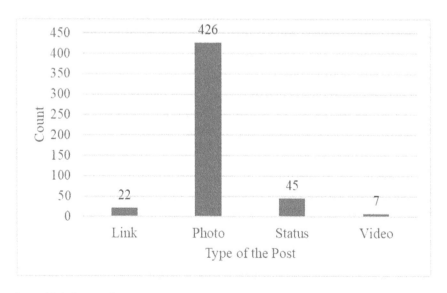

Figure 10.1 Count of various posts in the dataset.

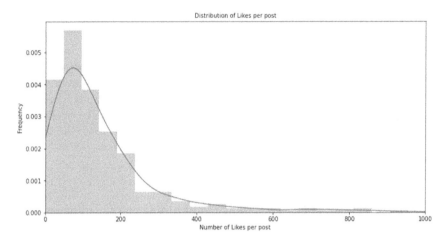

Figure 10.2 Distribution of likes per post.

of 0.001 scale. Maximum frequency is shown in the above figure for 100. Figure 10.3 shows the scatter plot of various attributes Vs total interactions. The total interactions are the sum of comment, share, and like attributes. A scatter (XY) plot is a type of vertical data visualisation tool that depicts the relationship between two sets of data. It is a graphical representation of data that is represented by a succession of dots plotted in a two-dimensional or three-dimensional plane. The "page total likes" metric counts how many people liked the page when the post was published. The remaining measures are less obvious. Customer conversations regarding a brand in online social networks are strong mindset facilitators that may have a significant influence on brand growth. It is decided that "total interactions" can be the target variable for this regression model.

Figure 10.4 shows the heatmap of the dataset. When there are numerous variables to compare, a heatmap is a handy visualisation approach for illustrating multivariate data. A heatmap is a pattern of coloured squares that shows values for an important variable along two axes. The axis variables are divided into ranges, much like a bar diagram or histogram, and the colour of each cell corresponds to the value of the primary variable in the associated cell range. The numerical numbers included within the cell demonstrate the relationship between the two variables. Positive numbers represent a positive connection, whilst negative values reflect a negative connection. Use correlation heatmaps to find potential correlations between variables and rate their strength. It is observed that 'Post Weekday', 'Post Hour' attributes are the negatively correlated with the target. 'Page total likes' have less correlation with target. These features can be discarded from the predictive model development.

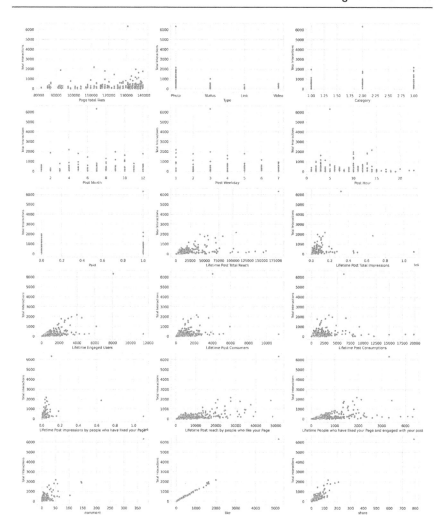

Figure 10.3 Scatter plot of various attributes Vs total interactions.

10.3.4 Machine Learning Algorithms

ML is an artificial intelligence and computer science discipline that uses data and algorithms to simulate how humans learn, gradually improving its accuracy. Three categories of ML exist: supervised, unsupervised, and reinforcement learning. Simply expressed, ML enables a user to send massive volumes of data to a computer algorithm, and the computer will assess and provide data-driven recommendations and conclusions based only on the input data. In this situation, ML approaches were employed to generate the regression model [21]. A regression model is a mathematical representation

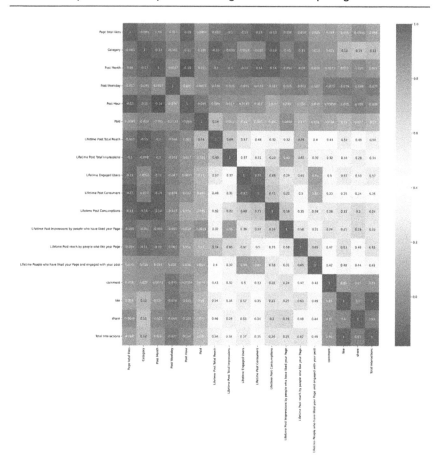

Figure 10.4 Heatmap of the dataset.

of the connection between one or more independent variables and a goal, response, or dependent variable. Three categories linear, multiple linear, and nonlinear are used to categorise regression analysis. Nonlinear regression analysis is widely used when working with difficult to manage data sets when the relationship between the dependent and independent variables is nonlinear. The vast majority of real-world datasets are nonlinear in nature. In this model development, supervised ML algorithms such as LightGBM, RF, AdaBoost, and XGBoost have been adopted.

10.3.4.1 Light Gradient Boosting

The advantages of LightGBM [22], including sparse optimisation, parallel training, multiple loss functions, regularisation, bagging, and early stopping, are similar to those of XGBoost. The main difference between the two is the structure of trees. The majority of other implementations develop a tree row by row, whereas LightGBM does not.

Light GBM, also known as a distributed gradient boosting framework for ML, is an acronym for 'light gradient boosting machine'. It is a DT approach that is employed in both classification and regression problems. The algorithm is prediction-based. Performance and accuracy are its two key focus areas according to its characteristics and properties. Gradient-based one side sampling and exclusive feature bundling are aspects of LightGBM.

10.3.4.1.1 Gradient-Based One Side Sampling (GOSS)

It's a method that gains from GBDT's lack of native weights for data samples. Since different gradients play different roles in the estimate of information gain, instances with bigger gradients will offer a greater quantity of information gain. As a consequence, GOSS randomly discards instances with small gradients while keeping samples with big gradients in order to preserve the correctness of the data. Approximately 80% of weight of low gradient instances and 20% from high gradient instances takes randomly. By this gradient is decreases for a newly trained model and performance and accuracy increases.

10.3.4.1.2 Exclusive Feature Bundling (EFB)

A nearly lossless technique for reducing the overall number of usable characteristics is EFB. Numerous characteristics in a sparse feature set are nearly mutually incompatible, which shows that they seldom take nonzero values simultaneously. The best illustration of unique features is one-shot encoded features. By combining these attributes, EFB reduces the number of dimensions while maintaining a high degree of accuracy. An exclusive feature bundle is a collection of exclusive features combined into a single feature.

10.3.4.2 Random Forest (RF) Regression

A supervised learning method called RF [23] uses a lot of DTs and an ensemble learning methodology. There are no interactions between DTs as they are built since RF is a bagging approach, which means all computations are done in parallel. Both classification and regression issues might be handled using RF.

The name 'RF' is derived from the bagging concept of data randomisation (Random) and the construction of numerous DTs (Forest). The basic concept of ensemble learning is straightforward. Multiple ML algorithms will be used, and their predictions will be merged in some fashion. It is known as the ensemble approach. This method produces more accurate forecasts than any particular model. Similarly, the RF algorithm will forecast using an ensemble technique.

10.3.4.3 Adaptive Boosting (AdaBoost) Regressor

AdaBoost [24] was one of the earliest boosting algorithms that was utilised for the purpose of problem solving. When using AdaBoost, the data for each training sample (x_i, y_i) is transformed by the application of a weight $(w_1, w_2, \ldots, w_N)$. At the beginning of the process, the basic learner gives equal weight to all of the observations. Once weights have been assigned to each observation, the weak learner can then be utilised for prediction. As a result of this, the misclassified observations made by the weak learner are given more weight in the predictions made by the base learner that comes after it. This process will be carried out until the tth iteration, at which point the T_i base learning algorithm will have reached its maximum potential. It is possible to develop a more robust learner by integrating the outputs of the weak learners, which also increases one's ability to foresee future events.

10.3.4.4 Extreme Gradient Boosting (XGBoost)

Boosting is the process of combining multiple weak classifiers into a single robust model in order to improve its overall accuracy. Boosting is a technique that was developed by expanding upon the groundwork that was set by gradient boosting [25]. This expansion resulted in the creation of XGBoost. In terms of computational speed, scalability, and generalisation performance, XGBoost is a version of gradient boosting that outperforms its parent algorithm. When utilising XGBoost, the organisation of data comes before anything else. Due to the fact that XGBoost will only accept numeric vectors as input, any categorical data will be transformed into their respective numeric equivalents. This encoding change can be accomplished by using One Hot Encoding. In the following step, the process of feature engineering and data cleansing is carried out. By utilising the universal function, we are able to obtain the estimated model, which can be represented by the formula:

$$\hat{y}_i^t = \sum_{k=1}^{t} f_k(x_i) = \hat{y}_i^{(t-1)} + f_t(x_i) \tag{1}$$

where,

$\hat{y}_i^t$ = forecasts at the stage t
$f_t(x_i)$ = a learner at stage t
x_i = the input variable
$\hat{y}_i^{(t-1)}$ = forecasts at the stage t-1

10.4 RESULTS AND DISCUSSION

The train-test split is used to assess if ML algorithms are appropriate for prediction-based algorithms or applications. This method is a rapid and simple technique to evaluate the output of our individual ML model to output from other machines. The 80:20 data split has been carried out. The developed regression model performance has been computed using regression evaluation metrics.

10.4.1 Regression Evaluation Metrics

An assessment metric measures the performance of a prediction model. A common method for doing this is to train a model on one dataset, use it to predict the future values on a holdout dataset that wasn't used during training, and then compare the forecasts to the holdout dataset's projected values. The common evaluation metrics for regression problems were described below.

10.4.1.1 Mean Absolute Error

Mean absolute error (MAE) is the mean of the absolute value of the errors. A fairly straightforward statistic called MAE determines the exact difference between real and anticipated values. MAE is expressed as,

$$MAE = \frac{1}{n}\sum_{i=1}^{n}|y - \hat{y}| \tag{2}$$

Here the n indicates the number of data, y is the real output and $\hat{y}$ is the predicted output.

10.4.1.2 Mean Squared Error

Mean squared error (MSE) is the mean of the squared errors.

There is a little degree of mean absolute error fluctuation in the most widely used and fundamental metric, MSE. The phrase 'mean squared error' relates to finding the squared difference between the real and projected value. MSE is expressed as,

$$MSE = \frac{1}{n}\sum_{i=1}^{n}(y - \hat{y})^2 \tag{3}$$

If the dataset contains outliers, the estimated MSE is higher since the outliers are penalised the most. In general, it lacks the robustness to outliers that MAE has.

10.4.1.3 Root Mean Squared Error

Root mean squared error (RMSE) is the square root of the mean of the squared errors. It is expressed as,

$$RMSE = \sqrt{\frac{1}{n}\sum\nolimits_{i=1}^{n}(y-\hat{y})^2} \tag{4}$$

Due to its ability to be interpreted in 'y' units, RMSE is even more widely used than MSE.

10.4.1.4 R-Squared

R-Squared (R^2) is an indicator of how much of the variance for a dependent variable in a regression model is explained by one or more independent variables. It is expressed as,

$$R^2 = 1 - \frac{Squared\,sum\,error\,of\,regression\,line}{Squared\,sum\,error\,of\,mean\,line} \tag{5}$$

The R^2 value should typically be between zero and one, such as 0.8, meaning that the model should be able to account for 80% of the variance in the data.

10.4.2 Discussion of Results

The research's conclusions and analyses were based on tests done on a particular set of Facebook posts from a cosmetic brand in 2014. Data mining algorithms depend on understanding patterns hidden in data since they are entirely data driven. Figure 10.5 displays the results of implemented models such the LightGBM, Random Forest Regression, AdaBoost, and XGBoost. The numerical values of assessment metrics can be found from Table 10.2. It is observed that RF-based regression model provided better results for the Facebook metrics dataset for the 'total interactions' target variable. A good model must fit all of the input information such that the projected values are as near to the actual values as feasible. As a consequence, we calculated the absolute difference between the predicted and actual numbers for each post first. We also calculated the percentage difference to examine the forecasts' relative deviation. Finally, for each model, we calculated the R^2 value, which is a prominent statistic for assessing the efficacy of regression models based on relative difference. The highly relevant features with target variable 'total interactions' are 'like', 'share', 'comment', and 'Lifetime Post Impressions by people who have liked your Page'. The model is less influenced with 'Post Weekday', 'Post Hour', 'Post Month', 'Page total likes', 'Paid',

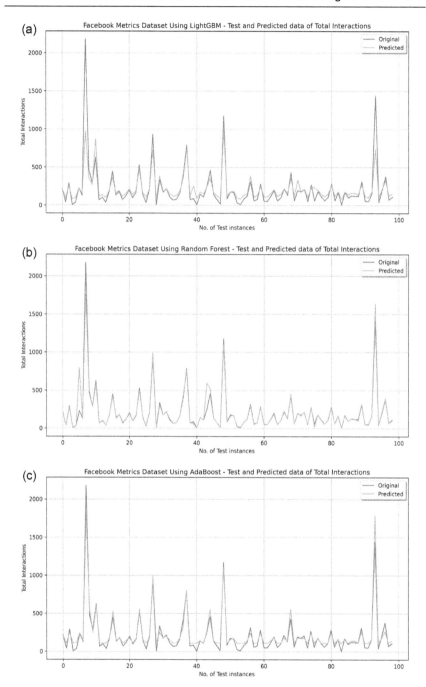

Figure 10.5 Performance of proposed model (a) LightGBM (b) Random Forest Regression (c) AdaBoost (d) XGBoost.

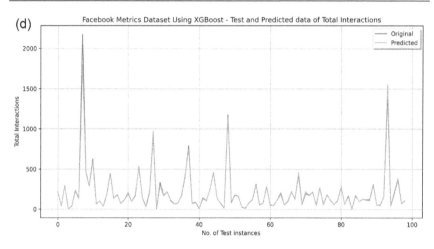

Figure 10.5 (Continued)

Table 10.2 Regression evaluation metrics comparison

ML Algorithm	MAE	MSE	RMSE	R² Square
LightGBM	68.281	24031.993	155.022	0.732
Random Forest Regression	24.344	6798.362	82.452	0.924
AdaBoost	39.98	2669.453	51.667	0.98
XGBoost	3.05	20.65	4.54	0.999

and 'Category' attributes. Models must be updated anytime data sources change, which might happen not just when evaluating other study as well as when the environment surrounding the company and the consumers naturally changes. Unforeseen circumstances can potentially significantly affect a model's capacity for prediction. As a result, data mining models must be constantly updated to reflect these changes. As a result, the reported results cannot be generalised. However, the experimental technique used may be extended to a different organisation and time period, revealing potentially relevant information.

10.5 CONCLUSION

Using data mining, this study focuses on predicting performance measures taken from postings published on a company's Facebook page. The publicly available Facebook metrics dataset is adopted from the UCI ML repository and the prediction model for social media performance metrics have been developed using the 'total interactions' attribute with 495 instances. The LightGBM, RF, AdaBoost, and XGBoost regression algorithms have been employed to develop the prediction model. Based on regression evaluation metrics, the XGBoost-based regression model performs better. The most and least relevant features have been identified. Customer feedback on products and services is always a concern for most large- and medium-sized businesses because it affects the financial success of the company. We believe that the developed model will help the concerned industry predict the performance of their Facebook page. This study generates several proposals for further investigation. The model may be enhanced with additional context characteristics. The comments on every post for customer trend analysis may indicate the feelings elicited by each post, and text mining may be utilised to gain new knowledge.

REFERENCES

[1] Moro, S., Rita, P., & Vala, B. (2016). Predicting social media performance metrics and evaluation of the impact on brand building: A data mining approach. Journal of Business Research, 69(9), 3341–3351.

[2] Facebook (2019). Company Info. Retrieved from https://tinyurl.com/n544jrt.

[3] Appel, G., Grewal, L., Hadi, R., & Stephen, A. T. (2020). The future of social media in marketing. Journal of the Academy of Marketing Science, 48, 79–95. https://doi.org/10.1007/s11747-019-00695-1

[4] Shahbaznezhad, H., Dolan, R., & Rashidirad, M. (2021). The role of social media content format and platform in users' engagement behavior. Journal of Interactive Marketing, 53(1), 47–65. https://doi.org/10.1016/j.intmar.2020.05.001

[5] Dwivedi, Y. K., Ismagilova, E., Hughes, D. L., Carlson, J., Filieri, R., Jacobson, J., . . . & Wang, Y. (2021). Setting the future of digital and social media marketing research: Perspectives and research propositions. International Journal of Information Management, 59, 102168. https://doi.org/10.1016/j.ijinfomgt.2020.102168.

[6] Tran, Q. M., Nguyen, H. D., Nguyen, B. T., Pham, V. T., & Le, T. T. (2021). Influence prediction on social media network through contents and interaction behaviors using attention-based knowledge graph. 2021 13th International Conference on Knowledge and Systems Engineering (KSE) (pp. 1–7). https://doi.org/10.1109/KSE53942.2021.9648712

[7] Chaudhary, K., Alam, M., Al-Rakhami, M. S., & Gumaei, A. (2021). Machine learning-based mathematical modelling for prediction of social media consumer behavior using big data analytics. Journal of Big Data, 8, 73. https://doi.org/10.1186/s40537-021-00466-2

[8] Senthil Arasu, B., Jonath Backia Seelan, B., & Thamaraiselvan, N. (2020). A machine learning-based approach to enhancing social media marketing. Computers & Electrical Engineering, 86, 106723. https://doi.org/10.1016/j.compeleceng.2020.106723.

[9] Sarath Kumar Boddu, R., Santoki, A. A., Khurana, S., Koli, P. V., Rai, R., & Agrawal, A. (2022). An analysis to understand the role of machine learning, robotics and artificial intelligence in digital marketing. Materials Today: Proceedings, 56(Part 4), 2288–2292. https://doi.org/10.1016/j.matpr.2021.11.637.

[10] Kanagarathinam, K., Sankaran, D., & Manikandan, R. (2022). Machine learning-based risk prediction model for cardiovascular disease using a hybrid dataset. Data & Knowledge Engineering, 140, 102042. https://doi.org/10.1016/j.datak.2022.102042

[11] Sekar, K., Kanagarathinam, K., Subramanian, S., Venugopal, E., & Udayakumar, C. (2022). An improved power quality disturbance detection using deep learning approach. Mathematical Problems in Engineering, 2022, Article ID 7020979. https://doi.org/10.1155/2022/7020979

[12] Kavaskar, S., Sendilkumar, S., & Karthick, K. (2020). Power quality disturbance detection using machine learning algorithm. In 2020 IEEE International Conference on Advances and Developments in Electrical and Electronics Engineering (ICADEE), Coimbatore, pp. 1–5. doi: 10.1109/ICADEE51157.2020.9368939.

[13] Nti, I. K., Akyeramfo-Sam, S., Bediako-Kyeremeh, B., & Agyemang, S. A. (2021). Prediction of social media effects on students' academic performance using Machine Learning Algorithms (MLAs). Journal of Computers in Education, 9(2), 195–223.

[14] Andy, A. U., Guntuku, S. C., Adusumalli, S., Asch, D. A., Groeneveld, P. W., Ungar, L. H., & Merchant, R. M. (2021). Predicting cardiovascular risk using social media data: Performance evaluation of machine-learning models. JMIR Cardio, 5.

[15] Kongar, E., & Adebayo, O. (2021). Impact of social media marketing on business performance: A hybrid performance measurement approach using data analytics and machine learning. IEEE Engineering Management Review, 49, 133–147.

[16] Khan, W., Ghazanfar, M. A., Azam, M. A., Karami, A., Alyoubi, K. H., & Alfakeeh, A. S. (2022). Stock market prediction using machine learning classifiers and social media, news. Journal of Ambient Intelligence and Humanized Computing, 1–24.

[17] Salminen, J. O., Mustak, M., Corporan, J., Jung, S., & Jansen, B. J. (2022). Detecting pain points from user-generated social media posts using machine learning. Journal of Interactive Marketing, 57, 517–539.

[18] Rustam, F., Khalid, M. A., Aslam, W., Rupapara, V., Mehmood, A., & Choi, G. S. (2021). A performance comparison of supervised machine learning models for Covid-19 tweets sentiment analysis. PLoS One, 16.

[19] Moro, S., Rita, P., & Vala, B. (2016). Predicting social media performance metrics and evaluation of the impact on brand building: A data mining approach. Journal of Business Research, 69(9), 3341–3351.

[20] Dataset URL. Retrieved from https://archive.ics.uci.edu/ml/datasets/Facebook+metrics

[21] Nicodemo, C., & Satorra, A. (2022). Exploratory data analysis on large data sets: The example of salary variation in Spanish Social Security

Data. BRQ Business Research Quarterly, 25(3), 283–294. https://doi.org/10.1177/2340944420957335

[22] Liao, H., Zhang, X., Zhao, C., Chen, Y., Zeng, X., & Li, H. (2022). Light-GBM: An efficient and accurate method for predicting pregnancy diseases. Journal of Obstetrics and Gynaecology, 42(4), 620–629. https://doi.org/10.1080/01443615.2021.1945006

[23] Danandeh Mehr, A., Torabi Haghighi, A., Jabarnejad, M., Safari, M. J. S., & Nourani, V. A. (2022). New evolutionary hybrid random forest model for SPEI forecasting. Water, 14, 755. https://doi.org/10.3390/w14050755

[24] Rani, S., Kumar, A., Bagchi, A., Yadav, S., & Kumar, S. (2021). RPL based routing protocols for load balancing in IoT network. Journal of Physics: Conference Series, 1950, 012073. https://doi.org/10.1088/1742-6596/1950/1/012073.

[25] Rani, S., Tripathi, K., Arora, Y., & Kumar, A. (2022). Analysis of anomaly detection of Malware using KNN. In 2022 2nd International Conference on Innovative Practices in Technology and Management (ICIPTM), pp. 774–779. https://doi.org/10.1109/ICIPTM54933.2022.9754044.

Chapter 11

How Does Clustering Help Us with Better Understanding in Social Text Streams?

Data Clustering and Classification with ML and DL

[1]Tajinder Singh and [2]Madhu Kumari

[1]Sant Longowal Institute of Engineering and Technology, Longowal, Sangrur, Punjab, India

[2]DIT, Dehradun, Uttrakhand, India

11.1 INTRODUCTION

Social networks and social media are quite well known these days among online users. The information explosion is facilitated by a number of social media sites. These platforms assist information seekers in identifying diverse patterns of information. Countless data segments known as real-time data arrive from numerous social media networks [1]. These data segments contain a variety of informational hidden patterns. Social media networks and media platforms are frequently used for a variety of purposes due to their simplicity and usability. It is difficult to assess the data that has been acquired, thus researchers employ social media to uncover hidden patterns for decision-making [2].

Numerous social media platforms participate in different events, which helps the social users to be a part of these events. Users share their opinions and experiences which helps the events to be more influential. In this way the diffusion rate of the event among social media also increases. At any social media platform, an event E is an instance on which the social users given their own opinions at different time intervals which are defined as $T = (t_1, t_2, \ldots\ldots t_n)$ where T is defining a time interval. Social text stream can be used to easily examine user behavior that changes over time. In order to make decisions and to investigate the contextual representation of semantics in social text streams, including social user behavior, hidden information can be examined. Decision-making involves the use of contextual knowledge, which is subject to change throughout time.

Text mining in social media event detection and classification plays a significant role which can be used to examine topic analysis and trend prediction [3, 4] etc. In social media text stream a stream of text S is represented as $(s_1, s_2, \ldots\ldots s_n)$ at a time T where $T = (t_1, t_2, \ldots\ldots t_n)$.

DOI: 10.1201/9781003329947-11

Data extracted from various social media platforms needs to be cluster for which clustering plays an important role. Semantics and lexicons can be combined together based on their similarity. The similarity index of various lexicons can be analyzed from the user's post in which user U is a set of various users $U = \{u_1, u_2, u_3, \ldots \ldots u_n\}$ located at different locations l.

In real-time data extraction, the process of extracting data can be based on open interval of time or can be based on closed interval which depends on the situation and analysis requirements [3, 5]. The start time of tweets in real time scenario is $t_{E_{start}}$ and event end time $t_{E_{end}}$. For a specific event e_α belongs to a series of events, $E = \{e_1, e_2, e_3, \ldots \ldots e_n\}$ a trend can be predicted by analyzing the rate of diffusion in a span of time [6]. This scenario also helps to know the event's impact and user's interest rate in particular scenario, which is usually measured in terms of peak time of an event $T_{e_{peak}}$. Thus, it is very much needed to analyze the behavior of events including user's participation in real-time. The main focus of this study is to analyze the role of clustering in social media which helps to compute the participation of users and provide an ease to analyze their diffusion rate.

11.2 LITERATURE SURVEY

Numerous researchers have given their own views and discussions on social media text stream. Therefore, based on their facts and figures it is observed that in social text stream, contextual information has a significant role. In any real-time analysis of data, it is important to consider context and based on this various surveys describing state-of-the-art social media event detection and classification have been explained [7, 8]. Authors have explained that in social media text stream, the former approaches which are explained by the various authors are classified in different ways, and it is important to classify the collected data into various units called cluster which are directly linked with their similarity. Prompt words and their context in terms of base topic is important to analyze during clustering, otherwise wrong decision will be taken due to lack of understand [2, 5, 9]. But it is also observed that in this whole process, authors have to pass through various phases to extract the required information patterns [1]. We all know that Twitter has a high profile which creates huge challenges. Despite these obstacles, it is used as a primary source of data in a variety of research tasks focusing on social text stream.

In text stream, the nature of the data will be unstructured so it is not easy to extract important semantics. Due to this reason, pre-processing is very important which helps to remove unwanted information from the collected text streams. As per the requirement and need, collected text can be filtered. Various symbols such as (@, #, etc., need to be removed so that a structured representation of data can be obtained [10]. It is also observed that in social media that users use short forms and abbreviations therefore, to handle this authors [11, 12] designed a pre-processing approach which helps to complete semantics into actual words [13]. Machine learning based approaches such as supervised and unsupervised can also be used for pre-processing [14].

For event classification and analysis content based machine learning approaches are used [15] which help the authors to analyze events from the social text stream. Clustering is also one from which to organize data into different class of clusters based on their similarity [16]. Various clustering mechanisms are available which help the users to organize data and its dynamic nature to make it more efficient and user friendly. Numerous applications such as social media tracking, topic detection, event analysis and tracking trend prediction including impact are using clustering [17].

In the current scenario, text stream clustering is widely used which helps to analyze huge data to extract informative patterns including their impact in terms of event detection, classification and tracking problem. Novel clustering mechanisms are given [18] which track social events and classify them as needed. They claimed that without analysis of content it is not possible to analyze the behavior of social events [19]. Online adaptive filtering adopted by various authors [20, 21] claimed that it helps to recognize evolving events based on the content.

Fourier transformation and wavelet based event detection also analyze events in social media text stream at different temporal and spatial scales [22]. Various tools and visualization methods are available such as graphs to view extracted patterns of analyzed data which makes comparison easy.

With the comparison of data, there exists a loss of data during preprocessing [23] and due to this sometimes important data is lost which is very important for decision making. Therefore, due to this reason spatial temporal information, including their contextual polarity which changes with time, is also required for accurate decision making [24]. Representation of various lexicons and their semantics also change with the context and in such scenarios a deep knowledge, including the sensitivity of the topic, helps to identify the exact meaning in an effective manner [25, 26]. This contextual information sensitivity is addressed [27] in which a dynamic drift in various semantics and lexicons with change of time is explained. The authors used the vector space model to represent semantics whereas, advance fixed vector dimension is used due to the fixed size of lexicons [28].

In existing studies to handle contextual polary in real-time data, Bayesian networks and Belief networks are frequently used [29] in which vector representation of text is very common using embedding. Various authors used embeddings in which [30] they provide a way by which text can be represented into vectors using embeddings. Language models such as trigram and n-grams are commonly used to analyze the impact of various semantics on neighboring lexicons [27, 31, 32]. For the classification purpose of semantic words, word2vec is commonly used. This model helps to organize huge data including neural networks [33]. A solid vector representation of various semantics is generated by word2vec in which weights represent words in the input to the neural network. Semantic vectors which make this task very easy helps the authors to analyze the data uniformly in required fashion [34].

In this representation of text to vectors the authors also used incremental clustering methods which are very helpful in real-time data analysis. In [35, 36] authors used the incremental clustering to analyze evolution of events. The incremental clustering methods will be updated whenever the novel data appears in the stream of text but due to the huge traffic of data, such models do not perform accurately because of their capability [37]. Therefore, it is important to analyze the case which helps to text the data feasibility in a real-time scenario to cluster them together in less time and complexity. As part of this online text stream, users extract data from social media for analysis. From the collected data, it is easy to analyze the impact of social media data in a real-time situation including context information [38]. For this purpose, various approaches are given in this chapter which can be adopted to analyze and detect various types of social media data in real-time including its influence impact in the future tweets.

11.3 SOCIAL TEXT STREAM: REPRESENTATION

In social text stream, data can be collected in continuous and discrete-time intervals. The extracted text needs to be pre-processed to remove unwanted information before further analysis. The crawled text (Twitter) contains unwanted information which is removed for further processing. Abbreviations, local words (slangs), short representations and OOV (out of vocabulary) are matched with the exact words to get the actual meaning. Therefore, for this purpose, pre-processing is implemented. As we are dealing with real-time data stream, it is quite difficult to obtain features from coming text to analyze them. In social text stream, data is a tweet t_w which consist of a major component such as user u and content c. In social media, every tweet t_w is associated with a social media user [2, 21]. The user profile contains a user name u_{name}, location l, time t and domain d. Therefore, for better understanding, we are describing some definitions as:

- *Text stream in social media:* A text stream in social media S is a set of all the collected data which is represented as $S = \{s_1, s_2, s_3, \ldots s_n\}$ in closed interval of time, $[t_1, t_2]$. Here the regular sequence of twitter data is defined as $T_w = (t_{w_1}, t_{w_2}, t_{w_3}, \ldots t_{w_n})$, where $t_{w_1}, t_{w_2}, t_{w_3}, \ldots t_{w_n}$ are the set of tweets extracted from the Twitter stream.
- *Topic analysis on social media:* In real-time social media data, topic is the combination of various tweets which are related to a particular context. Usually, a social media post p represents real world happenings. Multiple parameters such as time t, location l, user u can be

directly linked with start and ending time of tweets on a particular post p.

- **Clustering:** In data analytics, it is necessary to combine data according to their similarity. Clustering in text stream $S = (s_1, s_2, ...s_i, ...s_r, ...s_n)$, is a way by which data items are distributed among various clusters C which are represented as, $C = (C_1, C_2, ...C_j)$ where, $C_1, C_2, ...C_j \in S$, such that $S = \cup(c_1, c_2, ...c_j)$.
- **Cluster creation: In social text stream:** Cluster C is to be created on the basis of upcoming tweets in social media text stream on the basis of their similarity. Each of the tweets from text stream such as s_i belongs to the cluster C_j on the basis of similarity at time t_j where, $C_j \subset C$.
- **Life of a cluster:** C_{life} for the real-time data is directly associated with creation time of a cluster $C_{t_{create}}$ whereas, $C_{t_{end}}$ is the time when the last keyword is entered in a cluster. If we consider Ω is a survival time function for a cluster after creation (even no tweet added after creation time) of a cluster whereas Υ is a user defined; which indicates the dynamic nature of the cluster.
- **Novelty detection:** Novelty concept of any social media post p in text stream is associated with the creation of new cluster C_{new_i} is $p_{\beta_{novel}} \propto C_{new_i}$.
- **Similarity analysis:** Various clusters are created during event detection in text stream. Therefore, on the basis of similarity function cluster is assigned to a particular event. Thus, similarity function, $sim_f(s_f)$ holds the information about content changed within the clusters C and change in stream of text in closed time interval $[t_1, t_2]$.

11.4 ROLE OF MACHINE LEARNING IN TEXT MINING

Machine learning is a sub field of AI (Artificial intelligence). Various researchers used machine learning for various applications to help users for decision making. The machine learning approaches are based on algorithms. On the basis of data given to the designed algorithm, they perform and optimize their operations to provide better results. Intelligently, the machine learning algorithms sense the need of the current situation and accordingly they produce 'intelligent results' over time. In general there are four types of machine learning algorithms (Figure 11.1):

11.4.1 Supervised Machine Learning

In social text stream, supervised machine learning is based on examples in which data sets contains desired input and output as per the requirements. It is the responsibility of the machine learning algorithm to decide how

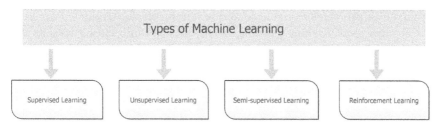

Figure 11.1 Types of machine learning.

to achieve that output based on the received input. Supervised approach analyzes the various patterns of data and on the basis of analysis it makes predictions. This process is continuing until the social text stream data is received by the user and doesn't achieve a high performance in terms of accuracy. Various types of supervised learning are:

- **Classification:** The main objective of classification is to depict a conclusion. The conclusion is depicted between the observed values and to analyze the class in which the observed belongs to. Identification of rumor and non rumor based posts on social media is an example of classification whereas, spam and non spam email identification also falls under classification.
- **Regression:** Relationship between various variables needs to be estimated and understood and for this purpose regression is used. For the purpose of prediction and forecasting based on various dependent variables and another variables regression can be used on priority.
- **Forecasting:** Forecasting is the way by which a user can analyze the predictions about the future based on historical data. The impact of various technologies and rumor posts on social media means users can be easily identified with forecasting. It also helps for trend prediction and analysis.

11.4.2 Semi-Supervised Learning

In this machine learning both labeled and unlabelled data are used. Meaning tags related information are associated with labeled data. With the help of this, the machine learning algorithm can easily understand the nature of data. On the other hand, unlabeled data does not contain such information. Therefore, with the combination, machine learning algorithms can learn to label unlabelled data accurately.

11.4.3 Unsupervised Learning

This machine learning helps to identify patterns. Various relations and correlations are identified by this approach on available data. It helps to interpret data to solve problems as per need and requirements. Generally we can say that unsupervised machine learning groups the data into cluster so that an organized representation can be formed. The organized representation of data enhances the clarity and decision making capacity from the collected data. The various types of unsupervised methods are:

- **Clustering:** Clustering helps to combine all similar lexicons and semantics together as per the define criteria. Data can be segmented using clustering and also helps to perform analysis on various data sets to extract patterns.
- **Dimension reduction:** To extract the required patterns which is required from the collected data, dimension reduction reduces the number of variables being considered.

11.4.4 Reinforcement Learning

This learning mechanism focuses on regimented learning processes. We know that in basic machine learning there exist actions, parameters and end values but in reinforcement learning usually it gains feedback from the past experiences. On the basis of historical information and past experiences, it learns to analyze data in response to generate better results. Various terms are used in reinforcement learning which are:

- **Agent:** Represents an entity which helps to recognize the environment.
- **Environment:** A stochastic environment which is random in nature by which reinforcement learning agents are surrounded by.
- **Action:** Various moves associated with agents within a specified environment.
- **State:** Defines the scenario given by the environment.
- **Reward:** To analyze and evaluate the action of the agents a feedback is given to the agent from environment.
- **Policy:** Policy is a plan applied by the agent for the next action which is usually based on current state or situation.

Including these all terms and representation, reinforcement learning is implemented by using various ways which are:

- Value-based.
- Model-based.
- Policy-based:
  - Deterministic
  - Stochastic

11.5 EVALUATION MECHANISM AND DATASET

In social media text mining, the major challenge includes data extraction in real-time. The various steps followed for data collection in text stream evaluation is explained subsequently in Figure 11.2 which depicts the real-time data extraction in Twitter.

- **Data Collection:** Tweets are extracted from the Twitter text stream and for this purpose Twitter API is used. In our research task, we concentrate on Twitter text stream. On the basis of pre-defined task the user can extract related data in a real-time scenario. Figure 11.3 (Snippet) is giving an idea to collect the tweets related to these data in real-time and accordingly event's related keywords using hashtags are applied at different time slots of streaming text for extracting similar data.
- **Mining the ground reality:** Hidden patterns of data in social media data which may include real facts and figures. Therefore, it is very important to extract all those features from data which are hidden and have a major role in the analysis of data in terms of context. Independently,

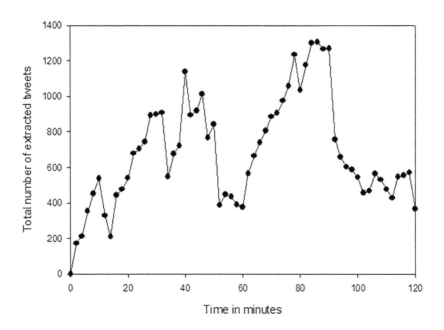

Figure 11.2 Twitter text stream extraction.

```
  def get_tweets(username):

          # Authorization to consumer key and consumer secret
          auth = tweepy.OAuthHandler(consumer_key, consumer_secret)

          # Access to user's access key and access secret
          auth.set_access_token(access_key, access_secret)

          # Calling api
          api = tweepy.API(auth)

          # 200 tweets to be extracted
          number_of_tweets=200
          tweets = api.user_timeline(screen_name=username)

          # Empty Array
          tmp=[]

          # create array of tweet information: username,
          # tweet id, date/time, text
          tweets_for_csv = [tweet.text for tweet in tweets] # CSV file created
          for j in tweets_for_csv:

                  # Appending tweets to the empty array tmp
                  tmp.append(j)

          # Printing the tweets
          print(tmp)

  # Driver code
  if __name__ == '__main__':

          # Here goes the twitter handle for the user
```

Figure 11.3 Real-time data extraction process.

a user cannot rely on visible features therefore, for that purpose manually features can be extracted. At various time spans, context of a topic
can be changed which is very important to study including multiple
sets of keywords in a particular time (same context) slot in which that
feature and theme appeared in conventional reports.

- **Topic Detection:** Extracted mechanism is based on a particular topic
  which decides the relevancy of the real-time data in terms of contextual
  polarity. Upcoming data stream which is to be evaluated in each time
  contains hidden patterns which are very important to extract based on
  topic and due to that reason the extraction mechanism is divided into
  various time slots and we merely consider text from stream as input
  with ground reality.
- **Evaluation of topic detection output with ground reality:** Evaluation
  of collected data in real-time can be evaluated in terms of loss before
  and after pre-processing with additional parameters such as split error
  and JS divergence.

  As described in Figure 11.2, tweets are extracted from the Twitter network. Each and every entity includes the structure of network, including
  user related information with location. Usually data is extracted based
  on query of keywords and features are considered as described [20].
  In text stream of Twitter, total 2356293 tweets from stream in various
  time slots are extracted. Every text available in text stream is related
  with different nodes. Every tweet from the Twitter nodes includes the
  information of sender and the receivers. After applying preprocessing

(filtering), various topics from the entire dataset are considered and these topics may or may not semantically be distinguishable.

11.6 PROPOSED METHODOLOGY OF CLUSTERING

In real-time data, the authors have been studying approaches for an efficient clustering mechanism for huge data. As we described previously, clustering is the important task of dividing the collected data into similar groups, called clusters. Clustering is quite a challenging task which includes various requirements of clustering in real-time data set which is described as:

- **Scalability:** Clustering mechanism deals with the huge number of data set which can be a million and due to that reason it can produce biased results. Therefore, there is a need to design a type of clustering approach which can handle huge features and produce scalable results.
- **Ability to deal with real time data:** Numerous clustering algorithms are designed for time-binary data. Whereas it is important to design the clustering approach which will handle real-time data effectively and efficiently.
- **Cluster requirement:** Input parameters from users are important to consider for analyzing cluster requirements. Deciding required clusters for real-time data is quite sensitive as parameters are very difficult to analyze. Therefore, an approach which can decide the requirement of clusters required for collected data in an effective way is needed.
- **Ability to handle noisy data:** Clustering approach should be designed in such a way that if any slang, out of vocabulary, short form of text arrives then an ability to handle it normally with good output results rather than compromising with performance.
- **Dimensionality in data:** Ability to handle sparse and highly skewed data as it may contain more than three dimensions and due to that reason it is a challenging task to handle data objects in high-dimensional space.
- **Interpretability of clustering:** Semantic representation and the ability to handle context based information is quite important during clustering. Therefore, to make it useable clustering mechanism should be comprehensive.
- Therefore, on the basis of data, a proposed clustering mechanism is designed (Algorithm 1) [21] which process all the real time data tweets and classifies them according to their similarity. The designed algorithm is not only clustering tweets but also taking care of contextual behavior of various semantics in the social text streams.

Algorithm 1: Procedure for event detection and classification in various text streams using fast clustering

---

Initialization:

1: **Input: A continuous stream of tweets:** Twitter text stream

$$T_w = (t_{w_1}, t_{w_2}, t_{w_3}, \ldots\ldots t_{w_n})_{t_w=1}^{t_w=n},$$

Cluster survival time η, t_c is a creation time of cluster, t_λ is the time when cluster will not accept more events t_η is the time span, and C_{life} is the life or survival life of a cluster.

Weight associated with text $\{w_j^{(T_w)} > 0\}_{t_w=1}^{t_{w_n}}$ and cluster number K. **Output:** Event detection and classification to analyze the active cluster C with collection of classified words w_i in terms of events from text streams S.

2: **Begin:**

for: $t_w = 1$ to t_{w_n} from text stream $(s_1, s_2, \ldots\ldots s_n) \rightarrow (t_{w_1}, t_{w_2}, t_{w_3}, \ldots\ldots t_{w_n})_{t_w=1}^{t_w=n}$

Compute indicator dataset of text stream corresponding to $W^{(T_w)}$ and constitute the indicator subset $C_{t_w}^{(0)}$ that indicates $T_{w()}$

end for

3: **Begin** loop initialize the K initial cluster center $\{t_{w_j}^{t_{w_n}}\}_{j=1}^K$ of $\{C_{t_w}^{(0)}\}_{t_w=1}^{t_{w_n}}$ and set the cluster label.

4: **for**

$t_w = 1$ to t_{w_n}

Divide $\{C_{t_w}^{(0)}\}_{t_w=1}^{t_{w_n}}$ into K cluster by using second step.

5: Re-compute the new cluster centers $\{t_j^{\wedge(t_{w_n})}\}_{j=1}^K$ of $(C_{t_w}^{(0)})$

Analyze the new cluster head and re-compute the new cluster centers as:

$\{t_j^{\wedge t_{w_n}} = t_j^{\wedge t_{w_n}}\}_{j=1}^K$

end for

end loop

The proposed approach for event classification will act as an asset to combine similar types of lexicons using clustering (Figure 11.4). The parameters used in this approach helps to give better performance in decision making and planning. Information which will be collected using various parameters such as user ID, location and information related to event, etc., save users time to track the particular topic efficiently. The criteria used to select the various parameters for clustering depends on the upcoming data in real-time scenario. In this case, it is observed that RFID and GPS based on cloud services also helps to track events effectively. The main challenge in tracking an event and clustering the similar lexicons together depends on the ability of storage. User's classification and their interest to participate in a particular

Accuracy of Proposed Clustering techniques in various text streams

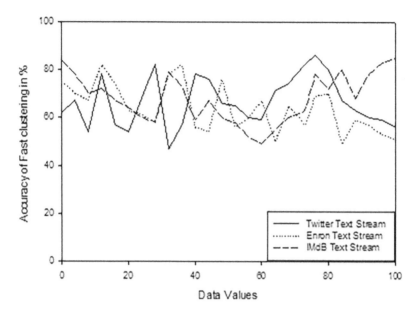

Figure 11.4 Accuracy of proposed clustering mechanism.

topic also plays a crucial role. Therefore, the effective selection of various parameters helps the users to track and trace several real-time events on the basis of origin, location and user including the historical information which is described in Figure 11.5.

11.7 WORKING OF CLUSTERING IN TEXT STREAM

As per the working principle of Algorithm 1, real-time tweets are clustered and if any novel keywords arrive then its score will be computed. An indicator is established and computed for text stream and the optimal value which will determine the requirements of clusters is computed using a gap statistic approach. The gap statistic method can work on any type of clustering approach. Updating the function is also used to update the value of cluster parameters on discovering a new text stream after assigning a cluster to a particular semantic word. Gradient descent method is used for updating the cluster value with weights. Performance of various cluster mechanisms are tested using various text stream and it is found that the Algorithm 1 is performing well in terms of accuracy using various text streams.

From the previous discussion we have seen the performance of the proposed clustering approach. Thus, it is also clear that every clustering mechanism operates on either a data matrix or a dissimilarity matrix. Representation of both clustering data structure is given subsequently in equation one and two.

$$
\begin{bmatrix}
x_{11} \ldots\ldots\ldots x_{1p} \ldots\ldots\ldots x_{1y} \\
x_{21} \ldots\ldots\ldots x_{2p} \ldots\ldots\ldots x_{2y} \\
\ldots\ldots\ldots\ldots\ldots\ldots\ldots\ldots\ldots \\
x_{n1} \ldots\ldots\ldots x_{np} \ldots\ldots\ldots x_{ny}
\end{bmatrix}
\tag{1}
$$

$$
\begin{bmatrix}
0 & & & \\
d(2,1) & 0 & & \\
d(3,1) & d(3,2) & 0 & \\
. & . & . & \\
. & . & . & \\
d(n,1) & d(n,2) & . & 0
\end{bmatrix}
\tag{2}
$$

11.8 REAL-TIME CASE STUDY OF TWITTER

The proposed algorithm of clustering is applied on real-time Twitter data to check its efficiency. The various features were selected and clustered in a fixed time as described in Figure 11.5. Features such as location, time, retweet, verified user, user and initial time of tweets are considered for analysis. Therefore, we can say that the advanced machine learning mechanisms are helpful to detect various features in efficient ways and outperform to sense the lexicons in various kinds of text streams (Figure 11.5).

It is also observed that during analysis of data in real-time, numerous users participated in different types of social media events. They help to spread information in a fast way and some dedicated users do this task to spread misinformation only. Therefore, to trust such user based information on social media is quite challenging. Existing studies indicate that the spread rate of false information will always be higher than the actual information and due to this reason various users can trust such information easily. Therefore, it is very important to cluster such dedicated users who play an active role in spreading wrong information in social media to mislead.

Figure 11.6 is depicting the various categories of social media users we have seen and that little information survived for a long time in society whereas some demise after a span of time. Therefore, the survival rate of any information is directly proportional to type of crowd (users) that how strongly they can trust on information.

Feature Evolution w.r.t. time window

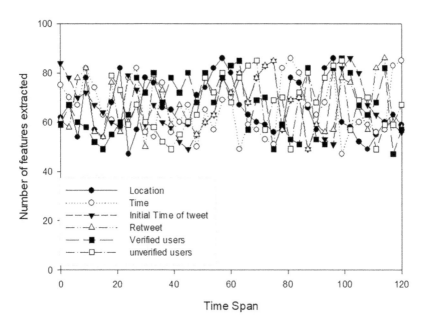

Figure 11.5 Real time feature analysis of Twitter.

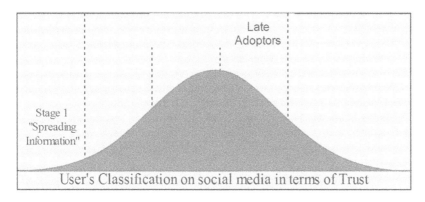

Figure 11.6 User classification on social media.

11.9 CONCLUSION AND FUTURE SCOPE

This chapter describes various factors which influence various social media semantics to cluster similar data objects. In real-time social text stream data is collected into different time intervals and the various steps used in clustering are explained. It is observed that the online clustering of data is a complex task due to the availability of text, symbols, images, abbreviations and slangs. Therefore, it is a big challenge to provide an efficient way to cluster heterogeneous input into synchronous and unified forms to make a right decision. On the basis of that, our discussion in this chapter brings novel findings about social media users and information shared by them. For the evaluation purpose, we considered Twitter for effective clarifications and easy to understand nature. A short period of analysis is also given which covers a less amount of distinct features based on rumor including user's participation. In the future, the analysis can be performed on images and video based data.

REFERENCES

[1] Jiang, X., Zhang, N., Huang, J., Zhang, P., & Liu, H. (2021). Analysis of prediction algorithm for forest land spatial evolution trend in rural planning. *Cluster Computing*, 1–9.

[2] Singh, T., Kumari, M., & Gupta, D.S. (2022). Real-time event detection and classification in social text steam using embedding. *Cluster Computing*. https://doi.org/10.1007/s10586-022-03610-6

[3] Kaliyar, R.K., Goswami, A., & Narang, P. (2021). FakeBERT: Fake news detection in social media with a BERT-based deep learning approach. *Multimedia Tools and Applications*, 80, 11765–11788.

[4] Santhosh Kumar, S., & Dhinesh Babu, L.D. (2020). Earlier detection of rumors in online social networks using certainty-factor-based convolutional neural networks. *Social Network Analysis and Mining*, 10, 20.

[5] Jiang, G., Li, S., & Li, M. (2020). Dynamic rumor spreading of public opinion reversal on Weibo based on a two-stage SPNR model. *Physica A: Statistical Mechanics and Its Applications*, 558.

[6] Eismann, K. (2021). Diffusion and persistence of false rumors in social media networks: Implications of searchability on rumor self-correction on Twitter. *Journal of Business Economics, 91*, 1299–1329.

[7] Jiang, M., Gao, Q., & Zhuang, J. (2021). Reciprocal spreading and debunking processes of online misinformation: A new rumor spreading–debunking model with a case study. *Physica A: Statistical Mechanics and Its Applications, 565*.

[8] Jung, A. K., Ross, B., & Stieglitz, S. (2020). Caution: Rumors ahead—a case study on the debunking of false information on Twitter. *Big Data and Society,* 7(2).

[9] Zhao, T. F., Chen, W. N., Kwong, S., Gu, T. L., Yuan, H. Q., Zhang, J., & Zhang, J. (2021). Evolutionary divide-and-conquer algorithm for virus spreading control over networks. *IEEE Transactions Cybernetics, 51*(7), 3752–3766. doi: 10.1109/TCYB.2020.2975530.

[10] Li, Q., Zhang, Q., & Si, L. (2019). Rumor detection by exploiting user credibility information, attention and multi-task learning. In *Proceedings*

of the 57th annual meeting of the association for computational linguistics (pp. 1173–1179). https://doi.org/10.18653/v1/P19-1113.

[11] Zhao, T. F., Chen, W. N., Kwong, S., Gu, T. L., Yuan, H. Q., Zhang, J., & Zhang, J. (2020). Evolutionary divide-and-conquer algorithm for virus spreading control over networks. *IEEE Transactions on Cybernetics, 51*(7), 3752–3766.

[12] Rout, R. R., Lingam, G., & Somayajulu, D. V. L. N. (2020). Detection of malicious social bots using learning automata with URL features in Twitter network. *IEEE Transactions on Computational Social Systems*, 1–15.

[13] Alsaeedi, A., & Al-Sarem, M. (2020). Detecting rumors on social media based on a CNN deep learning technique. *Arabian Journal for Science and Engineering, 45*, 10813–10844.

[14] Pan, T., Li, X., Kuhnle, A., & Thai, M. T. (2020). Influence diffusion in online social networks with propagation rate changes. *IEEE Transactions on Network Science and Engineering, 7*(4), 3100–3111. doi: 10.1109/ TNSE.2020.3015935

[15] Wang, J. J., Torelli, C. J., & Lalwani, A. K. (2020). The interactive effect of power distance belief and consumers' status on preference for national (vs. private-label) brands. *Journal of Business Research, 107*, 1–12.

[16] Wang, J., Wang, Z., Liu, X., Yang, X., Zheng, M., & Bai, X. (2021). The impacts of a COVID-19 epidemic focus and general belief in a just world on individual emotions. *Personality and Individual Differences, 168*, 110349. doi: 10.1016/j.paid.2020.110349

[17] Wang, Y. N., Wang, J., Yao, T., Li, M., & Wang, X. R. (2020). How does social support promote consumers' engagement in the social commerce community? The mediating effect of consumer involvement. *Information Processing & Management, 57*(5), Article 102272.

[18] Singh, T., & Kumari, M. (2021). Burst: Real-time events burst detection in social text stream. *The Journal of Supercomputing, 77*, 11228–11256. https://doi.org/10.1007/s11227-021-03717-4

[19] Li, J., Ni, S., & Kao, H. Y. (2020). Birds of a feather rumor together? Exploring homogeneity and conversation structure in social media for rumor detection. *IEEE Access, 8*, 212865–212875. https://doi.org/10.1109/ ACCESS.2020.3040263.

[20] Lin, Y., Chen, W. T., Li, X., Zuo, W. L., & Yin, M. H. (2019). A survey of sentiment analysis in social media. *Knowledge and Information Systems, 60*, 617–663.

[21] Singh, T., & Kumari, M. (2016). Role of text pre-processing in Twitter sentiment analysis. *Procedia Computer Science, 89*, 549–554.

[22] Ni, M. Y., Yang, L., Leung, C. M. C., Li, N., Yao, X. I., Wang, Y., Leung, G. M., Cowling, B. J., & Liao, Q. (2020). Mental health, risk factors, and social media use during the COVID-19 epidemic and cordon sanitaire among the community and health professionals in Wuhan, China: Cross-sectional survey. *JMIR Mental Health, 7*(5), e19009. doi: 10.2196/19009

[23] Bian, T., Xiao, X., Xu, T., Zhao, P., Huang, W., Rong, Y., & Huang, J. (2020). Rumor detection on social media with bi-directional graph convolutional networks. In *Proceedings of the thirty-fourth AAAI conference on artificial intelligence* (pp. 549–556). https://doi.org/10.1609/aaai.v34i01.5393

[24] Gorrell, G., Kochkina, E., Liakata, M., Aker, A., Zubiaga, A., Bontcheva, K., & Derczynski, L. (2019). SemEval-2019 task 7: RumourEval, determining rumour veracity and support for rumours. In *Proceedings of the 13th international workshop on semantic evaluation* (pp. 845–854). https://doi.org/10.18653/v1/S19-2147

[25] Song, C., Ning, N., Zhang, Y., & Wu, B. (2021). A multimodal fake news detection model based on cross modal attention residual and multichannel convolutional neural networks. *Information Processing and Management, 58*(1).

[26] Leal, J., Pinto, S., Bento, A., Goncalo Oliveira, H., & Gomes, P. (2014, August 23–24). CISUC-KIS: Tackling message polarity classification with a large and diverse set of features. In *Proceedings of the 8th international workshop on semantic evaluation (SemEval 2014)*(pp. 166–170), Dublin.

[27] Tasnim, S., Hossain, M. M., & Mazumder, H. (2020) Impact of rumors and misinformation on covid-19 in social media. *Journal of Preventive Medicine and Public Health, 53*(3), 171–174. https://doi.org/10. 3961/JPMPH. 20. 094

[28] Ahinkorah, B. O., Ameyaw, E. K., Hagan, J. E., Seidu, A.-A., & Schack, H. (2020). Rising above misinformation or fake news in Africa: Another strategy to control COVID-19 spread. *Frontiers in Communication, 5*, 45. https://doi.org/10.3389/fcomm.2020.00045

[29] Boukouvalas, Z., Mallinson, C., Crothers, E., Japkowicz, N., Piplai, A., Mittal, S., Joshi, A., & Adali, T. (2020). Independent component analysis for trustworthy cyberspace during high impact events: An application to covid-19. arXiv: 2006.01284.

[30] Busari, S., & Adebayo, B. (2020). *Nigeria records chloroquine poisoning after Trump endorses it for coronavirus treatment – CNN.* Retrieved August 3, 2021, from https://edition.cnn.com/2020/03/23/africa/chloroquine-trumpnigeria-intl/index.html

[31] Akon, S., & Bhuiyan, A. (2020). Rumors and its impact on youth during COVID-19 pandemic: The case of Bangladesh. Journal of Research in Education, Science, and Technology, 5, 26–35.

[32] Al-Rakhami, M., & Al-Amri, A. (2020). Lies kill, facts save: Detecting COVID-19 misinformation in Twitter. *IEEE Access,* 8, 155961–155970. https://doi.org/10.1109/ACCESS.2020.3019600

[33] Alkhalifa, R., Yoong, T., Kochkina, E., Zubiaga, A., & Liakata, M. (2020). QMUL-SDS at Check That! 2020: Determining COVID-19 tweet check-worthiness using an enhanced CT-BERT with numeric expressions. arXiv:2008.13160.

[34] Kaliyar, R., Goswami, A., & Narang, P. (2020). MCNNet: Generalizing fake news detection with a multichannel convolutional neural network using a novel COVID-19 dataset. In: *ACM international conference proceeding series* (p. 437). https://doi.org/10.1145/3430984.3431064

[35] Kaliyar, R., Goswami, A., & Narang, P. (2021). A hybrid model for effective fake news detection with a novel COVID-19 dataset. In: *ICAART 2021— proceedings of the 13th international conference on agents and artificial intelligence* (pp. 1066–1072). https://doi.org/10.5220/0010316010661072

[36] Alkhalifa, R., Yoong, T., Kochkina, E., Zubiaga, A., & Liakata, M. (2020). QMUL-SDS at CheckThat! 2020: Determining COVID-19 tweet checkworthiness using an enhanced CT-BERT with numeric expressions. arXiv: 2010.06906.

[37] Zarocostas, J. (2020). How to fight an infodemic. *Lancet (London, England)*, *395*(10225), 676. https://doi.org/10.1016/S0140-6736(20)30461-X

[38] Zhang, H., Kuhnle, A., Smith, J. D., & Thai, M. T. (2018). Fight under uncertainty: restraining misinformation and pushing out the truth. In *2018 IEEE/ ACM International Conference on Advances in Social Networks Analysis and Mining (ASONAM)*, 2018 (pp. 266–273), Barcelona, Spain. doi: 10.1109/ASONAM.2018.8508402

Chapter 12

AI/ML Revolutionizing Social Media and Business

A Comprehensive Study

*[1]Pooja Singh, [1]Lipsa Das, [1]Dev Bahubal,
[2]Sangeeta Rani, and [3]Ajay Kumar*

[1]Amity University, Greater Noida, UP, India
[2]Department of Computer Science and Engineering, World College of
Technology and Management, Gurgaon, India
[3]Associate Professor, Department of Mechanical Engineering, School of
Engineering and Technology, JECRC University, Jaipur, Rajasthan, India

12.1 INTRODUCTION

Artificial Intelligence (AI) and Machine Learning (ML) are rapidly growing fields that are changing the way we live and work. The significance of AI in businesses is increasing day by day and many people interact with AI on a regular basis without even realizing it. There are various applications of AI in everyday life, but its role in the workplace is even more profound. The field of AI dates back to 1956, but it took several decades of effort to make it a technical reality. AI helps to automate tasks, analyze data, and process natural language, which improves operational efficiency and streamlines processes.

One of the key benefits of AI is that it frees employees from repetitive and boring tasks, allowing them to focus on higher value work. Data analytics is another area where AI is making a difference, as it allows businesses to uncover new patterns and relationships in data, leading to previously unattainable insights. NLP also enhances accessibility for individuals with disabilities, making it easier for search engines and chatbots to be smarter.

Machine learning is a type of AI that allows computers to learn automatically from data sets and experiences. It does not require pre-defined algorithms or rules and the more data it has access to, the more it learns and makes accurate decisions. Machine learning techniques are being used in various industries, from chatbots and digital assistants, to autonomous vehicles and spam filters.

Machine learning has a number of commercial applications. For example, it allows for better predictive analysis in insurance, improved search results, better customer service, real-time buyer personalization, and identifying target markets.

DOI: 10.1201/9781003329947-12

The topic of this research is "How AI/ML Play a Vital Role in Social Media and Businesses." This study aims to examine the role of AI and ML in social media and businesses, connecting the two fields and exploring how they are changing the future of businesses. AI and ML is key to the future of businesses and this research aims to examine the trend of AI and ML in the field and how they are being used to analyze social media and marketing.

There have been multiple studies in this field, but not on the connection between AI, ML, social media, and businesses. The study will also explore the challenges and opportunities that come with using AI and ML in these contexts, and how businesses can leverage these technologies to achieve their goals. The findings of this study will be useful for businesses and individuals who are looking to stay ahead of the curve in this rapidly evolving field.

12.2 HISTORY

The history of Artificial Intelligence (AI) and Machine Learning (ML) in businesses and social media is a fascinating one that has evolved over the past several decades. AI has come a long way since its inception, and today it has become an integral part of many businesses and social media platforms. This essay aims to explore the evolution of AI and ML in businesses and social media and the impact it has had on the world.

The roots of AI can be traced back to the 1950s, when computer scientist John McCarthy coined the term "Artificial Intelligence." He defined AI as the science and engineering of making intelligent machines that can perform tasks that would normally require human intelligence [6]. The early years of AI were focused on developing rule-based systems that could perform specific tasks. This was followed by the development of expert systems, which could make decisions based on a set of rules and knowledge.

In the 1990s, the rise of the internet and the increasing power of computers brought about a new era of AI development. This era was characterized by the development of machine learning algorithms that could learn from data and make predictions or decisions without being explicitly programmed. This was a major milestone in the evolution of AI and ML, as it enabled computers to learn and adapt to changing circumstances, without human intervention.

The first business applications of AI and ML were seen in the financial services industry. Banks and other financial institutions used AI to analyze large amounts of data and make decisions about loans and investments. This was followed by the use of AI and ML in the retail industry, where companies used AI to analyze customer data and make recommendations about products and services.

The rise of social media in the early 2000s brought about a new era of AI and ML in businesses and social media. Social media platforms such as

Facebook, Twitter, and Instagram used AI to personalize the user experience, recommend content, and analyze user behavior. AI and ML were used to develop personalized news feeds, recommendations for friends, and recommendations for products and services. This was a significant shift from the early days of social media, when users were limited to simple text-based interactions with friends and family.

In recent years, AI and ML have become increasingly important in the business world. Companies are using AI and ML to automate many routine tasks, freeing up employees to focus on more important tasks. AI and ML is also being used to improve customer experience, by providing personalized recommendations and improving customer service. For example, chatbots powered by AI and ML are being used to answer customer questions and provide assistance, reducing wait times and improving the overall customer experience.

The impact of AI and ML on businesses and social media has been significant. AI and ML have enabled companies to make more informed decisions, improve customer experiences, and automate many routine tasks. This has resulted in increased efficiency, improved customer satisfaction, and increased revenue.

However, the impact of AI and ML has not been all positive. There are concerns about the potential for AI and ML to be used for malicious purposes, such as cyber-attacks and the spread of fake news. There are also concerns about the impact of AI and ML on employment, as many jobs may be automated in the future.

In conclusion, the history of AI and ML in businesses and social media is a story of rapid evolution and significant impact. AI and ML have become essential tools for companies, and have enabled them to improve efficiency, customer experiences, and revenue. As AI and ML continue to evolve, it is important that we consider the potential implications of these technologies and work to ensure that they are used for the benefit of society.

12.3 LITERATURE REVIEW

S. R. Hedberg [1996] [5] Artificial intelligence has been a significant contributor to the development of cutting-edge commercial applications for over a decade. The utilization of knowledge-based systems (KBS) have proven to be an asset for multiple Fortune 1000 organizations, aiding in the resolution of vital business problems, including scheduling of manufacturing operations and investment portfolio management. By enhancing productivity and reducing costs, AI has helped companies meet the demands of the competitive global economy. In recent years, company management has undergone a profound transformation with the advent of business process reengineering (BPR).

BPR aims to increase efficiency while reducing expenses by rethinking and streamlining business operations. It is therefore not surprising that many corporate leaders have turned to KBS methodologies, which have long been shown to achieve the goals of BPR, to facilitate this change. The first wave of AI-powered tools and applications for business process modelling (BPM) has now arrived, with companies such as IBM, EDS, the US Army, and Swiss Bank among the pioneers in using AI for business process management. Some companies have adopted traditional KBS technologies like ART*Enterprise and ProKappa, while others have opted for the newer AI tool, Rethink, specifically designed for BPM. In conclusion, the integration of AI and KBS in the business world have proven to be an asset, helping companies increase productivity and reduce costs while adapting to the demands of the competitive global economy. The advent of BPM has added a new dimension to the utilization of AI in the business world, with the first wave of AI-powered tools and applications already being implemented by leading companies.

V. R. Benjamins [2006] [8] The integration of artificial intelligence (AI) in business and society is seen as a key factor in bridging the gap between technology and mainstream markets. Consumers today expect more from the technology they interact with and are increasingly demanding features such as ambient intelligence, cognitive capabilities, and natural language speech. This shift towards higher user expectations highlights the importance of technology serving as an effective tool for users, rather than simply a source of innovation. It is crucial for technology developers to understand the needs and preferences of users, who can be considered the "clients" of technology. To meet these expectations, technology must evolve and adapt to align with the changing standards of the market. In summary, the ability of AI technology to innovate in the business and societal spheres is crucial to its mainstream adoption. Meeting user expectations, including those for ambient intelligence, cognitive capabilities, and natural language speech, is critical in ensuring the success and relevance of AI technology in the market.

K. A. Crockett, L. Gerber, A. Latham, and E. Colyer [2009] [40] The development of trustworthy artificial intelligence (AI) solutions is a complex process that requires careful consideration of a wide range of factors, including legal, ethical, social, environmental, and public opinion considerations. Despite the availability of a multitude of guidelines, principles, and toolkits, implementation remains limited, especially among small- and medium-sized enterprises (SMEs), due to a lack of knowledge, skills, and resources. In an effort to better understand SMEs' awareness of data and AI ethical principles, as well as the challenges they face in adopting ethical AI techniques, this study conducted qualitative consultations with SMEs across two events. Based on 33 assessment criteria, 77 published toolkits for establishing and promoting ethical and responsible AI activities were analyzed and ranked by independent experts. The findings of the study suggest that there is no one-size-fits-all solution for SMEs, and that the available toolkits are often lacking in practical application and instructions for use. The research provides a framework for SMEs to select the toolkits best suited to their needs, resources, and levels of ethical awareness, covering all stages of the AI lifecycle, from conception to implementation. In conclusion, the study highlights the need for more accessible and user-friendly toolkits for SMEs, as well as greater awareness of the importance of responsible AI practices. The findings provide valuable insights for researchers and practitioners working in the field of AI and ethics, and can inform the development of better tools and resources for SMEs looking to adopt ethical AI practices.

Brabazon, J. Cahill, P. Keenan, and D. Walsh [2010] [21] In this study, the authors explore the potential for using Artificial Immune Systems (AIS) in credit card fraud detection. With the increasing trend of online transactions, the need for efficient and effective methods to detect credit card fraud has become a pressing issue. Fraudsters are constantly adapting their techniques to bypass detection systems, making it challenging to develop systems that can keep up. AIS has been identified as a potential solution due to its ability to identify "non-standard" transactions without having been trained on all potential fraud patterns. The authors evaluate the performance of three AIS algorithms using a large dataset from an online shop and compared it with a logistic regression model. The results show that AIS algorithms have the potential for use in fraud detection systems but require further research to be fully realized in this field.

G. Shroff, P. Agarwal, and L. Dey [2011] [23] The emergence of social media platforms and specialized discussion forums have created a wealth of information on various topics, including products, services, and news events. This publicly available information holds great potential for large enterprises across different industries to gain insights into their operations and transactions, as well as the impact of external events on their businesses. In this study, we introduce the concept of Enterprise Information Fusion (EIF), which aims to combine internal and external information in real-time for effective decision-making. The proposed EIF framework utilizes traditional AI techniques such as the blackboard architecture and contemporary methods like locality sensitive hashing. The aim is to provide a comprehensive solution that helps enterprises to assess the impact of external events while also correlating them with known internal operations and transactions. In the study, the authors describe their preliminary experience in developing selected components of the EIF framework and outline the future research required to complete the solution. The results indicate that the EIF framework has the potential to provide valuable insights for large enterprises, but further research is needed to fully realize its benefits.

Xu, S. Gao, and X. Li [2011] [41] The use of internet marketing has become increasingly popular in recent years, offering businesses the opportunity to expand their reach and increase traffic to their website. This paper focuses on the application of internet marketing strategies at the Zhuhai New-Concept Training Centre (ZHNCTC), exploring various tactics aimed at increasing website traffic and boosting sales from existing customers. The tactics discussed include methods for improving website metrics such as "time on site" and "pages viewed," as well as proposed activities for driving more sales. The paper also provides suggestions for successfully adopting these internet marketing methods. This research highlights the significance of internet marketing in the modern business world, and the potential benefits it can bring to organizations looking to increase their online presence and reach new audiences.

V. Zamudio, P. Zheng, and V. Callaghan [2012] [42] The study presented in this work explores the concept of viewing a business as a collection of rule-based processes, similar to the set of rule-based coordinating agents in intelligent environments. The authors examine the application of directed graph theory, commonly used for stability analysis in systems of ubiquitous computing agents, to commercial systems. The report provides an overview of interaction networks and business process reengineering and demonstrates how they both rely on the concept of "process" and how they can be integrated. The study is a preliminary step towards the goal of investigating the full potential of AI for smart business monitoring and management.

S. Kosasi and Vedyanto [2015] [20] In this research, the focus is on the management of online cosmetics businesses and the identification of the gap value in the DS (Deliver and Support) and AI (Acquire and Implement) domains. The study aims to determine the level of information technology governance in each of these domains and its impact on customer turnover. The findings suggest that the average score for the DS Domain's information technology governance is lower compared to the AI Domain, indicating that there is a gap in the information technology governance in the DS Domain processes. The study also highlights the relationship between different information technology processes in the DS and AI domains, and their influence on the overall information technology governance. The results suggest that there is a need for more efficient information technology governance in the DS Domain to improve the management of online cosmetics businesses and reduce customer turnover. The study recommends the use of the COBIT 4.1 framework to ensure compatibility with information technology governance.

J. Kiruthika and S. Khaddaj [2017] [2] Virtual reality (VR) technology has been making an impact on various industries and when combined with Artificial Intelligence (AI), it offers a new dimension to businesses. Although not all businesses require VR, AI plays a more significant role. There is interest among stakeholders in identifying areas where VR/AI can have an impact on a company. The integration of VR with AI offers new possibilities and will bring a fresh range of experiences. This literature review focuses on some of these topics and presents a case study, highlighting recent advancements and challenges that must be addressed.

R. Ilieva and Y. Nikolov [2019] [4] In recent years, the use of technology, particularly Artificial Intelligence (AI), has become an increasingly important part of IT processes. This is due to the potential for AI to improve the efficiency and effectiveness of these processes, which play a critical role in managing events, incidents, normal operations, and performance reporting for technical components. By leveraging AI technologies, it is possible to optimize the management structure of IT processes, leading to a more efficient and effective use of resources. The trend towards incorporating AI into IT processes is seen as a way to improve the overall performance of these processes and ensure the success of the organization.

Mas'od, U. N. Idris, Z. Sulaiman, and T. A. Chin [2019] [19] The increase in popularity of online shopping has transformed the way consumers purchase goods and services. The growth of e-commerce has created opportunities for companies to reach consumers through social media, websites, and online platform apps. This study aims to examine the impact of likes, friend recommendations, comment posting, sharing posting, and Facebook advertizements on the buying intentions of Generation Y consumers. Generation Y, defined as individuals aged 19 to 37 years old, were selected as the target population for the study, with purposive sampling used to distribute online surveys in Johor and Selangor. The research focuses on examining the relationship between the mentioned factors and the buying intentions of Generation Y consumers who use Facebook and have made online purchases. The study contributes to the growing body of literature on e-commerce and online consumer behavior, providing insights into the impact of social media on purchasing decisions.

B. Thuraisingham [2020] [43] The use of social media platforms have become ubiquitous in society, connecting over a billion people and allowing for the sharing of information and communication. While these platforms have the potential to spread knowledge and facilitate discussions on important issues, they also have the potential to cause harm through the dissemination of false information and privacy invasions. As Artificial Intelligence (AI) systems continue to expand, their integration with social media platforms is changing the way people use these platforms. This literature review explores the role of AI and cyber security in social media systems and the advantages of AI for social media platforms, as well as the measures needed to ensure their safe and secure use.

C. Hahn, T. Traunecker, M. Niever, and G. N. Basedow [2020] [3] Artificial intelligence (AI) has the potential to revolutionize the way businesses operate by providing valuable insights and driving innovation. This literature review explores the concept of AI-driven business models, which leverage AI technology to construct at least one of the business model components. In contrast to data-driven business models, AI-driven business models are capable of learning and enhancing their performance without human intervention. The research highlights the potential benefits of adopting AI-driven business models for companies, including the potential for increased competitiveness in a rapidly changing business environment. The findings of the research provide decision-makers with important insights into the use of AI technology and its contribution to business practices.

IEEE SA [2020] [1] The increasing usage of Artificial Intelligence (AI) in organizations has led to the importance of AI ethics in their operations. This article highlights the significance of incorporating AI ethics in organizations and the methods of doing so. The article introduces an AI Ethics Readiness Framework to help organizations assess their preparedness in implementing AI ethics. It also covers the skills required and the ways to hire and staff for such an effort. Contributions from several industry professionals have been included in the article, which provides practical implementation of AI ethics based on their experiences as AI ethics leaders and practitioners in their respective fields. The article is part of the Aligned Design for Business series of The IEEE Global Initiative on Ethics of Autonomous and Intelligent Systems (A/ ISEthically) [7]. The series aims to inspire and provide mutual learning for the worldwide community of academics, data scientists, engineers, and tech entrepreneurs.

K. Feher [2020] [44] The concept of "new media" has become increasingly complex and difficult to define, due to the rapid changes in digital patterns. According to recent surveys, the most significant trends in new media are driven by technology, with a shift from digitalization to smart and narrow AI. These technological advancements have had a significant impact on society, culture, and business, changing media logics and presenting new challenges for identifying applicable definitions or theories. The goal of the study is to understand the evolving new media environment as it moves through the digital transition, using a trend-level analysis to better comprehend the forces, needs, and values that sustain these technological trends and economic models. The study incorporates the perspectives of industry professionals, drawing on their experiences as AI ethics thought leaders and practitioners. The Fjord trend report offers a human-focused perspective on the topic, exploring the creation of intelligence and unconventional commercial approaches. The study also examines the extreme outputs of technology-driven media, such as omnipresent or invisible media. Finally, the research summarizes the last few decades of paradigm developments in new media, resulting in the concept of NSAI (new-smart-AI) media.

Vania Sena and Manuela Nocker [2021] [46] This literature review explores the impact of AI on business models and the value creation in industries. The main hypothesis is that the integration of AI leads to new value creation mechanisms, resulting in the emergence of new firms and the decline in competitiveness of incumbent firms. The review focuses on qualitative investigations and grey literature to understand the evolution of business models in the AI era. The book is divided into six sections: (1) Introduction, (2) Overview of AI, (3) Value migration and business models in a sector, (4) Major elements of new AI-driven business models, (5) Influence on the formation of new business models, and (6) Concluding observations and thoughts on future research gaps. The goal of the review is to identify areas where formal research is needed to further our understanding of the relationship between AI and business models.

G. Shidaganti, S. Salil, P. Anand, and V. Jadhav [2021] [11] This literature review focuses on the use of AI and OCR to enhance Business Process Automation (BPA). Businesses often spend a considerable amount of time on repetitive and mundane tasks, such as data entry, employee ID validation, and meeting scheduling, reducing the time available for activities that bring value to the company. Robotic Process Automation (RPA) can automate these tasks, but its limitations and the need for immediate updates to the RPA application for any process modifications make it time-consuming to implement [10]. The study explores the use of AI, specifically Intelligent Process Automation (IPA), which combines the power of AI with RPA applications to create more intelligent and efficient systems. Additionally, the use of Optical Character Recognition (OCR) technology is analyzed as a means of extracting text from images and improving the automation of business processes. The research aims to examine the various ways in which AI and OCR can be integrated into BPA to improve efficiency and productivity.

Y. Zhao, T. Zhang, Y. Liu, Y. Zhu, and Y. Gao [2021] [13] This literature review focuses on the use of AI in customer service and its impact on customer satisfaction in the context of online buying. With the rapid advancement of digital technology, more and more sectors are turning to AI to minimize costs and increase productivity. AI customer service has become increasingly popular in recent years, with the use of intelligent robots, speech recognition, and other intelligent technologies. The study recognizes the importance of service innovation using AI technology, particularly in regards to its impact on customer satisfaction. The study employs a questionnaire and a structural equation model to analyze data from 289 users of major Chinese online shipping apps. The results showed that two external influence factors, as identified through the Technology Acceptance Model (TAM), have unique relationships and impact customer happiness. The findings indicate that reaction time, compatibility, correctness, optimism, and innovation have a positive impact on customer satisfaction, while discomfort and insecurity have a negative effect. The study highlights the importance of considering these factors in the implementation of AI customer service to ensure customer satisfaction.

S. M. Simionescu, A. Bădică, C. Bădică, M. Ganzha, and M. Paprzycki [2021] [14] This article explores the various business ecosystems enabled by blockchain technology, including those related to cryptocurrencies as well as those that utilize blockchain as a distributed and unalterable database. The article also proposes the creation of a marketplace aimed at democratizing access to General AI. The investigation provides insights into the different ways in which blockchain technology can be utilized for business purposes, highlighting the versatility and potential of this innovative technology. The proposed marketplace is an intriguing concept that has the potential to make General AI more accessible to a wider range of individuals and organizations.

S. Maitra, M. Rakib Ahamed, M. Nazrul Islam, M. Abdullah Al Nasim, and M. Ashraf [2021] [22] This research article delves into the issue of optimal spending for maximum profit in the era of big data and digital marketing. The focus is on identifying the right target group to allocate resources, which is a significant challenge for both customer acquisition and retention. The concept of customer lifetime value (CLV) is introduced as a potential solution, but conventional literature on its computation is deemed general. The study proposes an AI-powered CLV classifier utilizing transaction data from an online retail company. The method involves mining customer purchasing preferences from geographic, monetary, temporal, and category data and using them as input features for a neural network coded in TensorFlow to estimate future profitability [26]. The feature set is further improved through statistical inference and another iteration of the neural network. An SQL-backed recommender system is also proposed for cross-selling and up-selling customers based on their maximal inclinations. The study concludes by highlighting the importance of filtering elements that impact CLV and supporting the use of current soft computing in developing business-specific solutions using accessible customer datasets.

J. L. C. Sanz and Y. Zhu [2021] [18] The growth of Artificial Intelligence (AI) and Machine Learning (ML) has led to an increase in the number of methodologies available for data-driven modelling. Most ML algorithms can be applied to various industries and business processes. Open-source research fuels the development of ML, which is then distributed by software and cloud providers. However, the deployment of AI in finance has faced challenges, such as scalability and legal constraints. To overcome these challenges, AI should be developed with finance expertise and functional specialization from the start. This article presents an AI architecture for finance, with a focus on analytics and forecasting. The architecture is based on three interconnected axes: Design dimensions, modelling building blocks, and work practice. The aim is to help financial professionals manage the abundance of AI possibilities and expedite data monetization. The architecture is designed to be applicable to a wide range of financial scenarios, but with a focus on competencies in banking, financial markets, and chief financial officer (CFO) operations. The article presents the initial steps toward establishing a service practice and draws on years of experience in the finance industry and R&D in emerging finance technology.

Zarifis and L. Efthymiou [2022] [12] This literature review focuses on the importance of effective collaboration between new technology, particularly Artificial Intelligence (AI), and humans in achieving digital transformation in the educational sector. The review highlights the reality that not all colleges possess the necessary skills in the areas required for digital transformation and AI adoption. Therefore, new strategies and education business models must be developed to facilitate the adoption of AI in the education sector. The study proposes four AI-optimized education business models that can be selected from to optimize AI adoption. The review emphasizes the importance of having a well-defined plan for digital transformation as this builds trust between the digital transformation leader and the followers [9].

T. Meepung and P. Kannikar [2022] [15] The use of digital marketing techniques have become increasingly important in the modern business world. Understanding customer behaviour and the customer lifecycle is crucial in determining the most effective marketing strategy. The application of Artificial Intelligence (AI) and Machine Learning (ML) in digital marketing is growing in popularity as it offers numerous benefits. These benefits include faster information searching, improved results, and the ability to develop more personalized marketing materials. AI and ML can also be used to monitor customer behavior and segment individuals visiting a company's website, leading to more efficient marketing efforts. The integration of AI and ML into digital marketing can lead to increased sales and better connections with other businesses. The impact of AI and ML on digital marketing continues to evolve and there is a growing interest in understanding the best ways to leverage these technologies.

G. Jangra and M. Jangra [2022] [16] Over the past decade, the growth of the e-commerce industry has been substantial. The rise in online customers have made it imperative for e-commerce businesses to understand their needs and behaviors. To achieve this, e-commerce enterprises have incorporated Artificial Intelligence (AI) technology to gather information about customer demands and preferences for online products and services. The AI system analyzes customer data such as purchasing habits, average amount spent, and frequency of purchases. This provides e-commerce businesses with accurate and valuable information that they can use to adjust their products and services to meet the unique requirements and preferences of their customers. Furthermore, AI technology provides customers with personalized product suggestions, discounts, and offers that help them make informed purchase decisions. A study conducted on 200 individuals from different socioeconomic backgrounds in Haryana found a significant relationship between AI (such as voice and visual search, assortment intelligence tools, and virtual personal shoppers) and consumer buying behavior (such as trust, attitude, and perceived risk) in the context of online shopping. The study results indicated that AI has a strong and positive impact on consumer purchase decisions. The study used several characteristics to analyze purchase patterns, including preferred payment method, value of money spent on online shopping, frequency of online shopping, and electronic gadgets used in online shopping.

S. Singh, D. J. Greaves, and G. Epiphaniou [2022] [17] The growth of social media has raised concerns about the need for better data regulation in the filtering of online material to safeguard vulnerable individuals and groups. This study explores the drivers of data governance and social harm in social media, specifically focusing on the challenges faced by social media companies in moderating content. The study examines the impact of human interpretation, protected mediations, and machine learning content classification in determining how protection can be ensured. The research paper proposes a paradigm for social media website administration that integrates a socio-technical model of content control. The framework includes a proposed high-level system architecture for content moderation that considers the context-specific nature of social harm and behaviour that may require human interpretation. The architecture also includes a machine learning system to manage the vast amounts of information generated by social networks while maintaining privacy and protection for vulnerable stakeholders. Overall, the study highlights the importance of balancing the need for reducing the risk of harm with protecting the privacy and security of vulnerable groups in the context of social media [24].

12.4 METHODOLOGY

This study analyzes a study on the role of AI/ML in social media and businesses. We will be studying the literature review comprehensively to develop the relation between Artificial Intelligence and Machine Learning in social media and businesses. Also, a historical pathway study is done and analyzed in the paper to lay the entry of these technologies in the existing businesses and how they improvised their business models. The pattern of these technologies on organizations or software applications is studied and how it is beneficial for businesses is suggested. Also, this study is based on the theoretical secondary data which is recognized from various sources like published journals and other research generals.

12.4.1 Disney

Disney has integrated IoT and machine learning into its customer experience through the use of MagicBands. These wristbands use RFID technology to communicate with sensors throughout Disney's premises, allowing the system to track guests' activities and needs. MagicBands serve as tickets, FastPasses, credit cards, hotel keys, and more, reducing friction in the Disney experience. Disney's machine learning algorithm was also used to address the issue of long wait times for attractions, improving the overall customer experience. Disney recently filed a patent for a system that identifies customers based on their shoe sole. The company aims to enhance the visitor experience by creating a more personalized, seamless, and immersive environment. This next-generation system is designed to provide a unique experience for every guest.

12.4.2 Starbucks

Starbucks leverages machine learning and big data analytics to support its marketing efforts, business decisions, and sales. With over 90 million transactions per week across 25,000 stores worldwide, the company has a vast amount of data on its customers' buying habits. This information was collected through the launch of its mobile app and reward program, where users voluntarily provide data on their purchases, including the location, time, and type of product bought. Thanks to the data, Starbucks' system can identify customers' preferences, even when they visit an offline store. The app can also make personalized suggestions for new treats to go with their drinks. The digital flywheel program, a cloud-based artificial intelligence engine, drives these recommendations, offering customers new food and drink options they may not have known about. In summary, Starbucks uses machine learning and big data analytics to improve its customer experience and make more informed business decisions. Its digital flywheel program, powered by AI, enhances the customer experience by offering personalized recommendations and creating a seamless, connected experience both in-store and through the mobile app.

12.4.3 Amazon

AI and ML play a significant role in shaping Amazon's business strategy, impacting its products, warehouse operations, and Echo smart speaker. From its early days, Amazon has relied on machine learning to provide product recommendations to users based on their previous likes. Over time, these systems have been updated and improved to make the recommendations even more dynamic. One of Amazon's well-known products powered by ML is Alexa, a voice assistant that provides AWS users with access to cloud-based tools. Alexa enables shoppers to walk out of Amazon Go stores with their purchases, direct robots carrying products to the fulfilment centre, and more. The success of Amazon can largely be attributed to its Amazon Web Services (AWS), a cloud storage and server provider that has become the standard for many companies. AWS is utilized across a variety of industries, including retail, fashion, entertainment, real estate, healthcare, and more. Amazon caters its AI and ML services to meet the diverse needs of its customers, which range from experts with a Ph.D in machine learning to developers. In conclusion, AI and ML is integral to Amazon's business operations and drive its growth. The company's ability to tailor its machine learning and AI services to meet the needs of its diverse customer base has been a key factor in its success and rise to a near trillion-dollar company [38].

12.4.4 American Express

American Express is utilizing the power of big data and machine learning to enhance their customer experience. With a growing volume of data, including an increase in mobile transactions, Amex is using these technologies to gain insights into customer behaviour, detect fraud, acquire new customers, and provide personalized recommendations. Machine learning has allowed Amex to enhance their fraud detection capabilities, by monitoring online transactions and utilizing various data sources such as card membership, merchant information, and spending details. To acquire new customers, Amex has upgraded their online presence and website model, leading to a 40% increase in online engagement. When customers allow Amex to track their data, machine learning can analyze their history and provide tailored recommendations. Overall, American Express is leveraging the benefits of machine learning and big data to improve their services and provide a better experience for their customers.

12.4.5 ML Delivering Outstanding Customer Experience

Machine Learning consulting services have been instrumental in assisting large organizations in enhancing their customer experience. These companies have leveraged ML techniques to personalize the customer journey and create memorable experiences that keep their clients engaged and loyal. By employing go-to-market strategies, these companies have been able to delight their customers at every touchpoint and turn them into evangelists. In addition to this, Machine Learning has also proven useful in predicting customer issues and providing pre-emptive measures to address them. This has been made possible through predictive analysis, which enables companies to anticipate problems that customers may face soon and prepare an appropriate solution in advance. As a result, companies can deliver a superior experience that can convert a customer into a loyal customer and maintain a high level of retention. Machine Learning has the potential to transform customer experience, but it is crucial that companies use it in an ethical and responsible manner. Companies should ensure that they adhere to data privacy regulations and use customer data only for the purpose for which it was collected. In conclusion, Machine Learning has provided a powerful tool for companies to create personalized and memorable customer experiences. By leveraging predictive analysis, companies can anticipate customer issues and provide pre-emptive measures to address them, leading to increased customer satisfaction and loyalty. However, it is important for companies to use Machine Learning responsibly and ethically to protect customer data and maintain customer trust.

12.5 SOCIAL MEDIA APPS THAT IMPLEMENT AI/ML FOR BUSINESS

1. Lately

   Lately is an AI-powered platform designed to enhance your social media efforts. Its dashboard offers a range of tools to streamline scheduling and project management, making it a convenient solution for businesses looking to optimize their social media presence [25]. With Lately, you can generate numerous tweets related to any URL, document, or information, giving you a way to effectively promote your content. Additionally, the analytics feature of Lately allows you to determine the optimal times for posting on social media, giving you a wider reach and higher engagement with your audience. Some of the key features of Lately include:

- AI-driven dashboard of social media tools.
- Ability to produce multiple tweets.
- Scheduling of social media posts.
- Metrics analysis across various channels.

2. **Socialbakers**

Socialbakers is a well-regarded AI-powered social media management platform that offers a range of features to help with social media marketing [27]. Its main offerings include advanced audience insights, influencer discovery, and a comprehensive tracking dashboard. The platform's unified content feed allows users to see all posts across multiple social media platforms, providing a comprehensive view of their online presence.

In addition to these features, Socialbakers provides a smart scheduling tool that suggests the best times to post content. This is an important tool for maximizing the visibility of your content, ensuring that it reaches as many people as possible when they are most likely to be online and engaged. The platform also offers a multi-channel management system, which streamlines the process of managing multiple social media accounts.

Another key feature of Socialbakers is its influencer dashboard tool, which provides users with a way to identify and track influential individuals on social media. By analyzing their online presence, you can gain insights into the types of content that is likely to generate engagement and interest from your target audience. This information can be used to create more effective marketing campaigns and to better understand the needs and preferences of your target audience.

In conclusion, Socialbakers is a powerful AI tool for social media marketing, offering a range of features that can help you to understand your audience, track your social media performance, and create more effective campaigns [32]. With its advanced audience insights, influencer discovery tools, and smart scheduling features, this platform is well worth considering for anyone looking to maximize their social media presence.

3. **Heyday**

Heyday is a conversational AI tool for social media that helps businesses improve their customer service and drive sales. With its real-time interaction capability, Heyday allows customer service agents to handle high-value interactions with customers. This enhances the user experience and reduces the workload of customer service teams [45].

One of the key features of Heyday is its ability to create content for bots. This allows businesses to take advantage of the growing trend of conversational interfaces and AI-powered customer service. By providing an engaging and personalized experience, Heyday can help businesses stand out from the competition and retain customers.

Heyday uses natural language processing (NLP) and natural language generation (NLG) to customize product recommendations and support sales. This means that Heyday is able to understand customer inquiries and respond with relevant information and recommendations. By leveraging these advanced technologies, Heyday can help businesses increase their sales and improve customer satisfaction.

In conclusion, Heyday is a valuable AI tool for businesses looking to enhance their customer service and sales. With its real-time interaction capability, content creation for bots, and advanced NLP and NLG technologies, Heyday can help businesses stay ahead of the curve and provide a personalized and engaging customer experience.

4. **Wordstream**

Wordstream is an AI-powered tool designed to help businesses improve their advertising performance on social media. The platform uses machine learning (ML) to assess the effectiveness of pay-per-click (PPC) campaigns and provide data-driven recommendations [28]. This makes it an ideal solution for businesses of all sizes, including those in the online sales and marketing industries.

With Wordstream, businesses can easily determine the success of their PPC campaigns by analyzing data from across multiple social media channels. This information can then be used to make informed decisions about how to optimize campaigns and drive online growth. The platform's ML capabilities allow it to provide real-time insights and recommendations, so businesses can quickly adjust their strategies as needed.

In addition to its PPC assessment capabilities, Wordstream helps companies scale their online operations. By providing a comprehensive suite of tools and data-driven recommendations, Wordstream makes it easier for businesses to train teams, optimize their advertising strategies, and drive growth. Whether you're just starting out or looking to expand your online presence, Wordstream can help you achieve your goals.

In conclusion, Wordstream is a top AI tool for social media marketing. Its ML-based approach to PPC campaign analysis and optimization makes it a valuable resource for businesses of all sizes. By providing real-time insights, data-driven recommendations, and comprehensive support for growth, Wordstream is an ideal choice for businesses looking to maximize their advertising performance on social media [33].

5. **Cortex**

Cortex is an AI tool designed to help businesses optimize their social media content. The platform provides detailed analysis and recommendations for sharing content on social media, making it an ideal solution for businesses looking to improve their online presence.

One of the key features of Cortex is its ability to recommend the best times and frequency for posting content. Based on historical metrics, Cortex provides a schedule that maximizes engagement and ensures that your content is seen by the right people. The platform also offers a detailed analysis of your competitors, so you can see how your content stacks up and identify areas for improvement [47].

In addition to its analytical capabilities, Cortex also provides a user-friendly dashboard that makes it easy to manage your social media content. The dashboard provides an overview of your social schedule and highlights your recent posts, making it easier to stay on top of your social media activity.

When uploading photos to social media, Cortex can also help you make the best decision about which colours to use. The platform uses historical data to analyze which colours are most engaging to your audience, helping you ensure that your images are eye-catching and memorable.

In conclusion, Cortex is a great AI tool for businesses looking to optimize their social media content. With its detailed analysis, recommendations, and user-friendly dashboard, Cortex makes it easier to share optimized content and build a strong online presence. Whether you're looking to improve your metrics, increase engagement, or simply manage your social media activity more effectively, Cortex is a valuable resource.

6. QuillBot

QuillBot is a powerful AI tool designed to help businesses repurpose existing content into new and engaging social media posts. The platform uses advanced natural language processing algorithms to summarize and paraphrase existing content, creating new and unique versions that can be used on online newsletters and social media platforms [34].

QuillBot is widely regarded as one of the best rewriter tools on the market, and its flexibility and compatibility make it easy to use for businesses of all sizes. The platform can be used on any web browser or text editor, including popular tools like Microsoft Word and Google Docs, making it a versatile and flexible solution for content creation.

When rewriting content, QuillBot ensures that the original context of the content is retained while still highlighting the most important information. This means that businesses can create new and engaging content that accurately reflects their brand voice and messaging.

QuillBot also includes a vocabulary enhancement feature that helps users expand their vocabulary and write in a more engaging and compelling way. Whether you're looking to write more effectively for social media or simply want to improve your writing skills, QuillBot is a valuable resource.

In conclusion, QuillBot is a great AI tool for businesses looking to repurpose existing content into their social media strategies. With its advanced algorithms, versatility, and ease of use, QuillBot makes it easier to create fresh, engaging content that resonates with your audience. Whether you're looking to improve your writing skills or simply need a tool that can help you generate new and unique content, QuillBot is an excellent option.

12.6 CASE STUDY—INSTAGRAM

Instagram, a photo and video sharing platform, is one of the most popular social media networks in the world with over one billion monthly active users. The company has been using artificial intelligence (AI) and machine learning (ML) to enhance various aspects of its platform and provide better user experience and business opportunities. This case study will explore how Instagram is using AI/ML for business and its impact on the platform.

1. **Optimization of the Discovery Feed**
   One of the keyways Instagram has been using AI is to optimize its discovery feed. The discovery feed is the main feature that displays content to users based on their interests and previous interactions. Instagram uses AI to sort through millions of posts and curate a personalized feed for each user, ensuring that they see content that is relevant to them. This process involves analyzing users' behaviour, interests, and preferences, and using this data to rank posts in their discovery feed.

   Instagram has been using ML to enhance the discovery feed by continuously learning from users' behaviour. This allows the platform to provide more relevant and engaging content, resulting in higher engagement rates. The company has also been using AI to prevent the spread of harmful content on its platform, by using machine learning algorithms to detect and remove such content.

2. **Enhancing Advertising Experience**
   Another way Instagram has been using AI is to enhance the advertising experience for businesses. Instagram provides businesses with various advertising options, including in-feed advertisements, sponsored posts, and Stories ads. The company uses AI to target these advertizements to the right audience, ensuring maximum engagement and conversions. For example, businesses can target their advertizements to users based on their location, age, interests, and more. Instagram uses machine learning algorithms to analyze user data and provide businesses with insights and recommendations on how to optimize their advertizements for better results.

   Instagram has also been using AI to enhance the creative aspect of advertising. The company uses machine learning algorithms to analyze the effectiveness of advertizements and provide businesses with recommendations on how to improve them. This includes suggestions on the best colours, images, and content to use in their advertizements.

3. **Enabling Real-Time Customer Service**

Instagram has been using AI to provide real-time customer service. The company has been using chatbots powered by AI to respond to customer inquiries in real-time. These chatbots can handle a wide range of customer service inquiries, including account issues, technical support, and more. By using AI to handle customer service, Instagram has been able to improve the customer experience and reduce response times.

Instagram has also been using AI to enhance the content moderation process. The company uses machine learning algorithms to identify and remove harmful content on its platform. This includes detecting and removing spam, hate speech, and other harmful content. By using AI for content moderation, Instagram has been able to improve the safety and user experience on its platform.

Conclusion

Instagram has been using AI and ML to enhance various aspects of its platform, including the discovery feed, advertising experience, customer service, and content moderation. The company has been able to provide a more personalized and engaging experience for users, while also providing businesses with better opportunities to reach their target audience. By using AI and ML, Instagram has been able to improve the user experience, increase engagement rates, and provide real-time customer service. As AI and ML continue to evolve, it is likely that Instagram will continue to use these technologies to enhance its platform and provide better business opportunities.

12.7 ADVANTAGES OF AI/ML FOR BUSINESSES

Artificial Intelligence (AI) and Machine Learning (ML) have become the buzzwords in the business and technology industry, with both small and large organizations adopting these technologies to improve their operations, productivity and to remain competitive. In the world of social media, AI and ML have been used to create more personalized and engaging user experiences. In this article, we will explore some of the advantages that AI and ML bring to businesses and social media.

1. **Improved Customer Experience:** AI and ML technologies can help businesses better understand and predict customer behaviour, preferences, and buying patterns. This data can then be used to deliver more relevant and personalized experiences to customers, helping to build

stronger relationships, increase engagement, and loyalty. For example, Amazon uses machine learning algorithms to recommend products to customers based on their past purchases, making their shopping experience more convenient.

2. **Better Decision-Making:** AI algorithms can help organizations analyze large amounts of data to identify trends and patterns that can be used to make informed decisions. ML algorithms can be used to identify which products or services are selling better, what is driving customer churn, and which marketing strategies are most effective. This information can then be used to optimize business operations and strategies, helping organizations to make better decisions.

3. **Automation:** AI and ML can automate tasks such as data entry, customer service, and other manual processes, freeing up employees to focus on more strategic activities. This can increase efficiency, reduce costs, and increase productivity. For instance, chatbots powered by AI can respond to customer inquiries, reducing the burden on customer service teams.

4. **Increased Personalization:** AI algorithms can help social media platforms create a more personalized user experience, based on individual preferences and behaviours. This includes personalized recommendations for posts, videos, and advertizements. For example, Instagram uses ML algorithms to curate a personalized feed for each user, based on their interests, past behaviour, and engagement history.

5. **Fraud Detection:** AI algorithms can help businesses detect and prevent fraud. ML algorithms can identify unusual behaviour, such as unusual spending patterns, by analyzing vast amounts of data in real-time. This helps businesses to detect fraud early, reduce financial losses, and protect their customers.

6. **Improved Efficiency:** AI algorithms can help businesses automate time-consuming tasks and increase efficiency. For instance, AI-powered sentiment analysis can help businesses quickly identify negative customer feedback and respond accordingly, improving customer satisfaction [29, 34, 35].

7. **Cost Savings:** By automating processes and improving efficiency, AI and ML can help businesses reduce costs and save money. Additionally, AI algorithms can be used to identify areas where costs can be reduced, such as reducing waste and optimizing supply chains.

In conclusion, AI and ML technologies are increasingly being adopted by businesses and social media platforms to improve their operations, increase efficiency, and create a better user experience. With the rapid advancement of these technologies, organizations will continue to reap their benefits, helping to stay ahead of the curve and remain competitive [30].

12.8 CHALLENGES

Introduction: In recent years, Artificial Intelligence (AI) and Machine Learning (ML) have become increasingly popular in the business and social media industry. Despite the potential benefits, businesses and social media companies are faced with several challenges in implementing these technologies [31]. In this article, we will explore seven of the most common challenges businesses face when implementing AI and ML.

1. **Data Quality and Quantity:** One of the primary challenges businesses faces when implementing AI and ML is ensuring that the data they use is of high-quality and enough. AI and ML algorithms require large amounts of data to be trained, so it is important that businesses have access to clean and accurate data. If the data is poor, the results of the algorithms will also be poor. Businesses must invest time and resources into data collection, cleaning, and labelling.

2. **Integration with Existing Systems:** Another challenge businesses face is integrating AI and ML technologies into their existing systems. AI and ML algorithms often require new data structures, data access methods, and communication protocols, which can be challenging for existing systems to support. Businesses must invest in development and testing to ensure that AI and ML algorithms work effectively with existing systems.

3. **Expertise:** Businesses also face the challenge of finding and retaining personnel with the necessary expertise in AI and ML. This is particularly true in the social media industry, where a shortage of AI and ML experts can make it difficult for companies to implement these technologies effectively. Businesses must invest in training and development programs to help their employees acquire the skills they need to implement AI and ML effectively [36].

4. **Trust and Bias:** Another challenge businesses face is building trust in AI and ML systems, particularly when they are used in sensitive areas such as social media. AI and ML algorithms are only as good as the data they are trained on, so it is important that businesses are transparent about how their algorithms are trained and how they make decisions. Additionally, businesses must take steps to minimize bias in AI and ML algorithms, as biased algorithms can perpetuate discrimination and prejudice [37].

5. **Regulation:** Businesses also face challenges related to regulation, particularly in the social media industry. AI and ML technologies are rapidly evolving, and there are few legal and regulatory frameworks in place to govern their use. Businesses must stay up to date with regulations related to AI and ML and take steps to ensure that they comply with these regulations [39].

6. **Cost:** Implementing AI and ML technologies can be expensive, and businesses must invest in hardware, software, and personnel to implement these technologies effectively. Additionally, businesses must invest in ongoing maintenance and support, which can also add to the cost of implementing AI and ML.

7. **Privacy:** Finally, businesses face challenges related to privacy, particularly in the social media industry. AI and ML algorithms often collect and use personal data, which can be sensitive and subject to privacy regulations. Businesses must take steps to ensure that personal data is protected and that privacy regulations are respected.

Conclusion: In conclusion, businesses and social media companies face several challenges when implementing AI and ML technologies. From ensuring data quality and quantity, to addressing regulation and privacy concerns, businesses must invest time and resources into overcoming these challenges. By doing so, they can unlock the full potential of AI and ML and drive growth and innovation in their businesses and social media companies.

12.9 SUGGESTIONS

Implementing artificial intelligence and machine learning in businesses and social media businesses can be a complex and challenging process, but it can also bring significant benefits and profits if done correctly. Here are some suggestions on how to implement AI/ML in businesses and social media businesses to generate profits:

1. **Identify areas of the business that can benefit from AI/ML:** To effectively implement AI/ML in businesses, it's important to identify areas that can benefit from it. For example, businesses can use AI/ML to automate repetitive tasks, optimize marketing and sales, enhance customer service, and improve overall efficiency.

2. **Invest in data management and security:** AI/ML systems rely heavily on data, so it's crucial to have robust data management systems in place. This includes ensuring the accuracy and quality of data, as well as proper security measures to protect sensitive information.

3. **Collaborate with AI/ML experts:** Implementing AI/ML requires specialized knowledge and expertise, so it's important to work with AI/ML experts. This can include hiring AI/ML specialists, partnering with AI/ML companies, or working with AI/ML consulting firms.

4. **Develop a roadmap:** Implementing AI/ML in businesses requires a comprehensive and well-structured plan. A roadmap can help businesses stay on track and ensure the implementation is completed smoothly and efficiently.

5. **Continuously monitor and evaluate performance:** AI/ML systems can only be as effective as the data they are fed, so it's important to continuously monitor their performance. This includes regularly evaluating their results, adjusting algorithms and models as needed, and fine-tuning the systems for maximum performance.

6. **Train employees and customers:** To fully realize the benefits of AI/ML in businesses, employees and customers need to be trained on how to use the systems effectively. This includes providing training sessions, tutorials, and other resources to help employees and customers understand how to use the systems and achieve the best results.

7. **Invest in ongoing research and development:** AI/ML is an ever-evolving field, and it's important for businesses to invest in ongoing research and development. This includes staying up to date with the latest AI/ML technologies, attending conferences and workshops, and participating in AI/ML communities.

By following these suggestions, businesses and social media businesses can effectively implement AI/ML and reap the benefits of increased efficiency, improved customer experience, and increased profits. However, it's important to remember that AI/ML is not a one-time investment, but rather a continuous journey of improvement and refinement.

12.10 CONCLUSION

In conclusion, the research paper has analyzed the role of artificial intelligence (AI) and machine learning (ML) in businesses and social media companies. The paper demonstrated how these technologies have revolutionized the way businesses operate, by automating routine tasks, providing data-driven insights, and improving customer experiences. Additionally, the paper explored the benefits of AI and ML, such as increased efficiency, cost savings, and better decision making. However, the paper also acknowledged the potential risks associated with the integration of AI and ML in businesses, including the potential for job loss and ethical concerns. It is important for companies to be aware of these issues and take measures to mitigate their impact, such as upskilling employees and implementing ethical standards for AI. In summary, the paper emphasizes the importance of AI and ML in the modern business landscape and highlights their potential to drive growth and success. It also stresses the need for businesses to embrace these technologies with caution, and to ensure that their use aligns with ethical standards and regulations. The findings of this research paper can provide valuable insights for companies looking to integrate AI and ML into their operations and highlight the need for responsible and ethical use of these powerful technologies.

REFERENCES

1. Kiruthika, J., & Khaddaj, S. (2017). Impact and challenges of using of virtual reality & artificial intelligence in businesses. 2017 16th International Symposium on Distributed Computing and Applications to Business, Engineering and Science (DCABES), Anyang, pp. 165–168. doi: 10.1109/DCABES.2017.43.

2. Hahn, C., Traunecker, T., Niever, M., & Basedow, G. N. (2020). Exploring AI-driven business models: Conceptualization and expectations in the machinery industry. 2020 IEEE International Conference on Industrial Engineering and Engineering Management (IEEM), Singapore, pp. 567–570. doi: 10.1109/IEEM45057.2020.9309824.

3. Ilieva, R., & Nikolov, Y. (2019). AI integration in business processes management. 2019 International Conference on Creative Business for Smart and Sustainable Growth (CREBUS), Sandanski, pp. 1–4. doi: 10.1109/CREBUS.2019.8840086.

4. Hedberg, S. R. (1996). AI tools for business-process modeling. IEEE Expert, 11(4), 13–15. doi: 10.1109/64.511772.

5. Xu, A., Gao, S., & Li, X. (2011). Leveraging internet marketing to extend business reach: An empirical analysis of one language training centre. 2011 10th International Symposium on Distributed Computing and Applications to Business, Engineering and Science, Wuxi, pp. 92–95. doi: 10.1109/DCABES.2011.55.

6. Zamudio, V., Zheng, P., & Callaghan, V. (2012). Intelligent business process engineering: An agent based model for understanding and managing business change. 2012 Eighth International Conference on Intelligent Environments, Guanajuato, pp. 141–148. doi: 10.1109/IE.2012.59.

7. Benjamins, V. R. (2006). AI's future: Innovating in business and society. IEEE Intelligent Systems, 21(3), 72–73. doi: 10.1109/MIS.2006.41.

8. Feher, K. (2020). Trends and business models of new-smart-AI (NSAI) media. 2020 13th CMI Conference on Cybersecurity and Privacy (CMI) – Digital Transformation – Potentials and Challenges (51275), Copenhagen, pp. 1–6. doi: 10.1109/CMI51275.2020.9322725.

9. Crockett, K. A., Gerber, L., Latham, A., & Colyer, E. (2021). Building trustworthy AI solutions: A case for practical solutions for small businesses. IEEE Transactions on Artificial Intelligence, 4, pp. 778–791, Aug. 2023, doi: 10.1109/TAI.2021.3137091.

10. Shidaganti, G., Salil, S., Anand, P., & Jadhav, V. (2021). Robotic process automation with AI and OCR to improve business process: Review. 2021 Second International Conference on Electronics and Sustainable Communication Systems (ICESC), Coimbatore, pp. 1612–1618. doi: 10.1109/ICESC51422.2021.9532902.

11. Zarifis, A., & Efthymiou, L. (2022). The four business models for AI adoption in education: Giving leaders a destination for the digital transformation journey. 2022 IEEE Global Engineering Education Conference (EDUCON), Tunis, pp. 1868–1872. doi: 10.1109/EDUCON52537.2022.9766687.

12. Zhao, Y., Zhang, T., Liu, Y., Zhu, Y., & Gao, Y. (2021). Research on the influence mechanism of Artificial Intelligence (AI) customer service on user satisfaction with online shopping. 2021 2nd International Conference on Computer

Science and Management Technology (ICCSMT), Shanghai, pp. 253–260. doi: 10.1109/ICCSMT54525.2021.00056.

13. Simionescu, S.-M., Bădică, A., Bădică, C., Ganzha, M., & Paprzycki, M. (2021). On the role of blockchain in evolving the online business landscape. 2021 Conference on Information Communications Technology and Society (ICTAS), Durban, pp. 85–90. doi: 10.1109/ICTAS50802.2021.9395045.

14. Meepung, T., & Kannikar, P. (2022). Artificial Intelligence for digital business performance. 2022 Joint International Conference on Digital Arts, Media and Technology with ECTI Northern Section Conference on Electrical, Electronics, Computer and Telecommunications Engineering (ECTI DAMT & NCON), Chiang Rai, pp. 242–246. doi: 10.1109/ECTIDAMTNCON53731.2022.9720418.

15. Jangra, G., & Jangra, M. (2022). Role of Artificial Intelligence in online shopping and its impact on consumer purchasing behaviour and decision. 2022 Second International Conference on Computer Science, Engineering and Applications (ICCSEA), Gunupur, pp. 1–7. doi: 10.1109/ICCSEA54677.2022.9936374.

16. Singh, S., Greaves, D. J., & Epiphaniou, G. (2022). A framework for integrating responsible AI into social media platforms. Competitive Advantage in the Digital Economy (CADE 2022), Hybrid Conference, Venice, pp. 117–120. doi: 10.1049/icp.2022.2051.

17. Sanz, J. L. C., & Zhu, Y. (2021). Toward scalable Artificial Intelligence in finance. 2021 IEEE International Conference on Services Computing (SCC), Chicago, IL, pp. 460–469. doi: 10.1109/SCC53864.2021.00067.

18. Mas'od, A., Idris, U. N., Sulaiman, Z., & Chin, T. A. (2019). The influence of Facebook features and activities on consumers' purchase intention. 2019 6th International Conference on Research and Innovation in Information Systems (ICRIIS), Johor Bahru, pp. 1–6. doi: 10.1109/ICRIIS48246.2019.9073639.

19. Kosasi, S. (2015). The maturity level of information technology governance of online cosmetics business. 2015 3rd International Conference on New Media (CONMEDIA), Tangerang, pp. 1–6. doi: 10.1109/CONMEDIA.2015.7449140.

20. Brabazon, A., Cahill, J., Keenan, P., & Walsh, D. (2010). Identifying online credit card fraud using Artificial Immune Systems. IEEE Congress on Evolutionary Computation, Barcelona, pp. 1–7. doi: 10.1109/CEC.2010.5586154.

21. Maitra, S., Rakib Ahamed, M., Nazrul Islam, M., Abdullah Al Nasim, M., & Ashraf, M. (2021). A soft computing based customer lifetime value classifier for digital retail businesses. 2021 IEEE 12th Annual Ubiquitous Computing, Electronics & Mobile Communication Conference (UEMCON), New York, NY, pp. 0074–0083. doi: 10.1109/UEMCON53757.2021.9666546.

22. Shroff, G., Agarwal, P., & Dey, L. (2011). Enterprise information fusion for real-time business intelligence. 14th International Conference on Information Fusion, Chicago, IL, pp. 1–8.

23. Thuraisingham, B. (2020). The role of Artificial Intelligence and cyber security for social media. 2020 IEEE International Parallel and Distributed Processing Symposium Workshops (IPDPSW), New Orleans, LA, pp. 1–3. doi: 10.1109/IPDPSW50202.2020.00184.

24. Wang, Y., Ren, F., & Li, X. (2020). Social media analytics: A survey on big data and machine learning. Journal of Big Data, 7(1), 57.

25. Cui, Y., Qiu, J., & Wang, Y. (2021). A survey of deep learning applications in social media analytics. Information Fusion, 69, 140–153.
26. Yu, J., Li, X., Guan, X., & Shen, H. (2022). A remote sensing assessment index for urban ecological livability and its application. Geo-spatial Information Science, 1–22.
27. Raghupathi, V., & Raghupathi, W. (2019). AI applications in social media: A review. Journal of Big Data Analytics in Transportation, 1(1), 3.
28. Nguyen, T. H. (2020). Social media analytics: An overview of recent developments using machine learning. International Journal of Information Management, 50, 14–22.
29. Kaur, H., & Goyal, P. (2021). Machine learning techniques for sentiment analysis of social media data: A review. Artificial Intelligence Review, 54(5), 3747–3777.
30. Ture, M., & Yaylacı, M. E. (2021). Social media analytics and machine learning: A systematic literature review. Journal of Enterprise Information Management, 23, 455–463.
31. Saravanakumar, M., & Lakshmi, S. P. (2019). Deep learning techniques for social media analytics: A review. Journal of Ambient Intelligence and Humanized Computing, 10(11), 4523–4537.
32. Lu, X., & Yang, Z. (2020). An empirical study on the effectiveness of machine learning techniques for social media marketing. Internet Research, 30(2), 489–509.
33. Vanichpun, T., & Wannapiroon, P. (2021). A systematic review of machine learning in social media marketing. Computers in Human Behavior, 115, 106624.
34. Gruzd, A., Mai, P., & Kumar, M. (2021). Social media analytics and natural language processing: A literature review. International Journal of Information Management, 56, 102269.
35. Al-Maadeed, S. A., & Al-Karaki, M. A. (2020). Machine learning-based sentiment analysis for social media: A comprehensive review. Journal of Ambient Intelligence and Humanized Computing, 11(1), 1–22.
36. Wang, J., Guo, L., & Liang, Y. (2020). How social media analytics can inform business decisions: Lessons from the hospitality industry. Journal of Hospitality and Tourism Technology, 11(4), 543–560.
37. Kim, M. J., & Lee, H. J. (2019). Social media analytics in the hospitality industry: A review of empirical research. Journal of Travel and Tourism Marketing, 36(6), 631–643.
38. Boadh, R., Grover, R., Dahiya, M., Kumar, A., Rathee, R., Rajoria, Y. K., Rawat, M., & Rani, S. (2022). Study of fuzzy expert system for the diagnosis of various types of cancer. Materials Today: Proceedings, 56, 298–307.
39. Park, J. W., & Kim, Y. (2020). Understanding the impact of social media analytics on customer relationship management: A literature review and future research directions. Journal of Hospitality and Tourism Technology, 11(2), 186–204.
40. Crockett, K. A., Gerber, L., Latham, A., & Colyer, E. (2009). A framework for selecting and promoting AI toolkits in SMEs. In Proceedings of the AAAI Workshop on AI, Ethics, and Society.
41. Xu, S., Gao, Y., & Li, X. (2011). Application of internet marketing in Zhuhai New-Concept Training Centre. In 2011 International Conference on Business Management and Electronic Information (BMEI), Vol. 3, pp. 84–87. IEEE.

42. Zamudio, V., Zheng, P., & Callaghan, V. (2012). A graph-based approach to smart business process management. In Proceedings of the 2012 International Conference on Intelligent Systems Design and Engineering Applications (ISDEA), pp. 343–348. IEEE.
43. Thuraisingham, B. (2020). Artificial Intelligence for cybersecurity in social media systems: A literature review. In 2020 IEEE International Conference on Computational Science and Engineering (CSE) and IEEE International Conference on Embedded and Ubiquitous Computing (EUC), pp. 9–16. IEEE.
44. Feher, K. (2020). New media in the age of Artificial Intelligence. Fjord, Design and Innovation from Accenture Interactive, 3, 47–57.
45. Rani, S., Kumar, A., Bagchi, A., Yadav, S., & Kumar, S. (2021, August). RPL based routing protocols for load balancing in IoT network. Journal of Physics: Conference Series, 1950(1), 012073.
46. Sena, V., & Nocker, M. (2021). Artificial intelligence and business models: A literature review. European Management Journal, 39(1), 12–22.
47. Rajendra, P., Kumari, M., Rani, S., Dogra, N., Boadh, R., Kumar, A., & Dahiya, M. (2022). Impact of artificial intelligence on civilization: Future perspectives. Materials Today: Proceedings, 56, 252–256.

Chapter 13

Remote Sensing and Machine Learning

Charu Jhamaria and Tanisha Ameriya

Department of Environmental Science, IIS (deemed to be University), Jaipur 302020

13.1 INTRODUCTION

13.1.1 Remote Sensing and Its Application in Environmental Management

Remote sensing in the present time has become a popular field of interest and attracts scientists, researchers and policy makers across the globe. The term remote sensing is often misinterpreted with satellite based sensing but in its true sense, the term is commonly applied to the art and science of sensing and capturing information about the object with the help of specialized sensors placed on aircrafts, satellites, drones or even ground-based vehicles. It provides a synoptic view of the landscape at both global and local level. In addition, satellite-based remote sensing sensors have the ability to split the entire electromagnetic spectrum into multiple bands and can detect radiation in wavelengths other than the visible range, allowing for the differentiation of objects with varying optical qualities. This contactless information gathering system has enormous potential and is vital for studies related to environmental management. Over the years, remote sensing data have been used more and more for a wide range of applications, including disease control, monitoring natural resources, disaster management, environmental degradation and health management (Ghauri and Zaidi, 2015) (Table 13.1). Utilization of such data provides continuous monitoring and mapping at both spatial and temporal scale as opposed to the traditional approaches and strengthens the process of decision making. Moreover, technological advancements and the availability of RS data at reasonable prices enables continuous monitoring and prediction of environmental changes. With many benefits and greater data accessibility, remote sensing has emerged as a very promising tool in various scientific researches even though some of its aspects are not yet fully understood.

13.2 BASICS OF MACHINE LEARNING

Machine Learning is a branch of computer science that enables computers to learn without being explicitly programmed (Rajendra et al. 2022).

DOI: 10.1201/9781003329947-13

Table 13.1 Application of remote sensing in environmental studies

Atmospheric Parameters	Hydrological Parameters	Natural and Man-made Hazards	Land use Planning	Environmental Protection

• Aerosol
• Fog
• Black Carbon
• Dust Storm
  Ozone and
  other trace
  gases
	• Water Quality
	  Soil Moisture
	• Sea Surface
	  Temperature
	• Clouds Optical
	  Properties
	• Snow Cover
		• Floods,
		  Tsunami,
		  Earthquakes,
		  landslides
		  Mapping
		  and Risk
		  Assessment
		• Droughts
		• Epidemic
		  Mapping
		• Forest Fires
			• Land use/Land
			  cover changes
			• Urban Planning
			• Urban Heat
			  Islands
			• Agriculture
			  Forests (land and
			  coastal)
			• Coastal zone
			  monitoring
				• Environmental
				  Impact
				  Assessment

(*Source:* Ghauri and Zaidi, 2015)

It designs and constructs algorithms that allow the use of existing sets of data for classification and prediction-based analysis using specialized models. In the realm of big data, ML plays a significant role in handling data with great precision contrary to humans. In general, ML is broadly classified into supervised, unsupervised learning and reinforcement learning (Cohen, 2021).

Supervised learning, as the name suggests, uses a set of data labeled with correct answers to train the machine or system and based upon the learning, the test data is accurately processed. Supervised learning can be categorized into two types of algorithms—classification and regression. The classification method is used to classify the test data, and the regression technique is used to understand the relationship between the dependent and independent variables. Decision trees, linear regression, K-nearest neighbors, random forest, support vector machines are some of the widely used supervised learning algorithms.

Unsupervised learning uses algorithms to process an unlabeled dataset in order to understand the structure of the dataset, sort, and cluster that data based on the patterns and similarities. Unsupervised learning can be classified into two categories—clustering and association learning. Clustering methods deal with grouping the dataset into clusters based on the presence or absence of some predesigned criteria. In the association method of unsupervised learning, relationship between the variables in the large database are assessed. Some of the popular unsupervised learning algorithms are hierarchical clustering, K-means clustering, principal component analysis, independent component analysis, self-organizing maps, density estimations, etc.

In reinforcement learning the algorithm works in response to the environment. The agent (computer program or system) takes a sequence of actions for a problem in accordance with the environment and based on the output, it is either rewarded or punished. Unlike supervised or unsupervised learning, the agent itself discovers which actions yield maximum rewards. Markov model, Q-learning, and Deep-Q network are some of the major reinforcement learning algorithms.

These different types of learning algorithms are deployed in various sectors across the globe for better data handling, gaining new insights within the data and also for finding anomalies, if any. Furthermore, machine learning integrates approaches from various fields making it multidisciplinary and widely applicable (Figure 13.1).

13.3 USE OF MACHINE LEARNING IN REMOTE SENSING

The Earth is a complex system with interactions including the atmosphere, hydrosphere, biosphere, and lithosphere. Understanding and analyzing such interactions is extremely valuable in the present deteriorating world, where

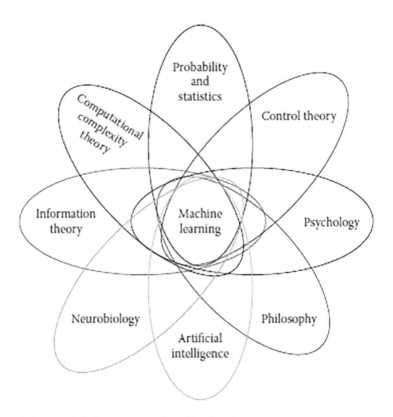

Figure 13.1 Multidisciplinary nature of machine learning.

sustainable development has become the need of the hour. For analysis of this dynamic earth, remote sensing and GIS proves to provide high resolution synoptical data. In order to handle and process such large amount of remote sensing data efficiently, ML methods are frequently utilized, although their usage in this sector is relatively new (Lary et al. 2015). In this section of the chapter, insights that will be focusing on the fundamental concept of algorithms from machine learning are addressed that are actively utilized in the field of remote sensing and GIS.

13.3.1 Maximum Likelihood Algorithm

Maximum likelihood algorithm has long been among the most popularly used classification method in remote sensing. The method classifies pixels based on its probability of belonging to different classes and assigns the pixel to the class with the highest probability. The algorithm assumes that the data or input bands are normally distributed and every pixel has equal probability for all the classes (Sisodia et al. 2014). It follows the Bayes Rule which states:

$$P(C_i | x) = P(x | C_i)\, P(C_i)/P(x) \tag{1}$$

Where,

x   = a vector with set of brightness values of a pixel in different bands
C_i = Spectral classes (i= 1, 2, 3. . . j)
$P(C_i | x)$ = conditional probability of class i given the feature vector x
$P(x | C_i)$ = conditional probability of feature vector x given that it belongs
               to class C_i
$P(C_i)$ = prior probability of occurrence of Class i in the image
$P(x)$ = probability of finding a pixel with measurement vector x in the
               image and can be denoted as:

$$P(x) = \sum_{i=1}^{n} P(x | C_i)\, P(C_i) \tag{2}$$

In the presence of complete sets of conditional probabilities $P(C_i | x)$ for a pixel, then the pixel can be classified as:

$$X \in C_i, \; if \; P(C_i | x) > P(C_j | x) \quad for \; all \; j \neq i \tag{3}$$

This equation explains that the probability of a given pixel to be in class i is greatest than for any other class.

Substituting from equation (1) in equation (3) we get more appropriate equation.

$$X \in C_i, \text{ if } P(x|C_i) \, P(C_i) > P(x|C_j) \, P\left(C_j\right) \quad \textit{for all } j \neq i \tag{4}$$

For ML classification, $P(x \mid C_i)$ is assumed to be distributed according to the multivariate normal distribution, also known as Gaussian distribution and the conditional probability $P(x \mid C_i)$ is represented by its mean vector μ and covariance matrix Σ_i

$$p\left(x|C_i\right) = \frac{1}{\sqrt{2\Pi\Sigma_i}} e\left(-\frac{(x-\mu)^2}{\Sigma_i(x-\mu)}\right) \tag{5}$$

This method is very efficient for classifying multi-spectral images however, it is more computation intensive and tends to over-classify the pixels.

13.3.2 Minimum Distance Classifier

Minimum distance classifier is a classification algorithm which classifies pixels to the class based on the distance mean values. The method determines the mean position (or mean vector) of the spectral classes from the each pixel and based on the training dataset, assigns the unclassified pixel to class with nearest mean value (Thakur and Maheshwari, 2017; Kamusoko, 2019). It uses Euclidean distance to measure the closest distance between the pixels and classes.

In Figure 13.2, Class 1, 2 and 3 are the training datasets and the small circular dot (let say 'x') in between the classes represents the unclassified pixel. The unclassified pixel will be assigned to the class with lowest Euclidean distance which is calculated using the subsequent equations (Razaque et al. 2021).

$$d_i(x) = x - m_i \text{ for } i = 1, 2, \ldots \ldots M \tag{6}$$

Where, M = number of classes. If $x = (p_1 q_1)$ and $m_i = (p_2, q_2)$, then

$$D_i\left(x^2\right) = \sqrt{(p1-p2)^2 + (q1-q2)^2} \tag{7}$$

This classification method is mathematically less complex but it gives poor results for the satellite data with high spectral variance and often leads to misclassification of pixels (Abinaya and Poonkuntran, 2019).

In a high-dimensional space, the approach constructs a hyperplane or multiple hyperplanes for classification or regression.

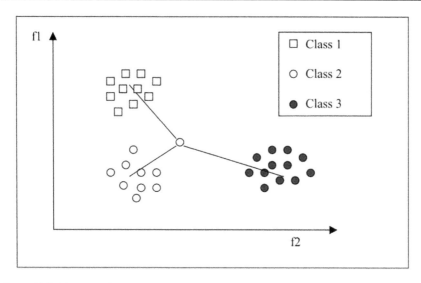

Figure 13.2 Minimum distance classification.

(*Source:* Mahesh Pal, 2014)

13.3.3 Support Vector Machines

Another supervised learning method is the support vector machine (SVM), which was developed by Vladmir N. Vapnik and Alexa Y. Chervonenkis in 1963. The approach creates a hyperplane or a set of hyperplanes in a high-dimensional feature space that can be used for classification and regression. In general, the higher the distance of hyperplane to its nearest data point on both sides, the better will be the classification (Figure 13.3) (Dönmez, 2013). The tool provides highly accurate predictive analysis and is less prone to over-fitting than other methods.

From Figure 13.3, it is clear that there can be more than one hyperplane for the classification of classes but the one with maximum margin is considered to be the best. This type of hyperplane is known as maximal margin hyperplane and this hyperplane can be constructed with the help of a subset of the training samples that lie on the margin, called support vectors. The support vectors aid in defining the margins of the hyperplanes (Figure 13.4).

Mathematically, SVM is illustrated generally using the subsequent equation (Dönmez, 2013):

$$\mathcal{D} = \left\{ \left(x_i, y_i \right) \middle| x_i \in \mathbb{R}^p, y_i \in \{-1, 1\} \right\}_{i=1}^{n} \tag{8}$$

Where, D is some training data, y_i is the class (either -1 or 1) to which point x_i belongs, and x_i is a p-dimensional real vector.

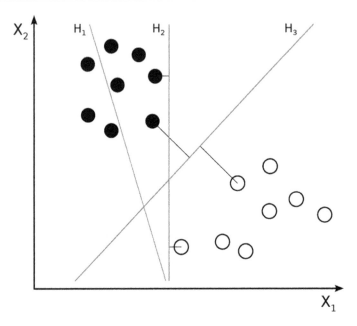

Figure 13.3 Concept of support vector machine. Here H1, H2 and H3 denote the three hyperplanes. H3 hyperplane separates the classes with highest margin then H2 and hyperplane H1 does not separate the classes at all. H2 hyperplane is also known as maximum margin classifier.

(*Source:* Dönmez, 2013)

Let's assume a hyperplane which is separating -1 class from +1 class. The point x which lies on the hyperplane should follow the equation (9).

$$w \cdot x + b = 0 \tag{9}$$

where, w = normal to hyperplane, (·) = dot product and $|b| / \| w \|$ = perpendicular distance from the origin to the hyperplane $\| w \|$ denotes the Euclidean norm of w.

Two hyperplanes can be chosen for the linear training dataset so that they completely divide the data, leaving no points in between. This region in between the hyperplanes is referred to as the margin. The hyperplanes can be formulated as:

$$w \cdot x + b \geq +1 \, for \, y_i = +1 \tag{10}$$

$$w \cdot x + b \leq -1 \, for \, y_i = -1 \tag{11}$$

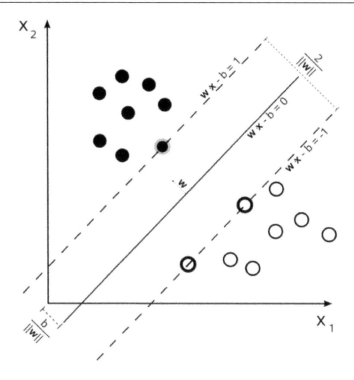

Figure 13.4 Maximum-margin hyperplane with support vectors.

Using the geometry, the distance between the two hyperplanes can be simple written as 2/ ‖ w ‖. Thus, the margin can be maximized by minimizing ‖ w ‖^2, given the constraint as mentioned in equation (12).

$$y_i(x_i + b) - 1 \geq 0 \tag{12}$$

SVM uses a variety of methods to create hyperplanes and concurrently minimize empirical classification error and maximize geometric margin, although the interpretation of parameters can be challenging sometimes in this algorithm (Dönmez, 2013).

13.3.4 Artificial Neural Network

Artificial Neural Network is a unique mathematical algorithm that mimics the functioning of the human brain, specifically the nervous system. Just as the human brain which consists of neuron nodes interconnected in a web-like fashion, the ANN system is also made up of large number of inter-connected and layered processing units called neurons that work together

(a)

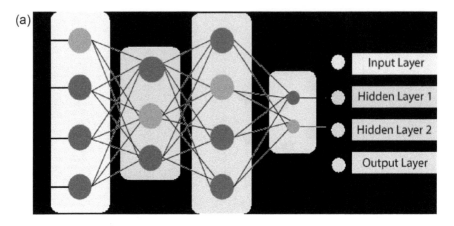

(b)

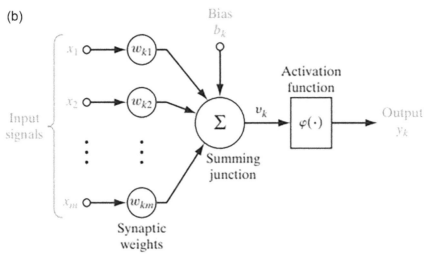

Figure 13.5 (a) Artificial neural network. Here, each circular node represents the neuron and arrows represents the connection. The input layer receives the data and the output layer generates the result. Between the two, one or more hidden layers that are necessary for data processing are present. (b) Basic functioning model of non-linear neuron named k.

for transmitting and processing the data (Figure 13.5a) (Dastres and Soori, 2021). Each connection has a connection weight which can be positive or negative based on the sign and these weights affect the intensity of signal at the connection. Each neuron has a threshold value above which the signal is transmitted and an activation function based on which the output is generated (Figure 13.5b). Here, activation function is governed by an activation value which is the summation of all the weighted signals (Gurney, 2018).

In mathematical terms, the neuron k can be described as follows (Haykin, 2009):

$$u_k = \sum_{j=1}^{m} w_{kj} x_j \tag{13}$$

and

$$y_k = \varphi(u_k + b_k) \tag{14}$$

Where, $x_1, x_2, \ldots x_m$ refers to the input signals; $w_1, w_2, \ldots w_m$ refers to the weight of the neuron k; b_k is the bias used in case of non-linear model; u_k (not depicted in Figure 13.5b) is the linear combiner output; $\varphi(\cdot)$ is the activation function and y_k is the output signal.

In the ANN system, networks can be feedforward, feedback or lateral depending upon the complexity of data and output requirements. Neural network has a wide applicability in the field of remote sensing due to its adaptivity, evidential response (along with classification provides decision making confidence), robust computation capability and uniformity in analysis and design (i.e. same notation is used everywhere in the data structure) (Gurney, 2018). However, this system can be slow to train which can produce non-optimal classification and often leads to overfitting of data (Maxwell et al. 2018).

13.3.5 Decision Tree and Random Forest

Decision tree classifier is a simple classifier which recursively splits the input data until no value is added to the model by the partition. As the name suggests, DT uses a trees like hierarchical structure to sort and represent the data which have the following components (Figure 13.6):

a) A *root node* which is a starting point with no incoming edge and many outgoing edges.
b) *Internal nodes* with one incoming edge and at least two outgoing edges. These nodes represent a test on an attribute or subset of attributes.
c) *Leaf or terminal nodes* which represent the class label. These nodes have only one incoming edge and no outgoing edge.

Decision tress can be mainly of two types: (a) classification tree and (b) regression tree, which are commonly addressed under an umbrella term, 'classification and regression tree (CART)'. In classification tree the leaf nodes represent the classes while in regression tree, the leaf nodes represent a continuous variable (Dönmez, 2013).

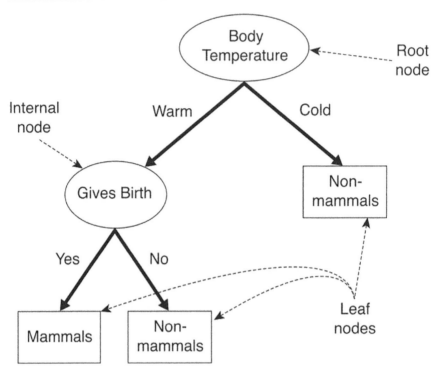

Figure 13.6 Example of decision tree representing the classification of mammals and non-mammals on the basis of temperature.

The DT considers every attribute of the dataset and selects the attribute which fits the best in providing maximum information about the problem. And all this is based on the concept of entropy, which states the randomness of the dataset. A set of data with similar attribute or value is said to have low entropy while data with random values is known to have high entropy. In DTs, we generally try to minimize the entropy in order to get accurate classification and prediction results (Cohen, 2021) (equation 15). The decision tress can also be created based on the concept of Gini impurity which measures the frequency at which any element of the dataset will be incorrectly labeled during random labelling (16).

For calculation entropy—

$$Entropy(s) = -(P+)log_2(P+) - (P-)log_2(P-) \qquad (15)$$

Where, s = sample, P+ = proportion of positive examples in sample s, and P- = proportion of negatives.

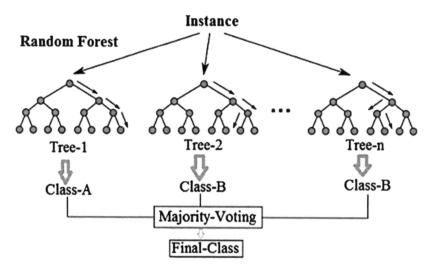

Figure 13.7 Simplified form of random forest classifier.

(*Source:* Cohen, 2021)

If all the examples belong to the same label or in case of pure split, entropy is zero while in the case of equally mixed examples, the entropy is one. Therefore, entropy value use to lie between zero and one.

For calculating Gini coefficient/Gini Index—

$$G.I. = 1 - \sum_{i=1}^{n} P^2$$
$$= 1 - [(P+)^2 + (P-)^2)]$$

(16)

Entropy and Gini impurity, both work on almost sample concept but Gini impurity is easier and quicker to compute in comparison to entropy.

DTs can be constructed in various ways using multiple trees for classification. These methods are commonly known as ensemble methods. One such method is bagging or bootstrap aggregating which uses multiple decision tress to make an ultimate decision by taking plurality of votes. Pal and Matter tried to assess the effectiveness of the decision trees in satellite image classification for land use land cover studies and by using the bagging method they found higher accuracy classification results (Kulkarni and Lowe, 2016).

Random forest method is one such ensemble method that is increasingly being used for land cover classification utilizing multispectral and hyperspectral satellite imageries (Figure 13.7). Random forest method integrates the idea of bagging and the random selection of features in order to overcome the drawbacks of the decision tree algorithm. In this method a subset of training samples is selected randomly and decision trees are created for each sample with the help of the bagging method. Finally, all the outputs of individual trees are combined to form the final output based on majority voting or averaging for classification or regression respectively (Pal, 2005).

Decision tree algorithms are very easy to understand and interpret; can handle both numerical as well as categorical data; robust and are capable of analyzing bulky datasets but they often lead to over-fitting of data and sometimes can become difficult to interpret. However, random forest classifiers are much more robust and accurate then simple DTs and are able to overcome the problem of over-fitting.

13.3.6 K-Nearest Neighbor

k-nearest neighbor algorithm is an instance-based learning algorithm that compares new problem instances directly to the training instances stored in the memory. Because of this, this method is usually referred to as memory-based learning or lazy learning. In this approach, the test sample is assigned to the common nearest class among its K-nearest neighbors, which are taken from the set of objects for which the class (k-NN classification) or the object attribute value (for k-NN regression) is known. Firstly, the training sample is prepared which consists of the vectors with a class label in a multidimensional space. The unlabeled vector is allocated to the class whose vectors appear most frequently in the k training samples nearest to the test vector using a user-defined constant k (Figure 13.7)(Pacheco et al. 2021). The distance from the unlabeled vector to the training vector can be measured using either Euclidean distance or Manhattan distance measures (equation 17 and 18). These distances for two points, x and y, with n attributes can be measured using the following formulas (Steinbach and Tan, 2009):

$$d(x,y) = \sqrt{\sum_{k=1}^{n}(x_k - y_k)^2} \text{ Euclidean distance} \tag{17}$$

$$d(x,y) = \sqrt{\sum^{nk=1}|x_k - y_k|} \text{ Manhattan distance} \tag{18}$$

KNN is a simplest ML algorithm widely used in remote sensing for classification and mapping burned areas. However, high computational cost and high-dimensional data greatly affects the performance of the algorithm (Figure 13.8).

13.3.7 K-Means Clustering

K-means clustering is the simplest unsupervised learning algorithm which classifies given datasets (pixels) into k clusters where each dataset or

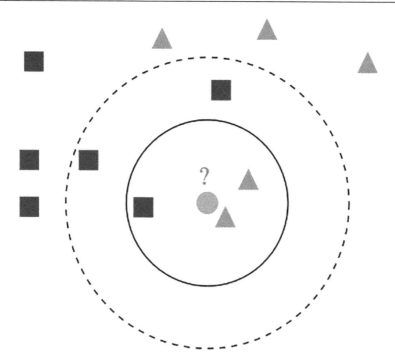

Figure 13.8 Example demonstrating k-NN classification. The unlabeled test sample or vector will be classified either to the class with blue squares (first class) or class with red triangles (second class). If k=3 (solid line) the test vector will be assigned to the second class and if k=5 (dashed line) it will be assigned to the first class.

observation belongs to a cluster with the nearest mean based on some pre-defined criteria (wavelength bands). For each cluster, k centroid is defined and the observation is assigned to the cluster with nearest centroid. After assigning all the observations to the clusters, positions of k centroids are recalculated and the process is repeated until the position of k centroid does not change. This leads to the classification of the observations into clusters from which the metric to be minimized can be calculated (Warf, 2014). While the algorithm is straightforward and simple to compute; number of cluster centers defined, the first cluster center selected, the sampling characteristics, the geometrical characteristics of the data, and clustering parameters may all have an impact on the K-means clustering outcome (Al-Doski et al. 2013).

13.3.8 ISODATA Clustering

ISODATA clustering stands for Iterative Self Organizing Data Analysis Technique. It is an unsupervised learning algorithm which is an advanced version of the K-means method. In remote sensing, the ISODATA method uses minimum spectral distance as a parameter to form clusters of pixels. The pixels or observations are assigned to the clusters in the way of K-means clustering. A convergence threshold is established, which is often set at 95%. It is the percentage of observations or pixels whose class value should remain unchanged during the iterations. By comparing the standard deviation values within each cluster and the distance between cluster centers to the threshold value, clusters can be split or merged. Clusters are divided when the standard deviation is greater than the threshold value and if the value is less than the threshold, the clusters are merged. When the distance values are on the higher side, the distribution is recalculated and splitting is done continuously until it drops below threshold (Merzougui et al. 2013).

13.4 CONCLUSION

The chapter attempts to concentrate on the conceptual workings of some machine learning algorithms that are widely used or have the potential to be used in remote sensing and GIS. Machine learning primarily focuses on computational and statistical methods for solving real-world problems with high accuracy and efficiency using large amounts of data. With the huge growth in remotely sensed data, it is becoming increasingly difficult to efficiently manage, analyze and interpret data. Given the extensive possibilities of ML, it appears to be a very effective method for handling this type of data. The majority of the algorithms described in the text are used for image classification, regression and prediction analysis, and the shortcomings of the algorithms provide future opportunities to researchers to develop new algorithms and models. The chapter focuses on the parameters that must be taken into account when processing data in order to produce the best results. In addition, sample size and quality of training data greatly impacts the accuracy of the models and hence underlines the usage of high-quality and high-resolution training data. Machine learning algorithms such as SVM, RF and ANN are found to be robust in complex data handling and have great value in classifying multispectral and hyperspectral satellite imageries. Though simple, techniques like k-NN, K-means, and minimum distance do not work well in complex feature spaces.

Utilizing machine learning in remote sensing has numerous advantages whereas, there are some drawbacks as well. Data accessibility, creating and validating the training data, and algorithm design issues prevent machine learning from being widely used in the field of remote sensing.

Despite the difficulties and disadvantages, current machine learning algorithms provide a powerful set of tools for information extraction from remotely sensed data and ought to be utilized to the fullest extent possible. Future advancements may also be anticipated to offer more ways to deal with poor training data, a complex feature space, and the requirement for user input in the form of user-defined parameters.

REFERENCES

Abinaya, V., & Poonkuntran, S. (2019). Classification of Satellite Image using Minimum Distance Classification Algorithm. SSRG International Journal of Computer Science and Engineering (SSRG-IJCSE), 1, 15–18.

Al-Doski, J., Mansor, S. B., Zulhaidi, H., & Shafri, M. (2013). Image Classification in Remote Sensing. Journal of Environment and Earth Science, 3(10), 141–148.

Cohen, S. (2021). The basics of machine learning: Strategies and techniques. In Artificial Intelligence and Deep Learning in Pathology. Elsevier Inc. https://doi.org/10.1016/b978-0-323-67538-3.00002-6

Dastres, R., & Soori, M. (2021). Artificial Neural Network Systems. International Journal of Imaging and Robotics (IJIR), 2021(2), 13–25. www.ceserp.com/cp-jour

Dönmez, P. (2013). Introduction to Machine Learning, 2nd ed., by Ethem Alpaydın. Cambridge, MA: The MIT Press 2010. ISBN: 978-0-262-01243-0. $54/£ 39.95 + 584 pages. Natural Language Engineering, 19(2), 285–288. https://doi.org/10.1017/s1351324912000290

Ghauri, D., & Zaidi, A. (2015). Application of Remote Sensing in Environmental Studies. Aerosol Science and Engineering, 1, 1–8.

Gurney, K. (2018). An Introduction to Neural Networks. CRC Press.

Haykin, S. (2009). Neural Networks and Learning Machines, 3/E. Pearson Education India.

Kamusoko, C. (2019). Chapter 4: Image classification. In Remote Sensing Image Classification in R (pp. 81–153). Springer. https://doi.org/10.1007/978-981-13-8012-9

Kulkarni, A. D., & Lowe, B. (2016). Random Forest Algorithm for Land Cover Classification. International Journal on Recent and Innovation Trends in Computing and Communication, 4(3), 58–63.

Lary, D. J., Alavi, A. H., Gandomi, A. H., & Walker, A. L. (2015). Machine Learning in Geosciences and Remote Sensing. Geoscience Frontiers, 7(1), 3–10. https://doi.org/10.1016/j.gsf.2015.07.003

Maxwell, A. E., Warner, T. A., & Fang, F. (2018). Implementation of Machine-Learning Classification in Remote Sensing: An Applied Review. International Journal of Remote Sensing, 39(9), 2784–2817. https://doi.org/10.1080/01431161.2018.1433343

Merzougui, M., Matsi, L., Nasri, M., & Matsi, L. (2013). Image Segmentation using Isodata Clustering with Parameters Estimated by Evolutionary Approach: Application to Quality Control. International Journal of Computer Applications, 66(19), 25–30.

Pacheco, A. D. P., Junior, J. A. D. S., Ruiz-Armenteros, A. M., & Henriques, R. F. F. (2021). Assessment of k-Nearest Neighbor and Random Forest Classifiers for Mapping Forest Fire Areas in Central Portugal using Landsat-8, Sentinel-2, and Terra Imagery. Remote Sensing, 13(7), 1–25. https://doi.org/10.3390/rs13071345

Pal, M. (2005). Random Forest Classifier for Remote Sensing Classification. International Journal of Remote Sensing, 26(1), 217–222. https://doi.org/10.1080/01431160412331269698

Pal, M. (2014). Factors Influencing the Accuracy of Remote Sensing Classifications: A Comparative Study. Thesis submitted to the University of Nottingham, January 2002.

Rajendra, P., Kumari, M., Rani, S., Dogra, N., Boadh, R., Kumar, A., & Dahiya, M. (2022). Impact of Artificial Intelligence on Civilization: Future Perspectives. Materials Today: Proceedings, 56, 252–256.

Razaque, A., Ben Haj Frej, M., Almi'ani, M., Alotaibi, M., & Alotaibi, B. (2021). Improved Support Vector Machine Enabled Radial Basis Function and Linear Variants for Remote Sensing Image Classification. Sensors, 21(13). https://doi.org/10.3390/s21134431

Sisodia, P. S., Tiwari, V., & Kumar, A. (2014). Analysis of Supervised Maximum Likelihood Classification for Remote Sensing Image. International Conference on Recent Advances and Innovations in Engineering (ICRAIE), 9–12. https://doi.org/10.1109/ICRAIE.2014.6909319

Steinbach, M., & Tan, P. N. (2009). kNN: k-nearest neighbors. In The Top Ten Algorithms in Data Mining (pp. 165–176). Chapman and Hall/CRC.

Thakur, N., & Maheshwari, D. (2017). A Review of Image Classification Techniques. International Research Journal of Engineering and Technology (IRJET), 4(11), 1588–1591.

Warf, B. (2014). Unsupervised Classification. Encyclopedia of Geography. https://doi.org/10.4135/9781412939591.n1179

Chapter 14

Revolutionizing Sales and Marketing
The Power of AI in Action

¹Pooja Singh, ¹Lipsa Das, ¹Raju Jha,
²Ajay Kumar, and ³Sangeeta Rani
¹Amity University, Greater Noida, UP, India
²Associate Professor, Department of Mechanical Engineering, School of
Engineering and Technology, JECRC University, Jaipur, Rajasthan, India
³Department of Computer Science and Engineering, World College of
Technology and Management, Gurgaon, India

14.1 INTRODUCTION

Machines that have been instructed to function and learn similarly to living beings are called AI systems. These gadgets can be programmed to do a variety of tasks, including speech recognition and decision-making. Weak AI and strong AI are the two basic divisions of AI technology. Strong AI, commonly referred to as AGI (Artificial General Intelligence), can carry out any intellectual work that a human can, in contrast to weak AI, which is focused on doing activities. Whereas AI in marketing and sales refers to the application of technology to many areas of the marketing and sales process to enhance and automate them. Using AI for personalisation, lead creation and scoring, customer service, predictive analytics, and ad campaign optimisation are a few examples of how this may be done (Figure 14.1).

- **Personalisation:** Artificial intelligence (AI) can examine consumer information and behaviour to tailor content and communication, such as tailored email campaigns or personalised product recommendations. Engagement and conversion rates benefit from this.
- **Lead generation and scoring:** AI can search through enormous collections of information to identify and rank high-value prospects. It can also assess leads based on how likely they are to convert. This may aid in enhancing the effectiveness of the sales procedure and raising return on investment.
- **Chatbots and virtual assistants:** Robo—advisors and chatbots powered by AI can assist qualify and nurture leads as well as provide round-the-clock support and assistance to customers. This can lower costs and increase customer satisfaction.

DOI: 10.1201/9781003329947-14

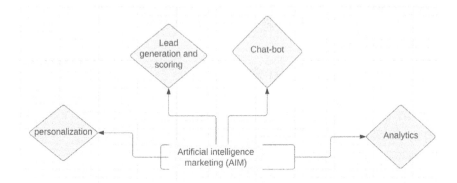

Figure 14.1 Scheme of artificial intelligence marketing.

Analytics that predict future behaviour: AI may examine client data to forecast behaviour and spot potential sales opportunities. This can enhance revenue and make marketing strategies work more effectively.

Setting policy in today's consumer driven sector is becoming more and more difficult. This implies identifying the user's desires and requirements and correlating the goods to their wants and needs. Making the best business decision necessitates a thorough understanding of altering customer behaviour. AI systems are transforming practically every aspect of a company, from finance to sales, R&D to operations, but the most profound influence of AI is being seen in marketing, where it has currently provided significant value and analysts anticipate it will remain to do so in the future. [2] While removing the possibility of human error, AI marketing solutions optimise and streamline campaigns. Marketers can use AI to develop marketing analytic strategies for focusing on prospective customers and designing unique customer experiences.

Today's marketing strategist routinely use AI to assist marketing departments and do more tactical tasks that do not require as much human delicacy. Compared to humans, AI can analyse tactical data more quickly and draw quick judgements about a campaign and its customers. Providing team members space to dedicate themselves to tactical tasks that can later direct advertising with AI assistance enhances the organisation.

Artificial intelligence (AI) in sales defines the application of technology to various areas of the sales process to support and improve them (Figure 14.2). Automating monotonous operations, using data analysis to guide sales strategies, personalising client communications, and other techniques fall under this category. Here are some instances of how AI can be applied in sales:

Lead generation: By monitoring information from several sources, such as social media, site traffic, and consumer information, AI may be used to discover potential consumers and produce leads.

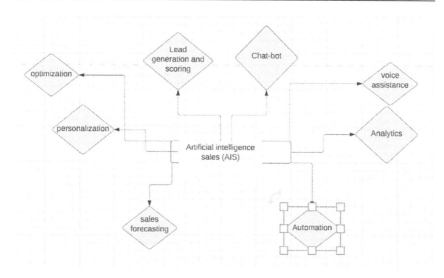

Figure 14.2 Artificial intelligence use in sales.

Sales forecasting: AI can evaluate data to estimate future sales, which can help sales teams focus their efforts and inform their strategy.

Predictive analytics: AI can be used to evaluate customer data and forecast customers' propensity to purchase, which can be used to guide sales strategy.

Automation: Artificial intelligence (AI) may automate monotonous operations like data input and customer follow-up, freeing up salespeople to work on higher-level projects.

Personalisation: AI can be used to make sales pitches and communications more relevant and effective for specific clients.

Chatbots: AI-driven chatbots can be used to communicate with customers, giving them information, responding to their inquiries, and assisting them in the purchasing process.

Voice Assistants: Customers can interact with voice assistants powered by AI to help them locate what they're looking for, provide personalised recommendations, and more.

AI can be used to improve sales processes by determining the ideal moment to get in touch with a customer, the best course of action to take, and the best offer to make to increase the effectiveness of sales channels.

14.2 HISTORY OF AI (TRACK OF AI GROWTH)

For academics, AI systems are not a recent concept or science. This science is far deeper than you might think. The mythologies of ancient Greece and Egypt also make mention of mechanised men. The following major moments

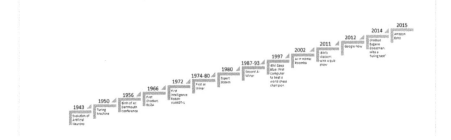

Figure 14.3 History chart of AI.

in AI history chart the path from its inception to the current state of development (Figure 14.3).

14.2.1 AI Progression (1943–1950)

1943: The original research that is now recognised as AI was finished in 1943 by Warren McCulloch and Walter Pits. An artificial neural architecture was proposed.

1949: In order to change the strength of brain connections, Donald Hebb created an upgrading rule in 1949. Hebbian learning is the term used to describe his rule.

1950: Mathematician Alan Turing from England created machine learning. The publication of "Computing Machines and Intelligence" by Alan Turing features a test idea. A Turing test can be used to evaluate a machine's ability to exhibit intelligent behaviour that is comparable to that of a person.

14.2.2 AI Inception (1950–1956)

1955: "Logic Theorist" was the name of the "first artificial intelligence software" created by Allen Newell and Herbert A. Simon. This programme proved 38 out of 52 mathematical theorems and found new, better justifications for several of them.

1956: The phrase "Artificial Intelligence" was first used by American scientist John McCarthy at the Dartmouth Conference. For the first time, artificial intelligence was presented as a field of study.

14.2.3 Golden Years for AI Milestones (1956–1974)

1966: The researchers prioritised the development of algorithms capable of solving mathematical issues. In 1966, Joseph Weizenbaum built the first chatbot, dubbed ELIZA.

1972: WABOT-1, the first conscious humanoid, was created in Japan.

14.2.4 Original Downfall of AI

Between 1974 and 1980, the first AI failure took place. The term "AI decline" refers to a time when data scientists experienced a severe lack of government funding for AI development.

As artificial intelligence (AI) fell out of favour, public interest in it decreased.

14.2.5 AI's Meteoric Rise (1880–1987)

1980: AI made a comeback with "Expert System" after a sabbatical throughout the fall. To replicate the capabilities of human experts in making decisions, expert systems were developed.

At Stanford University in 1980, the American Association of Artificial Intelligence held its first meeting.

14.2.6 Subsequent Downfall of AI (1987–1993)

The period from 1987 to 1993 was the subsequent downfall of AI.

Businesses and governments have once again halted financing for AI development owing of the high cost and inefficient results. Expert systems like XCON were incredibly cost effective.

14.2.7 Sophisticated Agents Development

1997: During the year 1997, IBM Deep Blue defeats global chess champion Gary Kasparov, becoming the first machine to do so.

2002: At that particular time, artificial intelligence (AI) entered the household in the shape of a vacuum cleaner, Roomba.

2006: AI did not enter the business sphere until 2006. Businesses such as Facebook, Twitter, and Netflix have also begun to use AI.

14.2.8 Other Milestones

2011: The IBM Watson computer won the Jeopardy game show, which featured challenging questions and puzzles. Watson has shown that it can understand natural language and provide quick solutions to challenging problems.

2012: Google released an Android app feature called "Google Now," which can forecast data for the consumer.

2014: Chatbot "Eugene Goostman" won a competition in the famed "Turing test."

2018: The IBM "Project Debater" disputed complicated themes with two professional debaters and fared admirably. Google showcased an AI application called "Duplex," which was a virtual assistant that took hairdresser appointments on call, and the person on the other end didn't realise she was speaking with the computer.

14.2.8.1 Why AI Technology is Required in Marketing

AI, a fascinating and cutting-edge technology, can supplement a company's current content strategy. It is a broad phrase that refers to a variety of technologies, such as machine vision, supervised learning, language processing, and advanced analytics. Due to its capacity for information evaluation and the provision of methodological approaches, supervised learning has a considerable impact on the environment of electronic marketing. As a result, it supports the use of needs-based evaluations by marketing professionals. Businesses that use AI solutions save time by focusing on other aspects of electronic marketing. AI is a massive and vigorous computing technology breakthrough with far-reaching implications. As a consequence, implementing AI in online marketing is urged in the next years to stimulate innovation and increase efficiency. [3]

In order to segment customers more effectively and move them to the next stage of their journey while providing the most value, marketers may use artificial intelligence (AI) to gather more detailed demographic information. By carefully analysing consumer data and comprehending what customers actually want, marketing companies can increase Return without spending money on ineffective projects. By eliminating unpleasant, unwanted advertising, they can also save time. [4] Many approaches will be used to personalise marketing with AI. In order to better satisfy the needs of their customers, several businesses are currently adopting AI to customise their websites, emails, social media postings, videos, and other resources. Automating tasks that traditionally required human intelligence is one of the main goals of AI. By reducing the amount of labour an organisation needs to complete a task or the amount of time employees must spend on tiresome tasks, significant efficiency improvements may be realised. [5, 6]

14.2.8.2 AI—Powered Marketing Versus Traditional Marketing

1. Improved Audience Interaction
   The internet is littered with customer-behaviour remnants. You may design a winning marketing plan using these breadcrumbs and artificial intelligence.

Marketing companies may use AI to fully understand their customers' demands and complaints. Furthermore, marketers may spend more time connecting with their audience. Hosting events in person and communicating on social media can help to establish relationships. As a consequence, consumer turnover is minimised, and strong brand grows.

When it comes to traditional marketing, you are not immediately linked with customers. Customers will just perceive you as a brand, and you will be unable to engage with them intellectually.

Advertisements, brochures, newspaper advertising, and other forms of conventional marketing are commonly used by firms to inform the public about their products and services. It is less successful since consumers may filter adverts and disregard flyers. As a result, AI marketing is recommended for greater audience interaction. You can collaborate with a social media marketing agency to find the best audience relationship network.

2. Application
   Manually inputting data, evaluating it, making elaborate charts, and even establishing email and social media plans have been made easier. The procedure is much faster using machine intelligence and automation.

Machine learning has become a critical tool for large technology organisations in order to automate these monotonous chores. Furthermore, by evaluating client behaviour, they aid in the creation of more relevant and tailored messaging.

Marketers will soon be able to "talk" to their CMS using voice-recognition technology. After the user specifies the modifications that need to be made, AI will automatically update the website or compose the blog post. Marketers today have more time to be creative and attend industry events to expand their expertise. Traditional marketing, on the other hand, cannot compete. Traditional advertising requires you to handle everything yourself, which is a time-consuming procedure. AI is an obvious winner in terms of advertising strategy that saves both time and money.

3. Competitively priced
   When it comes to expense, conventional marketing is clearly more expensive. It requires money to print and deliver booklets. Furthermore, television and print advertisements are expensive and do not produce enough income to provide the optimum ROI. Hire an SEO expert to develop a low-cost organic marketing campaign.

AI marketing is less expensive than traditional marketing. All you have to do is buy the programme once and you're done. You are not required to pay any additional fees. AI makes online marketing much easier. You don't need to pay a second person to speak with consumers, you don't need to worry about content moderation, and it doesn't take much work.

14.3 USE OF AI IN MARKETING AND SALES

AI is used in marketing techniques in a range of areas, including banking, governance, health, entertainment, and shopping. Each use case yields a unique outcome, such as improved quality metrics, a better client interaction, or more important promotional practices. Marketers are utilising AI through programmatic advertising to address a variety of issues. ML is used by programmatic platforms to place bids on current ad space that is pertinent to target consumers. AI may also help to reduce errors in the marketing process. [7] AI is more efficient than humans at performing specialised tasks as long as there is oversight and guidance. AI is more likely to deliver a greater investment return as it can dramatically accelerate the execution of promotional activities, save money, and boost efficiency. Machine learning is used in this technology to render quick judgements based on campaign and consumer context, and it can interpret performance data faster than people. The members of the group are given additional time to work on key initiatives that may later be used to influence AI-powered marketing. Rather of deferring AI judgements until the conclusion of a campaign, marketers may use legitimate data to choose better ads. [8]

Here are some examples of AI uses in sales and promotion:

Digital marketing:

> AI has had a big impact on digital marketing. Marketing professionals can utilise AI to understand consumer behaviour, actions, and indicators. They are able to quickly and effectively target the right people with the proper approach as a response. AI in marketing can help marketers swiftly process massive amounts of data from the Web, emails, and social media. It can work in tandem with conversion tracking to create data-driven decisions, have effective interaction, and have a positive impact on business outcomes. AI marketing supports data collection, consumer insight gathering, customer behaviour forecast, as well as the development of automating decision making. [9, 10]

Decrease in human error:

> AI has decreased human errors, especially in the most crucial sectors. Furthermore, this system may create and optimise information that is appealing to the recipients in a variety of email forms. Without a doubt, the purpose of AI is to minimise human involvement and eliminate the chance of human error. Many firms are concerned about their employees' capacity to protect client information and other crucial corporate data due to the prevalence of data security issues. AI may help with a variety of problems by learning, modifying, and addressing an organisation's information demands.

AI may replace many of the slash-and-burn resources that are usually employed to formulate and carry out a promotional campaign.

Connect business steps/methods:

Using the strength of information management, AI connects all aspects of corporate operations and provides a flawless performance. When it comes to marketing outputs in businesses, marketers that take advantage of AI's potential excel. Marketing professionals may develop and execute innovative marketing plans that are more individualised and human-centred thanks to AI technology. Customers are frequently thrilled by these strategies and become passionate brand supporters. The ability to influence customer micro-moments with technologies like AI may make interaction designs more enticing. The growing advantages of AI enable businesses to redefine marketing for a better user experience. [11, 12]

Allow for seamless customer service:

We can provide clients with knowledgeable, straightforward, and efficient customer care at every stage of their journey thanks to AI. A flawless and ideal customer experience depends on it. The foundation of Web analytics strategies is the automation of routine marketing tasks and processes. Marketing automation benefits greatly from AI applications. AI uses ML to acquire and analyse customer data in real-time, applying the results on a large scale. AI facilitates the separation, organisation, and prioritisation of this data. Tools for marketing automation powered by AI are revolutionising the field. By addressing needs that are changing in form, including the need for clients to receive hyper-personalised goods, upcoming platforms promises to strengthen marketing efforts. [13, 14]

Discovering user preferences:

Marketing teams may utilise AI to gain extensive, individualised knowledge about customer preferences and precise demographic information. This makes it possible for marketers to create customised experiences based on the tastes of their customers. This information may be used by advertising firms to provide a fuller picture of the target market, including whether the client would have read a headline without the graphics and how it might effect future means of communication. [15, 16]

Target market:

Customers' requirements and expectations must be understood by businesses so that they may satisfy them. AI marketing helps companies identify their target market so they can give each of their clients a more individualised experience. Conversion management solutions are elevated to new levels by AI. Marketers may now respond to complex strategic concerns by contrasting smart inbound communication to traditional KPIs. As technology advances, there is a growing need to provide highly individualised experiences as efficiently as feasible in the internet marketing, shopping, and corporate spheres. [17–19]

Building a forecasting model:

AI-powered technologies may help with data collection, model development, testing on real consumers, and model validation. Every customer may now receive personalised, relevant emails thanks to AI. Machine-learning programs may also help in spotting disengaged customer groups that are about to leave or go to a competitor. The study of omnichannel events and the detection of falling customer involvement is made easier with the help of AI-powered churn prediction. To keep consumers interested, it may send emails, push alerts, and relevant offers. When personalised content production and AI-powered churn prediction are combined, customer engagement increases, increasing lifetime value and revenue. [20–22]

Enhances the processing of data:

When creating successful AI-powered campaigns, the team may concentrate on organisational plans since AI accelerates data processing compared to human touch, assures clarity and security. Real-time operational data monitoring and collection by AI helps speed up business response times. They may be able to make better knowledgeable and fair decisions about what to do next based upon the data-driven reports. AI might help with drudgery and repetitive tasks. It reduces the amount of time workers are required to do such operations while eliminating mistakes. Hiring costs may be reduced significantly by re-purposing existing talent for more vital activities. [23, 24]

Large volumes of data for analysis:

AI is capable of analysing vast amounts of market data and predicting what a user would likely do next. It can analyse billions of search results to predict if a user will really make a purchase. AI also assists in identifying problems and taking appropriate remedial action. AI and machine learning have far-reaching consequences. While many of us are adept at coming to conclusions from massive amounts of data, the vast majority of us waste a significant amount of time attempting to locate relevant information in complex data. Artificial intelligence (AI) may be able to assist in certain circumstances by lowering load and saving time. [25, 26]

Improved marketing intelligence software:

Marketing automation tools that use AI help companies swiftly discover qualified prospects, improve lead nurturing programmes, and produce topical content.

Since they employ contextual emails to make what the organisation say more engaging and centre on what subscribers want to hear, another dynamic allocation emails in particular have been the most successful. Emails will always be relevant to subscribers because to dynamic content strategies that take their location-based, psychographics, observational methods, and insights into consideration. [27, 28]

Provide insightful insights:

By analysing each new data element and giving users with more pertinent information depending on their choices, AI apps simplify tasks. It must be seen as a tool for focusing marketing efforts on more challenging objectives. AI will surely assist marketers in their efforts to blend cutting-edge technology with human intelligence in order to read, interpret, and interact with modern customers on an individual level through hyper-personalised, relevant, and timely content.

A website visitor's behaviour is successfully analysed by algorithms, which then instantaneously change and display personalised ad content. Data is continuously gathered and used to inform future changes to ad content. AI will enable sellers to concentrate more on outcomes and help their clients by utilising personal and behavioural data. [29, 30]

Customise the way users' shop:

By engaging with virtual assistants and offering recommendations based on ML technologies, AI may create simulation models and customise shopping procedures. Many companies are interacting with their customers via AI. Based on previous searches, views, and sales, Amazon makes product recommendations using artificial intelligence.

These intelligent technologies are developing quickly and may soon be able to perform better than people in some capacities. Since AI has superior knowledge, data analysis, and input, it replaces humans in the task of identifying marketing techniques.

These may analyse data to forecast purchasing trends and activities of the customer base, and they may enhance the user interface to supply the audience with what they truly require. [31, 32]

Helping out marketers:

Aid in making wiser selections. Account marketers and account executives can concentrate on more important decisions, including campaign strategy, thanks to AI in Google Ads.

A more complicated subset of machine learning is deep learning. To identify complex patterns and correlations that can be used to understand consumer interactions and better individually targeted marketing and ROI, large data sets—including abstracted and distributed data—must be handled. As data becomes more accessible, businesses can now use AI to analyse it, predict trends, and improve the quality of their brand. [33, 34]

Enhanced income and client satisfaction:

AI may be used in marketing in a number of different contexts. Each application provides benefits like lower risk, faster processing, happier customers, higher revenue, etc. AI applications can quickly decide how to spend money across media channels, ensuring that customers are continually involved and that marketing is getting the most out of their budgets.

AI can assist in sending clients individualised messages at the ideal moment in their life. Using this technology, marketers may be able to spot clients who are at danger and offer them information that will persuade them to come back. AI-powered dashboards provide more specific data on what is effective, enabling it to be replicated across mediums and funding to be allocated correctly. [35, 36]

14.3.1 Obstacles That AI Has Recently Encountered in the Field of Marketing and Sales

The market is stacked with tons of opportunities as well as challenges that a business has to experience in case of any changes to their technology or policy, etc. The application of artificial intelligence in marketing and sales is consistent with this idea.

Here are some of the obstacles that AI has to face in the market:

Data Management:

In order to learn and generate predictions, AI needs a lot of data, yet this data may be biased, erroneous, or incomplete. This may result in subpar performance or bad judgement.

Presentation and communication:

AI models may be intricate and complicated to comprehend, making it difficult for corporations to justify their choices and actions to others.

Generalisation:

On the precise data sets they were trained on, AI models frequently perform well, but they may not generalise well to brand new, unexplored data.

Scalability:

AI models can be challenging to scale to accommodate big amounts of data or users since they might demand a lot of computing resources to develop and implement.

Security and dependability:

It is crucial to make sure AI systems are trustworthy and safe since they can make judgements that have real-world repercussions.

Prejudice and morality:

Corporations should take into account ethical and cultural ramifications while creating and using AI since models can reinforce or even magnify societal prejudices.

Human-in-the-loop:

Compared to human decision-making, automated decision-making can be more accurate and effective, but there are instances when it's crucial to have human monitoring and control to make sure the AI is functioning morally and in accordance with the company's principles.

Lack of IT infrastructure:

A strong IT infrastructure is necessary for a profitable marketing strategy. Because AI technology analyses a lot of data, it requires technology with excellent performance. As a result, installing the computer systems requires significant expense. This will guarantee regular upgrades and servicing to make sure they continue to function properly.

Changing the marketing environment:

Artificial intelligence causes disruption in daily marketing processes. The marketers must assess which jobs are being displaced and which are being generated as a result. According to a poll, artificial intelligence (AI) technology is predicted to replace nearly six out of ten current marketing analysts and specialists' positions.

Obtaining funding:

It is challenging for marketing teams to show how an investment in AI benefits a company. Additionally, it is simple to assess important performance indicators like efficiency and return on investment by demonstrating how AI has enhanced customer experience. The teams must ensure that they can quantify the benefits of investing in AI on a qualitative level.

Confidentiality and governance:

Consumers and businesses alike may be curious in how consumer data is utilised for business purposes. As a result, marketers must guarantee that they are utilising consumer data ethically. AI is concerned about these challenges. To comply with particular legal restrictions, AI technologies required to be properly taught. This will increase the acceptability of using client data for personalisation.

14.3.2 The Implications of AI Technologies in Marketing and Sales

There are numbers of benefits that Artificial intelligence can give to marketing agencies.
Some of them are:

- *Data analysis for Future Marketing*
  With massive amounts of data arriving every second, marketing teams struggle to analyse and derive insights from it. Business intelligence, which forecasts future behaviour using a variety of machine learning algorithms, models, and datasets, is one way that AI is assisting commercial teams in making the greatest use of data. This may be a huge assistance for marketing teams in understanding what sorts of things consumers would be shopping for and when, permitting them to better position advertisements.
- *Content Creation*
  AI-powered technology can make the tasks of content creators easier and more efficient. Though humans generate the majority of the material, you may use innovative approaches to boost the efficiency of your content team by robotic specific operations like as email content, personalised reviews, or social media content management.
- *Forecasting sales volume*
  Recognising and implementing the next step is what each company should strive for in order to surpass customers' expectations and grow revenue. With the use of AI in sales promotion, marketers may better

understand their customers and communicate with them based on data collected through interactions and previous purchases.

Using this technique, you can anticipate what customers will buy next and how much of a product will be sold. It assists you in deciding what to sell and to whom to recommend in order to increase sales. You may avoid overselling or reselling out-of-stock items by establishing business data and controlling your inventory.

- *Create a unique consumer experience*
  Artificial intelligence may be used by brands to improve customer experience by offering personalised information and offers, as well as outstanding customer support to each individual consumer.
  Consider your most recent online purchasing experience. You see a page with items you might be interested in as well as alternatives for exactly what you're going to buy. AI is used to evaluate prior purchases and recommend products that are a good fit for your requirements. This is an example of how AI may enhance the user experience through customisation.
- *Maintain data accuracy and confidentiality*
  AI has the ability to improve an institution's data quality and privacy when used correctly and successfully. Marketers frequently demand a significant amount of data at their disposal.
  As a result, in order to capitalise on machine learning solutions, it is vital to have high-quality data at a position where AI can perform its work. Consider using a modern data warehouse and implementing all-in-one data management software to reduce data quality issues caused by extensive data administration. AI improves data collection and secures this extensive data from dangers.
- *Faster and better judgement making*
  In comparison to human involvement, AI accelerates data processing, ensures authenticity and protection, and allows teams to focus on essential projects in order to generate effective AI-powered campaigns. Artificial intelligence (AI) can collect and monitor tactical data in real time, assisting marketers in making decisions now rather than waiting for initiatives to be finished. They could make better and more unbiased decisions about what to do next based on the data-driven reports. [37]

14.3.3 Future Scope of AI in Marketing and Sales

As AI progresses in the marketing industry, it will have a positive impact. What is the development of AI, despite its ability to perform any tough task? Increased usage of artificial intelligence in marketing does not reduce people's chances of discovering work. Instead, it will include smarter data in the job description, which will necessitate smarter personnel. Furthermore, it improves the brand's profits and effectiveness while also improving the customer engagement. With these advantages in mind, a variety of corporate sectors, including banking, technology, and even retail, have started to profit from sophisticated artificial intelligence that can foresee future trends using the pertinent data and spot possible dangers. The development of AI technologies is still in its early phases, despite its amazing qualities. According to PwC's Worldwide Machine Intelligence Study, by 2030, AI is expected to have a $15.7 trillion influence on the global economy. AI can help marketers analyse customer trends and patterns, anticipate results, and optimise advertising. It uses data, statistical tools, and cutting-edge AI technology to predict future trends. [37] When they analyse more data, AI systems learn how to provide better results and provide the best responses. Massive amounts of historical consumer data can be analysed by AI-powered ML algorithms to identify which advertisements are appropriate for consumers and at what stage of the purchasing process. AI will give organisations the optimisation benefits of providing material at the right time by utilising trends and data. There has never been a better time for marketers to begin experimenting with AI methods to aid in the creation of highly individualised client experiences. Since AI is expected to spread across all sectors and divisions, marketers should invest time and resources in testing new strategies and assuring that their marketing strategy is set up for ongoing success both now and in the future. [38]

14.3.4 Conclusion

The term artificial intelligence (AI) describes the methods that give machines the ability to do mental tasks that need human intelligence. Examples of these activities include learning, thinking, and interacting with the environment. Machine learning and deep learning are two of the most well-known AI techniques. AI can personalise brand experiences, making it simpler to boost customer loyalty and engagement. Language-based AI is used by marketers as engagement managers, payment processors, and sales tools to enhance the customer experience. Customers may now rely on chatbots to finish the shopping process for them rather than figuring it out for themselves. Language-based artificial intelligence is developing steadily, actively fine-tuning to deliver an even better experience the following time while "learning" from previous usages. With the help of observation, data collection, and analysis, AI may now be used to tailor content. This internet marketing tool helps advertisers maximise the effectiveness of their email campaigns. One of the digital marketing services that aids in targeting the right audience at the right time and ensuring effective conversion tactics is email marketing. Data analysis is the main perk of artificial intelligence in marketing. In order to provide marketers with information that is meaningful and practical, this technology will analyse enormous volumes of data.

REFERENCES

[1] S. Verma, Artificial intelligence in marketing: Systematic review and future research, Int. J. Inf. Manag. Data Insights (2021) 8.

[2] P. Kumari, Role of Artificial Intelligence (AI) in marketing, researchgate (2021) 14.

[3] A. Capatina, M. Kachou, J. Lichy, A. Micu, F. Codignola, Matching the future capabilities of an artificial intelligence-based software for social media marketing with potential users' expectations, Technol. Forecast. Soc. Change 151 (2020) 119794.

[4] B. Peyravi, J. Nekro˘siene, L. Lobanova, Revolutionised technologies for marketing: Theoretical review with focus on artificial intelligence, Bus. Theor. Pract. 21 (2) (2020) 827–834.

[5] P. Khokhar, Evolution of artificial intelligence in marketing, comparison with traditional marketing, Our Heritage 67 (5) (2019) 375–389.

[6] A. Murgai, Transforming digital marketing with artificial intelligence, Int. J. Latest Technol. Eng. Manag. Appl. Sci. 7 (4) (2018) 259–262.

[7] V. Sohrabpour, P. Oghazi, R. Toorajipour, A. Nazarpour, Export sales forecasting using artificial intelligence, Technol. Forecast. Soc. Change 163 (2021) 120480.

[8] S. Daskou, E. E. Mangina, Artificial intelligence in managing market relationships: The use of intelligence agents, J. Relatsh. Mark. 2 (1–2) (2003) 85–102.

[9] D. Shah, E. Shay, How and Why Artificial Intelligence, Mixed Reality and Blockchain Technologies Will Change Marketing We Know Today, in Handbook of Advances in Marketing in an Era of Disruptions: Essays in Honour of Jagdish N. Sheth, Sage Publications Pvt Ltd., 2019, pp. 377–390.

[10] J. Paschen, U. Paschen, E. Pala, J. Kietzmann, Artificial intelligence (AI) and value co-creation in B2B sales: Activities, actors and resources, Australas. Market J. 29 (3) (2021) 243–251.

[11] M. F. Sadriwala, K. F. Sadriwala, Perceived usefulness and ease of use of artificial intelligence on marketing innovation, Int. J. Innovat. Digit. Econ. 13 (1) (2022) 1–10.

[12] S. Yablonsky, Multidimensional data-driven artificial intelligence innovation, Technol. Innovat. Manag. Rev. 9 (12) (2019) 16–28.

[13] K. Buntak, M. Kova˘ci´c, M. Mutavd˘zija, Application of artificial intelligence in the business, Int. J. Quality Res. 15 (2) (2021) 403.

[14] K. Fish, P. Ruby, An artificial intelligence foreign market screening method for small businesses, Int. J. Enterpren. 13 (2009) 65.

[15] J. Spreitzenbarth, H. Stuckenschmidt, C. Bode, The state of artificial intelligence procurement versus sales and marketing, Hamburg International Conference of Logistics (HICL) 2021 (2021) 223–243.

[16] K. Siau, W. Wang, Building trust in artificial intelligence, machine learning, and robotics, Cutter Bus, Technol. J. 31 (2) (2018) 47–53.

[17] R. Dubey, D. J. Bryde, C. Blome, D. Roubaud, M. Giannakis, Facilitating artificial intelligence powered supply chain analytics through alliance management during the pandemic crises in the B2B context, Ind. Market. Manag. 96 (2021) 135–146.

[18] M. Giroux, J. Kim, J. C. Lee, J. Park, Artificial intelligence and declined guilt: Retailing morality comparison between human and AI, J. Bus. Ethics 178 (2022) 1027–1041.

[19] M. A. A. Daqar, A. K. Smoudy, The role of artificial intelligence on enhancing customer experience, Int. Rev. Manag. Market. 9 (4) (2019) 22.

[20] D. Vrontis, M. Christofi, V. Pereira, S. Tarba, A. Makrides, E. Trichina, Artificial intelligence, robotics, advanced technologies and human resource management: A systematic review, Int. J. Hum. Resour. Manag. 33 (6) (2022) 1237–1266.

[21] M. V. V. Yawalkar, A study of artificial intelligence and its role in human resource management, Int. J. Res. Anal. Rev. (IJRAR) 6 (1) (2019) 20–24.

[22] S. Sahai, R. Goel, Impact of artificial intelligence in changing trends of marketing. Applications of artificial intelligence in business and finance, Modern Trends (2021) 221.

[23] V. Kumar, B. Rajan, R. Venkatesan, J. Lecinski, Understanding the role of artificial intelligence in personalized engagement marketing, Calif. Manag. Rev. 61 (4) (2019) 135–155.

[24] T. Davenport, A. Guha, D. Grewal, T. Bressgott, How artificial intelligence will change the future of marketing, J. Acad. Market. Sci. 48 (1) (2020) 24–42.

[25] A. De Bruyn, V. Viswanathan, Y. S. Beh, J. K. U. Brock, F. von Wangenheim, Artificial intelligence and marketing: Pitfalls and opportunities, J. Interact. Market. 51 (2020) 91–105.

[26] R. Boadh, R. Grover, M. Dahiya, A. Kumar, R. Rathee, Y. K. Rajoria, M. Rawat, S. Rani, Study of fuzzy expert system for the diagnosis of various types of cancer, Mater Today: Proc. 56 (2022) 298–307.

[27] M. He, Z. Li, C. Liu, D. Shi, Z. Tan, Deployment of artificial intelligence in realworld practice: Opportunity and challenge, Asia-Pacific J. Ophthalmol. 9 (4) (2020) 299–307.

[28] I. V. Alyoshina, Artificial intelligence in an age of digital globalization, in: International Conference Technology & Entrepreneurship in Digital Society, 2019, 26–30.

[29] G. C. Tanase, Artificial intelligence: Optimizing the experience of digital marketing, Romanian Distribution Committee Magaz. 9 (1) (2018) 24–28.

[30] K. Buntak, M. Kovačič, M. Mutavdžija, Application of artificial intelligence in the business, Int. J. Quality Res. 15 (2) (2021) 403.

[31] K. Fish, P. Ruby, An artificial intelligence foreign market screening method for small businesses, Int. J. Enterpren. 13 (2009) 65.

[32] I. Pedersen, A. Duin, AI agents, humans and untangling the marketing of artificial intelligence in learning environments, in: Proceedings of the 55th Hawaii International Conference On System Sciences, 2022, January.

[33] L. T. Khrais, Role of artificial intelligence in shaping consumer demand in ecommerce, Future Internet 12 (12) (2020) 226.

[34] I. M. Enholm, E. Papagiannidis, P. Mikalef, J. Krogstie, Artificial intelligence and business value: A literature review, Inf. Syst. Front. 24 (2021) 1709–1734.

[35] V. Bader, S. Kaiser, Algorithmic decision-making? The user interface and its role for human involvement in decisions supported by artificial intelligence, Organization 26 (5) (2019) 655–672.

[36]   L. Tchelidze, Potential and skill requirements of artificial intelligence in digital marketing, Calitatea 20 (S3) (2019) 73–78.

[37]   S. Rani, A. Kumar, A. Bagchi, S. Yadav, S. Kumar, RPL based routing protocols for load balancing in IoT network, J. Phys. Conf. Ser. 1950 (1) (2021, August), 012073.

[38]   P. Rajendra, M. Kumari, S. Rani, N. Dogra, R. Boadh, A. Kumar, M. Dahiya, Impact of artificial intelligence on civilization: Future perspectives, Mater. Today: Proc. 56 (2022) 252–256.

Chapter 15

A Novel Framework for Stock Market Prediction Using Deep Learning Techniques

Siddharth Pandey and [2]*Tarun Biswas*

[1]National Institute of Technology Sikkim, India-737139
[2]Indian Institute of Information Technology Ranchi, India-834004

15.1 INTRODUCTION

A country's economy is directly connected with stock industry in modern civilization. Fundamentally, a stock market is the association of buyers and sellers of stocks or shares. The stock data is a sequence of the price of a given stock equally distributed by time intervals, that is, time series data. These data are very fluctuating and equivocal in nature. The stock traders mainly focused for accurate prediction of the shares so that profit can be maximized. These prediction procedures are further classified on behalf of traders and investors as fundamental analysis and technical analysis [1–6]. Fundamental analysis is a methodology of stock valuation by measuring its intrinsic value, that is, fair value [1]. On the other hand, technical analysis is a methodology where stock valuation is done based on charts and trends [2, 7]. Recently, several financial time series analysis using recurrent neural networks (RNN) are emerging. RNNs are a type of neural network in which the outputs from the previous step are fed as inputs to the current step. The study shows that the deployment of RNN based models for stock price prediction problem is effective [8] RNNs preserve and use the preceding data sequence to learn network weights while tracking of long-term input dependencies during training. Two variations of RNN, long short term memory (LSTM), and gated recurrent unit (GRU) are deployed to solve this problem [9]. There are many strategies to design the architecture for RNN. The stacked architecture uses two or more stacked unidirectional RNN layers where data processing is done in forward direction thorough the layers. On the other hand, the bidirectional architecture constitutes of two stacked layers of RNN to process data bidirectionally [10]. There are several RNN based models like the LSTM [10-13], GRU [14] and hybrid model with LSTM and GRU [15].

15.1.1 Motivation Challenge and Issues

While working with deep learning based classification, training of the model plays a pivotal role to enhance speed and accuracy. This is done

DOI: 10.1201/9781003329947-15

by incorporating transfer learning (TL) [16]. It is a technique in deep learning enabled approach in which the knowledge gained while solving one problem is stored and then applied to a different related problem [16] for further possible improvements. An enormous amount of money is involved in stock trading and even a fraction time difference in price prediction can result in huge profit or loss. Therefore, even a 1% improvement in the prediction model is highly valuable. Moreover, financial time series prediction is a big challenge because of its dynamic and highly volatile nature. Motivated by these facts, a deep learning based stock market prediction model using two-layered bidirectional long short term memory is proposed. The proposed BLSTM method is further enhanced by incorporating transfer learning (TL-BLSTM) technique. The proposed TL-BLSTM is tested on three different Indian stocks: ITC, ONGC, and SBI. These stocks are among the top 50 stocks listed on the National Stock Exchange (NSE), India [17]. The proposed TL-BLSTM prediction model compared with several existing algorithms in terms of minimum prediction error as LSTM [5, 10, 11], GRU [14], and hybrid model with LSTM and GRU [15].

15.1.2 Contributions

The overall contribution of the work is summarized:

- A deep learning based stock market prediction model is proposed using two-layered bidirectional long short term memory (TL-BLSTM) technique.
- The proposed TL-BLSTM model is further enhanced by incorporating transfer learning technique.
- The proposed model is first pre-trained with a large US-based dataset (S&P500 index) and then further trained on the training data sets generated from the reputed Indian stocks such as ITC, ONGC, and SBI [17].
- The proposed TL-BLSTM model is evaluated and compared with four other variants of RNN trained with the three different training methodologies.
- During evaluation, the proposed TL-BLSTM provides 10.5% (avg.) less mean absolute error (MAE) than the second-best performing model and training method for the three stocks.

The orientation of the work is as follows. Section 15.2 provides an overall background study of recent related stock market prediction models. The prerequisites models and problem statement with targeted objectives are discussed in Section 15.3. Section 15.4 describes the proposed

TL-BLSTM model for stock market prediction framework for three different stock data sets. Simulation over the various RNN based models are discussed in Section 15.5. The work is concluded with future directions in Section 15.6.

15.2 RELATED WORKS

Several deep learning techniques to address the classification problem are gaining attention a lot of researchers now a days. In this context people are also using deep learning techniques for financial time series analysis. Several recent related studies are described below. The authors Troiano et al. [5] have developed a model using a single layer of LSTM to learn trading rules by looking at the relationship between market indicators and decisions undertaken regarding entering or quitting a position. The experiment proved the ability of LSTM models to learn complex decision-making skills concerning financial time series. A two-layer stacked LSTM (SLSTM) based architecture is designed to predict the stock price for various industries in [14]. The SLSTM model gave good predictions for the test data sets however, it wasn't compared with other models.

Athelaya et al. [10] proposed deep learning models based on LSTM and GRU. Both bidirectional and unidirectional stacked architectures with multivariate inputs were employed to perform short- and long-term forecasting. The deep learning architectures were also compared to shallow neural networks using S&P 500 index historical data. Stacked LSTM architecture was found to be the best among all the models considered. A hybrid deep recurrent neural network based on LSTM and GRU units is designed to predict S&P 500 index price in [15]. The hybrid model performed better than vanilla LSTM and GRU based models. Minh et al. [14] proposed a framework to predict the directions of stock prices by using both financial news and sentiment dictionary. For this purpose, they used a two-stream GRU network and Stock2Vec—a sentiment word embedding trained on financial news data set. The TGRU network performed better than other models and proved that the addition of sentiment analysis can increase the efficiency of prediction systems. A deep learning model combining multiple pipelines of convolutional neural network and bi-directional LSTM is designed in [6]. The proposed model performs significantly better than a single pipeline deep learning model and support vector machine model on S&P 500 data set. It was also compared to several variations of single and multiple pipeline deep learning models based on different kernel sizes and number of BLSTM units. Ding et al. [4] proposed a multi-value associated network model of LSTM-based deep-recurrent neural network (Associated Net) to predict multiple prices of a stock simultaneously. It was also compared to vanilla LSTM

Table 15.1 Overview of related literature survey

Authors	Models Used	Description	Remarks
Troiano et al. [5]	LSTM	Replicated trading decisions using LSTM model.	Proved LSTM's ability to learn complex decision making. Some overfitting is observed.
Lin et al. [11]	Stacked LSTM (Two-Layered)	Predicted stock prices for various industries.	LSTM gave good predictions. The proposed model wasn't compared to other models.
Althelaya et al. [10]	Stacked and Bidi-rectional LSTM and GRU	Performed short-term and long-term predictions.	Stacked LSTM performed better than rest of the models.
Hossain et al. [15]	Hybrid of LSTM and GRU	Compared against other architectures based on LSTM and GRU.	Hybrid model performed the best among the tested models. Models were tested only on S&P500 dataset.
Minh et al. [14]	TGRU	Short term stock trends prediction.	TGRU performed better than LSTM ad GRU models. However, it uses long training time and huge computational resources.
Eapen et al. [6]	Combination of CNN and BLSTM	Compared against SVM and tested pipelines. with various	Proposed model showed improvements on previous methods.
Ding et al. [4]	Associated Net	LSTM based network to predict opening price, lowest price and highest price simultaneously.	Improved training accuracy. However, loss calculation method was not optimized.

model. The designed model showed considerate improvements in training accuracy compared to other models. The overview of literature report is presented in Table 15.1.

Point to be noted is that in [6, 10] have used bidirectional LSTM layer in their architectures however, training methodology is similar to normal method. To the best of our knowledge, this is the first use of a two-layered bidirectional LSTM model trained with transfer learning based approach. It is further evaluated and compared with to other stacked architectures based on LSTM, GRU, BGRU and hybrid approach [4, 5, 11, 12].

15.3 PROBLEM STATEMENT

Given historical data as $(O_1, O_2, \ldots O_n)$, $(L_1, L_2, \ldots L_n)$, $(H_1, H_2, \ldots H_n)$, $(C_1, C_2, \ldots C_n)$ and $(V_1, V_2, \ldots V_n)$ for a particular stock, predict C_{n+1} with the least amount of error.

Where, $(O_1, O_2, \ldots O_n)$ represents opening price of the stock for the first day, second day, and, n^{th} day respectively. Likewise, $(L_1, L_2, \ldots L_n)$, $(H_1, H_2, \ldots H_n)$, $(C_1, C_2, \ldots C_n)$ and $(V_1, V_2, \ldots V_n)$ denotes the lowest price, highest price, closing price and trading volume of the stock for first day, second day, and n^{th} day respectively. C_{n+1} denotes closing price of the stock for $(n + 1)^{th}$ day. Here, n is taken as 60 days. Four evaluation measures are considered while predicting the a price of stock such as mean absolute error (MAE), coefficient of determination (R^2), mean square error (MSE) and, root mean square error (RMSE).

- Mean absolute error (MAE) is a measure of errors between paired observations expressing the same phenomenon. MAE is calculated:

$$MAE = \left(\frac{1}{n}\right) \overset{n}{\underset{i=1}{X}} y_i x_i \tag{1}$$

x is the independent variable, y is the dependent variable and n is the number of samples.

- The Coefficient of Determination is denoted by R^2 which is the proportion of the variance in the dependent variable that is predictable from the independent variable(s). Its value ranges from zero to one and tells the goodness of the fit of a model.
  - Zerp indicates that the model doesn't fit the response data at all.
  - One indicates that the model fits exactly to the response data.
- Mean squared error (MSE) measures the average of the squares of the errors between the estimated values and the actual value. It is calculated:

$$MSE = \left(\frac{1}{n}\right) \overset{n}{\underset{i=1}{X}} (y_i \, x_i)^2 \tag{2}$$

- Root mean squared error (RMSE) is the square root of the mean square error. It is calculated as:

$$RMSE = \left(\frac{1}{n}\right) \overset{n}{\underset{i=1}{X}} (y_i - x_i)^2 \tag{3}$$

15.4 PROPOSED FRAMEWORK

A framework for accurate classification and prediction of the stock market using Two-Layered Bidirectional Long Short Term Memory (TL-BLSTM) is designed. The proposed TL-BLSTM framework is further enhanced by incorporating transfer learning technique. The detail stepwise procedure is

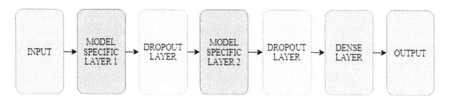

Figure 15.1 Proposed architecture.

Table 15.2 Specifications of each model

MODEL/LAYERS	LAYER 1		LAYER 2	
LSTM	**LSTM**		**LSTM**	
	Trainable Parameters	268288	Trainable Parameters	525312
GRU	**GRU**		**GRU**	
	Trainable Parameters	201984	Trainable Parameters	394752
TL-BLSTM	**TL-BLSTM**		**TL-BLSTM**	
	Trainable Parameters	536576	Trainable Parameters	1050624
BGRU	**BGRU**		**BGRU**	
	Trainable Parameters	403968	Trainable Parameters	789504
HYBRID	**HYBRID**		**HYBRID**	
	Trainable Parameters	268288	Trainable Parameters	394752

discussed as: The proposed TL-BLSTM is first pre-trained with a large US-based dataset (S&P 500 index) and then further trained on the training data sets generated from the Indian stocks as ITC, ONGC, and SBI [17]. The re-training is done on a small number of epochs on the training data sets. The proposed architecture is shown in Figure 15.1.

Here, each model has two model specific layers (256 units), two drop-out layers (0.2%) and a fully connected dense layer (one unit—257 trainable parameters). The detailed specifications of each model is shown in the Table 15.2. The first column describes the five models and the subsequent columns describe layer-wise specifications. Further, the number of trainable parameters of each layer of the respective models are defined. In case of bidirectional layers, the sum as merge mode is considered to combine the outputs of the forward and backward RNNs. Here, Adam optimizer and mean square error as the loss function are implemented during the evaluation process [18].

Remark 1: The proposed TL-BLSTM approach can produce better predictions than the simple LSTM and GRU networks because of its complexity and ability to learn deep relations from a large data set. The proposed framework used bidirectional LSTM to train the model based on the time series data. The input time series data are given as finite sequence to the model based on the assigned weight metric. To calculate the accurate value of a certain stock, bidirection LSTM enables additional training by traversing the input finite sequence data twice during the training phase. Due to additional training of the sequence data and assigned weight to each input the model used stochastic gradient method along with bidirection LSTM model which produce better prediction than normal LSTM technique. Learning computational complexity for LSTM model is $O(w)$ where, w denotes assigned weight metric.

15.4.1 Data and Pre-Processing

Very large US-based S&P 500 index data and three stocks listed on National Stock Exchange (NSE), India, namely ITC, ONGC, and SBI data sets are considered for training and testing purposes [17]. The date ranges from January 1950 to December 2019 for the S&P 500 index and January 2000 to December 2019 for the other three Indian stocks. Each data set has price history with one day intervals and each record of these data sets have the following seven attributes: date, open, low, high, close, adj close, and volume. The pre-processing of the data sets is done as:

- Import the data sets.
- Drop the columns "Date" and "Adj Close."
- Separate the training and testing data sets from the original data sets as follows:
    1. For in-domain and transfer learning methods:
        - Training Data: Considered as Indian stock data sets which range from January 2000 to December 2015.
        - Testing Data: Considered as Indian stock data sets which range from January 2016 to December 2019.
    2. For out-of-domain method:
        - Training Data: Considered as S&P 500 data sets which range from January 1950 to December 2019.
        - Testing Data: Considered as Indian stock data sets which range from January 2016 to December 2019.
- Normalize the data sets using min-max transformation which is obtained by the following equation:

$$X_{scaled} = \frac{(X - X_{min})}{(X_{max} - X_{min})} \tag{4}$$

where X_{scaled} is the new cell value, X is the original cell value, X_{min} is the minimum value of the column and, X_{max} is the maximum value of the column.

- Create new training and testing data sets from the old ones by concatenating rows to create a sliding window such that each row contains historical data of last 60 days.

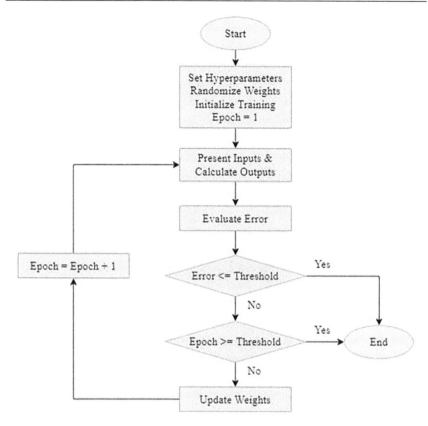

Figure 15.2 Learning process of RNNs using Backpropagation through Time algorithm [19].

15.4.2 Learning Process of RNNs

The model is trained using Backpropagation through Time algorithm [19, 20]. The Adam optimizer is used for learning purposes [18]. In each epoch, the model predicts the output for multiple batches of inputs and the error is calculated. The batch size is taken as 32. So 32 number of rows of data are processed at once and the corresponding output is predicted. The process is terminated when either the error is less than the threshold value or the number of epochs is greater than the threshold value. Otherwise, the weights of the network are updated based on the error and the training is continued. The overall stepwise computational procedure is shown in Figure 15.2.

15.4.3 Training Methodology

After successful design of the model, a good training strategy is needed. Here, three different training methodologies are used. The goal is to find the best

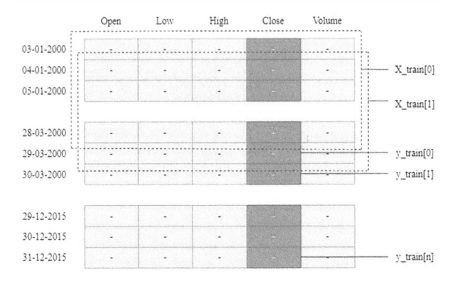

Figure 15.3 Sliding window based training procedure.

combination of a model as well as training method for predicting the stock accurately. The deployed methodologies are discussed as:

- In-domain training: This method is used by most of the recent studies [4–6, 10, 11, 14]. Here, the models are trained for each stock separately using a sliding window manner. In each pass (*i*), historical price data of 60 days is fed as input (X_train[i]) and the close price of the 61st day is targeted (y_train[i]). After every pass, the window moves forward by one day. The training data ranges from 03 January 2000 to 31 December 2015, for each stock. All the models were trained for 20 epochs. The overall procedure of the sliding window based training is presented in the Figure 15.3.
- Out-of-domain training: An important objective of this study is to find how effectively the models trained on a large US-based stock and predict the stock of Indian stocks. Hence, in this method, the models are trained using the S&P 500 Index data ranging from 03 January 1950 to 30 December 2019. The deployment method differs from the normal method in just the training data set while the sliding window process and the number of epochs remain the same.
- Transfer learning based training: Further enhancement of the model generated in the out-of-domain method, are now again trained for the Indian stock data sets. In this method, first, the model generated in out-of-domain method is loaded and separately trained on the Indian

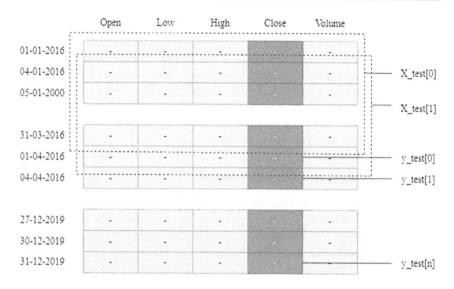

Figure 15.4 Sliding window based testing procedure.

stocks training data ranging from 03 January 2000 to 31 December 2015. The sliding window process remains the same however, the number of epochs in this method is reduced to 10.

15.4.4 Testing

The testing of the model is done by predicting the target (y_test) values for all the three stocks and calculating the errors. The test data set for all the three stocks ranges from 01 January 2016 to 31 December 2019. The prediction is done in a similar sliding window process as the training. After every prediction, the input window is moved forward by a day and the close price of 61st day is predicted. The overall testing procedure is shown in the Figure 15.4. Along with the proposed model, four other important RNN models based on LSTM [5, 11] GRU [14], BGRU [10] and, hybrid of LSTM and GRU [15] are also designed in a similar way to compare the results and find the better performing model.

15.5 EXPERIMENTATION SETTINGS AND RESULTS

In this section, Experimental Settings, Data Distribution for Model, and Results are discussed as follows.

15.5.1 Experimental Settings

Simulations are carried out on a workstation equipped with an Intel Core i7-8700 Processor, 3.2 GHz x6 with 8 GB RAM. The software environment used is Anaconda with Intel Distribution for Python. The model is implemented with Keras API, using Intel-optimized TensorFlow as backend engine. Scikit-learn library is used for normalization, NumPy library for mathematical operations, and Matplotlib library for plotting the results. The detail simulations are discussed as follows:

15.5.2 Data Distribution for Model

The complete database is divided into three segments as training data, testing data, and validation data. For training the model, we used 50% of the total data from aforementioned database in domain and transfer learning method. For testing the performance of the proposed model, 30% of the total database is used. The evaluation of the model is done based on the remaining data sets for validating system performance. Training data samples used fit the model for early classification. Moreover, validation data sets are used to provide an unbiased measurement of the model to fit on the training samples while tuning the model hyper parameters. Five cross validation strategy with the training samples (30%) are used. Test samples are used to provide unbiased evaluation of the final on the training samples data sets.

15.5.3 Results

The detail simulation results are as follows:

- In scenario one, models are implemented using in-domain training for each of the three Indian stock data sets. Evaluation indicators of various models for the three different stocks are presented in the Table 15.3–15.5. Figures 15.5–15.7 show the original price and the forecast for the first 100 days for the three stock data sets as ITC, ONGC, and SBI respectively.

In the case of ITC stock, GRU provides better predictions followed by BGRU. In the case of ONGC, LSTM gave the better predictions followed by

Table 15.3 Evaluation indicators for models trained using in-domain training for ITC

Models	Mean Absolute Error	R^2	Mean Square Error	Root Mean Square Error
LSTM	7.70	0.85	80.86	8.99
GRU	3.79	0.95	27.24	5.21
BGRU	4.11	0.94	28.23	5.31
HYBRID	5.89	0.89	56.46	7.51
TL-BLSTM	16.08	0.46	295.88	17.20

Table 15.4 Evaluation indicators for models trained using in-domain training for ONGC

Models	Mean Absolute Error	R^2	Mean Square Error	Root Mean Square Error
LSTM	2.56	0.97	12.17	3.48
GRU	3.06	0.96	14.71	3.83
BGRU	3.75	0.95	20.78	4.55
HYBRID	3.61	0.95	20.22	4.49
TL-BLSTM	2.69	0.96	13.36	3.65

Table 15.5 Evaluation indicators for models trained using in-domain training for SBI

Models	Mean Absolute Error	R^2	Mean Square Error	Root Mean Square Error
LSTM	5.48	0.95	59.84	7.73
GRU	9.34	0.91	121.22	11.01
BGRU	4.74	0.96	44.02	6.63
HYBRID	6.17	0.94	72.40	8.50
TL-BLSTM	10.46	0.88	161.42	12.70

Figure 15.5 ITC price prediction using in-domain training.

Figure 15.6 ONGC price prediction using in-domain training.

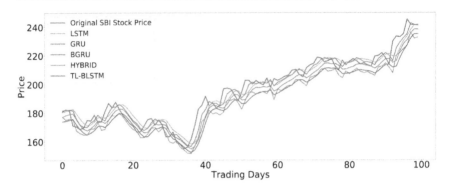

Figure 15.7 SBI price prediction using in-domain training.

TL-BLSTM. For the SBI stock, BGRU performs the best followed by LSTM. So, there's no concrete evidence of one model being better than the others in this training methodology. It is observed that the performance of the models also depends on the dataset instead of just the architecture. The increased complexity of BLSTM model doesn't help in this method as the data set is not very large and the complexity just affects the training in an inconvenient way. Based on the overall observation the learning computational complexity is increasing exponentially based on the input stock data sets which is non-linear time series data. The primary objective of this work is to reduce the computational complexity of learning LSTM model for prediction of the stock market. In order to reduce time complexity of the model, we used stochastic gradient decent optimization method along with bidirectional LSTM. The proposed model provides computational complexity $O(1)$ which is lesser than $O(w)$.

- Scenario two, the models are trained using out-of-domain training over US-based S&P 500 dataset and evaluated on the Indian stock data sets. Tables 15.6–15.8 show the evaluation indicators for the three stocks using out-of-domain training technique respectively. The overall performance study in terms of predicting the original price and the forecasted values during first 100 days are presented in Figures 15.8–15.10.

It is observed that the TL-BLSTM model provides better prediction for ITC as well as the SBI stock market rather than the second best one of ONGC. Predictions for out-of-domain training are worse compared to the results of the same models with the in-domain training. Since the training is done on a large data set, the learning of LSTM and BLSTM is definitely better. However, the training is done on the S&P 500 data set and not the actual stock data set. Therefore, overall predictions for out-of-domain training are as good when compared with the in-domain training.

Table 15.6 Evaluation indicators for models trained using out-of-domain training for ITC

Models	Mean Absolute Error	R^2	Mean Square Error	Root Mean Square Error
LSTM	5.62	0.91	48.83	6.98
GRU	5.08	0.92	39.43	6.27
BGRU	8.20	0.84	88.40	9.40
HYBRID	6.57	0.88	61.49	7.84
TL-BLSTM	4.69	0.93	36.25	6.02

Table 15.7 Evaluation indicators for models trained using out-of-domain training for ONGC

Models	Mean Absolute Error	R^2	Mean Square Error	Root Mean Square Error
LSTM	5.89	0.89	45.03	6.71
GRU	3.16	0.96	16.11	4.01
BGRU	8.30	0.81	82.45	9.08
HYBRID	3.46	0.95	18.99	4.35
TL-BLSTM	3.19	0.96	16.33	4.04

Table 15.8 Evaluation indicators for models trained using out-of-domain training for SBI

Models	Mean Absolute Error	R^2	Mean Square Error	Root Mean Square Error
LSTM	6.95	0.93	85.26	9.23
GRU	6.31	0.95	67.77	8.23
BGRU	9.61	0.90	131.04	11.44
HYBRID	7.77	0.92	99.65	9.98
TL-BLSTM	6.18	0.94	71.11	8.43

Figure 15.8 ITC price prediction using out-of-domain training.

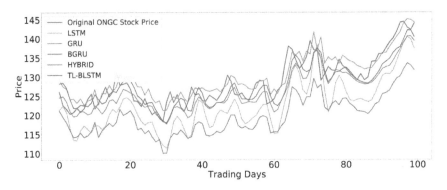

Figure 15.9 ONGC price prediction using out-of-domain training.

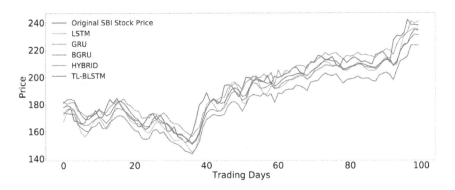

Figure 15.10 SBI price prediction using out-of-domain training.

- Scenario three, the models are further trained using transfer learning approach over the stock data sets using pre-trained models from scenario two. Performance evaluation indicators using transfer learning strategies are presented in the Table 15.9–15.11 according to the data sets. The overall performance issues in terms of predicting the original price and the forecasted values using transfer learning during first 100 days are presented in Figures 15.11–15.13.

From the simulation results, it is observed that the TL-BLSTM provides considerably better predictions while other models show varying performance for different stocks. It is observed that, because of its complex architecture, the TL-BLSTM model is able to learn deeper relations from the large data set from the S&P 500 data set while also tuning to the stock data set during further training. Other models have also performed decently in this experiment by taking advantage of this training methodology. It is also

Table 15.9 Evaluation indicators for models trained using transfer learning based training for ITC

Models	Mean Absolute Error	R^2	Mean Square Error	Root Mean Square Error
LSTM	6.60	0.86	73.07	8.54
GRU	5.88	0.90	50.51	7.10
BGRU	4.07	0.94	29.81	5.46
HYBRID	6.09	0.90	54.61	7.39
TL-BLSTM	3.29	0.96	20.52	4.53

Table 15.10 Evaluation indicators for models trained using transfer learning based training for ONGC

Models	Mean Absolute Error	R^2	Mean Square Error	Root Mean Square Error
LSTM	2.35	0.97	9.66	3.10
GRU	3.28	0.96	16.98	4.12
BGRU	2.37	0.97	10.26	3.20
HYBRID	2.65	0.97	12.43	3.52
TL-BLSTM	2.28	0.97	9.38	3.06

Table 15.11 Evaluation indicators for models trained using transfer learning based training for SBI

Models	Mean Absolute Error	R^2	Mean Square Error	Root Mean Square Error
LSTM	5.93	0.95	64.17	8.01
GRU	5.56	0.95	56.93	7.54
BGRU	5.26	0.96	55.42	7.44
HYBRID	6.48	0.95	67.18	8.19
TL-BLSTM	4.39	0.97	39.83	6.31

Figure 15.11 ITC price prediction using transfer learning based training.

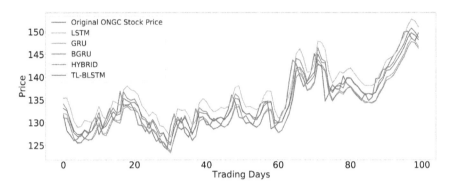

Figure 15.12 ONGC price prediction using transfer learning based training.

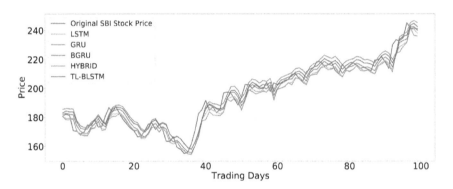

Figure 15.13 SBI price prediction using transfer learning based training.

observed that the TL-BLSTM model trained with transfer learning based training performs significantly better among all the models and all the training strategies. For ITC stock, TL-BLSTM model produces 3.29 MAE which is 13.19% less than the second best result (GRU model with normal method: 3.79 MAE) as shown in the Table 15.9. For ONGC stock, the TL-BLSTM model generates 2.28 MAE which is 10.93% less than the second best result (LSTM model with normal method: 2.56 MAE) as shown in the Table 15.10. For SBI stock, the TL-BLSTM model computes 4.39 MAE which is 7.38% less than the second best result (BGRU model with normal method: 4.74 MAE) as shown in the Table 15.11. On average, it is found that the TL-BLSTM model with transfer learning method gave 10.5% less error than the second best performing combination of the different models and training methodologies. The generalization of model is tested based on different validation data sets. We have used five cross validation settings to calculate average accuracy of the proposed model.

The originality in this manuscript is used for early classification of stock market data using deep learning technique. The computational complexity of model is lesser than $O(w)$. The advantages of the proposed model can be deployed in real-time stock industry for predicting the stock. It can be deployed as smart devices for different mobile applications for business purposes.

15.6 CONCLUSIONS AND FUTURE SCOPE

A deep learning based stock market prediction model is proposed using Two-Layered Bidirectional Long Short Term Memory (TL-BLSTM). The proposed TL-BLSTM framework is further enhanced by incorporating transfer learning technique. The proposed TL-BLTM based model is pre-trained with historical US-based price data sets of the S&P 500 index and further trained on the National Stock Exchange (NSE) of India data sets as ITC, ONGC, and SBI. The performance of the TL-BLSTM is evaluated through three different training strategies with four different stacked architectures based on LSTM, GRU, BGRU and hybrid of LSTM and GRU. Through the simulation results, it is observed that among the models trained using in- domain training, there is no single best model. Models trained using out-of-domain training gave the worst performance overall. Deployment method is generally not suitable for stock price prediction problems. Finally, the TL-BLSTM model trained using transfer learning produced significant improvement in predicting over the same model trained using a normal method.

In the future, parallel neural networks like CuDNN LSTM can be incorporated for further enhancing the speed of training. Sentiment analysis can also be added in the model to get better prediction accuracy. Evolutionary optimization algorithms can be incorporated for feature extraction and selection process.

Acknowledgments

We sincerely thank and acknowledge to Dr. Mitesh Khapra (Assistant Professor IIT Madras, India, for his support and guidance to prepare the research outcomes.

REFERENCES

[1] Fundamental Analysis, https://www.investopedia.com/terms/f/fundamentalanalysis.asp, [Online; accessed March 30, 2020].
[2] Technical Analysis, https://www.investopedia.com/terms/t/technicalanalysis.asp, [Online; accessed April 16, 2020].

[3] R. Zhang, B. Ashuri, Y. Deng, A novel method for forecasting time series based on fuzzy logic and visibility graph, Advances in Data Analysis and Classification 11 (4) (2017) 759–783.

[4] G. Ding, L. Qin, Study on the prediction of stock price based on the associated network model of LSTM, International Journal of Machine Learning and Cybernetics 11 (2019) 1307–1317.

[5] L. Troiano, E. M. Villa, V. Loia, Replicating a trading strategy by means of LSTM for financial industry applications, IEEE Transactions on Industrial Informatics 14 (7) (2018) 3226–3234.

[6] J. Eapen, D. Bein, A. Verma, Novel deep learning model with CNN and bidirectional LSTM for improved stock market index prediction, in: 2019 IEEE 9th Annual Computing and Communication Workshop and Conference (CCWC), IEEE, 2019, pp. 264–270.

[7] P. M. Rodrigues, N. Salish, Modeling and forecasting interval time series with threshold models, Advances in Data Analysis and Classification 9 (1) (2015) 41–57.

[8] A. Géron, Hands-on machine learning with Scikit-Learn, Keras, and TensorFlow: Concepts, tools, and techniques to build intelligent systems, O'Reilly Media, 2019.

[9] R. Zhao, D. Wang, R. Yan, K. Mao, F. Shen, J. Wang, Machine health monitoring using local feature-based gated recurrent unit networks, IEEE Transactions on Industrial Electronics 65 (2) (2017) 1539–1548.

[10] K. A. Althelaya, E.-S. M. El-Alfy, S. Mohammed, stock market forecast using multivariate analysis with bidirectional and stacked (LSTM, GRU), in: 2018 21st Saudi Computer Society National Computer Conference (NCC), IEEE, 2018, pp. 1–7.

[11] B.-S. Lin, W.-T. Chu, C.-M. Wang, Application of stock analysis using deep learning, in: 2018 7th International Congress on Advanced Applied Informatics (IIAI-AAI), IEEE, 2018, pp. 612–617.

[12] S. Hochreiter, J. Schmidhuber, Long short-term memory, Neural Computation 9 (8) (1997) 1735–1780.

[13] A. Graves, J. Schmidhuber, Framewise phoneme classification with bidirectional LSTM and other neural network architectures, Neural Networks 18 (5–6) (2005) 602–610.

[14] D. L. Minh, A. Sadeghi-Niaraki, H. D. Huy, K. Min, H. Moon, Deep learning approach for short-term stock trends prediction based on two-stream gated recurrent unit network, IEEE Access 6 (2018) 55392–55404.

[15] M. A. Hossain, R. Karim, R. Thulasiram, N. D. B. Bruce, Y. Wang, Hybrid deep learning model for stock price prediction, in: 2018 IEEE Symposium Series on Computational Intelligence (SSCI), 2018, pp. 1837–1844.

[16] J. Lu, V. Behbood, P. Hao, H. Zuo, S. Xue, G. Zhang, Transfer learning using computational intelligence: A survey, Knowledge-Based Systems 80 (2015) 14–23.

[17] NSE-national stock exchange of India ltd: Live Share/Stock Market News & Updates, Quotes (March 2020), https://www.nseindia.com/

[18] D. P. Kingma, J. Ba, Adam: A method for stochastic optimization, 3rd International Conference for Learning Representations, San Diego (2015), arXiv preprint arXiv:1412.6980

[19] P. J. Werbos, Backpropagation through time: What it does and how to do it, Proceedings of the IEEE 78 (10) (1990) 1550–1560.

[20] A. Graves, A. Mohamed, G. Hinton, Speech recognition with deep recurrent neural networks, in: 2013 IEEE International Conference on Acoustics, Speech and Signal Processing, 2013, pp. 6645–6649.

Index

9 781032 360300